Gypsy and Traveller

The Legal Action Group is a national, independent charity which campaigns for equal access to justice for all members of society.

Legal Action Group:

- provides support to the practice of lawyers and advisers
- inspires developments in that practice
- campaigns for improvements in the law and the administration of justice
- stimulates debate on how services should be delivered.

Gypsy and Traveller Law

Edited by Chris Johnson and Marc Willers

COMMISSION FOR
RACIAL EQUALITY

This edition published in Great Britain 2004
by LAG Education and Service Trust Limited
242 Pentonville Road, London N1 9UN
www.lag.org.uk

While every effort has been made to ensure that the details in this
text are correct, readers must be aware that the law changes and
that the accuracy of the material cannot be guaranteed and the
author and the publisher accept no responsibility for any losses or
damage sustained.

British Library Cataloguing in Publication Data
a CIP catalogue record for this book is available from the British
Library.

Crown copyright material is produced with the permission of the
Controller of HMSO and the Queen's Printer for Scotland.

ISBN-10   1 903307 26 0
ISBN-13   978 1 903307 26 0

Typeset and Printed by Hobbs the Printers, Totton, Hampshire

Foreword

by Trevor Phillips, Chair of the Commission for
Racial Equality

The disadvantage faced by Gypsies and Travellers extends beyond
site provision to all other walks of life including education, health
and criminal justice. And recent research suggests that the level of
racism and hostility experienced is at least as serious as that
experienced by any other community. It is still considered acceptable
by many to put up 'No Traveller' signs in pubs and shops and to
make overtly prejudiced remarks about Gypsies and Travellers in
public.

In the 16th Century laws were introduced requiring Gypsies to
leave England and to abandon their 'idle and ungodly life and
company' and adopt a sedentary way of life – the penalty for not
complying was execution. Times have changed but the
discrimination and disadvantage faced by these communities
persists.

Since 1994 there has not been a statutory duty on councils to
provide legal sites on which Gypsies and Travellers can live yet it is
virtually impossible for a Gypsy or Traveller to gain planning
permission on land they own, and there is a raft of eviction and
planning enforcement provisions that effectively criminalise a
nomadic existence.

The major shortage of sites for Gypsies and Travellers means that
we are left with a situation where thousands of families have
nowhere to go – and must either move into housing, camp
unlawfully or develop their own land unlawfully. This generates
considerable hostility from the local community, which in turn leads
to resistance to planning applications – creating a vicious circle by
exacerbating the lack of sites. A joined-up solution would have a
hugely positive impact on race and community relations.

Legal protection from discrimination does exist for Gypsies and
Travellers under race relations and human rights legislation. They
have rights within the planning system, rights to education, rights
connected to eviction and planning enforcement to name but a few.

Similarly, councils and other public authorities have responsibilities in these areas, and can be challenged where they fail in their obligations.

But the provisions that impact most on Gypsies and Travellers are highly complex, so that many are not adequately aware of their rights and not empowered to challenge injustice. Similarly, faced with a labyrinth of law, regulations, guidance and circulars, legal and other advisors struggle to determine exactly what their clients' rights are. There is now a rapidly developing body of case law relating to Gypsies and Travellers which many practitioners are not fully aware of, but which could be used to great effect in future cases – including landmark decisions made even as this book was being written.

I therefore take great pleasure in commending this book, which for the first time draws together all of the legislation and case law relating to Gypsies and Travellers. I hope that this book will empower people to secure their rights and enable those representing them both to provide effective advice on existing laws and bring improvements to the laws themselves.

Trevor Phillips
CRE Chair

August 2004

Preface and acknowledgements

For several years now the Legal Action Group (LAG) has organised an annual training day on the law relating to Gypsies and Travellers. At one such event in September 2002 a Romani Gypsy called out from the back of the room and asked us to write a book on the subject so that she and other Gypsies and Travellers could learn more about their rights.

We decided to take up the challenge and approached LAG with a rough plan for a book. The staff at LAG were very interested in the idea and agreed that there was a real need for a book that could highlight the law and issues that had an impact on the lives of Gypsies and Travellers. LAG then contacted the Commission for Racial Equality (CRE) and we were delighted to learn that it had been agreed that they would jointly publish the book.

Having been given the green light we approached Sasha Barton, Murray Hunt, Tim Jones, Angus Murdoch and David Watkinson to ask them to help produce the book. They all agreed without hesitation and as editors we would like to thank them all for their commitment to the book and their hard work.

We would also like to thank all the staff at LAG and, particularly, Esther Pilger for her enthusiasm and encouragement and Jan Cooper for his attention to detail. Special thanks are also due to our respective partners, Zoe and Sharon, for their support and patience whilst we edited the book.

The law as it relates to Gypsies and Travellers in England and Wales is correct as at 17 May 2004. However, there have been some major developments in some of the areas covered by this book since the text was finalised and these are reported in the section headed 'Recent developments in Gypsy and Traveller law'. Clearly, it is important that readers take these developments into account and we have made reference to the 'Recent developments' section in footnotes throughout the book to indicate when readers should refer back to them.

We are grateful to a number of people for providing us with information that has been inserted into the book and in particular would like to acknowledge: Inspector Ian Taggart of the Grampian

Police for information on the use of CJPOA 1994 s61 in Scotland; and Tim Shotton of Community Law Partnership for information on EU accession countries.

We must also acknowledge the other lawyers who have specialised in the representation of Gypsies and Travellers and have, through their case work, helped bring about many of the developments that we discuss in the book. In this regard, we would like to acknowledge: the Travellers' Advice Team at the Community Law Partnership (CLP) – namely, Sharon Baxter, Justine Compton and Roberta Kellie; the Gypsy and Traveller team at 2 Garden Court Chambers – namely, Stephen Cottle, Val Easty, Stephen Knafler, Adrian Marshall-Williams, Stephen Simblet and the rest.

It is important to make mention of the general support given by: the partners (Chris Esdaile, Mike McIlvaney and Rosaleen Kilbane) and other staff at CLP; and the administrative teams at 2 Garden Court Chambers and at 1 Pump Court (in particular, Ian Burrow and Mycal Thomas). We thank them all for their enthusiastic backing for the work that is done in this area and make the point that none of the cases that have been taken by CLP, 2 Garden Court and 1 Pump Court would have ever got off the ground without their devastating efficiency.

There is an enormous list of other academics, lawyers, planning consultants, researchers, support workers and campaigners who have inspired and assisted us in our work over the years, including: all those members of the Gypsy and Traveller Law Reform Coalition, Dr Donald Kenrick, Peter Kingshill, Jeremy Browne, Michael Cox and Philip Brown. Many of the others work with the organisations and bodies listed in appendix C. Special mention must also be made of the Traveller Law Research Unit at Cardiff Law School (now unfortunately 'in mothballs') and the inspiring work of Luke Clements and Rachel Morris.

Above all, our thanks must go to our Gypsy and Traveller clients who, by their courage, tenacity, enthusiasm and humour, have kept us going even after the worst setbacks.

We would like to dedicate this book to Johnny Delaney whose tragic death is reported in the first chapter. Hopefully, this book will help draw attention to the difficulties that Gypsies and Travellers face in our society and help them in their struggle to achieve equality.

Marc Willers and Chris Johnson
21 July 2004

Contributors

Sasha Barton works at the Commission for Racial Equality (CRE) as a senior policy officer, specialising in Gypsies and Travellers. The Commission for Racial Equality's work includes supporting cases of discrimination against Gypsies and Travellers and promoting equality of opportunity and good race relations across sectors. Sasha has responsibility for national policy in this area, and recently developed a three year strategy for the CRE. She works closely with central and local government, Gypsies and Travellers and other key stakeholders.

Murray Hunt is legal adviser to the Joint Parliamentary Committee on Human Rights. One of the founding members of Matrix chambers, Murray specialises in human rights law and public law. He is author of *Using Human Rights Law in English Courts* (Hart Publishing, 1997), joint editor of *A Practitioner's Guide to the Impact of the Human Rights Act 1998* (Hart Publishing) and contributing editor to a number of other works. He has written articles for *European Human Rights Law Review* and *Journal of Law and Society*.

Chris Johnson is a solicitor and one of the founding partners of Community Law Partnership, and member of the Travellers' Advice Team (TAT), in Birmingham. He travels the country representing Gypsies and Travellers as well as lecturing, training and writing to educate and support Travellers rights. He writes regularly for *Legal Action*.

Tim Jones is a barrister at No 5 Chambers, Birmingham, specialising in planning and local government law. He has appeared in numerous Gypsy and Traveller cases, including *Buckley v UK*, *Chapman v UK*, *R v Hereford and Worcester CC ex p Smith* and *Butler v Bath and NE Somerset DC*. His writing includes articles published in *European Human Rights Law Review*, *European Advocate*, *Justice Review* (Slovakia) and the *Law Society's Gazette*. He has spoken at numerous seminars including ones organised the Legal Action Group, European Roma Rights Center, National Association of Gypsy and Traveller Officers, Irish Traveller Movement and Council of Europe. He is a member of the Committee of the Administrative Law Bar Association and of the Bar Human Rights Committee. He is also a member of the Bars of Ireland and of Northern Ireland, and a Fellow of the Chartered Institute of Arbitrators.

Angus Murdoch is a partner of the Community Law Partnership in Birmingham and planning adviser to their Travellers Advice Team. The TAT provide specialist legal advice and representation to the Traveller community throughout England and Wales. He is an experienced trainer, lecturer and writer on Gypsy and Traveller issues.

David Watkinson is a barrister practising at Two Garden Court Chambers in London, specialising in housing law, judicial review and planning law as it affects Gypsies and Travellers. David is a contributor to *Law in a Housing Crisis* (1975); co-author of *Squatting, Trespass and Civil Liberties* (1976); *Civil Rights Guide* (1978); contributor to *Squatting: The Real Story* (1980); *Critical Lawyers Handbook* (1992). He has also contributed reviews, articles and case notes to *Legal Action, All England Legal Opinion* and *Solicitors Journal*. David has lectured on courses organised by Legal Action Group, Housing Law Practitioners' Association, South Bank Polytechnic, Warwick University, Central Law Training, Administrative Law Bar Association and Legal Services Commission. He is Executive member of the Administrative Law Bar Association and Housing Law Practitioners' Association, former member of the Civil Justice Council and current deputy chair of its housing and land sub-committee. He is also a member of the Legal Action Group and Haldane Society.

Marc Willers is a barrister, formerly at 1 Pump Court Chambers, now practising at Two Garden Court Chambers in London. He specialises in public law, human rights, and planning law and with a particular emphasis on the representation of Gypsies and Travellers. He is the treasurer of the Travellers Law Reform Coalition and a director of Friends, Families and Travellers. Marc has presented seminars organised by the Council of Europe and the United Nations High Commissioner for Refugees to train Russian judges and lawyers on the European Convention on Human Rights and its relevance to asylum-seekers, refugees and internally displaced persons. He has also presented a number of seminars on human rights, the law relating to Gypsies and Travellers and civil actions against the police and trains lawyers and advisers for Legal Action Group. He writes regularly for *Legal Action*.

Recent developments in Gypsy and Traveller law

Introduction

The law relating to Gypsies and Travellers is constantly evolving and there have been a number of developments since the chapters of this book were written.

How the Human Rights Act 1998 affects Gypsies and Travellers

Discrimination

The House of Lords recently gave judgment in *Ghaidan v Mendoza*[1] and, when doing so, expressed its broad approval of the '*Michalak*[2] questions' as a useful tool of analysis when a court considers whether there has been a breach of European Convention on Human Rights (ECHR) article 14. However, the House of Lords concluded that a fifth question needed to be asked in article 14 cases – namely, whether the difference in treatment is based on one or more of the grounds proscribed in article 14 – and warned against a rigidly formulaic approach being taken when determining such cases.[3]

Official sites

Security of tenure[4]

In both *Somerset CC v Isaacs and Secretary of State for Transport Local Government and the Regions*[5] and *R (Albert Smith) v Barking and*

---

1   [2004] UKHL 30, 21 June. See also chapter 2, paras 2.53–2.55.
2   *Michalak v Wandsworth LBC* [2003] 1 WLR 617.
3   See Hale LJ at paras 133–134 of the judgment.
4   See chapter 3 at paras 3.9–3.24.
5   [2002] EWHC 1014 Admin.

Dagenham LBC[6] it was held that there was sufficient justification for the fact that Gypsies and Travellers living on authorised council-run sites only received a very limited degree of security of tenure. However, the European Court of Human Rights (ECtHR) has recently delivered its judgment in the case of *Connors v United Kingdom*[7] and effectively overruled both those cases. Mr Connors and his family are Gypsies and they lived on a local authority site. Their licence to occupy the site was terminated as a result of allegations of nuisance. Mr Connors disputed those allegations and judicially reviewed the council's decision to seek their eviction. That application failed and the council obtained a possession order. Mr Connors complained to the ECtHR that the eviction of his family breached ECHR article 8. In its judgment the ECtHR indicated that:

- there was a positive obligation on the UK to facilitate the Gypsy way of life;
- the eviction was a serious interference with Mr Connors' article 8 rights and it required particularly weighty reasons of public interest by way of justification;
- it was not persuaded that there was any particular feature about local authority Gypsy sites which would render their management unworkable if they were required to establish reasons for evicting long-standing occupants;
- the power to evict without the burden of giving reasons which were liable to be examined on their merits by an independent tribunal had not been convincingly shown to respond to any specific goal or to provide any particular benefit to members of the Gypsy community,
- and the ECtHR concluded that the eviction could not be justified by a 'pressing social need' or proportionate to the legitimate aim pursued. As a consequence the ECtHR held that there had been a violation of ECHR article 8.

The decision ought to lead the government to change the law so that Gypsies and Travellers living on local authority sites are provided with full security of tenure.

---

6 [2002] EWHC 2400 Admin and [2003] EWCA Civ 385.
7 Application No 66746/01, 27 May 2004.

Planning law

Planning and Compulsory Purchase Act 2004[8]

The Planning and Compulsory Purchase Act (PCPA) 2004 received Royal Assent on 13 May 2004. The Act introduces provisions designed to reform and speed up the planning system.[9] Significantly, the PCPA 2004 provides that:

- there will be a regional spatial strategy (RSS) prepared for each region;
- that the RSS will be monitored and kept under review by a regional planning body (RPB);
- local planning authorities will be required to prepare local development documents (LDDs) and these will replace local plans, unitary development plans and structure plans;
- LDDs must be in general conformity with the RSS; and
- the Secretary of State has the power to revoke or direct a revision of an LDD.

It is understood that the government will soon be issuing guidance which will require that the accommodation needs of Gypsies and Travellers are assessed on a regional basis and met on a local level by the local planning authorities in their LDDs.

The Act also provides local planning authorities with a new discretionary power to serve temporary stop notices to halt breaches of planning control for a period of up to 28 days. When reviewing the PCPA 2004, the Joint Committee on Human Rights (JCHR) noted that the power could not be used to prohibit the use of a building as a dwelling house but could be used to prohibit the use of a caravan as a dwelling. Having done so, the JCHR expressed the view that the power would appear to discriminate against Gypsies and Travellers and that there seemed to be no justification for the difference in treatment. As a consequence the government has agreed that the power will not be brought into force until regulations are introduced which will ensure that it is not used in a discriminatory fashion.[10]

---

8 See chapter 4 at paras 4.54.10.
9 The provisions of the PCPA 2004 will come into force at different stages.
10 It is worth noting that a Gypsy has already challenged a local authority's use of a stop notice under Town and Country Planning Act (TCPA) 1990 s183 on the basis that the provision is incompatible with the ECHR – the decision is awaited.

Material considerations

Personal circumstances[11]

The case of *Porter v First Secretary of State and South Bucks DC*[12] concerned the grant of planning permission for a Gypsy site in the Green Belt. Mrs Porter, a Romani Gypsy, had lived in caravans on her land in the Green Belt since 1985 without planning permission. In 2000 the council obtained an injunction requiring her to cease her residential use of the land but that injunction was subsequently quashed.[13] Meanwhile, Mrs Porter applied for planning permission. Her application was refused by the council and she appealed to the Secretary of State against that refusal. At the subsequent planning inquiry it was accepted that the use of the land as a caravan site constituted inappropriate development in the Green Belt and the main issue was whether there were very special circumstances that clearly outweighed the harm by reason of inappropriateness. In the event the planning inspector concluded that: very special circumstances did exist given Mrs Porter's status as a Gypsy, her ill-health, her aversion to bricks and mortar and the fact that she had nowhere else to go; and that the grant of planning permission was justified.

The council's appeal against that decision was dismissed by Rich J but when the case came before the Court of Appeal, the grant of planning permission was quashed on the grounds that the inspector had failed to conduct a 'clear and cogent analysis' of the main issue and that he had failed to take into account the unlawfulness of her occupation of the site, which had been in persistent breach of planning control.[14] Mrs Porter then appealed to the House of Lords. On appeal the council argued that the Court of Appeal had been right to demand that the planning inspector gave a much fuller analysis of his reasons for granting planning permission on the facts of the case, as the Green Belt restrictions should not be 'watered down'. The House of Lords unanimously rejected that argument and restored the planning permission. When Lord Brown of Eaton-Under-Heywood gave his judgment he said:

> I cannot accept that submission. To my mind the inspector's reasoning was
> both clear and ample. Here was a woman of 62 in serious ill-health with a

---

11 See chapter 4 at paras 4.58–4.64.
12 [2004] UKHL 33, 1 July 2004.
13 See *South Bucks DC v Porter* [2003] 2 WLR 1547 and chapter 4 at para 4.106.
14 [2003] EWCA Civ 687, [2004] JPL 207, 19th May 2003.

rooted fear of being put into permanent housing, with no alternative site to go to, whose displacement would imperil her continuing medical treatment and probably worsen her condition. All of this was fully explained in the decision letter (and, of course, described more fully still in the reports produced in evidence at the public inquiry). Should she be dispossessed from the site onto the roadside or should she be granted a limited personal planning permission? The inspector thought the latter, taking the view that Mrs Porter's 'very special circumstances' 'clearly outweighed' the environmental harm involved. Not everyone would have reached the same decision but there is no mystery as to what moved the inspector.

The council also argued that the Court of Appeal had been right to conclude that the planning inspector had failed to take account of a material consideration, namely Mrs Porter's lengthy breach of planning control. However, this point was also unanimously rejected by the House of Lords. Though Lord Brown accepted that the unlawfulness of Mrs Porter's prior occupation of the site was capable of being a material consideration, he took the view that it would only be relevant if she was actually seeking to pray in aid her long period of occupation. However, as Mrs Porter was not relying on her continuing unlawful occupation in itself as constituting part of her hardship claim, the fact that she had occupied the site without planning permission since 1985 was of little if any materiality in the particular circumstances of the case.

Homelessness

The case of *Codona v Mid-Bedfordshire DC*[15] involved a homelessness application by a Gypsy woman and her extended family. The council offered bed and breakfast (B&B) accommodation for a limited period, stating that they had no sites or land available despite her accepted 'aversion to conventional housing'. While approving the judgment in *R (Margaret Price) v Carmarthenshire CC*,[16] the Court of Appeal concluded that, in the circumstances of this case, the offer of B&B did not fall below the minimum line of suitability of an offer of accommodation. It is expected that Ms Codona will be petitioning the House of Lords for leave to appeal.

---

15 [2004] EWCA Civ 925, 15 July.
16 [2003] EWHC 42 Admin, and see chapter 6 at paras 6.51–6.58, 6.95 and note 148.

Contents

Table of cases

Table of statutes

Table of statutory instruments

Table of circulars and guidance

Department for Education and Employment Circulars

Department of the Environment Circulars

Welsh Office

Reports

Guidance

Planning Policy Guidance Notes

Table of European legislation

Conventions

Directives

Abbreviations

ACAS	Advisory, Conciliation and Arbitration Service
ACPO	Association of Chief Police Officers
AONB	Area of Outstanding National Beauty
CA 1989	Children Act 1989
CJPOA 1994	Criminal Justice and Public Order Act 1994
CLS	Community Legal Service
CPR	Civil Procedure Rules
CRE	Commission for Racial Equality
CSA 1968	Caravan Sites Act 1968
CSCDA 1960	Caravan Sites and Control of Development Act 1960
DDA 1995	Disability Discrimination Act 1995
DfES	Department for Education and Skills
DFG	Disabled facilities grant
DoE	Department of the Environment
DPA 1998	Data Protection Act 1998
EA 1996	Education Act 1996
EA 2002	Education Act 2002
ECHR	European Convention on Human Rights
ECtHR	European Court of Human Rights
GP	General practitioner
GPDO 1995	Town and Country Planning (General Permitted Development) Order 1995
GSRG	Gypsy sites refurbishment grant
HA 1985	Housing Act 1985
HA 1996	Housing Act 1996
HA 2002	Homelessness Act 2002
HRA 1998	Human Rights Act 1998
LEA	Local education authority
LPA	Local planning authority
LSC	Legal Services Commission
MHA 1983	Mobile Homes Act 1983
NATT	National Association of Teachers of Travellers

NHS	National Health Service
NHSA 1977	National Health Service Act 1977
ODPM	Office of the Deputy Prime Minister
Ofsted	Office for Standards in Education
PCT	Primary care trust
PD	Practice Direction
PPG	Planning policy guidance
PPS	Planning policy statement
RRA 1976	Race Relations Act 1976
SENDA 2001	Special Educational Needs and Disability Act 2001
SHA	Strategic health authority
SSFA 1998	School Standards and Framework Act 1998
SSSI	Site of Special Scientific Interest
TCPA 1990	Town and Country Planning Act 1990
TLRC	Traveller Law Reform Coalition (now known as the Gypsy and Traveller Law Reform Coalition)

Introduction

Introduction

1.1   On 11 November 2003, BBC News Online reported:

> Police have arrested a total of six men on suspicion of inciting racial hatred after a bonfire society torched an effigy of a caravan with a gypsy family painted on the side. The tableau, which was burnt at Firle Bonfire Society's celebrations in East Sussex, caused outrage because of the controversial display. The society denies any claims the caravan, which had PIKEY written on the side ... was designed to be racist.[1]

1.2   The scene described above could easily have been taken from a medieval European genocide, but it was not: the caravan torching incident took place following problems in the area after a group of Travellers had set up camp near the village. The caravan in question was fortunately not occupied by real people but was made from plywood and adorned like a stereotypical modern Gypsy caravan, complete with paintings of Gypsy children on the side.

1.3   The Firle bonfire incident sparked a national debate in the media about the treatment of our Gypsy and Traveller population and about the racism they have experienced for many hundreds of years and which continues to the present day. The Commission for Racial Equality (CRE), subsequent to the Firle incident, launched a four-year strategy[2] aimed specifically at this group. Quoting from a MORI poll conducted in England, the strategy states:

> ... more than one-third of adults who took part admitted to being personally prejudiced against Gypsies and Travellers. This was greater than the levels of prejudice reported towards lesbians and gay men, other ethnic minorities and people with disabilities.[3]

1.4   Romani Gypsies and Irish Travellers are accepted as being racial groups for the purposes of the Race Relations Act 1976 and subsequent amendments.[4] Discrimination against them – as well as inciting racial hatred towards them – is prohibited by law in the United Kingdom. Those involved in the effigy burning defended their actions by saying that the objects of their anger were not the Gypsies and Travellers themselves, but the local authorities, whose lack of action in providing sufficient sites for Gypsies and Travellers in the area, inevitably led to more unsatisfactory locations being

---

1 BBC News Online, *Six arrests over burnt gypsy effigy,* 11 November 2003.
2 *Gypsies and Travellers: A strategy for the CRE, 2004–2007* (CRE, 2004).
3 *Gypsies and Travellers: A strategy for the CRE, 2004–2007,* p6.
4 See chapter 8, below, for an analysis of race relations legislation.

occupied. Gypsies and Travellers in their turn argue that the lack of authorised sites means that they have no option but to stop where they can, before being moved on again to some other village or town where another eviction will confront them in the near future.[5]

1.5 The Firle bonfire incident illustrates some of the issues which we will be considering in this book: the lack of lawful sites for Gypsies and Travellers; the role of the local authorities, the police, and the media; and how the law operates in relation to this minority group. However, before we can properly understand the contemporary treatment of Gypsies and Travellers in the UK, there is a need to place that matter within some kind of historical context. The remainder of this introduction tries to provide just such a context, starting with a brief examination of the vexed question of who the Gypsies and Travellers actually are.

Who are the Gypsies and Travellers?

1.6 The CRE has estimated that '[o]f the 200,000 to 300,000 Travellers in England, by far the largest group are Romani Gypsies, who have been in England since the early 16th century. Romani Gypsies have been recognised as a racial group since 1988 ... Irish Travellers, who have been travelling in England as a distinct social group since the 1800s, received legal recognition as a racial group in England and Wales in 2000 ...'[6] There are two other ethnic groups of Travellers in the UK, the Welsh Travellers (or Kale)[7] and Scottish Travellers, each of whom have separate origins and histories. Since this book deals with the law as it relates to England and Wales, and given the lack of information on the Kale (most of whom are now thought to be living in houses),[8] the following brief historical overview will concentrate on Romani Gypsies, Irish Travellers, and New Travellers.[9]

1.7 Most people have some idea of what is meant by terms such as 'Gypsies' and 'New Age' Travellers. In contemporary, anti-nomadic

5 See, for example, 'Decent homes for all', pamphlet, (Traveller Law Reform Coalition, 2004).

6 *Gypsies and Travellers*, p3, note 2.

7 There is considerable controversy among Gypsy and Traveller academics and writers about the existence of Kale as a separate type of Traveller group.

8 See, for example, the discussion in Kenrick & Clark, *Moving On: The Gypsies and Travellers of Britain* (University of Hertfordshire Press, 1996) pp38–39.

9 'New Traveller' is the term preferred by this (non-ethnic) group of Travellers themselves, though we will refer to 'New Age Traveller' where it is relevant in the historical context. See *Moving On*, pp117–136.

discourse, 'real Gypsies' occupy the top rung of a sliding-scale of authenticity, while 'New Age' Travellers, denied this status, are generally portrayed as pseudo-vagrants, criminals or the dispossessed underclass. While it is not denied that fundamental differences do exist between these groups (particularly in language and customs), the similarities between them – both in terms of their treatment by the state and (relatedly) their economic nomadism – are often overlooked.

Historical context

1.8 The Travellers who came to be known as 'Gypsies' were 'the first ... Asian immigrants to Europe'[10] and had migrated from India around 1000AD, with the first of three main waves arriving in Britain four or five centuries ago (the second at the end of the 19th century and the third in the 1960s). These early Gypsies had an itinerant economy and specialised in metal working, fortune telling, craft-making and musicianship.[11] Their preference for self-employment soon earned them the antipathy of some of the most powerful groups in society at the time, as such economic independence was perceived as a rejection of the master-servant relationship inherent in the guilds' monopoly of production, as well as 'a carnivalesque incitement to disorder.'[12]

1.9 There is some controversy around why they are called Gypsies, with many claiming that European states believed they had come from Egypt, perhaps fleeing religious persecution, and that 'Gypsy' is an adaptation of 'Egyptian':

> These long-haired tent-dwellers who appeared among villages and town-dwellers, defied classification, and they were given diverse names connected with an imagined origin or an imperfectly understood identity.[13]

10 Acton, *Gypsy Politics and Social Change* (Routledge, Kegan Paul, 1974) p27.
11 Many Gypsy groups reflect the predominant occupation in which they are involved. For example, the Kalderas, or copperworkers, from whom the word 'cauldron' has been appropriated in English. Liegeois, *Gypsies and Travellers: socio-cultural data, socio-political data* (Council of Europe, 1987) p39.
12 Stewart, *The Puzzle of Roma Persistence* (University of Hertfordshire Press, 1997) p85.
13 Liegeois, *Gypsies and Travellers: socio-cultural data, socio-political data* (Council of Europe, Strasbourg, 1987) p13.

1.10   Their dark skin colour[14] provided a ready focus for discrimination and the 'race' dimension is clearly evident in popular mythology of the time. The subsequent stereotyping of Gypsies invoked fears of the 'Black Heathen' alongside themes of idleness, indiscipline and depravity, themes which persist to this day. Thus, the historical oppression of Gypsy people can be seen to have ethnic, racial *and* class bases. These three factors are not mutually exclusive in Gypsy history; on the contrary, they are mutually reinforcing. Indeed, the three overlap to the extent that it is impossible to be sure where the influence of one ends and the others begin. Any such obvious deviations from established norms were subject to the most severe social and penal sanctions at the time and Gypsy nomads were particularly vulnerable to such punishment. In this way, their economic skills (which were a fundamental part of their nomadic identity) set them at odds with the dominant ideology of work in both feudal society (as 'masterless men'[15]), and in later capitalist societies (through their continued resistance to proletarianisation).

1.11   Within a short period of time after their arrival, Gypsies became seen as lazy, dirty, parasitic deviants and subject to repressive legislation aimed at expelling and, ultimately, exterminating the Gypsy population The first such law aimed explicitly against them was Henry VIII's Proclamation of 1530:

> Diverse and many outlandish people calling themselves Egyptians, have gone from place to place and used great and subtle means to deceive the people, bearing them in hand that they by palmistry could tell men's and women's fortunes ... and have deceived the people of their money and have also committed many heinous felonies and robberies.[16]

1.12   The punishment for being an 'Egyptian' at this time was banishment, but the state had trouble identifying exactly who was and who was not a 'Gypsy', as a great many indigenous dispossessed roamed the land during the Tudor period. The anti-Gypsy ideology combined with the anti-vagrant ideology of the time, a fact clearly reflected in the language of the increasingly draconian legislation, such as the 1554 'Order For the Avoiding of All Doubts and Ambiguities' which re-asserted the intended victims of the legislation as 'all such sturdy and false vagabonds of that sort living

---

14   Walvin, *There ain't no black in the Union Jack* (Routledge, 1973) makes the case that British people have 'always found blackness a peculiar and important point of difference, and is also relevant when considering anti-nomadism.

15   Fraser, *The Gypsies* (Blackwell, 1995) p35.

16   22 Henry VIII c10 of 1530.

only upon the spoil of the simple people [including those] in any company or fellowship of vagabonds commonly called or calling themselves "Aegyptians".'

1.13   The offence of being a Gypsy or living a nomadic life, carrying the death penalty, was thus created and remained on the statute books for over two centuries in Britain. These laws had a populist reflection in contemporary folk tales and mythology which demonstrate that, even by then, the stereotype was firmly fixed in the sedentary imagination that Gypsies were work-shy parasites worthy only of contempt:

> The local people, disconcerted by such unclassifiable originality in dress, language, way of life and possible mode of association, accused them of witchcraft, banditry and of spreading disease. In this way there grew up the dark and fearful image of a nomad with a soul as black as his skin, damned for all time in the eyes of a frightened society.[17]

1.14   It is important to underline the fact that the persecution of Gypsy people was not restricted to Britain but was a pan-European affair: during the 16th, 17th and 18th centuries, laws were passed in every single European state to control the 'Gypsy problem' in similarly repressive ways:

> For the next 200 years ... there is a depressing uniformity about the response of most European powers to the presence of Gypsies. They continued to be viewed as criminals simply because of their position in society and, on top of that, the special racial prejudices remained, together with religious hostility towards what was seen as their heathenish practices and sorcery. More generally, they suffered from the tide of repression that was arising everywhere against vagabondage and the 'sturdy beggar'. The authorities could not come to terms with masterless men, with no fixed domicile and useless as a workforce: in their eyes, that status was in itself an aberration, at odds with the established order, and had to be put right by coercion and pressure of the gyves.[18] Yet when the Gypsies offered legitimate services to the settled population, they were at risk from the ill-will attracted by transient traders and artisans who violated local monopolies, or from the abhorrence that occupations such as peddler or tinker or entertainer aroused among those in power.[19]

1.15   For the Gypsies who had migrated to Britain (as well as indigenous Travellers) commerce formed an important dimension

---

17   Liegeois, *Gypsies and Travellers: socio-cultural data, socio-political data* (Council of Europe, 1987) p44.

18   'Gyves' meaning shackles or fetters (The Chambers Dictionary, 1994).

19   Fraser, *The Gypsies* (Blackwell, 1995) p129.

of their economic survival, and while they may have strived to remain culturally independent of their sedentary neighbours, the fact that they traded goods and services with sedentary society, meant that economic inter-dependence became (and has remained) a feature of Gypsy life. Not only did nomadic groups hawk the wares they had made (or bought cheaply) in towns and villages which they passed on the road, but they frequently made their nomadic habits coincide with traditional horse and harvest fairs, and other meeting places. Here, not only were their skills in trade and craftsmanship in demand, but their musical and entertainment abilities could also earn them a living. By the 19th century, Gypsies had become familiar sights at these fairs, and many would make their annual travel routes so that they could attend fairs following the harvest, thus making a living from both:

> Fairs and race-meetings formed a major part of the Gypsy calendar, giving some structure to the timing and direction of their travels, and providing a meeting place for families and friends as well as allowing them to engage in the serious business of horse-dealing ... Once the harvests were in, the movement from town to country was reversed.[20]

1.16   Once again, it can be seen how their nomadism (while fundamental to their identity) is permeated with economic dimensions, primarily in terms of the historical bases of their persecution, but, also, in the fact that the patterns of their nomadism in Britain evolved in relation to the availability of viable economic niches in the wider society. This is demonstrated by the fact that many Gypsies moved with and for the harvest as agricultural workers and used these routes to ply their other trades, for example at the fairs. These sites in turn became a focus of cultural celebration for Gypsy people themselves, thus reinforcing the economic centrality of nomadism for their identity:

> For the Gypsy and the Traveller travelling has many functions. It permits social organisation, it sanctions adaptability and flexibility and makes the practice of trading possible ... Apart from its social function, travel has an equally important economic role. This is evident for certain occupations: nomadic trades observe the dates of holidays and fairs, cattle dealers those of cattle markets, agricultural workers the season for picking fruit, grapes and olives [in Europe]. Generally speaking, the essential characteristic of the occupations practised is self-employment, which in turn necessitates extensive prospecting with frequent

20 Fraser, *The Gypsies* (Blackwell, 1995) p110.

journeying, sometimes to distant parts in search of custom, for artisan or trader, for artist or merchant. Gypsies and Travellers cling to their occupational independence, which has so far guaranteed their adaptability.[21]

Racialising Gypsy people

1.17   Well into the 19th century, the persecution of Gypsy people by the populace at large was still encouraged by many European states. For example, in Holland, 'Gypsy hunts' were organised on a regional basis, and while it was an offence merely to be a Gypsy, it was perfectly legal to kill one. The racial dimension in this persecution is revealed in the vocabulary of intolerance used against them. Both the Dutch and Italian languages share the simile 'as black as a Gypsy'.[22]

1.18   In the 19th century, a new stereotype, the 'real Romani' or 'genuine Gypsy' evolved, alongside contemporary concerns with racial purity. In time, the pseudo-science of racial hygiene would come to concur with ill-informed 'Gypsyologists' and posit the existence of small, racially pure groups of 'genuine Gypsies' in the midst of a population of congenitally degenerate subproletariat people who had taken to the travelling life in order to avoid work, taxes and other social responsibilities.[23] In other words, the 'Gypsy problem' had become overtly racialised:

> From now onwards alongside the stereotype dirty, dishonest, child-stealing villain we have the dark, handsome, violin-playing lover-Gypsy, a 'noble savage', camping in the woodlands and living off the Earth ... It is allowed that there exists somewhere ... the true Romanies ... racially pure, clean in habits, noble in spirit. But they are never found; they are, of course, a phantom people. Parliamentary debates, in Britain and elsewhere, contain many references to these imaginary beings.[24]

1.19   The Nazi Holocaust provides the clearest example of how the articulation of this ancient hatred of nomads became translated into a national policy of racial hygiene. Ethnic Gypsies became the target of genocidal policies under the Third Reich and half a million of them lost their lives precisely because they *were* Gypsies. While the

---

21   Liegeois, pp52–53, note 13.
22   Kenrick and Puxon, *The Destiny of Europe's Gypsies* (Chatto-Heinemann, 1972) p113.
23   Kenrick and Puxon, p54.
24   Kenrick and Puxon, p30 and p41.

methods of mass destruction employed by the Nazis may have been unprecedented,[25] the targets of their repression were not. What was unique was that Nazi ideology was able to provide an inescapable biological racism which legitimised existing prejudices.

1.20 For example, the scientist in charge of 'Race Hygiene and Population Biology' at the Reich Department of Health, Dr Ritter, conducted 'research' on Gypsy genealogy, which ultimately formed part of the legitimation for the extermination policies which followed. His findings confirmed his belief that:

> Most gypsies are not gypsies at all, but rather the products of matings with the German criminal asocial subproletariat ... More than 90 per cent of so-called 'gypsies' are of mixed-blood. It has been demonstrated that gypsies, in their racial crosses in our homeland, have mated predominantly with Yenisch [non-Gypsy Travellers] and with asocial criminal elements and that this has lead to the formation of a Yenisch-gypsy lumpenproletariat which costs the state enormous sums in welfare costs ... The gypsy question can only be considered solved when the main body of asocial and good-for-nothing gypsy individuals of mixed-blood is collected together in large labour camps and kept working there, and when the further breeding of this population of mixed-blood is stopped once and for all.[26]

1.21 Thus the ideology of Gypsy romanticism was contrasted with the savage treatment of nomads in the real world. What the myth of the 'real Romani' legitimated, both in Britain and in Europe, was the persecution of Gypsies and Travellers who did not conform to the stereotypical notions of Gypsyhood held by the dominant society. As Okely puts it 'real Gypsies are those who best fit the stereotype of the observer.'[27] An important legacy from this period is that it remains a continuing 'sedentary obsession'[28] to attempt to distinguish these 'genuine Gypsies' from other nomads, and the state's attempts to divide nomads along these arbitrary lines continues to today. To take just one example, in a radio interview in 1999, the then Home Secretary, Jack Straw MP, sought to draw a distinction between genuine Romani Gypsies and 'travellers masquerading as law-abiding gypsies',[29] when referring to an incident involving Travellers in the West Midlands.

25 See Bauman, *Modernity and the Holocaust* (Polity Press, 1989).
26 Cited in Muller-Hill, *Murderous Science* (Methuesen, New York, 1988) p69.
27 Okely, *The Traveller-Gypsies* (Cambridge University Press, 1983) p27.
28 Fraser, *The Gypsies* (Blackwell, 1995) p27.
29 *Guardian*, 'Scattergun Straw', 20 August 1999.

Irish Travellers

1.22   There is a common presumption that Irish Travellers originated as the 'dispossessed' of the 'Great Famine' in the mid-19th century. In fact, there is reference to Travellers in Ireland long before the Romanies arrived on the shores of Britain. O'Riain states:

> There is evidence which points to the existence from the fifth century of indigenous nomadic groups in Ireland. In the twelfth century the name *Tynkler* or *Tynker* was given to a group of nomads who for a long time had maintained a separate identity, social organisation and dialect.[30]

1.23   Though Irish Travellers share the reliance on 'self-employment' and a distinct language (Shelta and Romani, respectively)[31] with Romani Gypsies, they have had a different experience of prejudice and discrimination. It has been made clear above how the prejudice against Romani Gypsies in Britain has continued unabated since they first came there. For Irish Travellers, the prejudice increased over time and now continues unabated. An important example of latter day prejudice within Ireland is the very presumption that Travellers first appeared at the time of the Great Famine. In this way, they can be seen as 'failed settled people'[32] rather than as a distinct ethnic group.

1.24   A large part of this different experience can be traced back to the colonial experience in Ireland and the history of mass emigration. MacLaughlin states:

> [U]nlike Elizabethan England ... those forced from relatively prestigious positions in Gaelic Ireland into vagrancy and mendicancy in colonial Ireland often retained the respect of the native dispossessed well into the eighteenth century.[33]

1.25   Yet that 'respect' was not to last:

> In the case of Ireland, the radical disavowal of 'tinkers'[34] and Travellers probably occurred much later than elsewhere in western Europe. It was

---

30   O'Riain, *Solidarity with Travellers* (Roadside Books, Dublin, 2000) p8.

31   These languages have different origins. Shelta is derived from Gaelic and Romani from Sanskrit.

32   Michael McDonagh, 'Origins of the Travelling People' in *Travellers: Citizens of Ireland* (Parish of the Travelling People, Dublin, 2000) p22.

33   MacLaughlin, *Travellers and Ireland: Whose Country, Whose History?* (Cork University Press, 1995) p11.

34   Nowadays a derogatory name for Irish Travellers.

particularly exacerbated by the decimation of plebeian agrarian society from the late nineteenth century onwards and the growth of a bourgeois Irish nationalism and clericalism after the Famine.[35]

1.26   Paradoxically, the Irish nationalism of the 19th century and the (eventual) independence of the south of Ireland in the 20th century led not to the inclusion but to the exclusion of Irish Travellers, who were subject to the same assumptions, prejudices and mythology as beset their nomadic counterparts in Britain:

> Nomadism on the other hand, and Travelling communities within Ireland, were looked on as social anomalies, relics from a 'barbarous' past that was best forgotten because they represented all that was backward, unstable and evil about Irish society.[36]

1.27   The experience Irish Travellers did share with, at least, the poor in Ireland was emigration. Thus, they arrived in Britain: 'Although Irish emigration to England began several centuries ago, the first reliable report of Irish Travellers dates from 1850.'[37]

1.28   Once in Britain, Irish Travellers experienced also the prejudice that the Romani Gypsies had long been experiencing and that the Irish Travellers had already experienced in Ireland itself. Without repeating the history of persecution and prejudice borne by Gypsies in Britain (as outlined above) the story can be brought up to date by reference to an incident that occurred in the same year, 2003, as the Firle bonfire:

> [T]hat year saw what most believed from the evidence was the racially motivated murder of Johnny Delaney, a teenage [Irish] Traveller, who was attacked in the vicinity of an unauthorised encampment, where members of his family lived and who he had been visiting. In court proceedings the jury were technically unable to identify a racial motive and punish the perpetrators accordingly.[38]

35 MacLaughlin, *Travellers and Ireland: Whose Country, Whose History?* (Cork University Press, 1995) p15.

36 MacLaughlin, *Travellers and Ireland: Whose Country, Whose History?* (Cork University Press, 1995) p28.

37 Kenrick and Bakewell, *On the Verge: The Gypsies of England* (University of Hertfordshire Press, 1990) p10.

38 Crawley, *Moving Forward: The provision of accommodation for Travellers and Gypsies* (The Institute for Public Policy Research, 2004) p60.

The end of the road for nomadism?

1.29   Stewart[39] argues that successive generations have prematurely rung the funeral knell for nomadism and have prophesied its impending destruction. We have been told that Gypsies in particular are ana-chronistic throwbacks whose allegedly pre-industrial employment patterns – such as fruit-picking, peg-making and horse-trading – have been made increasingly obsolete through technological and social change:

> Every age, ours as much as its predecessors, believes it will be the last to be blessed (or cursed) by the presence of Gypsies. Well-wishers and hostile commentators, romantics and cynics alike are of fixed opinion that the 'wanderers of the world' have at last been 'domesticated', their way of life finally outmoded and that the 'time of the Gypsies' has run out ... In truth, Gypsies all over Europe have been remarkably successful in preserving their way of life, adapting to changed conditions in order to remain the same.[40]

1.30   As Kenrick and Bakewell observe:

> [For Gypsy people] work is not an end in itself but a means of earning money while staying independent. Independence requires mobility and adaptability. The Gypsies ... have adapted their trades successfully to growing industrialisation. [They] rarely have one single occupation but practice a combination of trades, such as scrap-collecting, tarmacking, hawking, fortune-telling and so on. These trades also require minimum equipment which enables them to stay mobile ... Work patterns distinguish the Gypsy and Travelling people from other groups. There may be migrant workers but rarely do these remain as independent of wage labour as the Gypsies.[41]

1.31   However, while the increased speed of motorised transport meant that it was possible to cover further distances, it has also led to increased sedentarism as well as nomadism. Fraser provides a good example of some of the ways in which social change has been absorbed by Gypsies and Travellers:

> In the face of urbanisation, industrialisation and other European pressures, Gypsies showed themselves able to maintain their autonomy by exploiting opportunities created by the dominant system. They

39   Stewart, *The Puzzle of Roma Persistence* (University of Hertfordshire Press, 1997).

40   Stewart, *The Puzzle of Roma Persistence* (University of Hertfordshire Press, 1997), p82.

41   Kenrick and Bakewell, *On the Verge: The Gypsies of England* (University of Hertfordshire Press, 1990). pp14–15.

resisted temptations to go over to wage-labour, as so many others were doing. Most – even when settled – seem to have clung tenaciously to some ideal of community and independence and self-employment. In Britain, urbanisation did not prove incompatible with maintaining a degree of nomadism ... they moved from village to town where necessary and abandoned old trades in favour of new activities more suited to the times, but without compromising their freedom, their ethnic identity or their occupational and residential flexibility ... A less resilient culture might have succumbed completely; the Gypsies did not.[42]

Defining Gypsies in law

1.32   The relative influence of race, ethnicity and class in the history of the treatment of Gypsy and Traveller people has a contemporary reflection in the sometimes contradictory ways in which the British state has attempted to define who is and who is not a Gypsy in law. For the purposes of the Race Relations Act (RRA) 1976, for example, Gypsies are defined, by reference to belonging to a 'racial group' through birth or marriage and is thus an ethnic definition. In planning law, however, Gypsies (sometimes referred to as 'gipsies' in statutes and reported cases) are defined as 'persons of a nomadic habit of life, whatever their race or origin'[43] and the law is concerned with how the Gypsy or Traveller concerned makes their living, rather than the circumstances of their birth. That is, being a Gypsy or Traveller in Britain simultaneously involves racial/ethnic, as well as economic considerations.

1.33   The Highways Act 1959 created an offence that could only be committed by Gypsies or Travellers, that of living on or hawking goods on the roadside. The courts, convinced that parliament could not have intended to explicitly discriminate against ethnic Gypsies or Travellers, decided that the term 'Gypsy' must be concerned with one's lifestyle rather than ethnicity.[44] Following on from this, the definition contained in the Caravan Sites and Control of Development Act 1960 was that 'Gypsies' were 'persons of nomadic habit of life, whatever their race or origin.'[45]

42   Fraser, *The Gypsies* (Blackwell, 1995) p93.
43   For a full discussion of the definition of 'Gypsy' for planning law purposes, see chapter 4 at paras 4.38–4.55 below.
44   *Mills v Cooper* [1967] 2 All ER 100.
45   Caravan Sites and Control of Development Act 1960 s24(8).

Accommodation for Gypsies and Travellers

1.34   Sedley J (as he then was), in one of the leading cases involving Gypsies and Travellers (relating to the Criminal Justice and Public Order Act (CJPOA)1994), *Atkinson*,[46] gave a useful potted history of the post-war legislative history:

> It is relevant to situate this new and in some ways draconic legislation [CJPOA 1994] in its context. For centuries the commons of England provided lawful stopping places for people whose way of life was or had become nomadic. Enough common land had survived the centuries of enclosure to make this way of life still sustainable, but by section 23 of the Caravan Sites and Control of Development Act 1960 local authorities were given the power to close the commons to travellers. This they proceeded to do with great energy, but made no use of the concomitant power given to them by section 24 of the same Act to open caravan sites to compensate for the closure of the commons. By the Caravan Sites Act 1968, therefore, Parliament legislated to make the section 24 power a duty, resting in rural areas on county councils rather than district councils (although the latter continued to possess the power to open sites). For the next quarter of a century there followed a history of non-compliance with the duties imposed by the Act of 1968, marked by a series of decisions of this court holding local authorities to be in breach of their statutory duty; but to apparently little practical effect. The default powers vested in central government, to which the court was required to defer, were rarely if ever used. The culmination of the tensions underlying the history of non-compliance was the enactment of the sections of the Act of 1994 ... There followed, in section 80(1), the wholesale repeal of the material part, Part II, of the Caravan Sites Act 1968.[47]

1.35   The government's position on the repeal of the duty to provide sites by CJPOA 1994 was that, henceforth, Gypsy and Traveller sites would be provided solely through private endeavour by Gypsies and Travellers themselves through the planning system.[48] With no duty in place, public site provision effectively ground to a halt and the number of pitches available began to decline.[49] Private site provision, in the meantime, has manifestly failed to keep up with the demand and Gypsies and Travellers have continued to encounter enormous hurdles in their way when trying to establish private sites.

46   *R v Lincolnshire CC ex p Atkinson; R v Wealden DC ex p Wales; R v Wealden DC ex p Stratford* (1996) 8 Admin LR 529; [1997] JPL 65.

47   *Atkinson* (1996) 8 Admin LR 529 at 533–534.

48   See chapter 4 below.

49   See chapter 3 below.

1.36   Allied with the loss of traditional sites has been a concomitant decline in the health of Gypsies and Travellers,[50] due to the extremely poor environmental conditions that often exist on unauthorised sites, most of which will be without basic services, such as water, refuse collection or sanitation. The cumulative effect of poverty and the steady diminution of stopping places, has impacted on Britain's nomadic populations in serious ways. An analysis of research conducted on Gypsy and Traveller health found 'high levels of perinatal mortality, still-birth and infant mortality. Traveller children are between one-and-a-half and two times more likely to die in the first year of life than the children of settled communities. Generally ... travelling families [are] seriously disadvantaged in health and healthcare ...'[51]

1.37   A significant element of the Travelling community has also been impoverished, both through a reduction in trade with settled society, and through the loss of traditional stopping places. Even for those on official sites, restrictive licence conditions have often denied Gypsies and Travellers the opportunity of remaining economically active.[52]

1.38   This brings us back to the question of defining 'Gypsies' at law, since to qualify for provision under the relevant (and now repealed) Part II of the Caravan Sites Act (CSA) 1968, Gypsies and Travellers had to demonstrate that they were within the legal definition of 'Gypsy'. Over the years the courts have continued to emphasise the centrality of economy over ethnicity. The associations in the sedentary mind between Gypsies and this type of economic nomadism has now become so strong that such travel has become the essential element of Gypsy status in law. The implications of institutionalising the legal definition of 'Gypsy' in this way remain unresolved. This brings us to a consideration of 'New Travellers', since, arguably, it was this group which the definition was ultimately intended to exclude from provision.

New Travellers

Many people feel that the law operates unfairly in that it was intended to support the traditional way of life of Romani peoples but has been used

---

50 See chapter 7 below.

51 Hawes, *Gypsies, Travellers and the Health Service* (Policy Press, 1997).

52 See, for example, Hyman, *Sites for Travellers: a study in five London boroughs* (London Race and Housing Research Unit, 1989) p12.

by several groups of hippies, drug-takers and law-breakers who drive around in old cars and vans ...[53]

1.39   Quite in what way these 'hippies' were supposed to have used the CSA 1968 is not made clear by the authors of the above statement but it is untenable to imply that any significant number of them benefited from site provision under the Act.[54] Local authorities had failed to provide anywhere near adequate provision for traditional Gypsies and Travellers, let alone this new type of Traveller who were, if anything, even more despised than traditional (ethnic) Gypsies. Elsewhere, various arms of the state reinforced the view that the 'hippies' should be treated differently than traditional nomads:

> The situation has become more complex in recent years with the emergence of groups who do not wish to use the sites that are provided, may travel in large numbers, may not be nomadic and for whom the 1968 Act provisions may not have been provided. These may include some of the group colloquially known as New Age Travellers.[55]

1.40   The definition of 'nomadic' was at the centre of a court case in 1992 in which South Hams District Council in Devon argued that a group of 'New Age' Travellers encamped in their area were not Gypsies and were therefore owed no duty regarding site provision.[56] The court confirmed the economic meaning of nomadism, namely that to be a 'gipsy', one's travel must be related to how one makes a living:

> ... the definition of 'gypsies [in CSCDA 1960 s24(8) and CSA 1968 s16] imports the requirement that there should be some recognisable connection between the wandering or travelling and the means whereby the persons concerned make or seek their livelihood. Persons, or individuals, who move from place to place merely as the fancy may take them and without any connection between the movement and their means of livelihood fall outside these statutory definitions.[57]

---

53 C Barclay, Gypsy Caravan Sites, House of Commons Research Note 92/30.

54 There are currently believed to be three New Traveller local authority sites in England and none in Wales all of which were set up after the repeal of the duty to provide sites – information from the Travellers' Advice Team at the Community Law Partnership. No official statistics are available.

55 Consultation Paper, *Reform of the Caravan Sites Act*, Department of the Environment (DoE), March 1992.

56 *R v South Hams DC ex p Gibb* [1994] 4 All ER 1012.

57 [1994] 4 All ER 1012 at 1012.

1.41   This case established that Gypsy status could be gained and lost depending on the lifestyle of the individual Gypsy or Traveller. As such the case failed to exclude 'New Age' Travellers as a group – as many local authorities had hoped – but rather established a some-what paradoxical situation wherein a Romani Gypsy or Irish Traveller by birth living on a static caravan site could well fall outside the definition. An additional implication is that some New Travellers clearly might qualify as 'Gypsies', provided their travel had an economic purpose.

1.42   Kenrick and Puxon discern a historical pattern here:

> When the racial theories are swept aside, we find that the detractors have once more changed ground. Once again, they assert that the majority of people who call themselves gypsies are not gypsies at all. They are social misfits, the drop-outs of society who have taken up a pseudo-gypsy way of life to avoid social responsibilities, taxes and other inconveniences of modern life.[58]

1.43   As Fraser has stated:

> If excuse is needed for having plunged here into such legal niceties, it lies in the fact that we shall find the question of Gypsy identity has attended their passage through Europe ever since they first arrived, and these legal debates in the English courts serve very well to illustrate an important dilemma which refuses to go away in any discussion of Gypsies. Is it the way of life that is paramount in definition?[59]

1.44   While the media-hype around what became known (to everyone apart from themselves) as 'New Age Travellers' focused heavily on one particular group, the 'Peace Convoy', even by the early 1980s there were many 'alternative' Travelling groups staging festivals and fairs throughout the summer months. As well as performing as jugglers, musicians, clowns and fire-eaters, and trading things they had made or bought, many of these New Travellers also focused their nomadism around the fruit-picking and the fairs, and, like the Gypsies before them, their rejection of fixed wage-labour attracted particular prejudice. Free festivals themselves ultimately became expressly prohibited and were subject to repressive measures by the state – including a paramilitary assault against New Travellers by the police at the so-called 'Battle of the Beanfield' near Stonehenge in

---

58 Kenrick and Puxon, *The Destiny of Europe's Gypsies* (Chatto-Heinemann, 1972) pp30–31.
59 Fraser, The *Gypsies* (Blackwell, 1995) p5.

1985.[60] By these actions, the economic and social basis of the New Traveller community itself became criminalised.

1.45   There are profound similarities between the function of nomadism for traditional Gypsy people and that of New Travellers.[61] The courts have recognised these similarities since the earliest days of New Traveller culture, although both central and local government have been loathe to accept this reality in practice:

> In 1986, a Yorkshire court ruled that a group known as 'The Mutants' were Gypsies within the meaning of the [1968 Caravan Sites] Act. In Avon, a New Age Traveller, Mr Rexworthy, was ruled to be a Gypsy. [Yet] the Government has stated ... in Parliament that it does not on the whole see New Age Travellers as Gypsies, to be helped by the 1968 Act.[62]
> ...
> The distinction being made between acceptable 'true Gypsies' and unacceptable other travellers is akin to the 19th century concerns over the 'genuine Romani'. Like previous dividing practices, spoken tolerance for 'real Gypsies' is always expressed in relation to another, less defined group, be it 'half-breeds', Didicois, Irish travellers, tinkers, vagrants or New Age Travellers.[63]

1.46   The chronic shortage of sites, which has resulted from the policies described above, has sometimes, unfortunately, led to friction between Gypsy and Traveller groups themselves, all fighting for a minimal amount of provision. Thankfully, there are signs now that Gypsies and Travellers realise that the best way to progress their arguments is together:

> The major organisations representing Traveller and Gypsy communities have forged the Traveller Law Reform Coalition to campaign for the basic rights of somewhere to pitch a camp and access to basic services and have rallied behind the Traveller Law Reform Bill.[64] This is a unique alliance of Romani Gypsies, Irish Travellers and New Travellers who

60   See Kenrick and Clark, *Moving On: The Gypsies and Travellers of Britain* (University of Hertfordshire Press, 1996) pp121–122.
61   This fact is increasingly recognised in planning appeals. Many of the New Travellers discussed in chapter 4 below on planning law have been officially accepted as 'gipsies' due to their employment patterns.
62   Kenrick and Bakewell, *On the Verge: the Gypsies of England* (University of Hertfordshire Press, 1995) p50.
63   *On the Verge* p52.
64   Drafted by the Traveller Law Reform Unit at the University of Cardiff and moved (unsuccessfully on both occasions) as a private member's bill in 2002 and 2003. See further, chapter 9 below.

have previously found it challenging to work together, and in the past blamed each other for the loss of sites and the loss of public tolerance.[65]

Culture

1.47 It can be important, when considering this area of law, to have regard to cultural values of both Gypsies and other ethnic Traveller groups (a lot of which are shared). Some areas of commonality include:

- nomadism;
- the dominant position of the family and extended families;
- early and close kin marriage;
- work patterns;
- rituals surrounding death and marriage;
- relationship with the dominant settled society;
- language;
- the experience of discrimination.[66]

1.48 Where relevant, reference is made to Gypsy and ethnic Traveller culture throughout this book.

Outline of the book

1.49 This book is intended as a comprehensive coverage of the law as it relates to Gypsies and Travellers. It only covers the law as it relates to England and Wales.

1.50 Reference is made throughout to Gypsies (meaning 'Romani Gypsies') and Travellers (encompassing Irish, Scottish, Welsh and New Travellers) except where specific reference is made to a particular group. It is made clear in the text when a statutory definition of 'Gypsy' is being discussed.

1.51 Travelling Showpeople are discussed where relevant.[67] This book does not deal directly with houseboat dwellers or bargees ('Water Gypsies') since the law relating to them is very different and outside

---

65 Crawley, *Moving Forward* (IPPR, 2004) p24.
66 To give just one example, see Michael McDonagh, 'Ethnicity and Culture' in *Travellers: Citizens of Ireland* (Parish of the Travelling People, Dublin, 2000) pp26–31.
67 For a discussion of Travelling Showpeople, see Kenrick and Clark, *Moving On*, pp35–37.

the scope of this work.[68] However some of the discussion of the law (for example, on homelessness, education and health) will be of use to these groups.

1.52   Since it came into force on 2 October 2000, the Human Rights Act (HRA) 1998 has had an affect on all the areas of law covered in this book and its impact is discussed in chapter 2. Public provision of sites remains an essential subject and is dealt with in chapter 3. For those Gypsies and Travellers attempting to set up their own sites, as recommended by the government when bringing in the Criminal Justice and Public Order Act 1994, planning law is of vital importance and is dealt with in chapter 4. The need for adequate site provision of all sorts stems from the large numbers of Gypsies and Travellers who remain on unauthorised encampments and the law on this subject is dealt with in chapter 5. Over recent years the potential importance and use of the homelessness legislation has come to the fore and the law on this area is dealt with in chapter 6. Education and health are central concerns for Gypsies and Travellers and the law relating to these two areas is in chapter 7. As with the HRA 1998, discrimination legislation has an impact on all the areas of law discussed and is considered in chapter 8.

1.53   Each chapter flags up, either in the course of the chapter or in the conclusion to the chapter, potential or expected changes to the law, 'grey areas' and campaigns for changes to the law. There is a brief round-up of points for the future in chapter 9, the conclusion.

1.54   The appendices contain useful matters for reference. Appendix A deals with court and other procedures and should be referred to in conjunction with relevant parts of the various chapters.

1.55   The law as it relates to Gypsies and Travellers in England and Wales is correct as at 17 May 2004.[69]

---

68 For a discussion of Water Gypsies, see Sandford, *Rokkering to the Gorjios* (University of Hertfordshire Press, 1973) pp75–78.
69 See Recent Developments in Gypsy and Traveller Law at pxi above.

CHAPTER 2

How the Human Rights Act 1998 affects Gypsies and Travellers

The duties on public authorities under the Human Rights Act 1998

2.1   The main purpose of the Human Rights Act (HRA) 1998, which came fully into force on 2 October 2000, is to make the European Convention on Human Rights (ECHR, or the Convention) a part of UK law, so that the rights which it contains are made more practical and effective through being more directly accessible to people living in this country.

2.2   The HRA 1998 imposes new duties on all of the 'public authorities' with which Gypsies and Travellers are frequently in contact, including: government ministers and departments, the Planning Inspectorate, local planning authorities, the police, education authorities, health authorities, social services and the courts.[1]

2.3   HRA 1998 s6(1) makes it unlawful for a 'public authority' to act in a way which is incompatible with a Convention right, unless mandated to do so by legislation which cannot itself be read compatibly with Convention rights.

2.4   HRA 1998 s3(1) also requires all legislation to be read and given effect in a way which is compatible with Convention rights, 'so far as it is possible to do so'.

2.5   Most of the powers exercised by public authorities which most directly affect Gypsies and Travellers are broad discretionary powers conferred by statutes in wide and open-ended terms. Such powers must now be interpreted so as to be compatible with Convention rights, which means that the discretion which they give to public authorities must be exercised in a way which respects the Convention rights of Gypsies and Travellers.

2.6   To give an example, Town and Country Planning Act (TCPA) 1990 s187B confers very broad discretions on a local planning authority and the court to, respectively, apply for and grant injunctions to restrain breaches of planning control. To the extent that those discretions are each capable of being exercised incompatibly with the article 8 Convention rights of Gypsies and Travellers, HRA 1998 s3(1) requires that they be interpreted restrictively so as not to authorise such breaches of Convention rights. Since the discretion-conferring language of TCPA 1990 s187B is in terms very broad, and nothing in it compels a planning

---

1   HRA 1998 s6(3)(a).

authority or court to apply for or grant injunctions in breach of article 8, it is clearly 'possible' for the provision to be interpreted compatibly with article 8.

The most relevant Convention rights

2.7 The two Convention rights which are of most particular relevance to Gypsies and Travellers are articles 8 and 14. Article 8(1) provides that:

> (1) Everyone has the right to respect for his private and family life, his home and his correspondence.
> (2) There shall be no interference by a public authority with the exercise of this right except such as is in accordance with the law and is necessary in a democratic society in the interests of national security, public safety or the economic well-being of the country, for the prevention of disorder or crime, for the protection of health or morals, or for the protection of the rights and freedoms of others.

2.8 Article 8(1) has also recently been interpreted as guaranteeing the right to respect for the traditional way of life of a minority.[2] However, it is subject to justified limitations (under article 8(2)), where such interference is necessary in a democratic society in the service of various other enumerated interests, including most relevantly 'the protection of the rights of others', which has been interpreted to include the protection of the environment for others' enjoyment.[3]

2.9 Article 14 provides that:

> The enjoyment of the rights and freedoms set forth in this Convention shall be secured without discrimination on any ground such as sex, race, colour, language, religion, political or other opinion, national or social origin, association with a national minority, property, birth or other status.

Thus, it requires that no-one shall be discriminated against in the enjoyment of their Convention rights on any ground, including matters such as race, sex, national origin, or any other status. Article 14 is in principle relevant to any action or inaction by the State which treats different categories of people in different ways.

---

2 *Chapman v United Kingdom* [2001] 33 EHRR 399 at paras 71–74.
3 [2001] 33 EHRR 399 at para 82.

2.10   The right in article 14 is a right not to be discriminated against in the enjoyment of a Convention right. It is not therefore a free-standing equality provision, but relates only to differential treatment in relation to Convention rights. It is also important to appreciate that differences of treatment, even in relation to Convention rights, are capable of being objectively justified under article 14. Not every difference of treatment therefore amounts to a breach of article 14. What has to be established in order to make out a breach of article 14 is that other people in an analogous or relevantly similar situation have been treated more favourably, and that there is no objective or reasonable justification for such difference of treatment.

2.11   In deciding whether a difference of treatment is justified in this sense, a court will look to see whether the difference of treatment serves a legitimate aim, and whether the means employed to achieve that aim are proportionate.

2.12   Another Convention right which is of considerable relevance to Gypsies and Travellers is the right to education in article 2 of Protocol 1.[4]

The relevant Convention case law

2.13   HRA 1998 s6 requires public authorities to consider carefully the proportionality of their actions when making decisions which interfere with article 8 rights. Thus public authorities are required to undertake a systematic analysis of the relevant issues and to ensure that they have taken into account the answers to a properly articulated framework of questions before reaching such decisions.

2.14   Translating this requirement into practical reality for decision-makers on the ground is notoriously difficult. In order to make the task more intelligible, it is possible to distil from the most relevant Convention case law (in particular *Buckley v United Kingdom*[5] and *Chapman v United Kingdom*[6]) a number of discrete questions which public authorities must ask themselves and answer when deciding whether a particular decision or step would be compatible with the Convention rights of those Gypsies and Travellers affected.

---

4   See paras 2.63–2.64 and chapter 7 below.
5   [1996] 23 EHRR 101.
6   [2001] 33 EHRR 399.

Article 8: the nature of the rights in issue

2.15 It is clear that enforcement action against unauthorised development which is also somebody's home constitutes an interference with their article 8(1) rights which requires justification. It is also clear that article 8 is engaged wherever there is an interference with a de facto home: the fact that the home was established unlawfully in the first place does not prevent it from being within the scope of article 8. It is merely a factor to be taken into account in the overall balancing exercise in deciding whether or not the interference is justified (ie, proportionate).

2.16 However, the precise nature of the rights which are in issue under article 8(1) is important, because it will affect the approach which should be taken in assessing whether any interference with those rights is justified under article 8(2). In particular, it will affect the degree of deference (if any) which it is appropriate for a court to accord to the balancing exercise conducted by the public authority. Just as it is well-established in Convention case law that the nature of the right protected, and the nature of the activities being regulated, are important criteria in determining the appropriate scope of the 'margin of appreciation'[7] in a particular set of circumstances, so those factors will also be relevant to the degree of deference which is due to the judgment of the authority in making its own decision about whether the action proposed (eg, enforcement action) breaches article 8.

2.17 On this question of how to characterise the rights in issue under article 8(1), the European Court of Human Rights (ECtHR) in *Chapman v United Kingdom*[8] made a very clear finding which goes significantly beyond its earlier decision in *Buckley v United Kingdom*. Whereas in *Buckley*[9] the Court held that the case concerned the applicant's right to respect for her 'home' and considered it unnecessary to decide whether it also concerned the applicant's right

---

7 The 'margin of appreciation' is the concept developed by the European Court of Human Rights (ECtHR) to give a certain latitude to states in exercising the above mentioned balancing exercise, especially since the ECtHR itself is a supranational tribunal and at one stage removed from the matters involved. See also paras 2.31–2.35 below.

8 *Chapman v United Kingdom* [2001] 33 EHRR 399 at para 73.

9 *Buckley v United Kingdom* [1996] 23 EHRR 101 at para 54.

to respect for her 'private life' and 'family life', in *Chapman* the Court expressly held that:

> The applicant's occupation of her caravan is an integral part of her ethnic identity as a Gypsy, reflecting the long tradition of that minority of following a travelling lifestyle ... Measures which affect the applicant's stationing of her caravans have therefore a wider impact than on the right to respect for home. They also affect her ability to maintain her identity as a Gypsy and to lead her private and family life in accordance with that tradition.[10]

2.18   The ECtHR also observed that this was the case even though many Gypsies no longer live a wholly nomadic existence and increasingly settle for longer periods in one place in order to facilitate, for example, the education of their children.

2.19   The ECtHR's clear finding that measures affecting Gypsies' stationing of their caravans affect not merely the right to respect for their 'home' in the narrow sense, but their ability as members of an ethnic minority to continue to live according to their traditional travelling lifestyle, is of considerable significance to the approach which should be taken by public authorities when determining whether any interference with such an important right is justified in all the circumstances: the more important the Convention right, the greater the onus of justification on the public authority and therefore the greater the scrutiny that should be afforded to such justifications by the courts.

Nature and extent of interference with article 8 rights

2.20   In *Chapman* the ECtHR found that the decisions of the planning authorities refusing to allow the applicant to remain on her land in her caravans constituted an interference with her article 8(1) rights as identified above.[11] It is not enough, however, for the public authority to end its inquiry into the interference question there. It must also go on to consider the nature and extent of the interference with the article 8 rights of the Gypsy or Traveller.

2.21   This should involve the authority in deciding how serious the interference is in the circumstances of the particular case. The interference would be serious, for example, if a measure was taken imposing criminal sanctions if the Gypsies or Travellers continue to

---

10 *Chapman* [2001] 33 EHRR 399 at para 73.
11 [2001] 33 EHRR 399 at para 78.

use their land for the stationing of their caravans, in circumstances where there are no alternative sites available, leaving them with no other way in which they can continue to lead their traditional lifestyle within the law. Such a measure would affect the very essence of their rights under article 8 and as such the onus of justification upon the public authorities for such an interference would be a heavy one.

2.22   Any decision taken by a public authority which clearly constitutes an interference with an individual's article 8(1) rights calls for justification under article 8(2) as being 'in accordance with the law', pursuing a legitimate aim and as being 'necessary in a democratic society' in pursuit of that aim.

Interference in accordance with the law

2.23   In *Chapman* it was conceded that the various measures which had been taken by the planning authorities that interfered with the applicant's article 8 rights were 'in accordance with the law' for the purposes of article 8.[12] The requirement that any interference with article 8 rights be in accordance with the law means that there must not only exist a formal legal basis for the interference (for example, a statutory discretion), but that any law which confers a broad discretion must also give sufficient indication as to the scope of that discretion. As the ECtHR stated in *Malone v United Kingdom*:[13]

> It would be contrary to the rule of law for the legal discretion granted to the executive to be expressed in terms of an unfettered power. Consequently, the law must indicate the scope of any such discretion conferred on the competent authorities and the manner of its exercise with sufficient clarity, having regard to the legitimate aim of the measure in question, to give the individual adequate protection against arbitrary interference.

2.24   Generally, a public authority's powers in relation to Gypsies and Travellers, for example its powers of enforcement in relation to unauthorised developments, will satisfy both aspects of this requirement. If the authority is in any doubt as to whether a particular power which it intends to exercise satisfies this requirement, however, it should ask itself whether the provision in question satisfies the *Malone* test; that is, whether the provision indicates the scope of the discretion conferred on the authority, and

12 [2001] 33 EHRR 399 at para 79.
13 [1985] 7 EHRR 14 at para 68.

the manner of its exercise, with sufficient clarity to give individuals in the position of those affected adequate protection against arbitrary interference.

Legitimate aim

2.25   In *Chapman*, the government argued that the measures in question pursued the enforcement of planning controls which were in the interests of the economic well-being of the country and the preservation of the environment and public health. The ECtHR accepted the applicant's argument that the government had not put forward any detail to substantiate the aims allegedly pursued but relied on a general assertion; it found that the measures pursued the legitimate aim of protecting the 'rights of others' through preservation of the environment, and did not find it necessary to determine whether any other aims were involved.[14]

2.26   As with the nature of the rights in issue, the precise aim pursued by a measure is a matter of importance when it comes to justification, because as a matter of Convention case law the nature of the aim pursued is recognised to be one of the criteria which may affect the scope of the margin of appreciation to be afforded to the national decision-maker:

> ... the scope of the margin of appreciation is not identical in respect of each of the aims [in article 8(2)] justifying restrictions on a right.[15]

Similarly, as a matter of domestic law under the HRA 1998, the precise aim pursued by a measure may affect the degree of deference which is considered by a court to be due to the authority concerned.

2.27   Generally, the enforcement powers available to planning authorities will pursue the legitimate aim of protecting the rights of others in the sense of environmental protection. However, it remains necessary for the authority to be satisfied in any particular case that a particular enforcement measure is genuinely pursued for such a legitimate aim, and not for some other illegitimate purpose such as merely appeasing a vociferous or politically important local population or group who are objecting to the particular development.

---

14   *Chapman* [2001] 33 EHRR 399 at para 82.
15   *Dudgeon v United Kingdom* [1982] 4 EHRR 149 at para 52.

Necessary in a democratic society

2.28   The next stage in the structured analysis required by the Convention involves consideration of the question whether an interference with article 8 rights is 'necessary in a democratic society'. The abstract formulation of the test to be applied at this stage was restated in *Chapman* in familiar terms: an interference will be considered 'necessary in a democratic society' for a legitimate aim if it answers a 'pressing social need' and, in particular, if it is proportionate to the legitimate aim pursued.[16] This is what is often referred to as the 'proportionality requirement'.

2.29   Although the test for proportionality is easily formulated in the abstract, in practice precisely what proportionality requires in a particular context turns on the application to the facts of each case of general principles for assessing the proportionality of the interference. The general principles will be identified first before returning to consider the relevant factual matters which are to be taken into account by public authorities when deciding whether or not an interference with a Convention right is justified.

The general principles derived from *Buckley* and *Chapman*

2.30   The following general principles can be extracted from both the *Buckley v United Kingdom* and *Chapman v United Kingdom* decisions and will be followed by the ECtHR when assessing the proportionality of an interference with article 8 rights.

A wide 'margin of appreciation'

2.31   In principle, the national authorities enjoy a wide margin of appreciation 'in so far as the exercise of discretion involving a multitude of local factors is inherent in the choice and implementation of planning policies'.[17]

2.32   The rationale for this is also explained,[18] and is principally the common sense reason familiar to any court (whether exercising a reviewing or appellate jurisdiction), namely that, compared to the

16   *Chapman* [2001] 33 EHRR 399 at para 90.
17   [2001] 33 EHRR 399 at para 92 and *Buckley* [1996] 23 EHRR 101 at para 75.
18   *Chapman* [2001] 33 EHRR 399 at para 92.

primary fact-finder, the ECtHR is not well equipped to challenge judgments which have been made on detailed questions of local fact by a decision-maker who has visited the site and heard the evidence. Planning inspectors, in short, are much better placed to assess the impact of a particular use on the particular locality and therefore to assess the legitimacy of planning objections to that use. It is primarily a matter of relative institutional competence.

2.33   The effect of a presumptively wide margin of appreciation is that, in most cases concerning the exercise of planning judgment, the ECtHR will confine itself to a standard of review which is not at all intense and which centres on whether there has been a 'manifest error of appreciation by the national authorities.'[19]

Factors affecting the width of the margin of appreciation

2.34   Although the ECtHR's starting point is a presumptively wide margin of appreciation in this context, it also explicitly recognises in *Buckley*[20] and *Chapman*[21] that certain factors will affect the width of the margin of appreciation to be accorded in any particular case. These factors include:

1. the nature of the Convention right in issue;
2. its importance for the individual;
3. the nature of the activities restricted; and
4. the nature of the aim pursued by the restrictions.

2.35   The ECtHR in *Chapman*[22] also considered, but did not accept, the argument that a fifth factor should also be recognised as narrowing the margin of appreciation to be accorded to national authorities, namely the emerging international consensus among Council of Europe Member States recognising the special needs of minorities and an obligation to protect their security, identity and lifestyle.[23] The Court accepted that such an international consensus was indeed emerging, 'not only for the purpose of safeguarding the interests of the minorities themselves but to preserve a cultural diversity of value to the whole community',[24] and this clearly informed its analysis of

---

19 *Chapman* [2001] 33 EHRR 399 at para 92.
20 *Buckley* [1996] 23 EHRR 101 at para 76.
21 *Chapman* [2001] 33 EHRR 399 at para 91.
22 [2001] 33 EHRR 399 at paras 93–94.
23 The Framework Convention for the Protection of National Minorities, Strasbourg, 1/2/1195, Council of Europe Doc ETS 157.
24 *Chapman* [2001] 33 EHRR 399 at para 93.

the nature of the article 8 rights in issue, but it was not persuaded that the consensus was sufficiently concrete for it to derive any guidance as to the conduct or standards which States considered desirable in any particular situation. It therefore declined to reduce the margin of appreciation accorded to States in light of that recognition.

The importance of procedural safeguards

2.36   In determining whether the State has remained within its margin of appreciation when fixing the regulatory framework, the ECtHR regards the procedural safeguards available to the individual as being 'especially material'.[25] In particular, it will 'examine whether the decision-making process leading to measures of interference was fair and such as to afford due respect to the interests safeguarded to the individual by article 8.'[26]

2.37   Particular attention is paid to *procedural* safeguards in the decision-making process to compensate for the less intense standard of review adopted in relation to the *substance* of the measure which interferes with Convention rights.

2.38   Whether, in a particular case, an individual has yet had the opportunity of taking a procedural step which they wish to take, such as exercising a right of appeal to the secretary of state against the refusal of planning permission, should therefore be carefully considered by a planning authority when deciding whether or not to take enforcement action. Proceeding straight to enforcement, before allowing the Gypsy or Traveller an opportunity to persuade a planning inspector to grant planning permission may therefore be found to be precipitate.

Recognition of a positive obligation

2.39   The ECtHR has expressly recognised that the vulnerable position of Gypsies and Travellers as a minority means that some special consideration should be given to their needs and their different lifestyle both in the relevant regulatory planning framework and in arriving at decisions in particular cases,[27] and that to this extent there

25   *Chapman* [2001] 33 EHRR 399 at para 92 and *Buckley* [1996] 23 EHRR 101 at paras 76–77. See Recent Developments in Gypsy and Traveller Law at pxi above.

26   *Chapman* [2001] 33 EHRR 399 at para 92 and *Buckley* [1996] 23 EHRR 101 at paras 76–77.

27   *Buckley* [1996] 23 EHRR 101 at paras 76, 80, 84.

is a positive obligation imposed on States by article 8 to 'facilitate the Gypsy way of life'.[28]

Relevant factual matters

2.40   The general principles set out above should always guide any assessment of the proportionality of a given interference with article 8 rights. Against that background, the following can be identified as the most important factual matters which are taken into account by the ECtHR when applying its general principles to the concrete facts of a particular case in order to assess the proportionality of the interference:

- the seriousness of the impact of the measure on the most basic rights of the individuals concerned, including on the security of their accommodation, their family life, health, children's education and ability to maintain their traditional travelling way of life;[29]
- the availability of an alternative site, including its suitability for the individuals' particular needs, the financial circumstances of those affected, and the efforts made to find alternative sites;[30]
- whether there has been a full and fair opportunity for the individuals concerned to make their case for respecting their article 8(1) rights, including those arising from their Gypsy status, before the relevant administrative authorities, including a planning inspector;[31]
- whether the site was established unlawfully;[32]
- the strength of the reasons relied on as the justification for the interference (usually this will be the protection of the environment);[33]
- the seriousness of the enforcement measures taken, and whether other, less restrictive enforcement measures were available.[34]

---

28   *Chapman* [2001] 33 EHRR 399 at para 96.

29   [2001] 33 EHRR 399 at para 105.

30   [2001] 33 EHRR 399 at paras 103–104, 111–112 and *Buckley* [1996] 23 EHRR 101 at para 81.

31   *Chapman* [2001] 33 EHRR 399 at paras 106–109 and *Buckley* [1996] 23 EHRR 101 at para 80.

32   *Chapman* [2001] 33 EHRR 399 at para 102.

33   [2001] 33 EHRR 399 at para 110.

34   *Buckley* [1996] 23 EHRR 101 at para 83.

2.41   A properly conducted assessment of the proportionality of an interference should therefore involve consideration of evidence relating to as many of the above factual matters as are relevant in the particular case.

2.42   The approach of the ECtHR in both *Buckley* and *Chapman* was that the initial assessment of the necessity for a particular interference must be for 'the national authorities, who by reason of their direct and continuous contact with the vital forces of their countries are in principle better placed than an international court to evaluate local needs and conditions'.[35]

The relevant domestic case law post-Human Rights Act 1998

2.43   The combined effect of both the duties imposed on public authorities by the Human Rights Act (HRA) 1998 and the decision of the ECtHR in *Chapman* has recently been considered in a number of decisions of the domestic courts.

Article 8 and enforcement decisions

2.44   Local authorities wishing to evict Gypsies and Travellers from unauthorised sites on private land have increasingly been resorting to the power in the planning legislation to apply for an injunction to restrain a breach of planning control.[36] Before the HRA 1998, the well-established approach of the judiciary when dealing with such applications for injunctive relief was to treat the court's discretion as being narrowly circumscribed by the fact that the planning authorities had already decided what constituted a breach of planning control.[37] The judiciary in such cases regarded the planning authorities as having already struck the balance between the general public interest on the one hand and the interests of the individuals who were to be evicted on the other, and saw any role for the courts in considering questions such as the availability of alternative sites, or the hardship which would be caused by an injunction, as a usurpation of that policy-making function, and contrary to the will of

---

35   *Chapman* [2001] 33 EHRR 399 at para 91.

36   See Town and Country Planning Act 1990 s187B and chapter 4, para 4.109.

37   The leading authorities were two Court of Appeal decisions, *Mole Valley DC v Smith* [1992] 3 PLR 22 (decided under the predecessor power to grant injunctions) and *Hambleton DC v Bird* [1995] 3 PLR 8.

Parliament which had entrusted those powers to the planning authorities. In other words, they adopted an entirely submissive approach to the decisions of the planning authorities, subject only to a residual power to correct manifest errors or perverse decisions. It is exemplified by the decision of Hoffmann J at first instance in *Mole Valley DC v Smith*:[38]

> There can be no doubt that requiring [the Gypsies] to leave the site would cause considerable hardship. This court, however, is not entrusted with a general jurisdiction to solve social problems. The striking of a balance between the requirements of planning policy and the needs of these defendants is a matter which, in my view, has been entrusted to other authorities.

2.45   The central issue in the important case of *South Buckinghamshire DC v Porter*[39] was whether this approach survived the coming into force of the HRA 1998, or whether the fact that the article 8 rights of Gypsies and Travellers were engaged in such cases, meant that a court must now make an independent judgment in deciding whether or not to grant an injunction. *Porter* was a consolidated appeal against the decisions made in four separate cases by judges in the High Court. In each case, the judge at first instance had granted injunctions to restrain the use by Gypsies and Travellers of land for residential purposes in breach of planning control, and the question for the Court of Appeal and the House of Lords was, therefore, whether those judges had directed themselves correctly about the approach they should take in the exercise of their discretion.

2.46   In a judgment which was subsequently unanimously approved by the House of Lords, the Court of Appeal[40] set out the approach

38   Cited with approval in the Court of Appeal in the same case [1992] 3 PLR 22 at 31. See, to similar effect, Lord Donaldson MR at 32: 'it is not for the courts to usurp the policy decision-making functions of the Secretary of State ... by a side-wind', and Balcombe LJ at 33: 'the court is being asked to reverse the decisions of the authorities to whom Parliament has entrusted the relevant decision, not on grounds of illegality, but on grounds of policy'. The reasoning of Pill LJ in *Hambleton* at 15 was to precisely the same effect and he stated that the fact that the granting of an injunction is dependent on the court's discretion 'does not however entitle a judge ... to act as a court of appeal against a planning decision or to base a refusal to grant an injunction upon his view of the overall public interest.' The judge below in that case was criticised for having taken upon himself the role of assessing the benefits and disbenefits to the public as a whole, thereby 'taking upon himself the policy function of the planning authorities and housing authorities and their powers and duties.'
39   [2003] UKHL 26, [2003] 2 WLR 1547.
40   [2001] EWCA Civ 1549, [2002] 1 WLR 1359, [2002] 1 All ER 425 at paras 38–42.

which is to be applied by a court considering an application for an injunction brought under TCPA 1990 s187B in order to be consistent with the court's duty under HRA 1998 s6(1) to act compatibly with Convention rights. The Court of Appeal held that the judge hearing an application for an injunction under section 187B is not entitled to reach his or her own independent view of the planning merits of the case, which he or she is required to take as having been decided within the planning process.[41] However, in deciding whether or not to grant injunctive relief, the Court of Appeal held that the judge must consider a variety of factors which must be weighed in the balance, including:

- questions of hardship for the defendant and his or her family, including the impact on the family's health and education;
- the availability of alternative sites;
- the planning history of the site;
- the need to enforce planning control in the general interest;
- the degree and flagrancy of the breach of planning control;
- whether other enforcement measures had been tried in the past;
- whether there was any urgency in the situation;
- health and safety considerations;
- previous planning decisions;
- the local planning authority's decision to seek injunctive relief; and
- the degree of environmental damage resulting from the breach of planning control.

2.47   The Court of Appeal also recognised that the weight to be given to these considerations in the balancing exercise may vary depending on a number of other factors. For example, the relevance of, and weight to be attached to, previous planning decisions will depend on matters such as how recent they are, the extent to which considerations of hardship and availability of alternative sites were taken into account, and the strength of the conclusions reached on land use and environmental issues.[42] Similarly, the relevance and weight of the local planning authority's decision will depend on the extent to which they can be shown to have had regard to all the material considerations and to have properly posed and approached the article 8(2) questions as to necessity and proportionality.[43]

41 [2001] EWCA Civ 1549 at para 38.
42 [2001] EWCA Civ 1549 at para 38.
43 [2001] EWCA Civ 1549 at para 39.

2.48   Having identified these various factors as being relevant to the striking of the necessary balance between the competing interests, the Court of Appeal held[44] that the approach to TCPA 1990 s187B that it had adopted in the earlier decision in *Hambleton DC v Bird*[45] – which precluded consideration by the judge of questions of hardship – was not consistent with the court's duty to act compatibly with Convention rights contained in HRA 1998 s6(1). The Court of Appeal concluded that proportionality requires that the injunction not only be appropriate and necessary for the attainment of the public interest objective sought (the safeguarding of the environment), but also that it does not impose an excessive burden on the individual whose private interests (the Gypsy's private life and home and retention of his ethnic identity) are at stake. It was acknowledged by the Court of Appeal that a court's task in answering that question would not be an easy one, involving as it inevitably would the striking of a balance between competing interests of a very different character. The Court of Appeal stated that the task was unavoidable under the HRA 1998, and that 'provided it is undertaken in a structured and articulated way, the appropriate conclusion should emerge.'[46]

2.49   The Court of Appeal's approach in *Porter* was approved unanimously by the House of Lords.[47] The effect of these important decisions has been to require much more careful and explicit consideration of why measures taken against Gypsies and Travellers are justified.[48]

2.50   The decisions of the Court of Appeal and House of Lords in *Porter* represent an important advance on the position before the HRA

---

44 [2001] EWCA Civ 1549 at para 41.

45 [1995] 3 PLR 8.

46 [2001] EWCA Civ 1549 at para 42. Applying the new approach to the facts of the particular cases, the Court of Appeal held that in three of the four cases the judges below had determined the applications for an injunction by reference to the old approach which involved them in deferring excessively to the planning authorities' own views as to how the balance between the competing interests fell to be struck.

47 [2003] UKHL 26, [2003] 2 WLR 1547.

48 See, eg, *South Buckinghamshire DC v Coates* [2004] EWCA Civ 542, in which Sedley LJ, giving permission to appeal against a TCPA 1990 s187B injunction, giving Gypsies only one month to leave their land, said: 'Where a proportionality issue is raised, the first instance judgment should determine it not only by setting out as much as is necessary to find the relevant facts and appraise the relevant law, but by assembling in some short and tabular form the elements of the case which add up to a conclusion that the measures sought are either proportionate or disproportionate.'

1998 came into force.[49] However, the limitations of relying on article 8 to mitigate the effects of the overall shortfall of suitable sites are shown by the decision of the Court of Appeal in *Davis v Tonbridge and Malling BC*.[50] The case concerned an appeal by Travelling Showpeople against an injunction granted pursuant to TCPA 1990 s187B requiring them to leave the site which they had occupied in the absence of any alternative site being available for them in the whole of South East England. The evidence that, despite comprehensive searches, there was no alternative site for the Travelling Showpeople in South East England was clear and undisputed. It was also clear on the evidence that the Travelling Showpeople would suffer 'undoubted', 'real' and 'great' hardship if the injunction were granted. The judge at first instance therefore acknowledged that the case posed 'the stark question whether the appellants should be compelled to leave the site when they have nowhere else to go.' He nevertheless held that granting the injunction was not a disproportionate response to the continuing unlawful use of the site.

2.51   The Court of Appeal, after considering in full the decisions of the Court of Appeal and House of Lords in *Porter* and the decision of the ECtHR in *Chapman*, upheld the judge's decision. It held that the judge had correctly distinguished between the decision on the planning merits, which was for the planning authorities, and the decision on enforcement, which was for the court itself. Although there was inevitably considerable overlap between these two stages, because the same circumstances fell to be considered at each stage,[51] in the Court of Appeal's view, the judge had exercised his own jurisdiction on the issue of enforcement, and his reasoning in reaching his conclusion that enforcement was not disproportionate could not be faulted.[52] The decision that it was not a disproportionate interference with the article 8 rights of the Travelling Showpeople was therefore upheld, notwithstanding that this enforcement

---

49 Although it is worth noting that Lord Bingham of Cornhill expressed the view that it was 'very questionable whether article 8 of the European Convention has any bearing on the court's approach to an application under [TCPA s187B]' if the section is interpreted and applied in accordance with the approach enunciated by Simon Brown LJ in the Court of Appeal: see [2003] 2 WLR 1547 at 1565.

50 [2004] EWCA Civ 194.

51 [2004] EWCA Civ 194 at para 40.

52 [2004] EWCA Civ 194 at paras 42–55 and 59–65.

decision would cause them great personal hardship due to there being no alternative site available to them in the whole of South East England.[53]

2.52   The decision in *Davis* provides a salutary reminder that the protections against disproportionate enforcement action afforded by article 8 are no substitute for a legislative solution to the chronic under-provision of suitable sites for Gypsies and Travellers.

Discrimination

2.53   Gypsies and Travellers are among the most socially excluded groups in society and frequently suffer discrimination in their access to the most basic necessities of life. Although in theory Gypsies and Travellers enjoy the same entitlements to public services as the settled community, in practice they frequently experience discrimination in their access to such services. Some of the rights and interests which are protected by those basic services (for example, health and education) are within the scope of other Convention rights, such as the right not to be subjected to inhuman and degrading treatment (article 3), the right to respect for family life (article 8) and the right to education (protocol 1, article 2). The Convention's guarantee against discrimination in the enjoyment of Convention rights (article 14) can therefore be relied on where discriminatory access to basic services impinges on these Convention rights.

2.54   Precisely what the correct approach is to analysing whether there has been discrimination in the enjoyment of Convention rights, contrary to article 14, is a question which remains unsettled under the HRA 1998.[54] It has been considered a number of times at the

---

53   It is a curious feature of this case, however, that it was not expressly argued that the underlying planning decision, refusing planning permission for the development, was in breach of article 8: see, eg, [2004] EWCA Civ 194 para 46. This concession inevitably made it more difficult to argue that enforcement of that underlying decision was in breach of article 8.

54   One of the constraints on the utility of article 14 in the Convention case law has been the ECtHR's insistence that a complaint that breaches of a person's Convention rights were racially motivated must be proved 'beyond reasonable doubt': see eg, *Velikova v Bulgaria*, App No 41488/98, 18 May 2000, and *Anguelova v Bulgaria* [2004] 38 EHRR 31 paras 166–168. For a passionate and persuasive critique of the ECtHR's approach, see the partly dissenting opinion of Judge Bonello in *Anguelova*. For a sign that the ECtHR may now be moving away from its previously restrictive approach see *Nachova v Bulgaria* App No 43577/98, 26 February 2004 at paras 155–175.

level of the Court of Appeal and will shortly be considered by the House of Lords in a number of cases.[55]

2.55   For present purposes, the questions to be answered when considering whether there has been a breach of article 14 are:[56]

(i)   Do the facts fall within the ambit of one or more of the substantive Convention provisions?

(ii) If so, was there different treatment as respects that right between the complainant on the one hand and other persons put forward for comparison ('the chosen comparators') on the other?

(iii) Were the chosen comparators in an analogous situation to the complainant's situation?

(iv) If so, did the difference in treatment have an objective and reasonable justification: in other words, did it pursue a legitimate aim and did the differential treatment bear a reasonable relationship or proportionality to the aim sought to be achieved?

2.56   Attempts by Gypsies and Travellers to invoke article 14 have had mixed results to date. One of the most striking differences of treatment suffered by the Gypsy and Traveller population is the lack of legal protection for their security of tenure of their accommodation compared with the occupants of private caravan sites or tenants of local authority housing. Residents of Gypsy and Traveller sites provided by local authorities have only the most basic legal protection against harassment and eviction compared to other caravan dwellers or council tenants, and this difference of treatment is increasingly anomalous now that the majority of Gypsies and Travellers no longer pursue a wholly nomadic way of life. Article 14 provides a means of challenging such differential treatment.

---

55 See, eg, *Michalak v Wandsworth LBC* [2003] 1 WLR 617; *Aston Cantlow v Wallbank* [2002] Ch 51 (not affected on this point by the decision of the House of Lords [2003] UKHL 37); *R (S) v Chief Constable of South Yorkshire* [2002] 1 WLR 3223; *A v Secretary of State for the Home Department* [2003] 2 WLR 564; *Mendoza v Ghaidan* [2003] 2 WLR 478; *Carson v Secretary of State for Work and Pensions* [2003] EWCA Civ 797. Appeals in the cases of *A*, *Mendoza* and *Carson* are all due to be heard by the House of Lords in the course of 2004. See Recent Developments in Gypsy and Traveller Law at pxi above.

56 See *Michalak* [2003] 1 WLR 617 at 625 para 20. In *Carson* [2003] EWCA Civ 797 at paras 56–65, the Court of Appeal held that there is a degree of overlap between steps (iii) and (iv) in the structured approach to analysing discrimination claims outlined in *Michalak*, such that certain factors are capable of being relevant at both stages of the inquiry, and preferred a 'compendious' approach to a rigidly structured approach.

2.57   In *Somerset CC v Isaacs and Secretary of State for Transport, Local Government and the Regions*,[57] article 14 was relied on to challenge the differential treatment of Gypsy caravan occupiers on council sites compared to occupants of mobile homes sites. Caravan dwellers on mobile homes sites have had security of tenure since the passage of the Mobile Homes Act 1983, but that Act provides an exemption from those protections in relation to the occupiers of council sites. The argument was that such differential treatment in relation to the enjoyment of the right to respect for home lacked objective justification and was therefore in breach of article 14 in conjunction with article 8. The High Court gave the discrimination argument short shrift, however, holding that the exemptions from protection in the Caravan Sites Act (CSA) 1968 depended on the status of the site owner as a local authority, and not on any personal quality of the licensee or tenant, and it therefore raised no question of discrimination contrary to article 14.[58]

2.58   In *R (Albert Smith) v Barking and Dagenham LBC and Secretary of State for the Office of the Deputy Prime Minister*,[59] a Gypsy family who were seeking to prevent their eviction from a council site sought a declaration that the provisions of CSA 1968 Part I were incompatible with ECHR articles 8 and 14. The argument was that Gypsies and Travellers are not given the same protection against eviction by local authorities in CSA 1968 Part I as are given to secure tenants of conventional housing let by local authorities, and that this differential treatment of Gypsies and Travellers was without objective and reasonable justification and, therefore, in breach of article 14.

2.59   It was not disputed that the issue of security of tenure for Gypsies' and Travellers homes on caravan sites fell within the scope of article 8; eviction from a site clearly interfered with the right to respect for their home.[60] The differential treatment also could not be denied; Gypsies and Travellers' clearly enjoy lesser legal protection than that available to tenants of conventional housing. The Court also rejected the Secretary of State's argument that the chosen comparators, council tenants in conventional housing, were not in

57   [2002] EWHC 1014 Admin. See Recent Developments in Gypsy and Traveller Law at p00 above.
58   [2002] EWHC 1014 Admin at para 39.
59   [2002] EWHC 2400 Admin.
60   [2002] EWHC 2400 Admin at para 6. See Recent Developments in Gypsy and Traveller Law at pxi above.

an analogous situation to a Gypsy or Traveller living in a caravan on a council site.

2.60   On the question of whether the difference of treatment was justified, however, the High Court held that the Secretary of State had discharged the onus he bore of demonstrating that there was an objective and reasonable justification for continuing the absence of security of tenure for Gypsy and Traveller caravan dwellers on council sites. The High Court accepted the Secretary of State's argument that he was justified in maintaining the current position of a lack of security of tenure on local authority sites to allow for flexibility in meeting the accommodation needs of Gypsies and Travellers and to facilitate their nomadic way of life. If security of tenure were given to all long-term occupiers, the Court held, this might make matters worse for Gypsies and Travellers by reducing the number of sites available for them to enable them to pursue a nomadic way of life.[61]

2.61   The protection of article 14 has been invoked rather more successfully in relation to the relevance of an offer of conventional housing to Gypsies and Travellers when making decisions about planning permission or consequential enforcement. In *Clarke v Secretary of State for the Environment, Transport and the Regions and Tunbridge Wells BC,*[62] a planning inspector had found that conventional housing accommodation had been offered to the Gypsy family in question, and that they found the prospect distressing, having never lived in a conventional house. Nevertheless, the inspector went on to state that the offer of that accommodation detracted somewhat from the contention that the only alternative to the appeal site was an illegal roadside pitch. The High Court held that:

> ... in certain appropriate circumstances it can amount to a breach of articles 8 and 14 to weigh in the balance and hold against a Gypsy applying for planning permission, or indeed resisting eviction from

61 Although the discrimination challenge ultimately failed in this case, the public examination of the evidence going to justification of the current position is an important part of the ongoing public scrutiny of the social disadvantages suffered by the Gypsy and Traveller population, and will help maintain the momentum towards much needed law reform in this area. The court made clear in its judgment that its decision on justification was based on the evidence currently available, and that it expected the government to continue to monitor the present position and to obtain the necessary evidence to decide whether or not the present difference of treatment continues to be justifiable. For further discussion on this topic, see chapter 3 below. See Recent Developments in Gypsy and Traveller Law at pxi above.

62 [2001] EWHC 800 Admin; [2002] JPL 552; July 2002 *Legal Action* 23.

Council or private land, that he or she has refused conventional housing accommodation as being contrary to his or her culture.[63]

To treat such refusal as a relevant consideration in reaching a decision was just as impermissible as penalising a religious or strictly observant Christian, Jew or Muslim because they will not work on certain days, or to penalise a strictly observant Buddhist, Muslim, Jew or Sikh because they will not eat certain foods or wear certain clothing.

2.62   The onus was on the individual concerned to satisfy the planning inspector that they or their family do indeed have a genuine aversion to conventional housing, but once that has been established:

> ... it would be contrary to articles 8 and 14 to expect such a person to accept conventional housing and to hold it against him or her that he has not accepted it, or is not prepared to accept it, even as a last resort factor.[64]

Education

2.63   The Human Rights Act 1998 gives added weight to an important consideration which is all too frequently neglected in decisions affecting Gypsies and Travellers: the impact of those decisions on the education of Gypsy and Traveller children. Article 2 of Protocol 1 to the ECHR provides that no person shall be denied the right to education, which has been interpreted as guaranteeing a right of access to such educational facilities as exist.[65] In order for this right to education to be practical and effective, the children of Gypsies and Travellers require a minimum degree of stability in order to be able to attend the same school and receive continuous education.

2.64   On the traditional approach to planning law, which looked narrowly at land use considerations with only a narrow exception to consider 'personal circumstances' as a material consideration, the educational interests of Gypsy and Traveller children rarely, if ever, influenced decisions about whether or not to grant planning

63 [2001] EWHC 800 Admin at para 30.
64 [2001] EWHC 800 Admin at para 34. The decision was upheld on appeal by a unanimous Court of Appeal (see *Clarke v Secretary of State for Transport, Local Government and the Regions and Tunbridge Wells BC* [2002] EWCA Civ 819 at paras 5 and 15 of the judgment where the Court of Appeal endorsed the important point that an aversion to conventional housing may be grounded in a belief or understanding which is an integral part of a cultural identity as a Gypsy or Traveller).
65 See chapter 7 for a full discussion of issues with regard to education.

permission, or whether or not to enforce against unauthorised encampments. The enhanced status now given to the right to education means that this is a consideration which might make a real, practical difference in the circumstances of a particular case. In *Basildon DC v Secretary of State for the Environment,*[66] for example, the court upheld a decision of the Secretary of State in which the environmental harm caused by Gypsy caravan sites in the Green Belt was considered to be outweighed by the need for stable educational facilities for the younger children of the families concerned.

Culture

2.65   In *Chapman v United Kingdom*[67] the ECtHR recognised that Gypsies and Travellers have a right to respect for their traditional way of life and their culture and held that 'the applicant's occupation of her caravan is an integral part of her ethnic identity as a Gypsy, reflecting the long tradition of that minority of following a travelling lifestyle.'

2.66   In the case of *R v Tunbridge Wells BC ex p The Gypsy Council for Education, Culture, Welfare and Civil Rights and Eli Frankham,*[68] the High Court was asked to consider a case concerning the right of Gypsies to attend a traditional 'Horse Fair' that had been held in the village of Horsmonden, in Kent, for many years. A decision had been taken by the local authority to prohibit the holding of the annual Horse Fair on grounds that it would give rise to health and safety considerations.[69] It was the subject of an application for judicial review made by a respected elder of the Gypsy community and an organisation that works for the preservation of the Gypsy way of life. The decision was challenged on the basis that it breached articles 8, 11 (the right to freedom of association and assembly) and 14 of the Convention. However, the High Court accepted that the local authority had taken account of all relevant considerations and had struck the correct balance between the interests of the Romani Gypsy community and the interests of society in general. In addition the High Court held that the decision was necessary and proportionate, given the circumstances of the case and the fact that an alternative venue had been proposed some 20 miles away from Horsmonden.

---

66 21 December 2000 (unreported), Admin Ct.

67 *Chapman* [2001] 33 EHRR 399 at para 73.

68 7 September 2000 (unreported), Admin Ct.

69 The decision was made under the provisions of Public Order Act 1986 s14A (as amended by CJPOA 1994 s70) and was approved by the Secretary of State.

Summary of the approach required under HRA 1998

2.67   In light of both the Convention case law and post-HRA 1998 domestic decisions, we can return to the central question: what counts, as a matter of domestic law under the HRA 1998, as a proper assessment of the justification for a proposed interference with the Convention rights of Gypsies and Travellers?

2.68   As explained above, what an authority is required by the HRA 1998 to do is to conduct an overt and structured assessment of the proportionality of the interference it proposes, by asking a series of connected but discrete questions. The purpose of asking those questions is to identify the justification for interfering with a Convention right and to assist the authority in deciding whether the interference ultimately bears scrutiny as the sort of interference with a fundamental right that is acceptable in a modern democratic society.

2.69   There exist various formulations of the precise questions to be asked in conducting such a structured assessment of the proportionality of an interference with a Convention right. It is sufficient for present purposes to refer to the formulation relied on by Lord Steyn in *R (Daly) v Secretary of State for the Home Department*,[70] taken from the Privy Council's decision in *de Freitas v Permanent Secretary of Ministry of Agriculture, Fisheries, Lands and Housing.*[71]

2.70   On any formulation, a public authority such as a local planning authority, contemplating taking a measure which it knows will constitute an interference with any Convention right of Gypsies or Travellers, must ask itself at the very least the following four questions:

(i)   does the measure serve a legitimate aim (ie, is the objective sufficiently important to justify limiting a fundamental right)?

(ii)   is the measure rationally connected to that aim (ie, can it, in fact, serve to further that aim)?

(iii)   is it the least restrictive way of doing so (ie, are the means used no more than is necessary to accomplish the objective)?

(iv)   is it proportionate in the longstop sense that, viewed overall, the measure does not place too great a burden on the individual for the good of the community?

---

70   [2001] UKHL 26; [2001] 2 WLR 1622 at 1634.
71   [1999] 1 AC 69, PC.

2.71   Clearly, the proper conduct of this structured exercise in assessing proportionality should be conducted by the authority by close reference to evidence concerning the sorts of factual matters that the ECtHR has made clear are relevant to any assessment of the proportionality of an interference in this context: the impact on the individuals concerned; the availability and suitability of alternative sites; and so on.[72]

Conclusion

2.72   The HRA 1998 offers Gypsies and Travellers some important resources to be used in their struggle against the systemic discrimination and exclusion which they face. Requiring public authorities to justify interferences with Gypsies' and Travellers' way of life, and to demonstrate the necessity of treating members of those communities differently from the settled community, is a potentially empowering step for this most marginalised of groups. Used wisely, in a carefully thought-out litigation strategy, and at appropriate points in the policy-making and legislative process, the rights outlined above ought to help to hasten the day when public policy towards Gypsies and Travellers is no longer driven by the ignorance, fear and prejudices of some of the settled population.

---

72 See *R (Lee) v First Secretary of State* [2003] EWHC 3235 Admin at paras 23–27 for a recent example of the application of this more stringent approach to proportionality (Secretary of State's decision refusing a Gypsy planning permission quashed on basis that one sentence in a paragraph dealing with human rights was not sufficient to dispose of the claimant's argument that a refusal of temporary planning permission would amount to a disproportionate interference with his and his family's rights under article 8).

CHAPTER 3

Official sites

Introduction

3.1   This chapter is designed to explain:

1. what security of tenure Gypsies and Travellers have on local authority sites;
2. the effect of Human Rights Act (HRA) 1998 and the Disability Discrimination Act (DDA) 1995 on security of tenure;
3. the role of judicial review in relation to the allocation of and eviction from pitches on local authority sites;
4. the law affecting conditions of occupancy and repairs on authorised sites.

According to the Office of the Deputy Prime Minister (ODPM) Count of Gypsy caravans, nearly 50 per cent of the Gypsy and Traveller population at any one time will be accommodated on authorised local authority encampments. For example, in July 2003, the ODPM Gypsy Count showed that there were:

- 6,029 caravans on authorised council sites;
- 4,728 caravans on authorised private sites;
- 3,979 caravans on unauthorised sites; and
- a total of 14,736 caravans counted.

3.2   Although the Gypsy Count cannot be taken as completely accurate[1] it gives an idea of the significance of council provided sites so far as the accommodation of the Gypsy and Traveller population is concerned. This is so despite the closure of local authority sites since the repeal of the duty to provide accommodation by Criminal Justice and Public Order Act (CJPOA) 1994 s80.[2] The legal regime as it affects authorised council sites is, therefore, an important factor in the lives of nearly half of the Gypsy and Traveller population.

Provision of sites

3.3   The sites currently in existence have been established under different legal powers or duties. Under the Caravan Sites Act (CSA)

---

1   See Niner, *Counting Gypsies and Travellers: A Review of the Gypsy Caravan Count System* (ODPM, 2004).
2   For example, since 1994, 139 residential pitches have been lost due to site closure. See Niner, *The Provision and Condition of Local Authority Gypsy/Traveller Sites in England* (ODPM, 2002) p17.

1968, it was the *duty* of a county council, London borough, or (in Wales) a county borough to exercise their powers under Caravan Sites and Control of Development Act (CSCDA) 1960 s24 to 'provide adequate accommodation for gypsies residing in or resorting to their area'.[3] The CSA 1968 placed an obligation on county councils to determine what sites were to be provided and to acquire the land (subject to consultation and consideration of any objection through the planning process).[4] The district councils were obliged to exercise the other powers under CSCDA s24, and particularly the management of sites. The county councils were also expected to fix the charges made by the district councils for their provision and to pay the district councils any shortfall between their expenditure and receipts.[5] As a consequence 'the majority of public sites in non-metropolitan districts are owned by county councils and managed by district councils'.[6]

3.4 The CSA 1968 duty was repealed in 1994 by the CJPOA 1994, and now only the powers under CSCDA 1960 s24 remain. Those powers are wide:

(1) A local authority shall have power within their area to provide sites where caravans may be brought, whether for holidays or some other temporary purposes or for use as permanent residences, and to manage the site or lease them to some other person.

(2) ... a local authority shall have power to do anything appearing to them desirable in connection with the provision of such sites ...

3.5 For the purposes of CSCDA 1960 s24 the term 'local authority' is defined as including a county council, district council, London borough, and, in Wales, a Welsh county council or county borough.[7]

3.6 When the government repealed the CSA 1968 it envisaged that CSCDA 1960 s24 would become the vehicle for the provision of local authority caravan sites for Gypsies and amended CSCDA 1960 s24 by inserting a power to provide 'working spaces' for Gypsies and facilities for their normal activities.[8]

---

3 CSA 1968 s6.
4 CSA 1968 ss7 and 8.
5 CSA 1968 s7.
6 DoE Circular 18/94, Welsh Office 76/94 (hereafter DoE Circular 18/94) *Gypsy Sites Policy and Unauthorised Camping* para 19.
7 CSCDA 1960 s24(8) and s29(1).
8 CJPOA 1994 s80.

3.7   The government also envisaged that the network of existing sites would continue to be maintained after the repeal of the CSA 1968 duty. In Department of the Environment (DoE) Circular 18/94 local authorities were advised that:

> The Secretaries of State consider it appropriate that authorities should maintain their existing gypsy caravan sites, or should make suitable arrangements for their maintenance by leasing them to other persons who are willing and able to maintain them.[9]

3.8   The advice in Circular 18/94 also made it clear that the government expected that additional sites would continue to be provided by local authorities:

> The Secretaries of State also expect authorities to continue to consider whether it is appropriate to provide further permanent caravan sites for gypsies in their areas.[10]

The legal regime

Security of tenure

3.9   A Gypsy or Traveller living on a local authority caravan site has no real protection against eviction provided that he or she has been given four weeks' written notice and a court order has been obtained.[11] However, the CSA 1968 does afford residents some protection from eviction without a court order by making such an act a criminal offence. Similarly, the CSA 1968 protects residents from harassment by making acts calculated to affect the peace or comfort of the occupier and the withdrawal or withholding of services or facilities reasonably required a criminal offence.[12]

3.10   The lack of real protection against a 'lawful' eviction afforded to Gypsies and Travellers occupying local authority sites should be contrasted with the protection from eviction enjoyed by the occupiers of caravan sites covered by the Mobiles Homes Act (MHA) 1983 (which is similar to that enjoyed by secure tenants of conventional council housing).[13]

---

9 DoE Circular 18/94 para 21.
10 DoE Circular 18/94 para 22.
11 CSA 1968 ss2,3 and 4, which remain in force.
12 CSA 1968 s3.
13 Housing Act (HA) 1985.

3.11   MHA 1983 s5 specifically provides that land occupied by a local authority as a caravan site for Gypsies is not covered by the provisions of MHA 1983. Those occupying caravan sites regulated by MHA 1983 may not be evicted without a court order and then only if the owner of the site can establish one or other of the grounds set out in MHA 1983 Sch 1. The main grounds are:

- that the court is satisfied that the occupier is in breach of the licence agreement, and has failed to remedy that breach within a reasonable time, and it is reasonable for the agreement to be terminated;[14]
- that the occupier is not occupying the caravan or mobile home as his or her only or principal residence;[15]
- that the mobile home or caravan is having (or likely to have) a detrimental effect on the amenity of the site by virtue of its age and condition.[16]

In the event that a court is satisfied that a possession order should be made against a resident of a site covered by the MHA 1983 then it has the power to suspend its enforcement for such period, not exceeding 12 months, as it thinks reasonable and when doing so may impose such conditions as it thinks reasonable, including conditions as to the payment of rent or other periodical payments, or arrears of such rent or payments.[17]

3.12   Thus it can be seen that the protection enjoyed by MHA 1983 occupiers has some similarity to that of secure tenants of local authorities under the Housing Act (HA) 1985 (which provides that no possession order can be granted except on proof of grounds and the most used grounds being subject to it being reasonable to make an order).[18] The HA 1985 does not apply to caravan sites as it concerns only tenancies or licences of a dwelling-house.

---

14 MHA 1983 Sch 1 para 4.
15 MHA 1983 Sch 1 para 5.
16 MHA Sch 1 para 6. The Housing Bill 2004, currently before parliament, if it becomes law in its present form, would delete 'age' from this ground.
17 CSA 1968 s4(5). Note that this provision is not available to residents of local authority Gypsy sites.
18 HA 1985 s84 and Sch 2.

Security of tenure and the Human Rights Act 1998

3.13   The differences in security of tenure enjoyed by those living on authorised Gypsy sites and those living on sites protected by MHA 1983 on the one hand and local authority secure tenants under HA 1985 on the other hand, might be thought to be incompatible with the European Convention on Human Rights (ECHR); in particular articles 8 (right to respect for private and family life and the home) and 14 (prohibition of discrimination). However, in two cases, the High Court, backed by the Court of Appeal, has determined that there was no such incompatibility: *Somerset CC v Isaacs and Secretary of State for Transport, Local Government and the Regions*[19] and *R (Albert Smith) v Barking and Dagenham LBC and Secretary of State for the Office of the Deputy Prime Minister.*[20] Both cases concerned possession proceedings brought by the respective councils against the occupiers of pitches on official Gypsy caravan sites, who had been given notice terminating their occupation agreements.

3.14   In *Isaacs*, incompatibility with article 14 was argued on the basis of a comparison with the rights enjoyed by MHA 1983 occupiers and in *Smith*, on the basis of a comparison with the protection afforded to secure tenants by the HA 1985. In both cases it was argued that the provisions of the CSA 1968 were incompatible with articles 8 and 14 of the Convention on the basis that there was no justification for the difference in treatment experienced by Gypsies and Travellers. In argument reliance was placed on the following passage of the judgment of Sedley LJ in *Lambeth LBC v Howard,*[21] a case which concerned a local authority secure tenant:

> It seems to me that any attempt to evict a person, whether directly or by process of law from his or her home would on the face of it be a derogation from the respect, that is the integrity, to which the home is prima facie entitled.[22]

3.15   While the High Court accepted that the possession proceedings interfered with the article 8 rights of the occupants in each case and that there was a clear difference in treatment of Gypsies when compared to security enjoyed by other occupiers of local authority land and housing, it was held in both cases that the steps taken to

19   [2002] EWHC 1014 Admin.
20   [2002] EWHC 2400 Admin, and [2003] EWCA Civ 385. See Recent Developments in Gypsy and Traveller Law at pxi above.
21   [2001] EWCA Civ 468; [2001] HLR 636.
22   [2001] HLR 636 at 644.

evict them by both local authorities were justified under articles 8(2) and 14. When reaching his decision in *Isaacs*, Stanley Burnton J applied the judgment in *Rasmussen v Denmark*[23] and particularly the point made in that case that:

> ... for the purposes of article 14 a difference of treatment is discriminatory if it has no objective or reasonable justification, that is if it does not pursue a legitimate aim or if there is not a reasonable relationship of proportionality between the means employed and the aim sought to be realised.[24]

3.16   In *Isaacs* the Secretary of State justified the difference in treatment on the basis that security of tenure was not appropriate for those of nomadic habit of life (despite acknowledging that many Gypsies and Travellers occupy sites on a long-term basis) and in evidence the Secretary of State's witness made the following observations:

> The separate statutory framework allows for flexibility in meeting the accommodation needs of Gypsies. It appears that [Mr Isaacs] is effectively arguing in these proceedings in favour of a single statutory framework applicable to all caravan sites, including local authority Gypsy sites. In my view, such a single statutory framework would be detrimental to the interests of Gypsies throughout the country. If the security of tenure provisions of that framework applied equally to local authority Gypsy sites, it would undermine the flexibility that such sites provide in catering for the varied lifestyles of Gypsies. Some may move from site to site on a regular basis, while others may be more permanently based on a site, possibly travelling for a few months each year to take on seasonal work. If each Gypsy were able to rely on security of tenure then every site, whatever its designation, could potentially become a permanent site with no scope to accommodate short-term occupiers. Furthermore, if there were no longer a distinction in the statutory framework allowing flexibility for the provision of Gypsy sites, then there would be nothing to prevent any person residing in a mobile home seeking to occupy a Gypsy site, whether or not they pursue a nomadic lifestyle. Inevitably, fewer sites, if any, could be made available specifically for Gypsies pursuing a nomadic lifestyle ... Experience suggests that local authorities would face difficulties in managing sites if eviction were subject to broad discretionary powers of the courts to suspend or attach conditions to orders. There is a balance to be struck between the latter and the merits of flexibility (already mentioned) that such sites offer in catering for the varying accommodation needs of Gypsies.[25]

23 [1984] 7 EHRR 371.
24 [1984] 7 EHRR 371 at para 38.
25 *Isaacs* [2002] EHWC 1014 Admin at para 37.

3.17   In his judgment in *Isaacs* Stanley Burnton J, commented that he was:

> ... not over-impressed by the vagueness of the statement ... that 'experience suggests' ... [nevertheless] this evidence satisfied me that the exempting provisions are 'necessary in a democratic society' and a proportionate response to a social need, and do not amount to an infringement of article 8 [and article 14] ... In practice [site occupiers] ... are able to bring judicial review proceedings where the circumstances justify them, and I do not think that the absence of those safeguards substantially prejudices persons such as the defendant. Moreover, any such safeguards would detract from the flexibility that Parliament has decided is appropriate for exempted sites.[26]

3.18   It might be thought that, if flexibility is the true aim of the legislation then that could be achieved by the insertion into the agreements, by which each pitch is held, of terms that would provide for circumstances in which the council would: need to recover possession (for management or other purposes); and be able to do so if they were breached (subject to scrutiny by the court that such eviction was not in breach of article 8). For example, Mr Isaacs' licence conditions contained terms prohibiting the use of threatening words or behaviour against council employees and prohibiting him from leaving the site vacant for a period in excess of nine weeks – to meet the concern of pitches being left vacant which could otherwise be used by transit or short-stay occupiers. This could be seen as analogous to the grounds of possession under the HA 1985, which include 'management grounds' so as to enable works to be carried out and for under-occupation.

3.19   In *R (Daly) v Secretary of State for the Home Department*[27] Lord Steyn explained the way in which courts should assess whether an interference with Convention rights was 'proportionate':

> The contours of the principle of proportionality are familiar. In *de Freitas*[28] ... the Privy Council adopted a three-stage test ... that in determining whether a limitation (by an act, rule or decision) is arbitrary or excessive the court should ask itself: 'whether (i) the legislative objective is sufficiently important to justify limiting a fundamental right; (ii) the measures designed to meet the legislative objective are rationally connected to it; and (iii) the means used to impair the right or freedom are no more than is necessary to accomplish the objective'.

26 [2002] EHWC 1014 Admin at para 38.
27 [2001] AC 532 at 547; [2001] 2 WLR 1622 at 1634.
28 *de Freitas v Permanent Secretary of the Ministry of Agriculture, Fisheries, and Housing* [1999] 1 AC 69, PC.

3.20   It might be thought that the flexibility advocated by the government could be achieved by simple amendment of the legislation or by the publication of national guidance on site rules and agreements, and, if the issue is revisited in future cases, then it could be argued that the means used to achieve 'flexibility' are 'more than is necessary to accomplish the objective' and therefore disproportionate.

3.21   The Secretary of State's evidence in *Isaacs* was based on the assumption that the majority of Gypsies and Travellers continue to spend a substantial proportion of time travelling, leaving their pitches empty. However, in *Albert Smith* evidence was presented which indicated that because of the lack of sites 'the fact is that the nomadic way of life is ending for most gypsies and therefore the existing legislation is unsatisfactory'.[29] In *Albert Smith* the judge, Burton J, was also referred to the Niner report on *The Provision and Condition of Local Authority Gypsy/Traveller Sites in England*[30] and in particular the following passage of that report:

> On the case study residential sites, most families do not travel or travel only for a short period for family or holiday purposes. Some family members may travel leaving other family members behind. While there are exceptions, the general picture built up of residential Gypsy/Traveller sites is that they are stable, with long term residents who travel little during the course of a year. It may be that, for many residents, the attractions of a site lie in the possibilities of living in a trailer (attractive for cultural reasons and for leaving the travel option open), and of living within a culturally distinct community among friends and family ... For many residential site residents, nomadism appears to be a spiritual and cultural state of mind, rather than a day-to-day reality.[31]

3.22   In *Albert Smith* the government maintained the stance it had taken in *Isaacs* and indicated that it was still 'monitoring the position' and that 'the present position can be justified'.[32]

3.23   In his judgment, Burton J rejected the argument that the legislation was incompatible with the ECHR and said 'there is a very difficult question as to how to define gypsies, to whom security of tenure in such sites is to be given (if it is)'.[33] The judge repeated the

---

29 [2002] EWHC 2400 Admin at para 24.
30 (ODPM, 2002).
31 *The Provision and Condition of Local Authority Gypsy/Traveller Sites in England* at p29.
32 [2002] EWHC 2400 Admin at para 32.
33 [2002] EWHC 2400 Admin at para 32.

concern, expressed in *Isaacs*, that, without such a definition, people without Gypsy heritage or history would be able to occupy Gypsy caravan sites and noted that the government had indicated that it would 'give further thought to the position, and continue monitoring' and that '[m]eanwhile the safeguard of judicial review remains'.[34]

3.24   The Court of Appeal later refused permission to appeal the judgment in *Albert Smith*[35] and, when doing so, approved the judgment in *Isaacs*.[36] However, changing conditions and the results of continuing government monitoring may mean that this issue will return for reconsideration by the courts.[37]

Judicial review

3.25   The High Court, in both *Isaacs* and *Albert Smith*, referred to the remedy of judicial review as a protection against arbitrary eviction. It should be noted that judicial review proceedings can be used by Gypsies and Travellers to challenge a wide variety of public authority decisions. Examples of cases concerning Gypsies and Travellers include: *R v Hillingdon LBC ex p McDonagh*,[38] a case concerning an eviction from an unauthorised encampment; *R (Piggott) v Bedfordshire CC*,[39] a case concerning the allocation of pitches; and *R v Secretary of State for the Environment ex p Martin Ward*,[40] a case concerning a site closure.

3.26   However, judicial review can, of course, only be used when the public authority has made an error of law. Though the grounds for seeking judicial review are wide and include, for example:

- a misdirection or misunderstanding of the law;
- a failure to take account of a relevant matter;
- taking account of irrelevant matters; and
- the failure to give adequate reasons for a decision,

34 [2002] EWHC 2400 Admin at para 35.
35 [2003] EWCA Civ 385.
36 [2003] EWCA Civ 385 at para 16.
37 For discussion of the definition of 'Gypsy' for planning purposes, see chapter 4 at para 4.38 below. See Recent Developments in Gypsy and Traveller Law at pxi above.
38 [1998] HLR 531, and see para 3.27 below.
39 [2002] EWHC 77 Admin, see paras 3.27–3.29 below.
40 [1984] 1 WLR 835.

they do not permit a challenge to be made against a factual decision where no error of law has been made.[41] It follows that Gypsies and Travellers living on local authority run caravan sites are particularly vulnerable in circumstances where a decision to evict them from a site is based upon an assessment of disputed facts and involves no error of law. As the Niner report on *The Provision and Condition of Local Authority Gypsy/Traveller Sites in England*[42] shows, there is no uniform approach to the management of sites; there is no standard form residential contract; and there is a significant variation in the extent of the responsibilities of site managers and the level of training that they receive. When an allegation arises that might, if proved, lead to eviction, it is usually the site manager that will investigate and report to the local authority. The decision to evict a Gypsy or Traveller from a site is usually taken by the local authority but in some areas site managers have the power to reach such decisions. Either way, the site manager will have an extremely important role to play in the process and there is understandable concern amongst Gypsies and Travellers that many of the decisions that affect their homes are being made by, or based upon conclusions reached by, inexperienced and poorly trained site managers. Unfortunately, factionalism between families is not unknown on Gypsy sites. Who gets recommended for eviction may depend on who gets to the site manager first after a dispute. Once the decision has been taken and there is evidence to support it (although there may be evidence the other way), the decision may be very difficult to challenge by way of judicial review, even if the court itself might not have come to the same decision.

3.27   However, the same 'humanitarian considerations' come into play when a local authority is considering eviction from a pitch on an 'authorised' site as on an unauthorised encampment.[43] This would seem to be obviously so when the Gypsy or Traveller has, in effect, 'squatted' a pitch on an authorised site (as happened in both *McDonagh*[44] and *Piggott*[45] where the claimants occupied pitches

---

41 See, for example, *Associated Provincial Picture Houses v Wednesbury Corporation* [1948] 1 KB 223, *Tower Hamlets LBC v Nipa Begum* [2001] 1 WLR 306, and *Runa Begum v Tower Hamlets LBC* [2003] UKHL 5.

42 (ODPM, 2002) p25.

43 See chapter 5 and *R v Hillingdon LBC ex p McDonagh* [1998] HLR 531 at 533.

44 [1998] HLR 531.

45 [2002] EWHC 77 Admin.

which had been vacated by the previous occupiers). However, in one case the judge said:

> ... different considerations arise when a local authority is considering the management of an authorised encampment rather than the tolerance, or retention, of an unauthorised encampment.[46]

He went on to say:

> Nonetheless, the matters personal to a traveller and his family that a local authority should consider before exercising its powers to evict are relevant and must be considered whether the question is their eviction from an unauthorised encampment or from a plot on an authorised encampment.[47]

It can also be said that there is no real difference between an unauthorised encampment outside an authorised site and one inside – and, even in the case of an authorised pitch, by the time the decision to take possession proceedings occurs the pitch inside *will* be unauthorised as the site owner will have terminated the Gypsy's or Traveller's right to occupy by notice (see paragraph 3.9 above). So the same obligations not to act precipitately, and to make inquiries to establish the relevant facts and come to a proper decision, apply.

3.28   Additionally, a Gypsy or Traveller 'squatting' on an authorised site may be able to challenge by way of judicial review a decision to take possession proceedings by arguing that the local authority has failed to apply its allocation system correctly. That was the case in *Piggott*.[48] After occupying the pitch as a trespasser, Mrs Piggott applied for a pitch on the site (she wanted to be on that particular site as her daughter and other members of her family were living there, she was seriously ill and needed their care and support). It was agreed that the fact that Mrs Piggott was a squatter did not prevent her from making an application (although the council had initially taken that view). Burton J held that the council should have considered three matters: (1) the needs of the applicant; (2) the needs and requirements of others (also applicants) 'who should not be prejudiced by the unauthorised jumping of the gun of the applicant'; and, (3) the jumping of the gun itself to see whether it should make any difference at all or how far it should make a difference.[49] The

46 *R (Ward) v Hillingdon* [2002] EWHC 91 Admin; [2001] LGR 457 at 460 per Stanley Burnton J.
47 [2001] LGR 457 at 460.
48 [2002] EWHC 77 Admin.
49 [2002] EWHC 77 Admin at para 34.

council had failed to make a comparison of her position with that of the others on the waiting list for a pitch. Even though the council had offered Mrs Piggott a pitch on another site, it was held that she was entitled to be considered for a pitch on the site where she was camped.[50]

3.29   In *Piggott*, the court emphasised that unauthorised activity by Gypsies or Travellers on a site was not to be encouraged 'not least in the interest of other travellers'.[51] Nevertheless, the case shows that a Gypsy or Traveller facing eviction from an authorised site may have additional arguments to those on unauthorised encampments, particularly with respect to the question of any application for a pitch and how the local authority deals with the process of allocation of pitches. In the light of the decision in *Piggott* it would be advisable for local authorities to have clear and fair written allocation policies which are made available to all Gypsies and Travellers who request a copy.

3.30   It may be that a Gypsy or Traveller facing eviction for non-payment of rent would be able to argue that eviction was a disproportionate measure, for instance, because the amount is too small, or because the failure to pay is the result of faulty administration by the council's own housing benefit department, or because the council had failed to take into account an offer to discharge the arrears within a reasonable period of time. If the reason for notice to leave involves an allegation of anti-social behaviour, then it might be the case that the decision has been taken without listening to the Gypsy's or Traveller's side of the story. In the homeless person's case of *R v Gravesham BC ex p Winchester*,[52] Simon Brown J (as he then was) said:

> The applicant must be given the opportunity to explain matters which the local authority is minded to regard as weighing substantially against him ... [53]

3.31   The Disability Discrimination Act (DDA) 1995 makes it unlawful by reason of his or her disability to discriminate against a disabled person by evicting him or her.[54] A disabled person is someone who

---

50 [2002] EWHC 77 Admin at para 40. Mrs Piggott was subsequently offered and accepted a licence of a pitch on the site.
51 [2002] EWHC 77 Admin at para 29.
52 [1986] HLR 207.
53 [1986] HLR 207 at 214–215.
54 DDA 1995 s22(3)(c).

has a disability defined, for the purposes of DDA 1995, as a 'physical or mental impairment which has a substantial and long term adverse effect on his ability to carry out normal day to day activities.'[55] However, a landlord can argue that the action is 'justified'[56] and that the eviction is necessary 'in order not to endanger the health or safety of any person (including the disabled person)' and that 'it is reasonable in all the circumstances of the case' for the landlord to hold that opinion.[57] The DDA 1995 applies to 'premises', the definition of which 'includes land of any description'.[58] A local authority Gypsy or Traveller site will come within the provisions of the DDA 1995. In a case involving a tenant of a dwelling house, *North Devon Homes Ltd v Brazier*,[59] Mrs Brazier was involved in persistent anti-social behaviour. At first instance, the landlord obtained a possession order. Mrs Brazier successfully appealed against this order on the basis that evicting her was contrary to the above provisions of the DDA 1995. The High Court noted that there was no evidence that the landlord had ever directed its mind to these requirements. However, the High Court also stated that:

> The respondent [landlord], having adopted a proper review of the situation in accordance with the express terms of the Act, may conclude in the future that the health and safety of her neighbours are prejudiced and thus steps should be taken to evict the appellant [tenant].[60]

3.32   Thus, it is important to note that the DDA 1995 does not prohibit the eviction of a person with a disability. Nevertheless, it seems clear that a local authority will not be able to take possession proceedings against a Gypsy or Traveller who suffers from a disability (as defined in DDA 1995) unless and until proper consideration of the provisions of DDA 1995 has taken place.

Conditions of occupancy and repairs

3.33   While local authorities have powers as to the provision of facilities, organisation and management and there is guidance from central

---

55   DDA 1995 s1(1). See also DDA 1995 Sch 1.
56   DDA 1995 s24.
57   DDA 1995 s24.
58   DDA 1995 s68(1).
59   [2003] HLR 59 at 905; (2003) 6 CCLR 245.
60   [2003] HLR 59 at 913.

government,[61] there is little by way of obligations owed to Gypsies or Travellers by local authorities, which can be enforced by them in respect of the conditions of their occupation of authorised sites. Virtually the only obligations are those referred to in para 3.9 above. There are no obligations implied to carry out repairs to what is provided on the pitch (for example, the amenity block containing day room, toilet, bathroom/shower, or kitchen) or to repair or maintain the facilities on the site (for example, lighting or access ways). There is no equivalent to Landlord and Tenant Act 1985 s11 which puts repairing obligations on landlords of dwelling-houses let for less than seven years.[62] However, it has been possible to imply terms putting obligations on local authority landlords by using the principle of 'necessary implication' from contract law. Using that principle, Gypsies and Travellers have argued successfully that terms as to the maintenance of the site were to be implied into their agreements and they were able to recover damages for breach of them.[63] In the *Berry* case, the court eventually held that the following obligations on the local authority should be implied: to mark out pitches; to provide hardstanding; to provide chemical toilets and an emptying point for them; to provide waste receptacles; and to manage the site.

3.34 Usually the Gypsy's or Traveller's obligations will be set out in a written agreement provided when he or she agrees to occupy a pitch. The terms of such an agreement may deal with: the length of time of occupation (for example, for a year); consideration of renewal; termination; the number of caravans on a pitch; the maximum time permitted away from the site before the right to return is lost; restricting the use of the pitch (for example, no business use); and conduct on the pitch and site.[64] They rarely, if at all, impose

---

61 DoE Circular 14/89 *Caravan Sites and Control of Development Act 1960 – Model Standards*.

62 Although see para 3.42 below, on the Environmental Protection Act 1990.

63 *Berry v Wrexham Maelor County Borough Council* August 2001 *Legal Action* 25.

64 It should be noted, however, that in *Newham LBC v Khatun* [2004] EWCA Civ 55; (2004) LS Gaz 13 May p28 (a case involving a 'settled' homeless applicant), the Court of Appeal decided that the Unfair Contract Terms in Consumer Contracts Regulations 1999 SI No 2083, applied to contracts relating to land. These regulations will, therefore, apply to Gypsies and Travellers who are licensees on local authority (and other) sites. Under the regulations an unfair term is one which, contrary to the requirement of good faith, causes a significant imbalance in the parties' rights and obligations to the detriment of the Gypsy or Traveller concerned (the 'consumer' in terms of the regulations – reg 4).

obligations on the local authority but simply detail the Gypsy's or Traveller's obligations. Many adult Gypsies or Travellers are not literate or have poor literacy skills and this fact can create problems in itself as they may be unaware as to what they have agreed unless it is also explained verbally to them.

Rent/site fee

3.35　Caravan Sites and Control of Development Act (CSCDA) 1960 s24(3) provides that:

> The local authority shall make in respect of the use of sites managed by them, and of any services or facilities provided under this section, such reasonable charges as they may determine.

This provision enables local authorities to charge rent or site fees. Those financially eligible can apply for housing benefit to meet the charge in whole or part, depending on their income, and the calculations carried out under the housing benefit regulations.[65] Practical difficulties can arise when Gypsies or Travellers try to claim housing benefit. The fact that the work of many Gypsies and Travellers is of a seasonal/casual nature and that payment is often by cash can complicate the calculation of housing benefit entitlement. Local authority policies also vary from one area to another in relation to collection of the shortfall between the contractual site fee and the local reference rent assessed by the rent officer under the regulations as the amount eligible for housing benefit.[66] As a result Gypsies and Travellers tend to find that the cost of a pitch on local authority run sites can vary quite considerably. This point was highlighted in the Niner report on *The Provision and Condition of Local Authority Gypsy/Traveller Sites in England:*

> Overall this anomaly is resented almost as much for its arbitrary unfairness and irrationality as for the very real problems it can make for those affected.[67]

---

65 Housing Benefit (General) Regulations 1987 SI No 1971, reg 10(1)(g) in particular.

66 For further information on this, and other welfare benefits issues, see *Welfare Benefits and Tax Credits Handbook* (Child Poverty Action Group, 2003/2004).

67 (ODPM, 2002) p36.

Provision of facilities

3.36   CSCDA 1960 s24(2) states that local authorities have specific powers
'to provide for the use of those occupying caravan sites any services
or facilities for their health or convenience',[68] and 'to provide, in or in
connection with sites for the accommodation of gypsies, working
space and facilities for the carrying on of such activities as are
normally carried on by them'.[69] Those are powers, however, not
duties – so the local authority is not *obliged* to make such provision.
The power in respect of the provision of working space was
introduced by the Criminal Justice and Public Order Act 1994.[70]
However, in practice it is quite common for local authorities to
impose restrictions on the business use of their sites, despite the
recommendations contained in DoE Circular 1/94, Welsh Office
2/94 (hereafter DoE Circular 1/94), *Gypsy Sites and Planning,* that:

> Local Planning authorities should, wherever possible, identify in their
> development plans gypsy sites suitable for mixed residential, and
> business uses having regard to the safety of the occupants and their
> children.[71]

3.37   It is also part of Gypsy and Traveller culture to keep animals such
as horses or ponies. This can lead to problems about obtaining a
pitch on a local authority site – the agreements often do not permit
a resident to keep more than a dog or a cat and sometimes prohibit
all pets.

Fire precautions

3.38   The only other specific statutory provision relating to conditions on
sites refers to fire precautions. CSCDA 1960 s24(2A) states that:

> Before exercising the power to provide a site the local authority shall
> consult the fire authority, if they are not themselves the fire authority –
>
> (a) as to measures to be taken for preventing and detecting the outbreak
>   of fire on the site; and
> (b) as to the provision and maintenance of means of fighting fire on it.

---

68 CSCDA 1960 s24(2)(b).
69 CSCDA 1960 s24(2)(c).
70 CJPOA 1994 s80(2)(a).
71 DoE Circular 1/94 para 16.

Somewhat surprisingly, local authorities need only consult with the fire authority and do not necessarily have to follow the advice given to them as a result of such consultation.

3.39   The Secretary of State has published model standards under CSCDA 1960 s5(6) making precise recommendations as to the facilities to be provided on caravan sites, for example, as to the provision of fire alarms, fire extinguishers, water supply, and the distance of caravans from each other. However, none of them apply to Gypsy caravan sites and there is no obligation on local authorities to abide by the recommendations.[72]

3.40   An example of an attempt to sue a council for failure to provide/maintain fire-fighting equipment on its Gypsy caravan site, allegedly resulting in the destruction of the claimant's caravan and contents, was *Horace Piggott v Sheffield CC.*[73] HHJ Mettyear dismissed the claim finding:

1. there was no duty of care imposed by law in the circumstances of the case;
2. had there been a duty of care he would have found a breach of duty;
3. however, on the facts, he found that the loss would have occurred even if there had been no breach of duty, that is, the breach of duty made no difference.

This was a case in which the council had decided to carry out major renovation works to the site and all fire-fighting equipment was removed from the site including fire-extinguishers and means of alarm, leaving only two standpipes. The judge accepted the council's contention that the purpose of measures for dealing with fire on a caravan site (for example, fire extinguishers, a telephone or alarm system) was not to protect the occupier or property of the occupier of the caravan in which the fire started but to prevent the spread of fire from one caravan to another. Accordingly, there was not proximity sufficient to establish a duty of care, nor was it fair, just and reasonable to impose liability, although the reduction of ability to fight fires as a result of the council's actions was foreseeable (an appeal would have been pursued against this part of the learned judge's findings had it not been for 3. above). If there had been a duty of care he would have found a breach as the water pressure in

---

72 DoE Circular 14/89 *Caravan Sites and Control of Development Act 1960 – Model Standards.*
73 23 January 1998, Sheffield County Court, HHJ Mettyear, (unreported).

the standpipes was too low for fire-fighting. However, on the evidence, he found that even if the water pressure had been sufficient, the caravan would still have been destroyed.

Other site facilities

3.41 The guidance from central government in DoE Circular 1/94 also makes reference to the provision of site facilities. Circular 1/94 essentially aims to give guidance as to the exercise of local authorities' planning powers. At paragraph 17 it identifies three main types of sites: sites for settled occupation; temporary stopping places; transit sites. At paragraph 18, it states that for all sites 'consideration must be given to vehicular access from the public highway ... provision for parking, turning and servicing on site and road safety for occupant and visitors'. Landscaping is also advised for screening and privacy purposes. Annex B sets out characteristics of the sites said to be 'for illustrative purposes only'. They include: the provision of basic facilities for transit sites – 'refuse collection point', 'access to a drinking water supply', and 'sewage disposal'; the addition of hard surfaced access and hardstanding for caravans and vehicles for temporary stopping places; working spaces, safe play area for children, electricity, water supply, sanitation per pitch and a marked site boundary (fence or hedge) for settled sites.

Environmental Protection Act 1990

3.42 In relation to the conditions on a site, a Gypsy or Traveller can prosecute the local authority as the person responsible for a statutory nuisance under Environmental Protection Act (EPA) 1990 s82. A statutory nuisance within the meaning of EPA 1990 s79(1)(a) includes 'premises in such a state as to be prejudicial to health'. The phrase 'prejudicial to health' is further defined as 'injurious or likely to cause injury to health'.[74] The defendant in (what are commonly known as) 'section 82 proceedings' is 'the person responsible for the nuisance' defined as 'the person to whose act, default or sufferance [permission] the nuisance is attributable'.[75] The owner of the premises is the proper defendant if the person responsible cannot be found.[76] Statutory nuisance proceedings are often brought by local

74 EPA 1990 s79(7).
75 EPA 1990 s82(4)(a) and s79(7) respectively.
76 EPA 1990 s82(4)(c).

authorities against private owners[77] but by EPA 1990 s82, a private individual who is 'aggrieved' (that is, affected) by the conditions can bring a prosecution. A notice specifying the problem must first be served 21 days before the proceedings can be commenced. Section 82 proceedings are dealt with by the magistrates' court. The court can convict, fine,[78] and order compensation, works and costs. Tenants or other occupiers of houses have frequently used these proceedings in respect of conditions not covered by their tenancy agreements, for example, damp caused by excessive condensation.

3.43   Section 82 proceedings can be problematic. The burden of proof is to the criminal standard ('beyond a reasonable doubt') rather than the civil standard ('the balance of probability').[79] No public funding is available for representation although proceedings may be conducted by a lawyer paid on a conditional fee basis, that is, on the basis that the representative will only be paid if successful.[80] However, a lawyer instructed on such a basis is not entitled to charge an additional success fee in cases brought under EPA 1990. In addition it should be remembered that the prosecutor may well be ordered to pay the local authority's costs if the case is rejected. Though public funding is available to obtain an expert's report (for example, from an independent Environmental Health Officer) before the trial, it will not cover the cost of the expert's attendance at court. Additionally, the Gypsy or Traveller prosecuting the case needs to consider any possible effect on his continuing occupation of the site bearing in mind what has been said above about security of tenure. However, if it could be shown that a local authority's motivation for seeking eviction was that the Gypsy or Traveller had prosecuted the local authority under EPA 1990, then a 'public law challenge' by way of judicial review would lie on the basis that such action was unreasonable (that is, an action that no reasonable local authority would take).

3.44   A Gypsy or Traveller might use section 82 proceedings when the local authority have failed to deal with dampness caused by condensation in an amenity block or have failed to properly deal with rodent infestation, to give just two examples. Gypsies and Travellers have gained advantages by using such proceedings. For example, in

---

77   EPA 1990 s80.
78   Up to level 5 on the standard scale.
79   *R v Newham Justices ex p Hunt* [1976] 1 WLR 420.
80   Access to Justice Act 1999 s27(1).

Day v Sheffield CC,[81] a wide ranging order was achieved, requiring a programme to deal with rat infestation, internal site lighting, hard surfacing, provision of a dustbin for each pitch, and weekly refuse collection.

Grants

3.45   The CJPOA 1994 also repealed the Secretary of State's power to pay grants to local authorities for the provision of sites. However, since 2001/2002, the Government has made available £17m for repair and maintenance works to existing sites (not for the provision of new sites, although some has been made available for transit sites) and has invited local authorities to submit tenders for grants on an annual basis. This is known as the Gypsy Sites Refurbishment Grant (GSRG) challenge fund. The GSRG has now continued beyond the initial three-year period. The Niner report on *The Provision and Condition of Local Authority Gypsy/Traveller Sites in England,* commented that:

> ... the GSRG will have made a very valuable contribution to bringing sites up to standard, but that expenditure needs to be sustained.[82]

The report calculated that a grand total of £123.5m was needed to bring sites up to standard over a 30-year period.[83]

3.46   At present disabled facilities grants (DFGs), which assist in adapting dwelling-houses for the assistance of disabled residents, are not available for Gypsies or Travellers on local authority sites. The government proposes to address this issue in the Housing Bill 2004, currently before parliament, by amending the relevant legislation.[84] Social services have a general duty to assist disabled children within their area under Children Act (CA) 1989 by 'providing a range and level of services appropriate to their needs'.[85] CA 1989 defines a disabled person as a person who '[is] blind, deaf or dumb, suffers from mental disorder of any kind or is substantially and permanently handicapped by illness, injury or congenital deformity

---

81   August 1988 *Legal Action* 19.

82   (ODPM, 2002) p22.

83   *The Provision and Condition of Local Authority Gypsy/Traveller Sites in England* at p21, Table 3.

84   See Housing Bill 2004 clause 187 and the Housing Grants, Construction and Regeneration Act 1996.

85   CA 1989 s1(1).

or other such disability as may be prescribed.'[86] A service may (in other words, it is for the local authority to decide) include the provision of accommodation, and assistance in kind or in cash (and may be provided for the family of the child as well).[87] It is suggested that these provisions of the CA 1989 could be used to improve conditions for a disabled Gypsy or Traveller child whether they live on official or private sites.

Conclusion

3.47   When the duty to provide caravan sites for Gypsies was repealed in 1994, the government in its place sought to encourage provision by Gypsies and Travellers themselves. Though many have attempted to do so, it is apparent that a significant proportion of Gypsies and Travellers still live on unauthorised, roadside sites and that they require public site provision. Meanwhile, those living on official sites have limited rights as to security and very limited rights with regard to the allocation of pitches, their conditions of occupation and the provision of facilities, although there have been some achievements in recent years. The Commission for Racial Equality have tabled amendments to the Housing Bill 2004 which are designed to put Gypsies and Travellers on an equal footing with those living under the protection afforded them by MHA 1983. With security of tenure, Gypsies and Travellers could have greater confidence in enforcing their rights and in attempting to extend their rights. Whether the government adopts the suggested changes remains to be seen, but if no action is taken to redress the balance then it is likely that the issue will return to the courts for further consideration in the future.

86 CA 1989 s17(11).
87 CA 1989 s17(3), (6) and (7).

CHAPTER 4

Planning law

continued overleaf

Introduction

4.1   For many years there have been Gypsies and Travellers who have bought their own land, placed their caravans on it and used it as a base from which to travel. However, from 1970 to 1994 a significant number of sites for Gypsies and Travellers were established by local authorities acting in accordance with the duty under Caravan Sites Act (CSA) 1968 s6 'so far as may be necessary to provide adequate accommodation for gipsies residing in or resorting to their area ...'. When the Criminal Justice and Public Order Act (CJPOA) 1994 repealed CSA 1968 s6, the government rightly forecast that this was 'expected to lead to more applications for private gypsy sites'.[1] Since then planning law has played an increasingly important role in attempts to provide places where Gypsies and Travellers can place their caravans and live in them. Sadly, while in general most planning applications are allowed, most applications by Gypsies and Travellers are refused. As Lord Bingham said in his judgment in *South Buckinghamshire DC v Porter*:[2]

> In the case of Gypsies, the problem was compounded by features peculiar to them. Their characteristic lifestyle debarred them from access to conventional sources of housing provision. Their attempts to obtain planning permission almost always met with failure: statistics quoted by the European Court of Human Rights in *Chapman v United Kingdom*[3] ... showed that in 1991, the most recent year for which figures were available, 90 per cent of applications made by Gypsies had been refused whereas 80 per cent of all applications had been granted. But for many years the capacity of sites authorised for occupation by Gypsies has fallen well short of that needed to accommodate those seeking space on which to station their caravans.[4]

4.2   This situation was forecast in a forceful speech by Lord Irvine in the House of Lords debate on the CJPOA 1994:

> There is humbug at the heart of the Government's policy. The humbug is not simply that what they are suggesting is unrealistic as a solution to the problem of unauthorised sites; it is also that at the same time as they

---

1 Department of the Environment (DoE) Circular 1/94, Welsh Office 2/94 (hereafter DoE Circular 1/94), para 4.

2 *South Buckinghamshire DC v Porter; Chichester DC v Searle; Wrexham CBC v Berry; Hertsmere BC v Harty* [2003] UKHL 26; [2003] 2 WLR 1547, [2003] 3 All ER 1.

3 *Chapman v United Kingdom* [2001] 33 EHRR 399 para 66, [2001] 10 BHRC 48, (2001) *Times*, 30 January, ECtHR.

4 [2003] 2 WLR 1547 at 1554.

suggest that private site provision is the solution on which we should rely, they are making such provision more difficult by altering national planning policies. The real effect of the legislation, which they dare not openly avow, is to make those who have no lawful place to reside in their vehicles disappear through the imposition of criminal sanctions.[5]

4.3   Unfortunately, those strong comments did not lead to any positive change to the laws and policies relating to the public and private provision of sites for Gypsies and Travellers when the government changed in 1997.

4.4   This chapter seeks to ensure that those who represent Gypsies and Travellers are aware of key points of planning law and policy.

Structure of the planning system

Legislation

4.5   Since 1948 the development of land in England and Wales has been subject to controls imposed by the Town and Country Planning Acts. The present law is contained in the Town and Country Planning Act (TCPA) 1990 as amended (principally by the Planning and Compulsory Purchase Act 1991).[6] Similar regimes exist in Scotland and Northern Ireland.

4.6   TCPA 1990 is divided into 14 parts, of which the most important for Gypsies and Travellers are:

- Part II – Development plans which deal with the principal source of local planning policy;
- Part III – Control over development which includes the need for planning permission, consideration of applications for planning permission and appeals against refusal of planning permission;
- Part VII – Enforcement which provides for various means of enforcing against breaches of planning control; and
- Part XII – Validity which provides for challenges to various decisions related to planning, including the decisions of planning inspectors on development control and enforcement appeals.

---

5 Lord Irving of Lairg (then Shadow Lord Chancellor) during the House of Lord's Debate on the provisions in the CJPOA 1994, *Hansard* HL Debates, 11 July 1994.

6 It will be subject to further amendment when the Planning and Compulsory Purchase Bill 2004 is passed. See Recent Developments in Gypsy and Traveller Law at pxiii above.

Given the complexity of planning law,[7] this chapter concentrates on those aspects most relevant to Gypsy and Traveller cases.

Planning authorities

4.7 Most planning decisions are taken by the local planning authority (LPA) for the area concerned. In most English Gypsy and Traveller cases the relevant LPA will be the district council, London borough or national park authority. Where they exist, county councils are also LPAs, having responsibility for structure plans and for minerals and waste planning. Planning in national parks is the sole responsibility of national park authorities.[8] In Wales the LPA will be the county council, county borough, or national park authority.

The development plan

4.8 Local planning policy is contained in the development plan. In London boroughs, metropolitan district councils and some other unitary authorities, this is a single document known as the 'unitary development plan'. In parts of the country where there are both county councils and district councils and in some unitary authorities there are structure plans prepared by the county council (sometimes with a unitary authority) or a group of unitary authorities, and local plans prepared by the district council or unitary authority, which together (along with minerals and waste plans) constitute the development plan. Although emerging new or revised plans are often relevant to planning decisions,[9] it is the formally adopted plan that constitutes or is part of the development plan.

4.9 Development plans are extremely important in most aspects of town and country planning. As a result major economic concerns such as housebuilders and the minerals industry keep an eye on development plans to ensure that their interests are fully borne in mind. A major cause of inequality between the planning system's provision of accommodation for house-dwellers and its provision of accommodation for Gypsies and Travellers is that, while powerful and well-financed bodies ensure that the interests of housebuilders

7 Sweet and Maxwell's *Encyclopedia of Planning Law and Practice* now occupies seven volumes with a separate index.

8 For the detailed provisions in respect of planning authorities see TCPA 1990 ss1–9.

9 Planning Policy Guidance (PPG) Note 1 (General Policy and Principles) (1997), para 48.

are recognised, Gypsies' and Travellers' organisations do not have the resources to monitor emerging development plans and to challenge the absence of adequate policies to meet the needs of Gypsies and Travellers.[10] As a result, while the amendment of Green Belt boundaries to meet the need for housing has taken place on many occasions, it has never been changed to meet the needs of Gypsies and Travellers.

4.10   It is anticipated that when the Planning and Compulsory Purchase Bill 2004 is enacted and brought into force, the development plan will be comprised of: a regional special strategy produced by a regional planning board; and adopted or approved development plan documents produced by the local planning authority.[11]

Development control

4.11   The definition of 'development' is central to the system of development control:

> Subject to the following provisions of this section, in this Act, except where the context otherwise requires, 'development', means the carrying out of building, engineering, mining or other operations in, on, over or under land, or the making of any material change in the use of any buildings or other land.[12]

4.12   This definition is divided into two limbs:

- 'building, engineering, mining or other operations', known as 'operational development'; and
- material change of use.

Various operations and uses are deemed not to be development, including use of land for the purposes of agriculture or forestry.[13] The stationing of a residential caravan on land for the purposes of agriculture, for example, fruit or hop picking, or to attend ewes during lambing, will therefore not constitute development.

---

10 The only legal application where a Gypsy or Traveller has successfully challenged a development plan is *Butler v Bath and North East Somerset DC and others* [2003] EWCA Civ 1614; (2003) *Times* 4 November. There have been many by housebuilders and other developers.

11 Part 3 of the Planning and Compulsory Purchase Bill 2004. See Recent Developments in Gypsy and Traveller Law at pxiii above.

12 TCPA 1990 s55(1).

13 TCPA 1990 s55(2).

4.13   A common mistake in Gypsy and Traveller planning cases is to treat the placing of a caravan on land as an operational development. In itself, it is not, although it may involve associated operational development, such as the construction of roadways, hardstanding and amenity blocks. The stationing of a caravan on land for residential purposes, where the planning unit has previously had a wholly non-residential use (for example, a field in agricultural use), will be a material change of use and thus constitute development.[14] Usually this will require express planning permission.[15] If the previous use of the land is for another type of caravan site, such as a site for Travelling showpeople or a touring caravan site, it will be a question of fact and degree whether the change of its use to a site for Gypsies and Travellers is sufficient to be material.

4.14   The definition of 'caravan' that applies in TCPA 1990 is that contained in the Caravan Sites and Control of Development Act (CSCDA) 1960 s29(1), namely:

> 'caravan' means any structure designed or adapted for human habitation which is capable of being moved from one place to another (whether by being towed, or by being transported on a motor vehicle or trailer) and any motor vehicle so designed or adapted, but does not include –
>
> (a) any railway rolling stock which is for the time being on rails forming part of a railway system,
> (b) any tent.[16]

4.15   The word 'caravan' also covers certain structures composed of not more than two sections capable, when disassembled, of being moved by road.[17] The phrase 'mobile home' as used in mobile homes legislation has the same meaning as 'caravan' in caravan sites legislation.[18] It follows that while 'caravan' and 'mobile home' convey different meanings in everyday English, in law they are synonymous and cover almost everything that would be called a caravan, caravanette, a trailer-home or a mobile home.

14 *Restormel BC v Secretary of State for the Environment* [1982] JPL 785.
15 For circumstances where express permission is not required for the stationing of a caravan see below at paras 4.16–4.17 and DoE Circular 1/94 paras 29–32.
16 *Wyre Forest DC v Secretary of State for the Environment* [1990] 2 AC 357; [1990] 2 WLR 517; [1990] 1 All ER 780, HL. Caravan Sites and Control of Development Act (CSCDA) 1960 s29(1) also defines 'caravan site'.
17 For the full extended definition, see Caravan Sites Act (CSA) 1968 s13.
18 Mobile Homes Act 1975 s9(1) and Mobile Homes Act 1983 s5(1).

Planning permission

4.16   Planning permission is required for the carrying out of any development of land[19] unless the operation or use is lawful and immune from enforcement.[20]

4.17   Some matters (mainly of a minor nature) are granted planning permission by statutory instruments, known as development orders, the most important of which is the Town and Country Planning (General Permitted Development) Order (GPDO) 1995.[21] These include:

- certain minor operations, such as the erection of gates, walls and fences below specified heights;[22]
- certain temporary buildings and uses, such as moveable structures required in connection with building or engineering operations;[23]
- and certain caravan uses, such as use by a person travelling with a caravan for one or two nights.[24]

They are subject to conditions, which must be checked before relying on them. These permitted development rights may be withdrawn by a direction under GPDO 1995 art 4(1) made in respect of a specified area. This will not affect the legality of development that has already been carried out under the GPDO.[25]

4.18   However in most cases it will be necessary to apply for planning permission to the LPA.[26] A fee must be paid to cover the cost of such

---

19 TCPA 1990 s57.

20 TCPA 1990 s191 provides that 'uses and operations are lawful at any time if – (a) no enforcement action may then be taken in respect of them (whether because they did not involve development or require planning permission or because the time for enforcement action has expired or for any other reason); and (b) they do not constitute a contravention of any of the requirements of any enforcement notice then in force.' A person wishing to find out whether an existing use or operation is lawful may apply to the LPA for a certificate of lawfulness under TCPA 1990 s191 (or TCPA 1990 s192 in the case of a proposed use or operation).

21 SI No 418.

22 GPDO Class 2.

23 GPDO Class 4.

24 GPDO Class 5.

25 R v Epping Forest DC ex p Strandmill Ltd [1990] JPL 415.

26 TCPA 1990 s62.

an application.[27] In general there is no limit to the number of times that an application for planning permission can be made, although an LPA has a limited power to decline to determine applications within two years of the secretary of state dismissing an appeal or refusing an application provided they consider that 'there has been no significant change since the refusal or ... dismissal'.[28] An applicant who wishes to make a further application after an adverse decision of the secretary of state should therefore consider whether it can wait until the expiry of the two-year period or whether it can be changed significantly.

4.19   Applications for planning permission should be determined in accordance with the development plan, unless material considerations indicate otherwise.[29] It follows that those advising Gypsies and Travellers, like others advising people interested in the use and development of land, should consider objecting to the absence of appropriate policies in revised development plans[30] before they are adopted.

Material considerations

4.20   In the majority of cases concerning Gypsies and Travellers the proposed use of a piece of land as a Gypsy caravan site will conflict with some policies contained in the development plan. In such circumstances, Gypsies and Travellers will only be granted planning permission if they can show that there are material considerations that outweigh the development plan policy objections and justify the grant of planning permission. The phrase 'material considerations' is broad. As Cooke J stated in *Stringer v Minister of Housing and Local Government*:

> In principle ... any consideration which relates to the use and development of land is capable of being a planning consideration.

---

27 The Town and Country Planning (Fees for Applications and Deemed Applications) Regulations 1989 SI No 193, as amended.

28 TCPA 1990 s70A. It is anticipated that the Planning and Compulsory Purchase Bill 2004 will extend this power. See Recent Developments in Gypsy and Traveller Law at pxiii above.

29 TCPA 1990 s54A read with s70(2).

30 Which, after the commencement of the Planning and Compulsory Purchase Bill 2004, will consist of regional spatial strategies and development plan documents. See Recent Developments in Gypsy and Traveller Law at pxiii above.

Whether a particular consideration falling within that broad class is material in any given case will depend on the circumstances.[31]

4.21   Considerations that may be of particular relevance to applications for planning permission made by Gypsies and Travellers include:

- government advice;
- emerging development plans and supplementary planning guidance;
- designated areas and site location;
- Gypsy status;
- the need for Gypsy and Traveller sites;
- the applicant's need for a Gypsy or Traveller site;
- personal circumstances, and
- human rights.

Government advice

4.22   Government advice, including that contained in Planning Policy Guidance Notes (PPGs),[32] circular advice, and publications such as the ODPM Guidance on 'Managing Unauthorised Camping[33] are all capable of being material considerations.[34] Government guidance on Gypsy Sites and Planning is currently contained in DoE Circular 1/94.[35] This declares that one of its three main intentions is 'to provide that the planning system recognises the need for accommodation consistent with gypsies' nomadic lifestyle.'[36]

4.23   DoE Circular 1/94 provides that local planning authorities should 'make adequate gypsy site provision in their development plans, through appropriate use of locational and/or criteria based policies.'[37] 'Local Plans ... should wherever possible identify locations suitable for gypsy sites whether local authority or private sites.

---

31   [1971] 1 All ER 65 at 77.
32   These are to be replaced by Planning Policy Statements (PPSs). Consultation drafts of some PPSs have already been issued.
33   Published by the Office of the Deputy Prime Minister (ODPM). In force since 27 February 2004.
34   PPG 1, para 52.
35   DoE Circular 1/94 is being reviewed and it is anticipated that fresh guidance will be published in late 2004. DoE Circular 18/94, Welsh Office 76/94, Gypsy Sites Policy and Unauthorised Camping (hereafter DoE Circular 18/94) can also be relevant.
36   DoE Circular 1/94 para 1.
37   DoE Circular 1/94 para 9.

Where this is not possible they should set out clear, realistic criteria for suitable locations, as a basis for site provision policies ...'[38] In other words LPAs should always include locational policies in their local plans unless it is impossible to do so. If, and only if, it is impossible, should they include criteria-based policies. In practice most LPAs seem to have ignored this advice.[39] Gypsies and Travellers who look at development plans are given no idea where they are likely to obtain planning permission to locate their caravans and are often faced with having to satisfy unclear and unrealistic criteria.

4.24   Central government, which frequently intervenes in other aspects of local planning policy to ensure compliance with its own policies, has to-date left local plan policies that conflict with DoE Circular 1/94 in place. This situation may change. As Lord Rooker said on behalf of the government in a debate on the provisions of the Planning and Compulsory Planning Bill 2004:

> The central issue is to establish the policy and to ensure that we put in place a process within the new planning system whereby it is not possible to avoid providing the required number of sites. The need must be measured and assessed openly. The connection between the regional spatial strategy and local development documents does not allow a local authority to opt out and say, 'We are not having such a measure. We have no need of it' ... we shall ensure that local development plans by and large conform to the regional spatial strategy. We can solve this problem for the foreseeable future, not just for a few years. This is a generational issue for our fellow citizens. We shall do our best to come up with something that is acceptable to all parties concerned, including, of course, as a priority, Gypsies and Travellers themselves.[40]

4.25   A letter was sent by the Department of the Environment, Transport and the Regions to chief planning officers on 16 November 1999 to remind them of the emphasis in DoE Circular 1/94 on the identification of suitable locations for Gypsy sites in plans, wherever possible, and described this as 'the key message of the circular'. There is also the Court of Appeal judgment in *Butler v Bath and North*

---

38 DoE Circular 1/94 para 12.

39 ACERT and Wilson, *Directory of Planning Policies for Gypsy Site Provision in England* (Policy Press, 1997), a planning project carried out from 1995 to 1997 by the Advisory Council for the Education of Romani and other Travellers.

40 *Hansard*, HL Debates, col 978, 20 January 2004: col 978. The government is currently reviewing DoE Circular 1/94 and may well produce fresh guidance on Gypsy sites and planning later in 2004.

Somerset DC,[41] which pointed out that 'National policy draws a clear distinction between the identification of actual locations in a local plan and the setting of policy criteria. The preference is for the former.'[42]

4.26   Planning Policy Guidance (PPG) 3[43] contains government advice on housing. Paragraph 13 of PPG 3 advises LPAs to work jointly with housing departments to assess the range of Gypsies' and Travellers' needs.

4.27   PPG 12[44] contains government advice on development plans. Paragraph 4.14 states:

> As Circular 1/94 (Gypsy Sites and Planning) makes clear, plans should wherever possible identify locations suitable for Gypsy sites, whether local authority or private sites. Where this is not possible, they should set out clear, realistic, criteria for suitable locations as a basis for site provision policies. They should also identify existing sites which have planning permission, whether occupied or not, and should make a quantitative assessment of the amount of accommodation required.

4.28   Where a LPA fails to comply with the advice in DoE Circular 1/94 that fact may well constitute a material consideration that will count in favour of the grant of planning permission (if only on a temporary basis until such time as the LPA complies with the advice in DoE Circular 1/94).[45]

Emerging development plans and supplementary planning guidance

4.29   Account can be taken of policies in emerging development plans which are going through the statutory procedures towards adoption (or approval). The weight to be attached to such policies will depend upon the stage of plan preparation or review that has been reached.[46] Supplementary Planning Guidance produced by an LPA is also capable of being a material consideration.[47] Such guidance may be vulnerable to challenge by judicial review.[48]

---

41 [2003] EWCA Civ 1614.
42 [2003] EWCA Civ 1614 at para 28.
43 PPG 3 (Housing) (2000).
44 PPG 12 (Development Plans) (1999).
45 See, eg, *the Pylon Site* case (a decision of the Secretary of State dated 25 April 2002) (Application No TP/2001/0361).
46 PPG 1 (General Policy and Principles) para 48.
47 See PPG 12, paras 3.18 and 3.19.
48 See appendix A for details of judicial review procedure.

Designated areas and site location

4.30 Much of England and Wales is designated, usually under an adopted development plan. In 1995 approved Green Belts covered 12 per cent of England.[49] In 1992 National Parks and Areas of Outstanding National Beauty (AONB) alone covered about 22 per cent of England and Wales.[50] The overlap between Green Belts on the one hand, and National Parks and AONBs on the other is comparatively small.[51] In addition to these designations there are Sites of Special Scientific Interest (SSSI), World Heritage Sites and many other (principally local) designations. An applicant for planning permission in open land or a Green Belt will have to address DoE Circular 1/94 paragraph 13, which provides:

> As a rule it will not be appropriate to make provision for gypsy sites in areas of open land where development is severely restricted, for example, Areas of Outstanding National Beauty, Sites of Special Scientific Interest, and other protected areas. Gypsy sites are not regarded as being among those uses of land which are normally appropriate in Green Belts ...

4.31 DoE Circular 1/94 paragraph 13 gives very different advice to previous guidance that had expressly recognised that it may be necessary to accept the establishment of Gypsy sites in protected areas. It creates practical difficulties for Gypsies and Travellers, who are by and large, rural people, unable to afford urban land prices, and unfamiliar with the planning system. The combined effect of land prices, scarcity of available land, local opposition and the difficulties of dealing with the planning system makes the prospects of a Gypsy or a Traveller (whether or not he or she is well-educated and informed) being able to establish a lawful site in an urban area extremely poor.

4.32 The reality is that most Gypsies and Travellers will want to live in rural areas and will in any event be unable to live elsewhere. Paragraph 13 makes it clear where sites will not normally be allowed, without a clear statement as to where they will be permitted. By a

49 PPG 2 (1995) (Green Belts), para 1.3.
50 PPG 7 (1992), since replaced by PPG 7 (1997) (The Countryside: Environmental Quality and Economic and Social Development) and see now draft PPS 7 (2003). The percentage of land now covered by National Parks and AONBs has increased since 1992 as a result of further designations.
51 See the maps in PPG 2 and PPG 7.

process of elimination, it appears to favour areas that are neither 'open land' nor 'protected areas'.[52] In some parts of the country this creates a situation that is neither morally nor practically defensible: all rural areas are excluded because they are all protected land, while all available urban land is excluded because the Gypsy or Traveller cannot outbid the housebuilder. The situation is probably most serious in the countryside around London. This area contains the largest Green Belt, AONBs, and very high land prices. Parts of it have a long history of under-provision of public sites.[53] These factors combine to create a situation where disputes between Gypsies and Travellers and local planning authorities are almost inevitable.

4.33   In areas where there is a substantial amount of undesignated rural land it ought, with good will from all concerned, to be relatively easy to locate suitable sites for Gypsies and Travellers. Unfortunately, that good will is often lacking. In other areas, the fact that most land is designated will not remove the need to provide for Gypsies' and Travellers' accommodation. In such circumstances it is suggested that three approaches might be considered.

4.34   First, DoE Circular 1/94 paragraph 13 refers to 'open land'. There may well be sites on designated land that nobody using normal English would call 'open'. Former military sites such as anti-aircraft emplacements and redundant utility sites, such as a former sub-station, may well have natural screening that has developed over the years and be at a price that Gypsies and Travellers can afford. Although these may in many respects be suitable for Gypsy and Traveller sites, advisers should be aware that such sites may be contaminated and should give their clients a clear warning of this possibility. They should firmly advise site investigation before purchase.[54] Some former quarries may also be suitable, although physical safety in them should be given particular consideration.

4.35   Second, a 'sieve map' process may be adopted to determine preferred areas. Under this process the land of greatest importance within the LPA's area is excluded first. In assessing importance, national designations such as AONBs and SSSIs are clearly of

52 See also DoE Circular 1/94 para 22.
53 *R v Secretary of State for the Environment and Hertfordshire CC ex p Lee* [1987] 54 P&CR 311; [1985] JPL 724; *R v Secretary of State for the Environment and Surrey CC ex p Hilden* [1988] COD 3.
54 Gypsies and Travellers should be advised to instruct a conveyancing solicitor or a licensed conveyancer.

greater importance than local ones such as landscape protection areas. Further areas may be excluded in order of importance, but the process stops before the area of land remaining is too small to permit a realistic search for sites. In an area that was mainly undesignated land, all designated land might be excluded by this method. In an area that was wholly designated land, sites would be permitted in areas carrying the designation(s) of least importance. This is an entirely appropriate method of meeting a planning need.[55]

4.36   Third, an approach based on the needs of Gypsies and Travellers can be adopted. This is likely to lead to a search for sites reasonably close to (but not immediately adjoining) settlements of sufficient size to contain basic facilities such as a primary school, doctor's surgery and shop(s) with access to a road appropriate for a lorry towing a caravan. At its best, such an approach can lead to the identification of sites where Gypsies and Travellers' accommodation needs can be met in areas where they wish to live. However, if not done properly, such an approach can result in the adoption of a policy consisting of so many mandatory criteria that it is unrealistic to expect that a site could be found which would comply with its requirements. The criteria used should be reasonable. Thus in *Stirrup v Secretary of State for the Environment*,[56] a district council had interpreted a county council's policy as meaning that all Gypsy and Traveller sites should have main services readily and economically available. The High Court held that 'a requirement of mains services for a single caravan might well be *Wednesbury*[57] unreasonable'.

4.37   While the reference to 'open land' in paragraph 13 of DoE Circular 1/94 points primarily to the use of land that cannot be classified as 'open', the need to find somewhere for Gypsy and Traveller sites may well override that consideration, particularly where the land can be effectively screened by new planting. DoE Circular 1/94 paragraph 23 recognises that landscaping may make an application acceptable.

55 *Buckinghamshire CC v Hall Aggregates* [1985] JPL 634, CA.
56 (1993) 3 December, CO/383/93, Local Authority Law 1/94 2.
57 *Associated Provincial Picture Houses Ltd v Wednesbury Corporation* [1948] 1 KB 223; [1947] 2 All ER 680, CA.

Ethnic Gypsies and Travellers and Gypsy status

4.38   There is no doubt that Romani Gypsies are a separate racial group for the purposes of RRA 1976.[58] Irish Travellers are also recognised as a separate ethnic group.[59]

4.39   Article 8 of the European Convention on Human Rights (ECHR) protects, among other things, 'the traditional lifestyle of a minority'[60] and therefore, the cultural traditions of Romani Gypsies and Irish Travellers.' Article 14 of the ECHR prohibits discrimination in respect of Convention rights 'on any ground such as ... race ... national or social origin, association with a national minority, property, birth or other status'.

4.40   Race Relations Act (RRA) 1976 ss19A and 71, when read together, provide that local authorities must ensure that they exercise their planning function with due regard to the need to eliminate unlawful discrimination, including discrimination against Romani Gypsies and Irish Travellers.

4.41   Somewhat confusingly, the word 'Gypsies' is defined for the purposes of planning law not on grounds of ethnicity but as meaning:

> ... persons of nomadic habit of life, whatever their race or origin, but does not include members of an organised group of travelling showmen, or persons engaged in travelling circuses, travelling together as such.[61]

4.42   This is the definition applicable to the government guidance in DoE Circulars 1/94, 18/94 and PPG 12.[62] It follows that a Gypsy or

---

58 *Commission for Racial Equality v Dutton* [1989] QB 783; [1989] 1 All ER 306, CA.

59 *O'Leary v Allied Domecq* (2000) 29 August (Case No CL 950275–79), HHJ Goldstein, Central London County Court (unreported). For further consideration of this point see chapter 8. Compare the Race Relations (Northern Ireland) Order 1997 art 5, which for the avoidance of doubt makes express provision for Irish Travellers. Note also that since 19 July 2003 both Romani Gypsies and Irish Travellers have been protected by the EU Race Equality Directive (Directive 2000/43/EC; 2000 OJ L180/22). For a detailed consideration of this Directive see [2003] EHRLR 515.

60 *Buckley v United Kingdom* [1996] 23 EHRR 101; [1997] 2 PLR 10; [1996] JPL 1018, ECtHR, Opinion at para 64.

61 CSCDA 1960 s24(8). The same definition was formerly contained in CSA 1968 s16 and stems from the decision of the Divisional Court in *Mills v Cooper* [1967] 2 WLR 1343. For guidance in respect of Travelling showpeople, see DoE Circular 22/91, Welsh Office 78.91.

62 PPG 12 (1999) (Development Plans).

Traveller who seeks planning permission for a Gypsy caravan site and wishes to rely upon the positive government guidance in support of the application must first prove that he or she falls within the statutory definition.

4.43   In *Greenwich LBC v Powell*,[63] Lord Bridge of Harwich stated that a person could be a statutory Gypsy if he led a nomadic way of life only seasonally.

4.44   The case of *R v Shropshire CC ex p Bungay*,[64] concerned a Gypsy family that had not travelled for some 15 years in order to care for their elderly and infirm parents. An aggrieved local resident in the area of the family's recently approved Gypsy site sought judicial review of the local authority's decision to accept that the family had retained their Gypsy status even though they had not travelled for some considerable time. Dismissing the claim, the judge held that a person could remain a Gypsy even if he or she did not travel, provided that their nomadism was held in abeyance and not abandoned.

4.45   In the later case of *Hearne v National Assembly for Wales*,[65] a traditional Gypsy was held not to be a Gypsy for the purposes of planning law as he had stated that he intended to abandon his nomadic habit of life, lived in a permanent dwelling and was taking a course that led to permanent employment.

4.46   In *R v South Hams DC ex p Gibb*,[66] the Court of Appeal considered the statutory definition further and qualified it by holding that there should be some recognisable connection between the travelling of those claiming to be Gypsies and the means whereby they made or sought their livelihood:

> ... the definition of 'Gypsies' ... imports the requirement that there should be some recognisable connection between the wandering or travelling and the means whereby the persons concerned make or seek their livelihood. Persons, or individuals, who move from place to place merely as the fancy may take them and without any connection between the movement and their means of livelihood fall outside these statutory definitions ...[67]

4.47   The latter part of the Court of Appeal's interpretation of the statutory definition of 'Gypsy' involves a consideration of whether

---

63 [1989] 1 AC 995; [1989] 2 WLR 7 at 15.

64 [1991] 28 HLR 195.

65 22 October 1999, (QBENF 1999/0648/C); (1999) *Times* 10 November.

66 [1995] QB 158; [1994] 4 All ER 1012, CA.

67 [1994] 4 All ER 1012 at 1021.

the individual concerned travels to seek or make their livelihood and this point has been considered further in a number of cases. For example, in *Maidstone BC v Secretary of State for the Environment and Dunn*,[68] it was held that a Romani Gypsy who bred horses and travelled to horse fairs at Appleby, Stow-in-the-Wold and the New Forest, where he bought and sold horses and remained away from his permanent site for up to two months of the year, at least partly in connection with this traditional Gypsy activity, was entitled to be accorded Gypsy status. More recently, in *Basildon DC v First Secretary of State and Rachel Cooper*,[69] the Court of Appeal accepted that a Romani Gypsy woman was a statutory Gypsy, in circumstances where she travelled to traditional Gypsy fairs during the summer months and sold craft items at those events.

4.48   LPAs often go to considerable lengths to try to 'prove' that the Gypsies or Travellers seeking planning permission are not statutory 'Gypsies'.

4.49   The Welsh Assembly's Equality of Opportunity Committee[70] has recognised this tendency and has argued that the weaknesses in the planning system are indicated by the increasing consideration of the provisions of the Human Rights Act (HRA) 1998 in relation to legal action being taken by Gypsies and Travellers on planning issues. The Committee has noted the:

> ... apparent obsession with finding ways to prove that an individual is not a 'Gypsy' for the purposes of the planning system. This approach is extremely unhelpful ... and there can be no doubt that actual mobility at any given time is a poor indicator as to whether someone should be considered a Gypsy or a Traveller.[71]

4.50   Recently, the courts have also returned to consider the question of whether an individual can lose her or his Gypsy status, particularly in relation to cases where old age and ill health has led to Gypsies and Travellers not being able to travel.

4.51   In *Wrexham CBC v The National Assembly for Wales and Berry*,[72] a planning inspector had allowed a planning enforcement appeal for an ethnic Irish Traveller family in Wrexham, only to see the decision challenged in the High Court on the grounds that the elder

---

68 [1996] JPL 584.

69 [2004] EWCA Civ 473.

70 *Review of Service Provision for Gypsies and Travellers* (National Assembly for Wales, 2003).

71 *Review of Service Provision for Gypsies and Travellers* at p58.

72 [2002] EWHC 2414 Admin.

breadwinner in the family, Mr Berry, was no longer a 'Gypsy' because he had become too ill to continue to travel for work.

4.52   In his judgment, Sullivan J decided that he could not see anything in *R v South Hams DC ex p Gibb*[73] to suggest that, had the Court of Appeal been confronted with what might be described as a 'retired' Gypsy, it would have said that he had ceased to be a statutory Gypsy because he had become too ill and/or too old to travel in order to search for work. Indeed, Sullivan J stated that he believed:

> ... such an approach would be contrary to common sense and common humanity ... It would be inhuman pedantry to approach the policy guidance ... upon that basis ...[74]

4.53   Soon after *Berry* was heard by Sullivan J, the High Court considered another challenge to Gypsy status in the context of the refusal of planning permission in the case of *O'Connor v First Secretary of State and Bath and North East Somerset DC*.[75] This time the case involved an inspector's decision that the Irish Traveller concerned was not a Gypsy because she had become too ill to travel.

4.54   Field J decided that it was not enough, as the inspector had done, simply to focus on the travelling currently being undertaken or likely to be undertaken in the future, but that the inspector should instead consider such circumstances as:

- the person's history;
- the reasons for ceasing to travel;
- the person's future wishes and intentions to resume travelling when the reasons for settling have ceased to apply; and
- the person's attitude to living in a caravan rather than a conventional house.

4.55   In *Berry*, Wrexham CBC appealed against the decision of Sullivan J and the Court of Appeal allowed the appeal.[76] In doing so Auld LJ stated the following propositions of law should be applied:

> ...
> (2) Whether applicants for planning permission are of a 'nomadic way of life' as a matter of planning law and policy is a functional test to be applied to their normal way of life at the time of the

---

73   [1995] QB 158; [1994] 4 All ER 1012, CA.
74   [2002] EWHC 2414 Admin at para 20. Note that the decision of Sullivan J was overturned by the Court of Appeal – see para 4.55 below.
75   [2002] EWHC 2649 Admin.
76   [2003] EWCA Civ 835.

determination. Are they at that time following such a habit of life in the sense of a pattern and/or a rhythm of full time or seasonal or other periodic travelling? The fact that they may have a permanent base from which they set out on, and to which they return from, their periodic travelling may not deprive them of nomadic status. And the fact that they are temporarily confined to their permanent base for personal reasons such as sickness and/or possibly the interests of their children, may not do so either, depending on the reasons and the length of time, past and projected, of the abeyance of their travelling life. But if they have retired permanently from travelling for whatever reason, ill health, age or simply because they no longer wish to follow that way of life, they no longer have a 'nomadic way of life'. That is not to say they cannot recover it later, if their circumstances and intention change ... But that would arise if and when they made some future application for permission on the strength of that resumption of the status.

(3) Where, as here, a question is raised before a Planning Inspector as to whether applicants for planning permission are 'gypsies' for the purpose of planning law and policy, he should: (i) clearly direct himself to, and identify, the statutory and policy meaning of that word; and (ii) as a second and separate exercise, decide by reference to that meaning on the facts of the case whether the applicants fall within it ...

(4) In making the second, factual, decision whether applicants for planning permission are gypsies, the first and most important question is whether they are – to use a neutral expression – actually living a travelling life, whether seasonal or periodic in some other way, at the time of the determination. If they are not, then it is a matter of fact and degree whether the current absence of travelling means that they have not acquired or no longer follow a nomadic habit of life.

(5) On such an issue of fact and degree, the decision-maker may find any one or more of the following circumstances relevant and, if so, of varying weight: (i) the fact that the applicants do or do not come from a traditional gypsy background and/or have or have not followed a nomadic way of life in the past – the possible relevance in either case being that respectively they may be less or more likely to give it up for very long or to abandon it entirely; (ii) the fact that the applicants do or do not have an honest and realistically realisable intention of resuming travelling and, if they do, how soon and in what circumstances; (iii) the reason or reasons for the applicants not living a travelling way of life at the time of the determination and their likely duration.[77]

The need for Gypsy and Traveller sites

4.56   The case of *Hedges and Hedges v Secretary of State for the Environment and East Cambridgeshire DC*,[78] is authority for the fact that the national, regional and local need for additional site provision is capable of being a material consideration in planning applications made by Gypsies and Travellers.

4.57   *Hedges* is also an authority for the proposition that the personal need of a Gypsy or Traveller for a site is a material consideration that should be considered independently of the question of personal circumstances and hardship.[79]

Personal circumstances

4.58   The traditional approach in planning law to land-use factors and personal circumstances is contained in Lord Scarman's speech in *Great Portland Estates plc v Westminster CC*:

> ... the principle ... is now well settled. It was stated ... in one sentence in *East Barnet Urban District Council v British Transport Commission* ... Lord Parker CJ said ... 'what is really to be considered is the character of the use of the land, not the particular purpose of a particular occupier.' These words have rightly been recognised as extending beyond the issue of change of use: they are accepted as a statement of general principle in planning law. They apply to development plans as well as to planning control ... However, like all generalisations, Lord Parker CJ's statement has its own limitations. Personal circumstances of an occupier, personal hardship, the difficulties of businesses which are of value to the character of a community are not to be ignored in the administration of planning control. It would be inhuman pedantry to exclude from the control of our environment the human factor. The human factor is always present, of course, indirectly as the background to the consideration of the character of land use. It can, however, and sometimes should, be given direct effect as an exceptional or special circumstance. But such circumstances, when

77 Mr Berry was refused permission to appeal against the Court of Appeal's decision and has lodged an application with the ECtHR which has yet to be considered. Gypsy and Traveller women who are single parents may be faced with LPA decisions that they are not statutory 'Gypsies' since they do not travel for an economic purpose. In such circumstances, they may be able to argue that their economic nomadism is in abeyance (see *R v Shropshire CC ex p Bungay* [1991] 28 HLR 195). Alternatively, they may be able to argue that such a conclusion amounts to indirect sex discrimination under the Sex Discrimination Act (SDA) 1975, though there is currently no case-law on this matter.

78 [1996] 73 P&CR 534 at 545.

79 [1996] 73 P&CR 534 at 545.

they arise, fall to be considered not as a general rule but as exceptions to a general rule to be met in special cases. If a planning authority is to give effect to them, a specific case has to be made and the planning authority must give reasons for accepting it.[80]

4.59   In DoE Circular 1/94 paragraph 22 the government advised LPAs that:

> As with any other planning applications, proposals for Gypsy sites should continue to be determined solely in relation to land-use factors.

However, this guidance has been criticised by the High Court in two cases: *Webb v Secretary of State for the Environment*[81] and *Rexworthy v Secretary of State for the Environment*,[82] and unless the phrase 'land-use factors' is interpreted so as to include personal circumstances, the advice in paragraph 22 would conflict with the House of Lords decision in *Great Portland Estates*. Indeed, in so far as it makes an assertion in respect of other planning determinations, it is clearly wrong.

4.60   While personal circumstances carry little or no weight in the vast majority of planning cases, they are often of crucial importance when Gypsies and Travellers apply for planning permission. This is particularly so where the proposed site is situated within an area of national designation such as a Green Belt.

4.61   PPG 2 paragraph 3 states that there is a general presumption against inappropriate development within the Green Belt. Paragraph 3.2 states that inappropriate development is, by definition, harmful to the Green Belt and such development should not be approved, except in 'very special circumstances'. It is for the applicant to justify inappropriate development and 'very special circumstances' will not exist unless the harm by reason of inappropriateness, and any other harm, is clearly outweighed by other considerations.

4.62   Gypsy and Traveller sites are not categorised as 'appropriate development' and in practice a Gypsy or Traveller seeking planning permission for a site within the Green Belt will have to show that there is a pressing need for further sites and/or that their personal circumstances justify the grant of planning permission.

---

80 [1985] AC 661 at 669–670; [1984] 3 All ER 744, HL. See also PPG 1 (General Policy and Principles) (1997) para 38.
81 [1995] EGCS 147; [1996] 71 P&CR 411.
82 [1998] JPL 864, in which the inspector's decision was quashed as a result of it taking a narrow view of DoE Circular 1/94 para 22 and subordinating the Gypsy's circumstances to development plan policies.

4.63 In *Doncaster MBC v Secretary of State for the Environment, Transport and the Regions*[83] and *R (Chelmsford BC) v First Secretary of State and Draper*,[84] Sullivan J emphasised the importance of the guidance in PPG 2 and, in *Doncaster*, emphasised the fact that it is important that the need to establish the existence of '"very special circumstances" ... is not watered down'.[85] That approach has since been endorsed by the Court of Appeal.[86]

4.64 The education of the children of Gypsies and Travellers may be of particular relevance in a planning application and if those needs are sufficiently strong then they may be sufficient to clearly outweigh the objections to the use of land within the Green Belt as a caravan site (on their own or in conjunction with other considerations).[87] Similarly, health considerations are often a very important factor in planning cases and can prove to be crucial.

Human rights as a material consideration

4.65 Local authorities, planning inspectors, the Secretary of State and the courts are all public bodies for the purposes of Human Rights Act (HRA) 1998 s6(3) and are therefore subject to the duty imposed by HRA 1998 s6(1) to act compatibly with the European Convention on Human Rights (ECHR) when dealing with applications for planning permission made by Gypsies and Travellers.[88]

4.66 In 2001 the European Court of Human Rights (ECtHR) gave its judgment in five cases brought by British Gypsies who had been refused planning permission to place their caravan homes on their

---

83 [2002] EWHC 808 Admin.

84 [2003] EWHC 2978 Admin.

85 [2002] EWHC 808 Admin at para 74.

86 *South Buckinghamshire DC v Secretary of State for Transport, Local Government and the Regions and Porter* [2003] EWCA Civ 687; (2003) *Times* 23 May. See Recent Developments in Gypsy and Traveller Law at pxiii above.

87 *Basildon DC v Secretary of State for the Environment, Transport and Regions* 21 September 2000 (unreported) (CO/3315/2000) at para 34 of the judgment where Ouseley J stressed that the educational needs of children are an important aspect of wider land use considerations in the provision of Gypsy sites and that there is considerable public interest in the planning system for providing stable educational opportunities for Gypsy and Traveller families. Compare *Doncaster* [2002] EWHC 808 Admin and *Draper* [2003] EWHC 2978 Admin.

88 For a detailed consideration of the HRA 1998 as it affects Gypsies and Travellers see chapter 2.

own land.[89] The United Kingdom government settled a sixth case, in which the European Commission of Human Rights had previously found a breach of the Convention, by a payment of £60,000 and full costs.[90]

4.67   The applicants in each case had complained of breaches of various Convention rights, notably article 8. This provides:

(1) Everyone has the right to respect for his private and family life, his home and his correspondence.

(2) There shall be no interference by a public authority with the exercise of this right except such as is in accordance with the law and is necessary in a democratic society in the interests of national security, public safety or the economic well-being of the country, for the prevention of disorder or crime, for the protection of health or morals, or for the protection of the rights and freedoms of others.

4.68   The lead case, *Chapman v United Kingdom,*[91] concerned a Gypsy woman who had bought land in the Three Rivers District of Hertfordshire. This district contained no provision for Gypsies and was in a county that had a history of under-provision for Gypsies, which had led to a High Court declaration that it was in breach of the (now repealed) statutory duty to provide Gypsy caravan sites.[92] Mrs Chapman's land was however situated in a Green Belt.

4.69   The ECtHR first considered whether the prima facie rights contained in article 8(1) were in issue. It unanimously held that they were, not only in the case of the right to respect for home (which in the light of an earlier decision of the ECtHR in *Buckley v United Kingdom*[93] the government had conceded), but also in the case of the right to respect for private and family life. As the ECtHR said:

... the applicant's occupation of her caravan is an integral part of her ethnic identity as a Gypsy, reflecting the long tradition of that minority

---

89   *Chapman v United Kingdom* [2001] 33 EHRR 399; [2001] 10 BHRC 48; (2001) *Times* 30 January, ECtHR (Commission [1998] HRDC IX 386). See also *Beard v United Kingdom* [2001] 33 EHRR 442, *Coster v United Kingdom* [2001] 33 EHRR 479, *Smith (Jane) v United Kingdom* [2001] 33 EHRR 712 and *Lee v United Kingdom* [2001] Application No 25289/94.

90   *Varey v United Kingdom* (Application No 26662/95).

91   *Chapman* [2001] 33 EHRR 399.

92   *R v Secretary of State for the Environment ex p Lee* [1987] 54 P&CR 311.

93   [1996] 23 EHRR 101; [1997] 2 PLR 10; [1996] JPL 1018, (1996) *Times* 9 October, ECtHR (Commission [1994] JPL 536; [1995] JPL 633; 19 EHRR CD20).

of following a travelling lifestyle. This is the case even though, under the pressure of development and diverse policies or from their own volition, many Gypsies no longer live a wholly nomadic existence and increasingly settle for long periods in one place in order to facilitate, for example, the education of their children. Measures which affect the applicant's stationing of her caravans have therefore a wider impact than on the right to respect for home. They also affect her ability to maintain her identity as a Gypsy and to lead her private and family life in accordance with that tradition.[94]

4.70   The judges of the ECtHR disagreed on whether the interference by the State was justified as 'necessary in a democratic society'. A majority of 10 of the 17 judges held that it was, while a minority dissented. There was a distinct difference between the Western European judges, a majority of whom found in the applicants' favour, and the Eastern European ones who, with the exception of the Slovak judge, found in favour of the UK government. Schiemann LJ, the ad hoc UK judge, also found in the government's favour.

4.71   The majority recognised that 'there may be said to be an emerging international consensus amongst the Contracting States of the Council of Europe recognising the special needs of minorities and an obligation to protect their security, identity and lifestyle [see ... in particular the Framework Convention for the Protection of Minorities[95]], not only for the purpose of safeguarding the interests of the minorities themselves but to preserve a cultural diversity of value to the whole community'.[96] However they were 'not persuaded that the consensus is sufficiently concrete for it to derive any guidance as to the conduct or standards which Contracting States consider desirable in any particular situation'.[97] In so stating they left open the possibility that the consensus may harden sufficiently for the Court to bear it in mind in future judgments.

4.72   The majority also held that:

> As intimated in the *Buckley* judgment, the vulnerable position of Gypsies as a minority means that some special consideration should be given to their needs and their different lifestyle both in the relevant regulatory planning framework and in arriving at the decisions in particular cases

---

94 *Chapman* [2001] 33 EHRR 399 at para 73.

95 Framework Convention for the Protection of National Minorities, Strasbourg, 1/2/1195, Council of Europe Doc ETS 157.

96 *Chapman* [2001] 33 EHRR 399 at para 93.

97 [2001] 33 EHRR 399 at para 94.

> ... To this extent there is thus a positive obligation imposed on the Contracting States by virtue of Article 8 to facilitate the Gypsy way of life ... [98]

4.73   However the majority relied upon the doctrine of 'margin of appreciation'[99] to find for the government, holding:

> ... a margin of appreciation must, inevitably, be left to the national authorities, who by reason of their direct and continuous contact with the vital forces of their countries are in principle better placed than an international court to evaluate local needs and conditions. [100]

It should be noted that this doctrine depends on the international nature of the Court. It will therefore not apply to a national court acting under the Human Rights Act (HRA) 1998. [101]

4.74   While the government succeeded, it did not escape criticism from the majority, who commented:

> ... the issue for determination ... is not the acceptability or not of a general situation, however deplorable, in the United Kingdom in the light of the United Kingdom's undertakings in international law, but the narrower one whether the particular circumstances of the case disclose a violation of the applicant's, Mrs Chapman's, right to respect for her home under article 8 ... [102]

4.75   The minority delivered a strong dissenting judgment in respect of article 8. They accepted 'that the examination of planning objections to a particular use of a site is not a role for which this Court is well-suited ... Where town and country planning is concerned, the Court has previously noted that this involves the exercise of discretionary judgment in the implementation of policies adopted in the interest of the community ...'[103]

4.76   However the dissenting judges took a different approach to the treatment of minorities stating:

> There is an emerging consensus amongst the member States of the Council of Europe recognising the special needs of minorities and an obligation to protect their security, identity and lifestyle, not only for the

---

98 [2001] 33 EHRR 399 at para 96.

99 See chapter 2 at paras 2.31–2.35.

100 *Chapman* [2001] 33 EHRR 399 at para 91.

101 See the Court of Appeal decision in *South Buckinghamshire DC v Porter; Chichester DC v Searle; Wrexham CBC v Berry; Hertsmere BC v Harty* [2001] EWCA Civ 1549; [2002] 1 All ER 425; [2002] 1 WLR 1359; July 2002 *Legal Action* 22, at para 25 per Simon Brown LJ.

102 *Chapman* [2001] 33 EHRR 399 at para 100.

103 *Chapman* [2001] 33 EHRR 399, joint dissenting opinion at p435.

purpose of safeguarding the interests of the minorities themselves but also in order to preserve a cultural diversity of value to the whole community. This consensus includes a recognition that the protection of the rights of minorities, such as Gypsies, requires not only that Contracting States refrain from policies or practices which discriminate against them but that also, where necessary, they should take positive steps to improve their situation through, for example, legislation or specific programmes. We cannot therefore agree with the majority's assertion that the consensus is not sufficiently concrete or with their conclusion that the complexity of the competing interests renders the Court's role a strictly supervisory one ...[104]

4.77   The dissenting judges bore in mind the difficulties of Gypsies, stating:

The long-term failures of local authorities to make effective provision for Gypsies in their planning policies is evident from the history of implementation of measures concerning Gypsy sites, both public and private ... the Government is already well aware that the legislative and policy framework does not provide in practice for the needs of the Gypsy minority and that their policy of leaving it to local authorities to make provision for Gypsies has been of limited effectiveness ... it is in our opinion disproportionate to take steps to evict a Gypsy family from their home on their own land in circumstances where there has not been shown to be any other lawful, alternative site reasonably open to them. It would accordingly be for the authorities to adopt such measures as they consider appropriate to ensure that the planning system affords effective respect for the home, private life and family life of Gypsies such as the applicant.[105]

4.78   In addition to joining the dissenting opinion, Judge Bonello emphasised Hertfordshire County Council's proven non-compliance with the law. In a separate opinion he stated:

A public authority owes as great an obligation to comply with the law as any individual. Its responsibility is eminently more than that of individuals belonging to vulnerable classes who are virtually forced to disregard the law in order to be able to exercise their fundamental right to a private and family life – individuals who have to contravene the law due to the operation of the prior failures of the public authorities. In the present case, both the public authorities and the individual had undoubtedly trespassed the boundaries of legality. But it was the public authority's default in observing the law that precipitated and induced the subsequent default by the individual. That failure of the authorities has

104 [2001] 33 EHRR 399 at pp435–436.
105 [2001] 33 EHRR 399 at p438.

brought about a situation which almost justifies the defence of necessity. Why a human rights court should look with more sympathy at the far-reaching breach of law committed by the powerful, than at that forced on the weak, has not yet been properly explained.[106]

4.79   Though the applicants in *Chapman* were unsuccessful, the HRA 1998 principles derived from that case are of general application and will be relevant in almost every case where Gypsies and Travellers seek planning permission for use of land as a caravan site.

Human rights and offers of conventional housing

4.80   Significantly, the provisions of HRA 1998 and the ECHR have been applied by the domestic courts to determine whether the availability of conventional housing should be taken into consideration (that is, a material consideration) when Gypsies and Travellers seek planning permission for their own caravan sites.

4.81   In *Clarke v Secretary of State for the Environment, Transport and the Regions and Tunbridge Wells BC,*[107] an inspector dismissed an appeal against the local planning authority's refusal of planning permission to site a Gypsy caravan in a special landscape area. Mr Clarke argued that the inspector had wrongly taken into account an offer by the authority of conventional housing accommodation and that this was in breach of articles 8 and 14[108] of the ECHR.

4.82   At first instance Burton J held:

> ... it can amount to a breach of articles 8 and 14 to weigh in the balance and hold against a Gypsy applying for planning permission, or indeed resisting eviction from ... land, that he or she has refused conventional housing accommodation as being contrary to his or her culture. Such circumstances ... are and should be, limited, just as they are if, for example, it is to be alleged similarly to be impermissible, in relevant circumstances, to hold it against or penalise a religious or strictly observant Christian, Jew or Muslim because he or she will not, and thus cannot work on certain days, or to hold it against, or penalise, a strictly observant Buddhist, Muslim, Jew or Sikh because he eats or will not eat

---

106 [2001] 33 EHRR 399 at page 441.

107 [2001] EWHC 800 Admin; [2002] JPL 552; July 2002 *Legal Action* 23; (2001) *Times* 9 November.

108 See para 4.67 above for article 8. Article 14 provides: 'The enjoyment of the rights and freedoms set forth in this Convention shall be secured without discrimination on any ground such as sex, race, colour, language, religion, political or other opinion, national or social origin, association with a national minority, property, birth or other status.'

certain foods, or will not wear certain clothing. It is not, and cannot be, a formality to establish this, and the onus is upon the person such as a Gypsy who seeks to establish it.[109]

4.83 After considering the need to establish Gypsy status, he said:

... if such be established then ... bricks and mortar, if offered, are unsuitable, just as would be the offer of a rat-infested barn.[110] It would be contrary to articles 8 and 14 to expect such a person to accept conventional housing and to hold it against him or her that he has not accepted it, or is not prepared to accept it, even as a last resort factor.[111]

4.84 The inspector's decision was quashed on the basis that he either took into account impermissible factors relating to conventional housing or made insufficient findings in respect of such factors.

4.85 The LPA's appeal was dismissed and the Court of Appeal held that the approach of Burton J was entirely in accord with the approach of the ECtHR in *Chapman*.[112] Buxton LJ held:

What the judge seems to me to be ... rightly directing the inspector to, is a careful examination of the objections of the Clarke family to living in conventional housing in order to determine the extent to which article 8 is truly engaged, and the nature of its engagement by the combination of their Gypsy identity and their opposition to conventional housing. Only when the inspector has made that determination in clearer terms than he adopted in his present letter will it be possible for him properly to engage in the balancing consideration that Burton J envisages ... This was a case where a Convention right was potentially engaged and in such cases a more intense scrutiny of the facts upon which that right is asserted needs to be engaged in before the court can indulge in the balancing exercise that article 8(2) imposes on it.[113]

Making an application for planning permission

4.86 Advisers settling an application for planning permission should include the following:

- a plan showing the boundaries of the site; and
- the application fee.

109 [2001] EWHC 800 Admin at para 30.
110 As to which see *R v South Herefordshire DC ex p Miles* [1983] 17 HLR 82 per Woolf J (as he then was).
111 [2001] EWHC 800 Admin at para 34.
112 *Chapman* [2001] 33 EHRR 399.
113 [2002] EWCA Civ 819 at para 15.

The site area should be specified in the application form, preferably in square metres or hectares. Although a high degree of mathematical precision is seldom essential, guesses can cause difficulty at a later stage.

4.87   Advisers may also wish to consider submitting information on the following matters:

- Evidence of the applicant's statutory Gypsy status and of Gypsy ethnicity, including details of travelling by the applicant and by family members for the purpose of work and copies (not originals in case they are lost) of family photographs.
- Where applicants and their families have ceased travelling temporarily, evidence of any intention to resume travelling.
- Details and evidence of any factors relevant to the personal circumstances of members of the family, in particular any health, educational or other welfare needs.
- Details and evidence of attempts to find alternative sites.
- Evidence of aversion to conventional housing.
- Occupational needs.
- Any specific need for accommodation that would assist Romani Gypsies and Irish Travellers who keep animals, particularly horses and ponies.

Appealing against a refusal of planning permission

4.88   If the local planning authority refuses permission the applicant may appeal to the secretary of state[114] within three months of the date of refusal of permission.

4.89   Most appeals are determined by an inspector from the Planning Inspectorate. A small proportion are determined by the secretary of state or Welsh Assembly (in reality a civil servant acting on his or its behalf) after consideration of a report prepared by an inspector. There are four procedures for an appeal:

- written representation,[115]
- a hearing,[116] or

114 Town and Country Planning Act (TCPA) 1990 s78.
115 Town and Country Planning (Appeals) (Written Representations Procedure) (England) Regulations 2000 SI No 1628.
116 Town and Country Planning (Hearings Procedure) (England) Rules 2000 SI No 1626.

- an inquiry determined by an inspector,[117]
- an inquiry determined by the Secretary of State.[118]

These are governed by different procedural rules. The time limits imposed by these must be obeyed. Failure to do so may disadvantage the applicant considerably.

4.90   An appeal is a fresh determination of the merits of an application. Applicants' advisers should, therefore, include in the appeal documentation the material adduced in support of the application. In addition they should also answer the local planning authority's (LPA's) refusal reasons and bring their evidence up-to-date (particularly in the case of welfare needs and evidence of travelling). Where the LPA is relying upon policies that conflict with central government advice (for example, criteria that in practice are too difficult to meet) this should be stated. Where racist material is included in the papers before the inspector, for example objectors' letters containing offensive assertions against Romani Gypsies or Irish Travellers, the inspector's attention should be drawn to the Race Relations Act (RRA) 1976 s19A.[119] Thorough preparation is necessary. If a point is omitted it will not normally be possible to raise it before the High Court.[120]

An application to the High Court[121]

4.91   An appeal decision may be challenged by an application to the High Court on the ground that the appeal decision was not within the powers of, or did not comply with, the relevant requirements of TCPA 1990.[122] Such a challenge can only be made within six weeks of the date on the decision letter. This period cannot be extended under any circumstances. These applications are heard in the

---

117 Town and Country Planning (Appeals) (Determination by Inspectors) (Inquiries Procedure) (England) Rules 2000 SI No 1625.

118 Town and Country Planning (Inquiries Procedure) (England) Rules 2000 SI No 1624.

119 Similarly, New Travellers would be able to object to discriminatory material by reference to ECHR articles 8 and 14.

120 *Smith v Secretary of State for the Environment Transport and the Regions and Wyre Forest DC* [2001] EWCA Civ 1550. In that case it had not been argued at the planning inquiry that the development plan did not comply with DoE Circular 1/94.

121 And see appendix A on procedures.

122 TCPA 1990 s288.

Administrative Court, almost always either in London, or, for Wales, in Cardiff.

4.92   The principles affecting a statutory review under TCPA 1990 s288 were conveniently summarised in *Seddon Properties v Secretary of State for the Environment:*[123]

- decision-makers must not act perversely;
- they must not take into account irrelevant matters or fail to take into account that which is relevant;
- they must abide by statutory procedures;
- and they must not depart from the principles of natural justice.

4.93   Reasons must be proper, adequate and intelligible.[124] It is important to bear in mind that the appeal decisions must be read as a whole in a reasonably flexible manner and not as a contract or statute,[125] that questions of planning judgment are for the decision-maker not the court,[126] that the requirement to take into account all relevant considerations is limited to those matters which might cause the decision-maker to reach a different decision,[127] and that the decision-maker, while required to have regard to every material consideration need only state reasons in respect of the principal controversial issues.[128] So, for example, a secretary of state's decision was quashed where he had to deal with the issue of the grant of temporary planning permission and proportionality in the context of ECHR article 8 but had failed to do so.[129]

123 [1981] 42 P&CR 26–28 per Forbes J.

124 *Save Britain's Heritage v No 1 Poultry Ltd* [1991] 1 WLR 153, HL, per Lord Bridge of Harwich at 165–168. In *South Buckinghamshire DC v Secretary of State for Transport, Local Government and the Regions and Linda Porter* [2003] EWCA Civ 687, the Court of Appeal quashed the decision to grant Mrs Porter planning permission on the basis that there had been a failure by the decision-maker to provide a 'clear and cogent analysis' of the reasons why it had been concluded that there were very special circumstances that clearly outweighed the objections to the grant of planning permission. Mrs Porter has appealed against that decision to the House of Lords. See Recent Developments in Gypsy and Traveller Law at pxiii above.

125 *Save Britain's Heritage v No 1 Poultry Ltd* [1991] 1 WLR 153, HL, per Lord Bridge of Harwich at 165.

126 *City of Edinburgh v Secretary of State for Scotland* [1997] 1 WLR 1447, per Lord Clyde at 1458–1459.

127 *Bolton MBC v Secretary of State for the Environment* [1990] 61 P&CR 343, CA, per Glidewell LJ, at 352–353.

128 *Bolton MBC v Secretary of State for the Environment* [1995] 3 PLR 37 at 42–43, HL.

129 *Lee v First Secretary of State* [2003] EWHC 3235 Admin.

4.94　　In applications where only one party is represented on each side, costs normally follow the event. Where there is multiple representation, costs are in the discretion of the court and there are no absolute rules.[130]

Enforcement

Statutory provisions

4.95　If a development is carried out without the grant of the required planning permission, the local planning authority may:

- issue an enforcement notice if it considers it expedient to do so having regard to the provisions of the development plan and to any other material considerations;[131]
- seek a planning injunction;[132]
- take no action.[133]

Government guidance

4.96　Department of the Environment (DoE) Circular 1/94,[134] and Planning Policy Guidance (PPG) 18 contain the principal guidance on enforcement against Gypsies and Travellers who are using land for residential purposes in breach of planning control. The guidance in PPG 18 relating to small businesses applies to Gypsy and Traveller sites.[135] PPG 18 requires the LPA:

> ... to explore – in discussion with the owner or operator – whether the [use] can be allowed to continue operating acceptably on the site at its current level of activity, or perhaps less intensively. The LPA should carefully explain the planning objections to the current operation ... and,

---

130　Normal practice is however set out in *Bolton MBC v Secretary of State for the Environment* [1995] 3 PLR 37 at 51.

131　TCPA 1990 s172(1). In addition TCPA 1990 s183 provides that an LPA can issue a stop notice if they consider it expedient that an activity should cease before the expiry of the period of compliance with an enforcement notice. Breach of a stop notice is a criminal offence. For further discussion on the use of stop notices see chapter 8 para 8.113 and Recent developments in Gypsy and Traveller law at pxiii above.

132　TCPA 1990 s187B.

133　PPG 18 (1991) (Enforcing Planning Control) para 5.

134　DoE Circular 1/94 at paras 26–28.

135　PPG 18 at para 15.

if it is practicable, suggest ways to overcome them. This may result in the grant of a mutually acceptable conditional planning permission, enabling the owner or operator to continue ... at the site without harm to local amenity ...[136]

In addition PPG 18 advises LPAs that:

Unless it is urgently needed, formal enforcement action should not come as a 'bolt from the blue'... It should be preceded by informal discussion about possible means of minimising harm to local amenity caused by the ... activity; and, if formal action will clearly be needed, by discussion of the possible relocation ... to another site ...[137]

4.97   DoE Circular 1/94 paragraph 26 provides that:

The existence or absence of policies for gypsy sites in development plans could constitute a material consideration in matters of enforcement.

It follows that those advising Gypsies and Travellers should check whether the development plan policies accord with the advice in DoE Circular 1/94. Where the development plan is deficient, then that point can be raised in enforcement proceedings, eg, as a defence to injunction proceedings or as mitigation.

Considerations of common humanity

4.98   *R v Lincolnshire CC ex p Atkinson*[138] concerned the exercise of powers under CJPOA 1994 s77 in relation to unauthorised encampments.[139] Commenting on DoE Circular 18/94, *Gypsy Sites Policy and Unauthorised Camping*, paras 9–13, Sedley J said:

Detailed analysis of these passages and debate about what legal force, if any, an advisory circular of this kind possesses has been made unnecessary by the realistic concession of counsel for both local authorities that whether or not they were spelt out in a departmental circular the matters mentioned in the paragraphs ... would be material considerations in the public law sense that to overlook them in the exercise of a local authority's powers under sections 77 to 79 of the Act ... would be to leave a relevant matter out of account and so jeopardise the validity of any consequent step. The concession is rightly made because those considerations in the material paragraphs which are not

136 PPG 18 at para 16.
137 PPG 18 at para 16.
138 *R v Lincolnshire CC ex p Atkinson; Wealden DC ex p Wales and Stratford* [1997] JPL 65; [1996] 8 Admin LR 529; (1995) *Times*, 22 September.
139 See chapter 5 at para 5.111 below.

statutory are considerations of common humanity, none of which can properly be ignored when dealing with one of the most fundamental human needs, the need for shelter with at least a modicum of security.[140]

4.99   The considerations of common humanity identified in DoE Circular 18/94 must be taken into account in reaching decisions in relation to enforcement action.[141] The ODPM Guidance on 'Managing Unauthorised Camping' will also be relevant.[142]

Enforcement notices

4.100   An LPA may issue an enforcement notice where it appears to them that there has been a breach of planning control and that it is expedient to issue the notice, having regard to the provisions of the development plan and to any other material considerations.[143] TCPA 1990 s171B provides that:

- an enforcement notice must be issued within four years of the date of the breach of planning control where it relates to a breach consisting of –
  (i) the carrying out without planning permission of building, engineering, mining or other operations in, on, over or under land; or
  (ii) the making without planning permission of a change of use of any building to use it as a single dwelling house;
- in the case of any other breach of planning control, no enforcement action may be taken more than 10 years after the date of the breach.

Enforcement notices should state 'the matters which appear to the local planning authority to constitute the breach of planning control' and 'specify the steps which the authority require to be taken, or the activities which the authority require to cease, in order to achieve whole or partial remediation.'[144]

4.101   An enforcement notice must specify the date on which it is to take effect and service of the notice shall take place not more than 28 days after its date of issue and not less than 28 days before the date

---

140 [1997] JPL 65 at 72; [1995] 8 Admin LR 529.
141 *R v Kerrier DC ex p Uzell* [1996] 71 P&CR 566 at 571.
142 See chapter 5 below.
143 TCPA 1990 s172(1).
144 TCPA 1990 s173(1)(a), (2) and (4).

specified in it, as the date on which it is to take effect.[145] It has been
held that an enforcement notice that required immediate compliance
was a nullity, without legal effect and incapable of amendment.[146]

Enforcement notice appeals

4.102 There is a right of appeal against an enforcement notice to the
Secretary of State on one or more of the following seven grounds:

(a) that, in respect of any breach of planning control which may be
constituted by the matters stated in the notice, planning
permission ought to be granted or, as the case may be, the
condition or limitation concerned ought to be discharged;

(b) that those matters have not occurred;

(c) that those matters (if they occurred) do not constitute a breach of
planning control;

(d) that, at the date when the notice was issued, no enforcement
action could be taken in respect of any breach of planning control
which may be constituted by those matters;

(e) that copies of the enforcement notice were not served as required
by section 172;

(f) that the steps required by the notice to be taken, or the activities
required by the notice to cease, exceed what is necessary to
remedy any breach of planning control which may be constituted
by those matters or, as the case may be, to remedy any injury to
amenity which has been caused by any such breach;

(g) that any period specified in the notice in accordance with section
173(9) falls short of what should reasonably be allowed.[147]

4.103   In considering ground (f) it is important to consider whether the
enforcement notice enforces against existing rights such as fencing
and gates permitted by the GPDO.[148] An appellant who wishes to rely
on ground (f) should specify, without prejudice to his or her position
on other grounds, the arguments in relation to existing rights and

---

145 TCPA 1990 s172(3).

146 *R (Lynes) v West Berkshire DC* [2002] EWHC 1828 Admin, Harrison J, 24 July
2002.

147 TCPA 1990 s174(2) as substituted by the Planning and Compensation Act
1991 s6.

148 See para 4.17 above.

indicate the variations of the notice that would be appropriate if the other grounds of appeal failed.[149]

4.104 The enforcement appeal system was reformed to bring it in line with development control appeals with effect in England from 23 December 2002.[150] As with all planning appeals the timetable for these appeals should be strictly observed.

4.105 There is a further right of appeal on a point of law to the High Court against a decision on an appeal against an enforcement notice pursuant to TCPA 1990 s289.[151] Such an appeal may be brought in circumstances where it can be argued that:

- the decision was perverse;
- there was an absence of evidence to support a finding of fact; or
- the decision-maker took account of irrelevant factors or failed to bear in mind relevant factors.

The appeal should be brought within 28 days.[152]

4.106 Non-compliance with an enforcement notice is a criminal offence contrary to TCPA 1990 s179. It is an offence triable either way and is punishable in the magistrates' court with a fine not exceeding £20,000 and in the Crown Court with an unlimited fine. When determining the amount of any fine to be imposed the court 'shall in particular have regard to any financial benefit which has been accrued or appears likely to accrue to [the defendant] in consequence of the offence'.[153]

---

149 *Taylor v Secretary of State for the Environment, Transport and the Regions* [2001] EWCA 1254; New Law Digest 101088201; (2001) *Times* 16 October.

150 This has been brought about through five statutory instruments: the Town and Country Planning (Enforcement Notices and Appeals) (England) Regulations 2002 SI No 2682; the Town and Country Planning (Enforcement) (Written Representations Procedure) (England) Regulations 2002 SI No 2683; the Town and Country Planning (Enforcement) (Hearings Procedure) (England) Rules 2002 SI No 2684; the Town and Country Planning (Enforcement) (Determination by Inspectors) (Inquiries Procedure) (England) Rules 2002 SI No 2685; and the Town and Country Planning (Enforcement) (Inquiries Procedure) (England) Rules 2002 SI No 2686. Advice on these is contained in DoE Circular 2/02 *Enforcement Appeals Procedures*. There are almost identical rules for Wales.

151 See appendix A on procedures.

152 In *Jarmain v Secretary of State for the Environment, Transport and the Regions* [2001] EWHC 1140 Admin, Gibbs J, it was held that an appeal against a decision made in respect of an enforcement notice appeal must be made pursuant to TCPA 1990 s289 and not s288.

153 TCPA 1990 s179(9).

4.107   In such a prosecution it must be shown that the 'enforcement notice' issued by the LPA is formally valid (and has not been set aside) and that it is not possible to challenge its vires.[154] Where an owner of land is prosecuted for breach of an enforcement notice, he or she will have a defence if he or she can show that everything that could be expected to be done to secure compliance with the notice was done.[155] It is not open to a defendant to challenge the validity of the enforcement notice on any of the grounds upon which appeal may be made to the secretary of state.[156]

4.108   Where any steps required by an enforcement notice are not taken within the period for compliance with the notice, the LPA may enter the land and take those steps. It may then recover from the owner of the land any expenses reasonably incurred by them in doing so.[157]

Enforcement injunctions

4.109   TCPA 1990 s187B(1) provides that where an LPA considers 'it necessary or expedient for any actual or apprehended breach of planning control to be restrained by injunction, they may apply to the court for an injunction.'

4.110   The judgment of the House of Lords in *South Buckinghamshire DC v Porter*[158] is not only the most important decision on the use of TCPA 1990 s187B against Gypsies and Travellers, but it is also a helpful source of dicta in other fields of planning law and practice. This judgment related to four consolidated appeals. In each case Gypsies/Travellers, who were living in caravans on land without the requisite planning permission, were defendants to proceedings brought by the LPAs for planning injunctions under section 187B. Each court at first instance had granted an injunction requiring the Gypsies/Travellers to move off their land. The Gypsies and Travellers appealed to the Court of Appeal raising human rights arguments as to why the injunctions should not have been granted. The Court of Appeal unanimously allowed their appeals, holding that *Hambleton DC v Bird*,[159] which had greatly limited the power of a judge to refuse

---

154   *R v Wicks* [1998] AC 92, HL.
155   TCPA 1990 s179(3). See also *R v Clarke* [2002] JPL 1372 and *R v Wood* [2001] EWCA Crim 1395; [2002] JPL 219.
156   TCPA 1990 s285.
157   TCPA 1990 s178.
158   [2003] UKHL 26; [2003] 2 WLR 1547.
159   [1995] 3 PLR 8, CA.

a section 187B injunction, was no longer good law (if it ever had been such).[160]

4.111   Simon Brown LJ giving the leading judgment in that case, stated that a judge:

> should not grant injunctive relief unless he would be prepared if necessary to contemplate committing the defendant to prison for breach of the order, and that he would not be of this mind unless he had considered for himself all questions of hardship for the defendant and his family if required to move, necessarily including therefore, the availability of suitable alternative sites.[161]

4.112   Simon Brown LJ indicated that a judge was entitled to take account of countervailing considerations against the need to enforce planning control, for example:

- the degree and the flagrancy of the (postulated) breach;
- whether conventional enforcement measures had been tried;
- the urgency of the situation;
- health and safety considerations;
- whether the injunction was intended to remove a Gypsy or Traveller from a site or prevent him moving on to a site; and
- previous planning decisions – the relevance of which would depend upon a variety of matters including their age, the extent to which considerations of hardship and the availability of alternative sites was taken into account, the strength of the conclusions reached on the land use and environmental issues and whether a defendant had the opportunity to make his or her case for at least a temporary personal planning permission.

4.113   Simon Brown LJ added that:

> ... whilst it is not for the court to question the correctness of the existing planning status of the land, the court in deciding whether or not to grant an injunction (and if so, whether and for how long to suspend it) is bound to come to some broad view as to the degree of environmental damage resulting from the breach and the urgency or otherwise of bringing it to an end. In this regard the court need not shut its mind to the possibility of the planning authority itself coming to reach a different planning judgment in the case.[162]

---

160 *South Buckinghamshire DC v Porter; Chichester DC v Searle; Wrexham CBC v Berry; Hertsmere BC v Harty* [2001] EWCA Civ 1549; [2002] 1 All ER 425; [2002] 1 WLR 1359; July 2002 *Legal Action* 22.

161 [2002] 1 WLR 1359 at 1377.

162 [2002] 1 WLR 1359 at 1377–1378.

4.114   Finally, Simon Brown LJ stated that:

> ... the court's discretion is absolute and injunctive relief is unlikely unless properly thought to be 'commensurate' – in today's language, proportionate ... whatever view one takes of the correctness of the *Hambleton* approach in the period prior to the coming into force of the Human Rights Act 1998, to my mind it cannot be thought consistent with the court's duty under section 6(1) to act compatibly with Convention rights. Proportionality requires not only that the injunction be appropriate and necessary for the attainment of the public interest objective sought – here the safeguarding of the environment – but also that it does not impose an excessive burden on the individual whose private interests – here the gipsy's private life and home and the retention of his ethnic identity – are at stake.[163]

4.115   The House of Lords unanimously dismissed the LPA's appeals and endorsed the guidance given by the Court of Appeal.[164]

4.116   Having considered the arguments and previous decisions, Lord Bingham stated that the power to grant an injunction under TCPA 1990 s187B was a discretionary power, and that 'the court is not obliged to grant an injunction because a local authority considers it necessary or expedient for any actual or apprehended breach of planning control to be restrained by injunction' and that 'the court must decide whether in all the circumstances it is just to grant the relief sought'.[165]

4.117   A little later Lord Bingham added:

> ...the Secretary of State was entitled to have regard to the personal circumstances of the Gypsies ... When application is made ... under section 187B, the evidence will usually make clear whether, and to what extent, the local planning authority has taken account of the personal circumstances of the defendant and any hardship an injunction may cause. If it appears that these aspects have been neglected and on examination they weigh against the grant of relief, the court will be readier to refuse it. If it appears that the local planning authority has fully considered them and nonetheless resolved that it is necessary or expedient to seek relief, this will ordinarily weigh heavily in favour of granting relief, since the court must accord respect to the balance which the local planning authority has struck between public and private

---

163 [2002] 1 WLR 1359 at 1378.
164 *South Buckinghamshire DC v Porter and others* [2003] UKHL 26; [2003] 2 WLR 1547.
165 [2003] 2 WLR 1547 at 1562.

interests. It is, however, ultimately for the court to decide whether the remedy sought is just and proportionate in all the circumstances ...[166]

4.118 Lord Bingham continued explaining that:

The court should ordinarily be slow to make an order which it would not at that time be willing, if need be, to enforce by imprisonment.[167]

He doubted that article 8 of the European of Convention on Human Rights added to domestic law, stating in respect of the *Buckley*[168] and *Chapman*[169] judgments:

... when asked to grant injunctive relief under section 187B the court must consider whether, on the facts of the case, such relief is proportionate in the Convention sense, and grant relief only if it judges it to be so. Although domestic law is expressed in terms of justice and convenience rather than proportionality, this is in all essentials the task which the court is in any event required by domestic law to carry out.[170]

4.119 Lord Bingham concluded his judgment by stating that:

The guidance given by the Court of Appeal in the judgment of Simon Brown LJ ... was in my opinion judicious and accurate in all essential respects and I would endorse it.[171]

4.120 Lord Steyn agreed, adopting similar reasoning to Lord Bingham, and stated, having referred to article 8:

Even if it had previously been possible to ignore great or marked hardship in the exercise of discretion under section 187B – a hypothesis which I do not accept – such an approach is no longer possible.[172]

4.121 Commenting on the fact that TCPA 1990 s187B empowers a LPA to apply for an injunction, whether or not they have exercised or are proposing to exercise any of their other planning enforcement powers, Lord Clyde said:

... that does not mean that the court may not take account of the facts regarding any other remedy which the authority have pursued or the fact that they have not pursued any other remedy.

166 [2003] 2 WLR 1547 at 1564.
167 [2003] 2 WLR 1547 at 1565.
168 *Buckley v United Kingdom* [1996] 23 EHRR 101.
169 *Chapman v United Kingdom* [2001] 33 EHRR 399.
170 [2003] 2 WLR 1547 at 1566.
171 [2003] 2 WLR 1547 at 1566.
172 [2003] 2 WLR 1547 at 1572.

The key words of his opinion are:

> ... section 187B(2) allows and has always allowed the court in the exercise of its discretion in granting an injunction to weigh up the public interest in securing the enforcement of planning policy and planning decisions against the private interests of the individuals who are allegedly in breach of planning control. In particular I would hold that it is open to the court to consider questions of hardship, particularly as regards health, arising out of the effect on such individuals of a grant of an injunction.[173]

Lord Clyde also pointed out that in Gypsy cases 'considerations of humanity may be particularly acute owing to their particular traditions and lifestyle'.[174]

4.122   Lord Hutton said:

> ... it is not for the court to act merely as a rubber stamp to endorse the decision of the local planning authority to stop the use by the particular defendant in breach of planning control. Moreover the court is as well placed as the local planning authority to decide whether the considerations relating to the human factor outweigh purely planning considerations; the weight to be attached to the personal circumstances of a defendant in deciding whether a coercive order should be made against him is a task which is constantly performed by the courts.[175]

4.123   Lord Scott of Foscote dealt with the criteria that govern the grant of section 187B injunctions:

> ... the court must take into account all or any circumstances of the case that bear upon the question whether the grant would be 'just and convenient'. Of particular importance, of course, will be whether or not the local planning authority can establish not only that there is a current or apprehended breach of planning control but also that the ordinary statutory means of enforcement are not likely to be effective in preventing the breach or bringing it to an end. In a case in which the statutory procedure of enforcement notice, prosecution for non-compliance and exercise by the authority of such statutory self-help remedies as are available had not been tried and where there was no sufficient reason to assume that, if tried, they would not succeed in dealing with the breach, the local planning authority would be unlikely to succeed in persuading the court that the grant of an injunction would be just and convenient.[176]

---

173 [2003] 2 WLR 1547 at 1574 and 1576.
174 [2003] 2 WLR 1547 at 1577.
175 [2003] 2 WLR 1547 at 1580.
176 [2003] 2 WLR 1547 at 1584.

4.124 He also stated that the jurisdiction to grant TCPA 1990 s187B injunctions 'is one of great delicacy and to be used with caution'.[177]

The option to take no action

4.125 LPAs are not obliged to take enforcement action.[178] Rather they are only entitled to take enforcement action where they consider it expedient.[179]

Exceptional funding for planning inquiries

4.126 CLS funding ('legal aid') is not normally available to cover the cost of representation at planning inquiries. However, Access to Justice Act 1999 s6(8)(b) empowers the Lord Chancellor to authorise funding in individual cases, following a request from the Legal Services Commission (LSC – formerly the 'Legal Aid Board') so long as the person seeking funding is financially eligible for legal aid. The Lord Chancellor's Guidance indicates that the client must show that no alternative means of funding is available. Under the Guidance, the Lord Chancellor will be prepared to consider funding (known as 'exceptional funding') where:

(i) there is significant wider public interest; or
(ii) the case is of overwhelming importance to the client; or
(iii) there is convincing evidence that there are other exceptional circumstances such that without public funding for representation it would be practically impossible for the client to bring or defend the proceedings, or the lack of public funding would lead to obvious unfairness in the proceedings.

'Exceptional funding' has been obtained under these provisions for Gypsies and Travellers for representation at planning inquiries. The provisions are complex and solicitors or advisers should refer to the details in the latest edition of the LSC Manual. Applications will need to be made to the LSC Area Office in London.[180]

177 [2003] 2 WLR 1547 at 1584–1585.
178 PPG 18 Enforcing Planning Control, para 5.
179 *R (Prokopp) v London Underground Ltd* [2003] EWCA Civ 961; New Law Property Digest 103076201, 7 July 2003 (Kennedy, Schiemann and Buxton LJJ).
180 And see Murdoch, *Gypsies and Planning Appeals: the right to a fair and impartial hearing* [2002] JPL 1056.

Conclusion

4.127   The HRA 1998 has led to a series of far-reaching legal cases concerning Gypsies and Travellers and the planning system that, in the main, have supported their attempts to continue to follow their traditional way of life. Perhaps most significantly, the House of Lords in *Porter* held that the vulnerable position of Gypsies and Travellers as a minority group deserves more sympathetic attention than had hitherto been the case and stated that:

> ... there is force in the observation attributed to Vaclav Havel, no doubt informed by the dire experience of central Europe: 'The Gypsies are a litmus test not of democracy but of civil society.'[181]

---

181 [2003] 2 WLR 1547 at 1564.

© James Lampard

© James Lampard

© K. Westley

© Elisabeth Blanchet

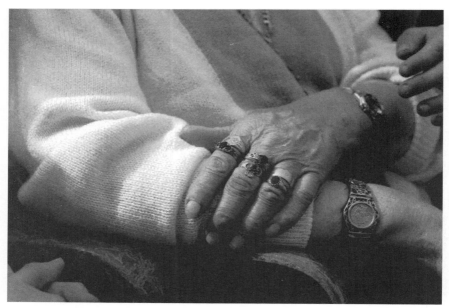

© Elisabeth Blanchet

© Yasmin Worrell

© Yasmin Worrell

© K. Westley

© Simon Evans

CHAPTER 5

Evictions from unauthorised encampments

continued overleaf

Introduction

5.1   Before the duty to provide caravan sites was repealed by the Criminal Justice and Public Order Act (CJPOA) 1994,[1] it was possible to challenge a local authority's decision to take eviction action against an unauthorised encampment by making an application for judicial review and arguing that the local authority in question had failed to provide sufficient (or any) sites.[2] At the same time as the CJPOA 1994 repealed the duty, it armed local authorities with 'draconic'[3] new eviction powers. The use of these far-reaching powers has been circumscribed, to some extent, by the effect of government guidance and the fact that public bodies have had to comply with their duty to act compatibly with the European Convention on Human Rights (ECHR) since October 2000.[4] Recent developments in homelessness legislation[5] have also had a significant impact on the use of eviction powers by local authorities.

5.2   There are many other bodies and individuals that may be involved in the eviction of Gypsies and Travellers from unauthorised encampments, including: the police; government departments; other public authorities; and private landowners.

5.3   This chapter begins by detailing the different 'methods' that can be used in the eviction of those living on unauthorised encampments and by explaining which method is available to which body or individual and what 'substantive defences' might be available to those facing eviction in each case. The term 'substantive defence' is used to indicate a defence that can be raised in any court of first instance. The chapter then moves on to indicate what (if any) 'public law challenges' might be available to those facing eviction, that is, challenges that could be made by way of judicial review in an attempt to prevent eviction taking place.[6] It should be emphasised at the outset, that 'substantive defences' will not often be of practical

---

1   For further discussion, see chapter 1 at paras 1.34–1.36, above.

2   See, for example, *West Glamorgan CC ex p Rafferty; R v Secretary of State for Wales ex p Gilhaney* [1987] 1 WLR 457.

3   Described as such by Sedley J in *R v Lincolnshire CC ex p Atkinson; Wealden DC ex p Wales and Stratford* [1995] 8 Admin LR 529 (hereafter referred to as 'the *Atkinson* case').

4   HRA 1998 s6.

5   See below at para 5.126 and chapter 6.

6   A 'public law challenge' will not be available against an individual. For more detail on judicial review, see appendix A below.

use in cases where a public body uses its powers to evict Gypsies and Travellers from unauthorised encampments and that it is much more likely that the eviction will be prevented or at least postponed if a 'public law challenge' is mounted and it can be shown that the public body's decision to seek eviction was unlawful.

5.4　　　One starts from the position that a landowner has a basic right to obtain possession against people who are trespassing on his or her land. It is not necessary to discuss the political, philosophical and cultural clashes between nomadism and sedentarism but clearly some of those issues colour the legal position.[7] After the introduction of the Human Rights Act (HRA) 1998 in October 2000, the question arose as to whether it would be possible for a trespasser to raise a defence under ECHR article 8 (the right to respect for private and family life and the home) before the court of first instance in eviction proceedings. The House of Lords answered that question in the negative when it determined the case of *Harrow LBC v Qazi*.[8] In that case a local authority tenancy was held jointly by a husband and wife. When the wife left, she gave notice to quit. The tenancy then terminated and the husband became a trespasser. The local authority sought possession and the husband relied upon article 8 in his defence. A majority of the judges in the House of Lords held that people without any proprietary interest in the land in question would be unable to rely on such a defence in a court of first instance, though it was accepted that they could potentially rely on article 8 in any public law challenge.[9]

7　For a wider discussion of these issues see Derek Hawes and Barbara Perez, *The Gypsy and the State: The Ethnic Cleansing of British Society* (The Policy Press, 1996).

8　[2003] 3 WLR 792.

9　For example, Lord Millet stated, at 795: '[O]nce it concludes that the landlord is entitled to an order for possession [ie, aside from HRA 1998], there is nothing further to investigate. The order is necessary to protect the rights of the landlord; and making or enforcing it does not show a want of appropriate respect for the applicant's home ... In the exceptional case where the applicant believes that the local authority is acting unfairly or from improper or ulterior motives, he can apply to the High Court for judicial review.'

Methods of eviction and substantive defences

Civil Procedure Rules Part 55[10]

Who can use it?

Anyone with sufficient interest in the land including, potentially, a licensee.[11]

5.5 Civil Procedure Rules (CPR) Part 55 has taken the place of County Court Rules Order 24 (in the county court) and Rules of the Supreme Court Order 113 (in the High Court), both of which had previously provided the procedures for the eviction of trespassers.

5.6 CPR Part 55.1(b) states:

> ... 'a possession claim against trespassers' means a claim for the recovery of land which the claimant alleges is occupied only by a person or persons who entered or remained on the land without the consent of a person entitled to possession of that land but does not include a claim against a tenant or subtenant whether his tenancy has been terminated or not.

5.7 A tenant whose tenancy is terminated will not become a 'trespasser' for the purposes of CPR Part 55 but a licensee, whose licence is terminated, will. Gypsies or Travellers residing on official caravan sites will normally be licensees. If a Gypsy or Traveller lives in caravans or vehicles on land with the consent of the owner or occupier of the land, even if a rent or fee is paid to the owner or occupier, they will be a licensee. Once such a licence is terminated,[12] they will come within the scope of CPR Part 55.1(b).

5.8 Possession claims must normally be commenced in a county court[13] but exceptionally they can be commenced in the High Court.[14] CPR Part 55.6 deals with service of claims against 'trespassers':

> Where, in a possession claim against trespassers, the claim has been issued against 'persons unknown' [as it usually is[15]], the

---

10 Throughout this section on CPR Part 55, reference should be made to *Civil Procedure* ('The White Book') (Sweet & Maxwell, 2004).

11 *Manchester Airport Authority v Dutton* [1999] 2 All ER 675.

12 See chapter 3 at paras 3.9–3.32 above, for the details of termination of a licence on an official site.

13 CPR Part 55.3(1).

14 See para 5.12 below.

15 See CPR Part 55.3(4).

claim form, particulars of claim and any witness statements must be served on those persons by –

(a)(i) attaching copies of the claim form, particulars of claim and any witness statements to the main door or some other part of the land so that they are clearly visible; and

(ii) if practicable, inserting copies of those documents in a sealed transparent envelope addressed to 'the occupiers' through the letter box;[16] or

(b) placing stakes in the land in places where they are clearly visible and attaching to each stake copies of the claim form, particulars of claim and any witness statements in a sealed transparent envelope addressed to 'the occupiers'.[17]

5.9 A CPR Part 55 claim is commenced by using Claim Form N5 and, in a claim against trespassers, the standard Particulars of Claim Form, N121. Both these forms *must* be used.[18] However, in practice, if they have not been used, the judge may simply adjourn the matter for the correct forms to be produced rather than strike the claim out. The 'trespasser' does not have to file a defence,[19] but clearly would want to do so if he or she wishes to argue that he or she is not a 'trespasser' or wishes to raise one of the other 'substantive defences' listed below.

5.10 A solicitor or adviser instructed by a Gypsy or Traveller who is threatened with eviction should carefully consider whether the claimant has complied with the procedural rules and proved that he or she is entitled to possession. If there is no 'substantive defence' to a claim brought by a public body but the decision to evict is susceptible to judicial review,[20] then an adjournment of the possession proceedings should be sought so that a claim for judicial review can be made.[21]

---

16 This method of service may be relevant to Gypsies or Travellers parked within the curtilage of a building (area of land attached to a dwelling-house), especially where there are also 'trespassers' residing in the building itself.

17 This is the method of service normally employed for unauthorised encampments but it is also common for notices to be attached to vehicles on a site.

18 See CPR Practice Direction (PD) 55 para 1.5.

19 CPR Part 55.7(2).

20 See para 5.111–5.126 below.

21 *Avon CC v Buscott* [1988] 1 All ER 841.

Has title been proved?

5.11   The claimant will need to prove title to, or sufficient interest in, the land,[22] usually by the production of a witness statement or affidavit (from a person who has authority to do so) which will attach to it either office copy entries from the Land Registry, conveyances, leases or other relevant official documents proving title to the land. In the absence of such proof, the Gypsies' or Travellers' adviser may wish to do a Land Registry search themselves. Alternatively, the Gypsies or Travellers may wish to make enquiries of local residents who may be able to cast some light on the question of ownership of, or legal interest in, a piece of land.

Should the matter have been commenced in the High Court?

5.12   If brought in the High Court, a separate certificate from the claimant (verified by a statement of truth) explaining why this has been done is required.[23] CPR Practice Direction (PD) paragraph 1.3 states:

> Circumstances which may, in an appropriate case, justify starting a claim in the High Court are if –
>
> (1) there are complicated disputes of fact;
> (2) there are points of law of general importance; or
> (3) the claim is against trespassers and there is a substantial risk of public disturbance or of serious harm to persons or property which properly require immediate determination.

Was sufficient notice given and has service been properly effected?

5.13   CPR Part 55.5(2) states:

> In a possession claim against trespassers the defendant must be served with the claim form, particulars of claim and any witness statements –
>
> (a) in the case of residential property, not less than five days; and
> (b) in the case of other land, not less than two days, before the hearing date.

Simple failure of service may not be enough, in itself, to defend the claim. The defendant may need to show some prejudice to his case

---

22 CPR PD 55 para 2.6.
23 CPR Part 55.3(2).

or disadvantage as a result of the failure of service, for example, inability to investigate the question of title in the time allowed. It has to be said that the court is more likely to adjourn the hearing, rather than dismiss the claim, where service has been defective.

5.14   Gypsies or Travellers who are 'trespassers' and who are within the curtilage of a residential building (for example, in the yard of a disused house) will have to be served five clear working days before the hearing date while those camping on 'other land' will only have to be given two clear working days' notice.[24] For example, in an action taken against Gypsies and Travellers camping on a car park where the hearing date is on:

- a Thursday, then service should be effected on the Monday, provided that is a working day;
- a (working) Monday, then service should be effected on the previous Wednesday.[25]

5.15   There is provision for the court to shorten the above time limits.[26] CPR Practice Direction 55 at para 3.1 states:

Particular consideration should be given to the exercise of power if:

(1) the defendant, or a person for whom the defendant is responsible, has assaulted or threatened to assault:
  (a) the claimant;
  (b) a member of the claimant's staff;
  (c) another resident in the locality;
(2) there are reasonable grounds for fearing such an assault; or
(3) the defendant, or a person for whom the defendant is responsible, has caused serious damage or threatened to cause serious damage to the property or to the home or property of another resident in the locality.

---

24 Notes to CPR Part 55, 55.5.2. CPR 2.8(4) states: 'Where the specified period is – (a) five days or less and (b) includes (i) a Saturday or Sunday; or (ii) a Bank Holiday, Christmas Day or Good Friday, that day does not count.'
25 Defendants are given at least two clear working days' notice so that they can obtain legal advice, if it is required. If the hearing date was on a Monday and service was effected on the Friday, then the defendant might be unable to obtain such advice.
26 CPR Part 3.1(2)(a).

5.16   In such a case the claimant should make an application for abridgement of time on form N244.[27] If the application is allowed by the court, service could be shortened to the day before the hearing. Self-evidently, an adviser or solicitor assisting a Gypsy or Traveller on an unauthorised encampment who is facing such a short deadline, will have to make a very quick assessment of possible 'substantive defences' or 'public law challenges' and may be able to set aside an order for abridgement in circumstances where:

- the allegations are denied;
- responsibility for the persons who have caused or threatened to cause serious damage is denied, for example, the Gypsy or Traveller may be encamped with others over whom he or she has no responsibility;
- any assertion that the damage caused or threatened involves 'serious damage' is denied.

The hearing

5.17   If there is no defence to the claim for possession of land occupied by trespassers, or if the court rejects any defence raised, then it has no discretion and the court must order possession. In a claim against trespassers, the court has no power to suspend the enforcement of the possession order unless the claimant agrees (and then the court can only suspend an order for possession for up to six weeks).[28] However, in practice there will clearly be a delay before the bailiff (in the case of a county court order) or the High Court enforcement officer (in the case of a High Court order)[29] sets an eviction date. Moreover, while the court can only, with the claimant's agreement, give a six-week suspension before the possession order comes into effect, the claimant retains a discretion as to when to apply for a warrant (or writ in the High Court) of possession (which entitles the claimant to enforce the possession order and evict the trespassers). Failure by a local authority or other public authority to take into account new welfare considerations that arise after the date of the

27 Notes to CPR Part 55, 55.5.3.
28 CPR PD 55 para 8.2.
29 Previously a sheriff executed High Court writs but this practice was repealed by Courts Act (CA) 2003 s99. For further discussion of this change see (2004) *LS Gaz* 22 April p31.

possession order could give rise to a 'public law challenge'.[30] Though notice by the bailiff or High Court enforcement officer is not required,[31] it is common practice for the bailiff or High Court enforcement officer to notify the 'trespassers' of the date they have set for eviction. Nevertheless, this practice is not always followed and it is, therefore, a good idea to be pro-active and to contact the bailiff or High Court enforcement officer and ask whether a warrant (or writ) of possession has been issued and, if so, when they will be carrying out the eviction.[32] At the hearing, the Gypsy or Traveller could apply to be joined as a named party to the proceedings.[33] However, unless they have a defence to the proceedings, there is no point in applying to be joined since it will merely open up the possibility of an order for costs.

Warrants of possession and restitution

5.18   After obtaining a possession order under CPR Part 55 in the county court, the order must be served on the defendants.[34] Unless the defendants voluntarily vacate the land in question, the claimant will have to obtain a warrant of possession. The claimant will then have to request the county court bailiff to execute the warrant (in the High Court, the claimant will obtain a writ of possession and execution will be effected by the High Court enforcement officer). If a new incident of trespass occurs more than three months after the date on which the original possession order was granted, the claimant will have to apply for a warrant of restitution (writ of restitution in the High Court). Permission is required for a warrant (or writ) of possession which is sought more than three months after the date of the order and is also required for a warrant (or writ) of restitution regardless of when it is sought.[35] However, no

---

30 For a full discussion of 'public law challenges' see paras 5.111–5.139 below.
31 The Courts Service provides a form N54 to notify those subject to possession orders of impending eviction but there is no obligation to use it.
32 CPR Part 39, 39.3 sets out the circumstances in which a party who fails to attend the hearing may apply to set aside the order. The party must: act promptly; have a good reason for not attending; and, have a reasonable prospect of success at trial.
33 CPR Part 19, 19.4.
34 CPR Part 40, 40.4.
35 However, note that if the new incident of trespass (even if it does not involve all of the original trespassers) occurs within the three months following the order, a warrant (or writ) of possession can be sought without the need for permission.

notice of any of the above applications needs to be given to the defendants.[36]

5.19   Under CCR Order 24.6:[37]

> (1) Subject to paragraphs (2) and (3), a warrant of possession to enforce an order for possession, in a possession claim against trespassers under Part 55, may be issued at any time after the making of the order and ... a warrant of restitution may be issued in aid of the warrant of possession.
>
> (2) No warrant of possession shall be issued after the expiry of three months from the date of the order without the permission of the court, and an application for such permission may be made without notice being served on any other party unless the court otherwise directs.
>
> (3) Nothing in this rule shall authorise the issue of a warrant before the date on which possession is ordered to be given.

5.20   In *Wiltshire CC v Fraser*,[38] it was held that a warrant (or writ) of restitution will be issued to recover land from occupants who were neither parties to the original proceedings nor dispossessed by the original order, provided there is a plain and sufficient nexus (or link) between the order for possession and the need to effect further recovery of the land. In *Fraser*, a possession order against trespassers was obtained and executed in 1983. In 1985 there was a new incident of trespass and, among the trespassers, were two of the defendants named in the original proceedings. This was held to be a sufficient nexus.

5.21   Simon Brown J (as he then was) stated:

> Given that the writ of restitution can be issued to recover land from occupants who were neither party to the original proceedings nor dispossessed by the earlier writ of possession, in what circumstances should this be permitted? In my judgment this will always depend upon the particular facts of the individual case ... The writ of restitution being in aid of execution, it would be appropriate to permit its issue only in those cases where there was a plain and sufficient nexus between the original recovery of possession and the need to effect further recovery of

---

36 For circumstances where a warrant (or writ) might be set aside, see *Leicester CC v Aldwinkle* [1991] HLR 40, CA. Though this case involved the tenancy of a dwelling house, the principles outlined in it (especially with regard to oppressive use of warrants) may occasionally be of use to Gypsies or Travellers faced with a warrant, eg, if there was not a sufficient nexus or link with the previously obtained possession order.

37 Retained in force – see *Civil Procedure* ('The White Book') 2004, Vol 1, p1987.

38 [1986] 1 WLR 109.

the same land. Putting it another way, the court will be bound to ask itself: are the acts or episodes of trespass of which the owners complain during the overall period in question properly to be regarded as essentially one transaction?[39]

5.22   Clearly, therefore, where at least one defendant who was on the land in question at the time of the original order, returns to the same piece of land, the claimant will be able to obtain a warrant (or writ) of restitution. However, it is also common for a claimant to seek to obtain a warrant (or writ) in other circumstances. For example:

(a) where the trespassers involved in the later incident of trespass are acquaintances of a defendant or defendants who were involved in the original possession action;

(b) where the trespassers involved in the later incident of trespass were directed to the land or told about the land by a previous defendant or defendants;

(c) where a registration plate on a vehicle present on the land in question at the time the original possession order was obtained, is the same as the registration plate on a vehicle present at the later incident of trespass.

With regard to these examples, and ones like them, it is questionable whether a court would hold that there was 'essentially one transaction.'

5.23   Clearly, if there is no nexus or link between the original and the subsequent incidents of trespass, the claimant will not be able to obtain a warrant (or writ) of restitution and will have to seek a fresh possession order.

5.24   Regardless of whether a warrant (or writ) of restitution can be obtained, and regardless of whether some or all of the original defendants are involved in the subsequent incident of trespass, provided there is a sufficient period of time between the two incidents of trespass, the government guidance on welfare enquiries, applicable to local authorities and other public authorities, will still be relevant.[40] For example, even if exactly the same group of trespassers have returned to the same piece of land, there may have been a significant change of circumstances that the local authority or other public authority ought now to take into account before deciding whether to proceed with further eviction action.

39 [1986] 1 WLR 109 at 113.
40 For further discussion of the need for welfare enquiries, see paras 5.111–5.139, below.

Criminal Justice and Public Order Act 1994 s61

Who can use it?

The police

5.25   Criminal Justice and Public Order Act (CJPOA) 1994 s61 states:

> (1) If the senior police officer present at the scene reasonably believes that two or more persons are trespassing on land and are present there with the common purpose of residing there for any period, that reasonable steps have been taken by or on behalf of the occupier to ask them to leave and –
>
>   (a) that any of those persons has caused damage to the land or to property on the land or used threatening, abusive or insulting words or behaviour towards the occupier, a member of his family or an employee or agent of his, or
>
>   (b) that those persons have between them six or more vehicles on the land,
>
> he may direct those persons, or any of them, to leave the land and to remove any vehicles or other property they have with them on the land.

5.26   Failure to comply with such a direction to leave may result in arrest without a warrant[41] and impoundment of vehicles.[42] Section 61(4) contains the details of the 'offence':

> If a person knowing that a direction under subsection (1) above has been given which applies to him –
>
>   (a) fails to leave the land as soon as reasonably practicable, or
>
>   (b) having left again enters the land as a trespasser within the period of three months beginning with the day on which the direction was given,
>
> he commits an offence and is liable on summary conviction to imprisonment for a term not exceeding three months or a fine not exceeding level 4 on the standard scale, or both.

5.27   CJPOA 1994 s61 powers are regularly used by the police in England and Wales. It is noted, at the outset, that this is not the case

41 CJPOA 1994 s61(5).
42 CJPOA 1994 s62.

in Scotland.[43] The Association of Chief Police Officers (ACPO) Guidance for Scotland, states:

> There is a general presumption against prosecution of the unauthorised encampment of Gypsy Travellers relating to trespassory offences, although this presumption may be overridden by public interest considerations, dependent upon the circumstances ... Prosecution ... should only be considered as a last resort when all other options have been exhausted.

5.28   There are several 'hurdles' which the police must cross before being able to properly justify a CJPOA 1994 s61 eviction. Effectively each of these 'hurdles' presents the possibility for a 'substantive defence'.

'The senior police officer present'

5.29   CJPOA 1994 s61(3) states:

> A direction under subsection (1) above, if not communicated to the persons referred to in subsection (1) by the police officer giving the direction, may be communicated to them by any constable at the scene.

5.30   Since CJPOA 1994 s61(1) makes clear that the senior police officer must be present at the scene of the trespass, it must follow (if section 61(3) is to have any meaning) that the *'senior police officer present'* must be above the rank of constable, even if he or she does not personally communicate the direction to leave. It should be noted that there is no requirement for a section 61 removal direction to be in writing and commonly it is given verbally. However some police forces have a policy of giving a written notice and it can be important to be aware of any such written policies that exist. The ACPO Guidance on CJPOA 1994,[44] with regard to directions to leave land, states that 'it is suggested this is given both verbally and in writing. Providing unco-operative trespassers in a large gathering with both verbal and individual notices may be impossible.' An

---

43 CJPOA 1994 s61 applies equally to Scotland. Unauthorised encampments are not an unusual occurrence in Scotland. For example, in 2003, the Grampian Police Force experienced 34 separate encampments involving some 450 vehicles.

44 Latest version issued August 2000. It should be noted that ACPO have recently indicated that this Guidance is to be withdrawn and they will, from now on, be relying on the Office of the Deputy Prime Minister (ODPM) Guidance on Managing Unauthorised Camping, issued February 2004.

example of a notice is given and it is further stated: 'Although the notice is not a statutory requirement it should be used as a matter of good practice.'

'Two or more persons ... with the common purpose of residing'

5.31 Very occasionally one meets with a Gypsy or Traveller travelling alone. The police cannot use their CJPOA 1994 s61 powers against such a person. Additionally, if the Gypsies or Travellers have stopped for some purpose other than *'residing'* (for example, to make a hot drink or to change a flat tyre) then section 61 cannot be used. This is regardless of the perceived inconvenience of the location (for example, a supermarket car park). It should also be noted that, under section 61(9) – the definition section:

> ... a person may be regarded for the purposes of this section as having a purpose of residing in a place notwithstanding that he has a home elsewhere.

Thus, Gypsies and Travellers who, for example, have a pitch on an official site but are in the process of travelling for seasonal work, might be caught by section 61 if they stop on land without permission despite the existence of their 'home' elsewhere. It should also be noted that, unlike with the local authority powers of eviction under CJPOA 1994 s77,[45] the Gypsies or Travellers do not have to be in vehicles. Thus Gypsies and Travellers in tents or benders, for example, can be served with a direction even if they do not have a vehicle.[46]

'Trespassing on land'

5.32 Trespass has its ordinary meaning. By CJPOA 1994 s61(9):

> 'land' does not include –
> (a) buildings other than –
> (i) agricultural buildings within the meaning of, in England and Wales, paragraphs 3 to 8 of Schedule 5 to the Local Government Finance Act 1988 ...
> (ii) scheduled monuments within the meaning of the Ancient Monuments and Archaeological Areas Act 1979;
> (b) land forming part of –
> (i) a highway unless it falls within the classifications in section 54 of the Wildlife and Countryside Act 1981 (footpath, bridleway or

---

45 See para 5.66 below.
46 Providing CJPOA 1994 s61(1)(a) is satisfied. A 'bender' is a dome-shaped, tent-like structure, constructed by fixing tarpaulin over wooden rods or poles.

byway open to all traffic or road used as a public path) or is a cycle
track under the Highways Act 1980 or the Cycle Tracks Act 1984
...

5.33   Therefore, the police will not be able to serve a removal direction
under CJPOA 1994 s61 on Gypsies and Travellers who are camping
within the curtilage of a building or are camping on the highway
(subject to the exceptions detailed above). With regard to 'buildings',
it is not uncommon in urban areas for Gypsies or Travellers[47] to be
encamped within the yard or curtilage of a disused or empty
building. CJPOA 1994 s61 could not be used in such circumstances.
It is also quite common for Gypsies or Travellers to be encamped at
the end of dead-end roads, in cul-de-sacs, on lay-byes or on highway
verges. Once again section 61 cannot be used to evict them from
such a site.

'Reasonable steps ... by or on behalf of the occupier to ask them to leave'

5.34   The leading case on this issue is *R (Fuller and others) v Chief
Constable of the Dorset Constabulary and Secretary of State for the Home
Department*.[48] This case involved an unauthorised encampment on a
former rubbish tip owned by Weymouth BC. After a period of
'toleration', and following an incident at the site concerning a
confrontation between two police officers and certain of the
Travellers, the police and the local authority simultaneously served
removal directions which expired at the same time. This action was
quashed by the High Court. Giving judgment, Stanley Burnton J
gave a useful summary of the effect of CJPOA 1994 s61:

> In construing section 61 of the 1994 Act on the basis of common law
> principles, it is necessary to bear in mind that because it creates a
> criminal offence it is to be narrowly construed. Indeed, it creates a
> draconian procedure. I accept the claimants' point that Travellers are
> likely to comply with a direction under section 61 through fear of arrest
> and the forcible removal and detention of their vehicles although they
> may have an arguable justification for remaining on the land. Section 61
> must, I think, be all the more narrowly construed for that reason.

47 Especially New Travellers – based on the case-work of the Travellers' Advice
Team at Community Law Partnership. Criminal Law Act 1977 s6 (provisions
to prevent the use of violence for securing entry) may also be of relevance in
such circumstances. For more information on 'squatting', contact the
Advisory Service for Squatters – see appendix C below.

48 [2002] 3 All ER 57.

> The claimants submitted ... that section 61(1) assumes that the steps taken by the occupier to ask the trespassers to leave have been ineffective: ie, they have refused to leave. Whereas section 61(1)(a) applies to persons who have already been guilty of criminal or other misconduct, section 61(1)(b) applies to persons who may have been perfectly well-behaved. It seems to me that Parliament was unlikely to have intended to bring the criminal law to bear on such trespassers who had not refused to leave when asked. On this basis, section 61(1) is to be read as impliedly requiring that the trespassers have not complied with the occupier's request that they leave as a condition of the making of a direction by the police under the section.[49]

In other words, the occupier must give notice to leave before there can be any question of the police serving a section 61 removal direction. Thus, for example, a private landowner might give 48 hours' notice for the Gypsies or Travellers to leave. If they have not left at the end of that 48-hour period, then the police can decide to use section 61. However what is the position if the landowner or occupier is a local authority or other public authority?

5.35   In order to answer this question it is necessary to consider the extent to which local authorities and other public authorities must take account of welfare or humanitarian considerations before evicting trespassers from their land.[50] If a local authority (or other public authority) has failed to take account of humanitarian considerations before deciding to evict Gypsies or Travellers residing on their land without permission then it is arguable that their failure to do so may, in itself, mean that *reasonable steps* have not yet been taken by the occupier. In the *Fuller* case, Stanley Burnton J stated:

> In my judgment, a local authority must consider the Convention rights of trespassers and their human needs generally when deciding whether or not to enforce its right to possession of that land.[51]

It must be fairly clear, therefore, that a local authority must make enquiries into welfare issues before it can come to a decision on eviction.[52]

---

49 [2002] 3 All ER 57 at 69.

50 See 'public law challenges' at paras 5.111–5.139 below.

51 *Fuller* [2002] 3 All ER 57 at 74.

52 Other public authorities might also be required to carry out welfare enquiries, as discussed at paras 5.134–5.139, below.

Has one of the additional three criteria been met?

5.36   A removal direction cannot be issued unless the senior police officer present at the scene reasonably believes that the trespassers:

- have caused damage to land or property on the land;
- have used threatening, abusive or insulting words or behaviour; or
- have six or more vehicles between them on the land.

'Damage to land or property on land'

5.37   In terms of 'damage to land', CJPOA 1994 s61(9) defines 'property' as:

> (a) in England and Wales, property within the meaning of section 10(1) of the Criminal Damage Act 1971 ...

Criminal Damage Act 1971 s10(1) defines 'property' as:

> ... property of a tangible nature, whether real or personal, including money and – including wild creatures ... not including mushrooms growing wild on any land or flowers, fruit or foliage of a plant growing wild on any land.

Additionally, CJPOA 1994 s61(9), states that 'damage':

> ... includes the deposit of any substance capable of polluting the land.

Thus fly-tipping is probably within the definition. However it is unclear precisely what might be encompassed by the phrase 'damage to land'. In an old nineteenth century case, *Gayford v Chouler,* a farmer gained damages from someone who walked across his hay meadow thus damaging the crop.[53] It might be hoped that a modern court would consider 'damage' to mean something more significant than squashed grass. Some possibilities might include:

- the breaking of a lock to a gate;
- damage to a height barrier;
- cutting wood for fires.

However, without any extensive definition within CJPOA 1994 and with a dearth of case-law on this issue it is very difficult to predict what might be encompassed by the phrase. The ACPO Guidance on CJPOA 1994 contains certain suggestions: 'churned up ground

---

53 *Gayford v Chouler* [1898] 1 QB 316.

caused by heavy vehicles; diesel spillages; animal and human excrement; destroyed fencing and spoiled crops ... dumping of litter or rubbish ...'.

'Threatening, abusive or insulting words or behaviour'

5.38 Any 'threatening, abusive or insulting words or behaviour' must be directed to 'the occupier, a member of his family or an employee or agent of his.' 'Occupier', under CJPOA 1994 s61(9), means:

> ... in England and Wales, the person entitled to possession of the land by virtue of an estate or interest held by him ...

The rest of this criterion has its ordinary meaning and will turn on the evidence presented and the answers the Gypsies or Travellers have to any allegations that are made. It will be important for police officers to make sure that they treat Gypsies and Travellers fairly and that they do not jump to the conclusion that the evidence of the occupier or his agent should be preferred to that of the trespassers unless there are reasonable grounds for reaching such a conclusion.[54]

'Six or more vehicles'

5.39 The definition of 'vehicle' is extremely wide. CJPOA 1994 s61(9) states:

> 'vehicle' includes –
> (a) any vehicle, whether or not it is in a fit state for use on roads, and includes any chassis or body, with or without wheels, appearing to have formed part of such a vehicle, and any load carried by, and anything attached to, such a vehicle; and
> (b) a caravan as defined in section 29(1) of the Caravan Sites and Control of Development Act 1960.

Thus a caravan and its towing vehicle will constitute two vehicles. Three caravans and three towing vehicles will make the requisite six. Taking the ordinary meaning of the word 'vehicle' it can be implied that it is 'constructed'. Thus a motor-bike, barrel-top wagon or even a bicycle or derelict car may be covered by the term but clearly the horse that pulls the wagon will not. A 'caravan' is defined, under

---

54 See also paras 5.130–5.131 below.

Caravan Sites and Control of Development Act (CSCDA) 1960 s29(1), as:

> ... any structure designed or adapted for human habitation which is capable of being moved from one place to another (whether by being towed, or by being transported on a motor vehicle or trailer) and any motor vehicle so designed or adapted, but does not include –
> (a) any railway rolling stock which is for the time being on rails forming part of a railway system, or
> (b) any tent ...

Thus the term 'caravan' not only includes caravans as such but also camper vans, motor vehicles designed or adapted for human habitation (such as buses, lorries or removal vans) and mobile homes. Some Gypsies and Travellers have been known to park five or less vehicles on the land in question and to park the rest of their vehicles off the land, for example, on a nearby road, so as to avoid falling foul of section 61.

The statutory defence

5.40   The statutory defence to CJPOA 1994 s61 evictions is contained in section 61(6):

> In proceedings for an offence under this section it is a defence for the accused to show –
> (a) that he was not trespassing on the land, or
> (b) that he had a reasonable excuse for failing to leave the land as soon as reasonably practicable or, as the case may be, for again entering the land as a trespasser.

If Gypsies or Travellers can show that they have permission from the occupier of land to remain there, they are clearly not trespassers and the section cannot be used.

5.41   In the case of *Krumpa v DPP*,[55] the Divisional Court considered the meaning of the phrase 'reasonably practicable'[56] and concluded that the question whether something was 'reasonably practicable' should be considered objectively and was not a matter that could be determined solely by the police officer's view of what was reasonable. However, in *Fuller*, Stanley Burnton J adopted a very narrow

---

55 [1989] Crim LR 295.
56 In the context of the Public Order Act 1986 which first introduced the police powers of eviction against Gypsies, Travellers and other trespassers.

interpretation of the phrase in the context of removal directions and stated that:

> If the trespassers have failed to comply with the occupier's request, there is no reason for a direction not to take immediate effect.[57]

5.42 It is not uncommon for the police to use video evidence when dealing with an unauthorised encampment. The ACPO Guidance states that: 'When issuing a direction it is recommended, as best practice, to use video evidence gathering facilities to record both the verbal direction and service of notices.' Clearly, if the police were to take more intrusive video evidence (for example, by filming the interior of vehicles, as has been known to happen in the past) then they may commit an unjustified interference with the rights of the trespassers to respect for their private and family life and their homes protected by article 8 of the European Convention on Human Rights.[58]

Obtaining a court order

5.43 As will be seen above, Gypsies or Travellers who fail to comply with a valid removal direction under CJPOA 1961 s61 or who return to the land within the specified three-month period, can face arrest and impoundment of their vehicles (that is, their homes) without the need for any court order to be obtained. If arrest or impoundment has occurred, or if the Gypsies or Travellers remain on the land in defiance of the removal direction, the police will have to seek a further order from a magistrates' court. When the matter comes to court, the Gypsies or Travellers will have the opportunity of putting forward the 'substantive defences' mentioned above, if any apply. The very real practical problem for Gypsies or Travellers is that the threat of arrest and/or impoundment *before* the matter comes to court may (understandably) force them to leave the land on which they are encamped *even where* they or their advisers believe there is a 'substantive defence'. In such circumstances, a 'public law challenge' by way of judicial review may be mounted if the police have acted unlawfully, for example, by:

- failing to take into account a relevant matter,
- acting unreasonably in failing to properly address a defence raised by the trespassers, or

57 [2002] 3 All ER 57 at 70.
58 *See Campbell v MGN Limited* [2004] UKHL 22. For further discussion of ECHR article 8, see chapter 2 above.

- acting 'disproportionately' in terms of article 8 of the European Convention on Human Rights.

In practice such a 'public law challenge' will need to be lodged very swiftly.[59]

5.44   There may be grounds (other than the above) for a 'public law challenge' which will be examined later in this chapter.

CJPOA 1994 s62A

Who can use it?

The police

5.45   The Anti-Social Behaviour Act 2003 introduced a new section 62A to CJPOA 1994.[60] Section 62A exists alongside CJPOA 1994 s61, that is, the police can use either power provided, of course, the necessary criteria are met. Section 62A, which is entitled 'Power to remove trespassers: alternative site available', states as follows:

(1) If the senior police officer present at a scene reasonably believes that the conditions in subsection (2) are satisfied in relation to a person and land, he may direct the person –
   (a) to leave the land;
   (b) to remove any vehicle and other property he has with him on the land.

(2) The conditions are –
   (a) that the person and one or more others ('the trespassers') are trespassing on land;
   (b) that the trespassers have between them at least one vehicle on the land;
   (c) that the trespassers are present on the land with the common purpose of residing there for any period;
   (d) if it appears to the officer that the person has one or more caravans in his possession or under his control on the land, that there is a suitable pitch on a relevant caravan site for that caravan or each of those caravans;
   (e) that the occupier of the land or a person acting on his behalf has asked the police to remove the trespassers from the land.

---

59 For further discussion of judicial review see appendix A below. For further discussion of article 8 and 'proportionality', see chapter 2 above.

60 The Traveller Law Reform Coalition, when making submissions during the passage of the Anti-Social Behaviour Bill, pointed out that it was extremely insulting to Gypsies and Travellers to include unauthorised encampments per se within the scope of a measure designed to tackle anti-social behaviour.

(3) A direction under subsection (1) may be communicated to the person to whom it applies by any constable at the scene.

(4) Subsection (5) applies if –

    (a) a police officer proposes to give a direction under subsection (1) in relation to a person and land, and

    (b) it appears to him that the person has one or more caravans in his possession or under his control on the land.

(5) The officer must consult every local authority within whose area the land is situated as to whether there is a suitable pitch for the caravan or each of the caravans on a relevant caravan site which is situated in the local authority's area.

5.46 Though the provisions in section 62A are very similar to those in section 61 there are some subtle and important differences and these will be emphasised, where they occur, below.

'Senior police officer present'

5.47 Apparently a police constable could give such a direction though there will have to be a more senior officer present.[61]

'Trespassers'

5.48 CJPOA 1994 s62A(2)(a) refers to 'the person and one or more others' and it follows that a single Gypsy or Traveller, travelling on his or her own, would not therefore be caught by section 62A.[62]

'Common purpose of residing there'

5.49 If the Gypsies or Travellers are simply stopping on the way to somewhere else, for example, to have a meal, then the section would not apply.[63]

'Caravans'

5.50 CJPOA 1994 s62A refers to identifying a suitable pitch for a 'caravan'. The definition section[64] defines 'caravan' as having the same meaning as contained in the Caravan Sites and Control of Development Act 1960.[65] If the Gypsies or Travellers are residing in benders or tents the section does not apply. This differs from section

---

61 See the discussion at paras 5.29–5.30 above, which applies equally here.

62 See para 5.31 above.

63 See para 5.31, above.

64 CJPOA 1994 s62A(6).

65 For the definition of 'caravan', see para 5.39 above.

61 which can be used against Gypsies or Travellers residing solely in benders or tents.[66] However, it is nowadays fairly rare to come across Gypsies or Travellers residing in benders or tents, so there will be few cases where this issue arises in practice.

'Suitable pitch'

5.51   The inclusion of the word 'suitable' is important. No case-law exists at present to help in the definition of 'suitable pitch'. The draft guidance from the Office of the Deputy Prime Minister (ODPM)[67] states:

> The meaning of *suitable pitch* is not defined in the legislation. Of course, it is for the courts to interpret legislation, but the Secretary of State considers that a *suitable pitch* is one that provides basic amenities including water, toilets and waste disposal facilities. This could include an authorised transit site or stopping place. There should be a reasonable expectation that the pitch will be available for peaceful occupation for at least three months, except where the trespasser is expecting to move on before that time (emphasis in the text).

5.52   It seems unlikely that the police will be able to use CJPOA 1994 s62A to evict Gypsies and Travellers until local authorities provide sufficient sites for them. The report by Niner, *Local Authority Gypsy/Traveller Sites in England*[68] indicated that, on the 324 local authority Gypsy sites recorded by the January 2002 Gypsy Count, there were only 307 transit *pitches*.[69] Additionally, not all these transit pitches will have sufficient amenities for them to be deemed to be 'suitable'.

5.53   A pitch may not be suitable for a number of reasons. For example it may be on a site occupied by people that are in dispute with the Gypsies and Travellers that the police wish to evict. The ODPM *Guidance on Managing Unauthorised Camping*[70] states:

> There must be close working between site managers and local authority and police officers dealing with unauthorised camping over allocations of pitches on sites. Site managers may be aware of issues around

---

66 See para 5.31, above.

67 Issued 27 February 2004 and expected to be finalised by autumn 2004.

68 ODPM, 2003.

69 For a discussion of the Gypsy Sites Refurbishment Grant (GSRG), which now includes an amount set aside for the provision of new transit sites, see chapter 3 at para 3.45 above.

70 Issued 27 February 2004.

Gypsy/Traveller group and family compatibility, which must be taken into account when allocating pitches on residential sites.[71]

5.54   Therefore, the question of 'compatibility' of groups or families will also be relevant to the issue of whether the pitch offered is 'suitable'. Another important factor relevant to the issue of suitability will be related to the location of the pitch and its distance from schools, work and healthcare provision. Local authorities will also have to have regard to their allocations policy for any particular site to which it is suggested that a Gypsy or Traveller should be directed and ensure that that is also being followed.[72]

5.55   The pitch must be on a 'relevant caravan site' which is defined as:

... a caravan site which is –
(a) situated in the area of a local authority within whose area the land is situated, and
(b) managed by a relevant site manager.[73]

'Relevant site manager' is defined as:

(a) a local authority within whose area the land is situated;
(b) a registered social landlord.[74]

5.56   Therefore the site must either be managed by the local authority or by a registered social landlord, such as a housing association. If the site is managed by some other organisation, even if it is owned by the local authority in question, it will not be a 'relevant caravan site'. This is an important point for advisers or solicitors to be aware of.

5.57   It may also be the case that suitable pitches can only be identified for some of the Gypsies or Travellers parked on an unauthorised encampment and it is possible for the section to be applied to only a part of the group of Gypsies or Travellers in question. However, if the group is an extended family[75] or if certain members of the group

---

71 *Guidance on Managing Unauthorised Camping* para 4.8.
72 It will be important for a local authority to check on this to avoid court challenges from other Gypsies or Travellers awaiting a pitch on the site in question. See further the discussion on 'allocation' in chapter 3 paras 3.28–3.29 above.
73 CJPOA 1994 s62A(6).
74 CJPOA 1994 s62A(6). A housing association would be an example of a registered social landlord. To be a registered social landlord the body in question must be registered as such under Chapter 1 of Part 1 of the Housing Act 1996.
75 As is very common among Irish Travellers: see, for example, Michael McDonagh 'Nomadism' in *Travellers: Citizens of Ireland* (The Parish of the Travelling People, Dublin, 2000) pp33–46.

require special support from others within the group, those factors will also have to be taken into account, it is suggested, in assessing the suitability of a pitch or pitches offered.

'Occupier'

5.58   CJPOA 1994 s61 provided that the occupier must take 'reasonable steps'.[76] Under section 62A the occupier (or someone acting on his behalf) merely has to ask the police to remove the trespassers and he or she does not have to give any notice or make any request to leave to the Gypsies or Travellers in question. However, if the occupier is a local authority or other public authority, it seems they will still have to take account of welfare considerations before making a request to the police to use section 62A.[77]

'Communicated to the person'

5.59   As with CJPOA 1994 s61, there is no need for written notice to be given.[78] It appears that a Gypsy or Traveller, who is away from the land or otherwise not present when a direction to leave is communicated, may not be subject to the direction.

'Consult every local authority'

5.60   In England, this could involve not only a district council but also the relevant county council. No doubt local authorities and the police will need to have in place policies for liaison and sharing of information. Additionally this implies that the pitch offered could be on a county council site. If the latter site was a considerable distance away from the encampment, this might raise the question of whether the pitch was 'suitable'.[79] The draft guidance from the ODPM on CJPOA 1994 ss62A–E[80] states:

> In two tier authority areas, where a district council is situated within a wider county council area, the *suitable pitch* may be anywhere within the county council area.

76 See paras 5.34–5.35 above.
77 See further the discussion at paras 5.111–5.139 below.
78 But see what is stated above with regard to police forces who have a policy to use written notices and the possibility of challenging the failure to apply such a policy – para 5.30 above.
79 See paras 5.51–5.54, above.
80 Issued 27 February 2004 and expected to be finalised by autumn 2004.

As mentioned above, and especially where the county council area is extremely large, it might be doubted, in relation to distance from schools or healthcare, whether *anywhere* in the area would automatically be 'suitable', contrary to what is said in the draft guidance.

Offences

5.61 A person commits an offence if he knows that a direction under CJPOA 1994 s62A(1) has been given which applies to him/her and:

(a) he fails to leave the relevant land as soon as reasonably practicable,[81] or

(b) he enters any land in the area of the relevant local authority as a trespasser before the end of the relevant period with the intention of residing there.[82]

The 'relevant period' is three months from the day on which the direction is given.[83] Importantly it should be noted that this applies to *all land* in the relevant local authority area. However, the word 'relevant' qualifies 'local authority' in this context (contrast the position of an officer consulting the local authority or local authorities in the context of 'suitable pitch'). 'Relevant local authority' means:

(a) if the relevant land is situated in the area of more than one local authority (but is not in the Isles of Scilly), the district council or county borough council within whose area the relevant land is situated;

(b) ... the Council of the Isles of Scilly; in any other case, the local authority within whose area the relevant land is situated.[84]

Thus failure to comply with a direction under section 62A could result in an effective three-month ban from *that* local authority area (and not some wider county council area). However, if the Gypsies or Travellers, who have received a direction, stop on land in the area with the permission of the occupier, then they will not commit an offence.

---

81 For a discussion of the meaning of 'reasonably practicable' see para 5.41 above.

82 CJPOA 1994 s62B(1).

83 CJPOA 1994 s62B(2).

84 CJPOA 1994 s62E(6).

5.62   A person guilty of an offence is liable on summary conviction to imprisonment for a term not exceeding three months or a fine or both.[85] A constable may arrest a person committing an offence under this section.[86] A constable may also seize and remove any vehicles.[87]

Statutory defence

5.63   CJPOA 1994 s62B(5) states:

> In proceedings for an offence under this section it is a defence for the accused to show –
> (a) that he was not trespassing on the land in respect of which he is alleged to have committed the offence, or
> (b) that he had a reasonable excuse –
>   (i) for failing to leave the relevant land as soon as reasonably practicable, or
>   (ii) for entering the land in the area of the relevant local authority as a trespasser with the intention of residing there, or
> (c) that, at the time the direction was given, he was under the age of 18 years and was residing with his parent or guardian.

There is no case-law on the definition of 'reasonable excuse' in this context but it can be surmised that this might include mechanical breakdown or illness.[88] The exclusion of Gypsies or Travellers aged under 18 simply protects them from prosecution but will not normally (presuming they are travelling with adults) protect them from eviction. Again, as with section 61, it is likely that the section will normally be effective without the need to take the matter to court, since the threat of eviction and impoundment of their homes will usually be sufficient to persuade the Gypsies or Travellers to move.

5.64   As with CJPOA 1994 s61, if Gypsies or Travellers had been arrested[89] or have had their vehicles impounded[90] for failing to comply with a direction to leave under section 62A, or if they have not yet left the land (or returned to other land in the area) in defiance

---

85 The fine should not exceed level 4 on the standard scale. CJPOA 1994 s62B(3).
86 CJPOA 1994 s62B(4).
87 CJPOA 1994 s62C.
88 By analogy with CJPOA 1994 s77 – see further below at para 5.66 onwards.
89 Under CJPOA 1994 s62B(4).
90 Under CJPOA 1994 s62C.

of such a direction, the police would have to obtain a further order from the magistrates' court.[91]

5.65 Gypsy and Traveller support groups have voiced serious concerns about the use of CJPOA 1994 s62A.[92] The short deadlines that the police can give to Gypsies and Travellers mean that in practice it will be very unlikely that a court will hear a public law challenge before eviction takes place. However, the fact that the eviction has been carried out will not render a public law challenge academic, because the Gypsies or Travellers may wish to challenge the use of section 62A in order to avoid committing an offence if they return to the area within three months of the day when the direction was given.

CJPOA 1994 s77

Who can use it?

Local authorities

5.66 CJPOA 1994 s77 states:

> (1) If it appears to a local authority that persons are for the time being residing in a vehicle or vehicles within that authority's area –
> (a) on any land forming part of a highway;
> (b) on any other unoccupied land; or
> (c) on any occupied land without the consent of the occupier,
> the authority may give a direction that those persons and any others with them are to leave the land and remove the vehicle or vehicles and any other property they have with them on the land.

The offence is defined by CJPOA 1994 s77(3) as follows:

> If a person knowing that a direction under subsection (1) above has been given which applies to him –
> (a) fails, as soon as practicable, to leave the land or remove from the land any vehicle or other property which is the subject of the direction, or
> (b) having removed any such vehicle or property again enters the land with a vehicle within the period of three months beginning with the day on which the direction was given,
> he commits an offence and is liable on summary conviction to a fine not exceeding level 3 on the standard scale.

5.67 This is a very wide-ranging power and, though there is a specific statutory defence that is discussed at para 5.73 below, there are very

---

91 See further the discussion at para 5.43, above.
92 See further the conclusion at para 5.150 below.

few 'substantive defences'. Almost inevitably, it is the question of potential 'public law challenges' that is much more significant.[93] Nevertheless, the following 'substantive defences' are available.

'Consent of the occupier'

5.68   Virtually all land, regardless of whether or not it is owned by the local authority, is potentially covered by CJPOA 1994 s77 except for land where the Gypsies or Travellers have the consent of the occupier to be there. However, as can be seen below,[94] local authorities can utilise planning enforcement powers in those circumstances. An attempt to argue that land where there was no known owner or occupier was not within the section because the Gypsies themselves were the (adverse) occupiers, was unsuccessful at permission stage in the High Court.[95]

'Vehicle or vehicles'

5.69   In contrast to CJPOA 1994 s61, the Gypsies or Travellers must be residing in a vehicle or vehicles. Gypsies or Travellers who are not residing in vehicles (for example, in benders or tents) will not be covered by the section. However this is subject to the exception mentioned in the next paragraph.

'Written notice'

5.70   With regard to service of the required written notice of a removal direction under CJPOA 1994 s77, section 79 states:

> (2) Where it is impracticable to serve a relevant document on a person named in it, the document shall be treated as duly served on him if a copy of it is fixed in a prominent place to the vehicle concerned; and where a relevant document is directed to the unnamed occupants of vehicles, it shall be treated as duly served on those occupants if a copy of it is fixed in a prominent place to every vehicle on the land in question at the time when service is thus effected.

93 See paras 5.111–5.139 below.

94 At para 5.110

95 *R (Caroline Stephenson) v East Derbyshire Magistrates' Court and Amber Valley BC* [2003] EWHC 903 Admin, Sullivan J. In certain (rare) cases, where a Gypsy or Traveller has been residing on land that he or she did not own for 12 years or more without permission, he or she may be able to claim adverse possession of that land. However, the law on adverse possession is complex and has changed dramatically since the bringing into force of the Land Registration Act 2002. See Jourdan, *Adverse Possession* (Butterworths, 2003).

(3) A local authority shall take such steps as may be reasonably practicable to secure that a copy of any relevant document is displayed on the land in question (otherwise than by being fixed to a vehicle) in a manner designed to ensure that it is likely to be seen by any person camping on the land.

If a written notice is not placed on the vehicle(s) of a Gypsy or Traveller, that may constitute a defence. The catch-all phrase in section 77(1), 'any others with them', means that Gypsies or Travellers living on the land in tents or benders will be subject to the removal direction if they are with others who are residing in vehicles on the land. In those circumstances, section 79(3) makes similar provision to that which covers CPR Part 55 proceedings for display of notices on stakes or by other prominent methods.

'As soon as practicable'

5.71   It should be noted that, in contrast to CJPOA 1994 s61(4)(a), the word 'reasonably' has been omitted from CJPOA 1994 s77(3)[96] and Gypsies and Travellers can be prosecuted if they fail to leave the land 'as soon as practicable' after a removal direction has been given. What is 'practicable' in any given case will depend upon the facts but it is likely that a magistrates' court would convict a Gypsy or Traveller who had failed to comply with a short deadline in all but exceptional cases.

'Again enters the land ... within the period of three months'

5.72   The question whether a Gypsy or Traveller has returned to the land within three months of the original removal direction will be a simple matter of fact. In a case where Gypsies had ignored a removal direction and remained on the land for more than three months before being prosecuted under CJPOA 1994 s79 it was unsuccessfully argued that a removal direction could only be effective for a period of three months and that there was no power to prosecute a person after that period of time had expired.[97]

96 See further paras 5.40–5.41 above.
97 *R (Caroline Stephenson) v East Derbyshire Magistrates' Court and Amber Valley BC* [2003] EWHC 903 Admin.

Statutory defence

5.73   The statutory defence is contained within CJPOA 1994 s77(5) and can be relied on, like the other potential defences, if and when the matter comes before the magistrates' court. It states:

> In proceedings for an offence under this section it is a defence for the accused to show that his failure to leave or to remove the vehicle or other property as soon as practicable or his re-entry with a vehicle was due to illness, mechanical breakdown or other immediate emergency.

This is a fairly self-explanatory defence though there is currently no case-law to help us with the breadth (or otherwise) of the phrase 'other immediate emergency'. However, the practicalities of raising this statutory defence and any other substantive defence (and thus turning up at court and risking a removal order and a fine) are dealt with in the conclusion to this chapter.[98]

Obtaining a court order

5.74   Under CJPOA 1994 s78:

> (1) A magistrates' court may, on a complaint made by a local authority, if satisfied that persons and vehicles in which they are residing are present on land within that authority's area in contravention of a direction given under section 77, make an order requiring the removal of any vehicle or other property which is so present on the land and any person residing in it.
>
> (1) An order under this section may authorise the local authority to take such steps as are reasonably necessary to ensure that the order is complied with and, in particular, may authorise the local authority, by its officers and servants –
>
> (a) to enter upon the land specified in the order; and
>
> (b) to take, in relation to any vehicle or property to be removed in pursuance of the order, such steps for securing entry and rendering it suitable for removal, as may be so specified.
>
> (3) The local authority shall not enter upon any occupied land unless they have given to the owner or occupier at least 24 hours' notice of their intention to do so, or unless after reasonable enquiries they are unable to ascertain their names and addresses.

5.75   Normally, therefore, such a removal order will ensure that the Gypsies or Travellers who are subject to the order will have at least 24 hours after the order is obtained within which to leave the land. This will not be the case, however, if the local authority are both the

---

98 At para 5.150 above.

owner *and* the occupier of the land, or if the local authority cannot reasonably ascertain the identity of the owner or occupier. It has been the normal practice of local authorities, since this power of eviction was brought into force, to only seek a removal order and not to seek a conviction for the potential criminal offence under CJPOA s77(3).[99]

Highways Act 1980

Who can use it?

Local authorities and the police

5.76 A 'highway' is a way over which there exists a public right of passage, that is a right for all, at all seasons of the year, freely and at their will, to pass and re-pass without let or hindrance.[100] It should also be noted that a highway will include any footpaths or cycle tracks as well as the carriage way, and also any verge enjoyed by the public as part of the highway.[101]

5.77 If a person, without lawful authority or excuse, in any way wilfully obstructs the free passage along a highway, he or she is guilty of an offence.[102]

5.78 A lawful excuse will be established if it can be shown that the person causing the obstruction honestly but mistakenly believed, on reasonable grounds, that the facts were such as would make the conduct lawful.[103] However, proof of mens rea is not required to act wilfully, that is, one does not have to *intend* to cause an obstruction – if an obstruction is caused and the person responsible for the obstruction acted of their own free will, that is sufficient.[104] Thus the person responsible for the obstruction probably has a 'substantive defence' if their car has broken down and is thus causing an obstruction. Indeed, where the obstruction is of a temporary nature (as in the latter example), it will only be an offence if it is shown that the obstruction arose from unreasonable user of the highway.[105]

---

99 See para 5.66 above.
100 *Ex p Lewis* [1888] 21 QBD 191 at 197 per Wills J.
101 See *DPP v Jones* [1999] 2 WLR 625.
102 Highways Act 1980 s137(1). A person guilty of an offence is liable to a fine not exceeding level 3 on the standard scale.
103 *Cambridgeshire and Isle of Ely CC v Rust* [1972] 2 QB 426; [1972] 3 All ER 232.
104 *Arrowsmith v Jenkins* [1963] 2 QB 561.
105 *Nagy v Weston* [1965] 1 All ER 78, [1965] 1 WLR 280.

5.79   The case of *DPP v Jones*,[106] raises an interesting question with regard to the use of highways legislation to 'move on' Gypsies or Travellers. The case did not involve action for breach of the highways' legislation but for 'trespassory assembly'.[107] The defendants took part in a peaceful, non-obstructive assembly on a highway. They were campaigning for the right to hold a festival at Stonehenge and were on the roadside verge, adjacent to the perimeter fence of the monument at Stonehenge. The Court of Appeal allowed the defendants' appeal against the Divisional Court finding that this amounted to a 'trespassory assembly'. The Court of Appeal held that the public had the right to use the highway for such reasonable and usual activities, including peaceful assembly, as were consistent with the primary right to use it for passage and repassage, it being a matter of fact and degree for the court in each case to decide whether the user was reasonable and not inconsistent with that primary right. Lord Hutton stated:

> It is neither desirable in theory nor acceptable in practice for commonplace activities on the public highway not to count as breaches of the criminal law of wilful obstruction of the highway, yet to count as trespasses ... and therefore form the basis for a finding of trespassory assembly for the purposes of the Act of 1986. A system of law sanctioning these discordant outcomes would not command respect.

5.80   Gypsies or Travellers do not usually face actions on the basis of 'trespassory assemblies' but they do frequently stop for short periods on the verges of highways (which are, in terms of highways legislation, part of the highway). Indeed, Gypsies and Travellers have been stopping in such locations, for short periods, for hundreds of years in the United Kingdom. It could be argued that such an incident, where the Gypsies or Travellers are not obstructing any footpath or cycle track and are acting peaceably, comes within the

---

106 [1999] 2 WLR 625.

107 A 'trespassory assembly' is defined by Public Order Act 1986 s14A, as inserted by CJPOA 1994 s70, as: 'an assembly ... intended to be held in any district at a place on land to which the public has no right of access or only a limited right of access ... [which] is likely to be held without the permission of the occupier of the land or to conduct itself in such a way as to exceed the limits of any permission of his or the limits of the public's rights of access and ... may result – (i) in serious disruption to the life of the community, or (ii) where the land, or a building or monument on it, is of historical, architectural, archaeological or scientific importance, in significant damage to the land, building or monument ...'

ambit of a 'commonplace activity', as mentioned by Lord Hutton. Nevertheless, it is common for Gypsies and Travellers on the verges of a carriage way to be moved on for allegedly obstructing the highway. However, there is, as yet, no case-law on this situation.

5.81 It is also an offence for any person in charge of a vehicle to cause or permit it, or a trailer (which could include a caravan) drawn by it, to remain at rest on any road in such position, condition, or circumstances as to be likely to cause danger to other road users.[108]

5.82 On certain highways the keeper of any horses, cattle, sheep, goats or swine found straying on or lying on or at the side of the highway is guilty of an offence.[109]

5.83 The only possibility of impoundment of vehicles under the highways legislation is contained in Highways Act 1980 s149, as follows:

(1) If anything is so deposited on a highway as to constitute a nuisance, the highway authority for the highway may by notice require the person who deposited it there to remove it forthwith [and can apply to magistrates for a removal and disposal order].

(2) If the highway authority for any highway have reasonable grounds for considering –
  (a) that anything unlawfully deposited on the highway constitutes a danger (including a danger caused by obstructing the view) to users of the highway, and
  (b) that the thing in question ought to be removed without the delay involved in giving notice or obtaining a removal and disposal order ...

the authority may remove the thing forthwith.

5.84 The 'thing unlawfully deposited' could include vehicles. If sufficient danger is caused, impoundment could occur. Other than this circumstance, impoundment without an order is not possible.

5.85 Where a highway is created through the acquisition of land over which it passes, either by agreement or through the exercise of compulsory purchase powers, the highway authority are the owners both of the surface of the highway and the subsoil. However, where a highway is created by dedication (that is, with the permission of the landowner without releasing his or her rights over the land), the

---

108 Road Traffic Act 1988 s22. A person guilty of an offence is liable to a fine not exceeding level 3 on the standard scale and also discretionary disqualification.

109 Highways Act 1980 s155(1). A person guilty of an offence is liable to a fine not exceeding level 3 on the standard scale. The animal in question can also be removed to the common pound.

subsoil[110] beneath the highway remains in the ownership of the 'dedicating landowner'.[111] Moreover, in the case of those highways which are not maintainable at public expense, both the surface of the highway and the subsoil remain within the ownership of the dedicating landowner.[112] Where the dedicating landowner retains ownership of the surface of the highway and/or the subsoil, he or she will be able to take possession action (for example, CPR Part 55 proceedings) against any trespassers on the highway.

5.86   In a case where a Gypsy or Traveller is prosecuted under any of the above statutory provisions he or she will be able to defend the proceedings successfully if the prosecuting authority are unable to satisfy the magistrates' court that all the elements of the alleged offence have been proved.

Bye-laws

Who can use them?

Local authorities and certain other public authorities

5.87   A bye-law is an ordinance affecting the public and laid down by an authority which has been given statutory powers to do so.[113] If validly made, a bye-law has the force of law within its sphere of operation. Bye-laws made by local authorities must be confirmed by some central authority before they can have the force of law.[114]

5.88   A local authority can either be given power to deal with specific matters or may make bye-laws for the good rule and government of the whole or any part of the area they cover, as well as for the prevention and suppression of nuisances.[115]

---

110 The surface of the road was defined by Denning LJ, in *Tithe Redemption Commission v Runcorn UDC* [1954] 2 WLR 518, as: 'the top spit, or perhaps ... the top two spits, of the road' (at 530).

111 See *Truckell v Stock* [1957] 1 WLR 161; *Rolls v St George the Martyr, Southwark, Vestry* [1880] 14 Ch D 785.

112 See *Encyclopaedia of Highway Law and Practice* (Sweet & Maxwell, 2004) 1–002.

113 *Kruse v Johnson* [1898] 2 QB 91.

114 Local Government Act 1972 s236(3).

115 This applies to the council of a district, the council of a principal area in Wales, the council of a London Borough and the Council of the Isles of Scilly: Local Government Act 1972 s235(1) as amended by the Local Government (Wales) Act 1994 s66(5), Sch 15 para 49.

5.89   Bye-laws may not be made if they duplicate the provisions of other enactments.[116]

5.90   A copy of a bye-law or part of a bye-law must be provided to any person on request on payment of such sum as the authority may determine.[117]

5.91   A bye-law requires four elements for it to be valid:

(a) it must be intra vires (that is, within the power of the authority making it);
(b) it must not be 'repugnant' to the general law;
(c) it must be certain;
(d) it must be reasonable.

5.92   A bye-law must be intra vires. A local authority cannot take upon itself powers by means of a bye-law beyond the powers conferred on it by statute.[118]

5.93   A bye-law must not be repugnant to the general law. Therefore, a bye-law must not make something unlawful which the general law does not make unlawful.[119]

5.94   A bye-law must be certain. To be certain, a bye-law must contain a clear statement of the course of action required (or that should be avoided) and must contain sufficient information to allow people to know what is expected of them.[120]

5.95   A bye-law must be reasonable. To be reasonable, a bye-law must not be manifestly unjust, capricious, inequitable or partial in its operation, or involve oppressive interference with the rights of those subject to it. For example, in one case bye-laws imposing on landlords a duty to clean certain houses were held unreasonable where they applied to a landlord who had not reserved a right of entry to the property in question.[121]

5.96   A local authority may not waive the requirements of its bye-laws unless it has reserved the right to do so. Bye-laws made by local authorities should be interpreted benevolently and upheld if possible.[122]

---

116 See, for example, *Galer v Morrissey* [1955] 1 All ER 380.
117 Local Government Act 1972 s236(6) – currently the sum must not exceed 10p for every 100 words.
118 See, eg, *R v Wood* [1855] 5 E&B 49.
119 See, eg, *Powell v May* [1946] KB 330.
120 See, eg, *Percy v Hall* [1997] QB 924.
121 *Arlidge v The Metropolitan Borough of Islington* [1909] 2 KB 127.
122 *Kruse v Johnson* [1989] 2 QB 91 at 99, per Lord Russell of Killowen CJ.

5.97   The production of a printed copy of a bye-law made by a local authority which is endorsed with a certificate signed by the proper officer of the authority is prima facie evidence of the bye-law, provided the certificate states that:

(a) it was made by the local authority;
(b) the copy is a true copy;
(c) on a specified date the bye-law was confirmed.

5.98   Bye-laws may be enforced by the imposition of fines, the removal of offenders from the place to which the bye-law relates, or by injunction.

5.99   Other public authorities may be empowered to make bye-laws. For example, the Forestry Commission may make bye-laws:

- for the preservation of trees, timber and the Commissioners' property;
- for prohibiting or regulating any act or thing tending to injure or disfigure Forestry Commission land or amenities; and
- for regulating the reasonable use of the land by the public for the purposes of exercise or recreation.[123]

5.100   All of the principles with regard to validity and scope mentioned above also apply to bye-laws produced by other public authorities.[124]

5.101   If a local or other public authority prosecutes a Gypsy or Traveller for allegedly breaching a bye-law, the matters mentioned above with regard to validity may provide a 'substantive defence'.[125] However, it should be emphasised that the practice of most local and other public authorities tends to be to rely on other forms of possession action to evict Gypsies or Travellers from land, while at the same time quoting relevant bye-laws (sometimes as a way of justifying their action as being 'proportionate').[126]

---

123 Forestry Act 1967 s46(1). The Forestry Commission bye-laws currently in force are Forestry Commission Bye-laws 1982 SI No 648.
124 *Boddington v British Transport Police* [1999] 2 AC 143.
125 *Boddington v British Transport Police* [1999] 2 AC 143.
126 See chapter 2 above, for discussion of 'proportionality' in the context of the Human Rights Act (HRA) 1998.

Common law powers

Who can use them?

Anyone entitled to possession of the land, for example, landowner, tenant, licensee

5.102   If a trespasser peaceably enters or is on land, the person who is in, or is entitled to, possession may require him or her to leave, and, if the trespasser refuses to leave, may remove that person from the land, using no more force than is reasonably necessary.[127] The request to leave could, potentially, be a request to leave forthwith.

5.103   Such powers are available to all landowners. However, an attempt to use these powers by a local or other public authority does not preclude a potential public law challenge by way of judicial review.[128]

5.104   However, if a trespasser enters with force and violence, the person in possession may remove that person without a previous request to depart.[129] Once again, in the case of local or other public authorities, a potential public law challenge is not precluded, though the fact of the use of force or violence by the trespasser, may assist the authority to argue that their decision to evict is 'proportionate'.[130]

5.105   The use of more force than is 'reasonably necessary' could result in an action for trespass to the person or property and a compensation claim for any damage caused. The person(s) carrying out the eviction or the person in possession could also be charged with having committed a criminal offence such as assault or criminal damage if the trespasser is injured or property is damaged during the course of the eviction.

5.106   The Office of the Deputy Prime Minister (ODPM) *Guidance on Managing Unauthorised Camping*[131] states:

> The Government believes that local authorities should always follow a route which requires a court order. As local authorities and public bodies, authorities must have regard to considerations of common humanity or other statutory duties, and must ensure that the human rights of unauthorised campers are safeguarded.[132]

---

127 Halsbury, *Laws of England*, Butterworths, 1999, 4th edition, Vol. 45(2), para 522.
128 See paras 5.111 and 5.139 below.
129 See, for example, *Polkingham v Wright* [1845] 8 QB 197.
130 See, for a discussion of 'proportionality' and the HRA 1998, chapter 2 above.
131 Issued on 27 February 2004.
132 ODPM *Guidance on Managing Unauthorised Camping* at para 6.5.

This would seem to effectively preclude the use of common law powers by local and other public authorities.

5.107   The ODPM Guidance also contains recommendations for other landowners using common law powers of eviction:

> Good practice guidelines for common law evictions would seek to ensure that no more than necessary 'reasonable force' is used and might include:
> • Police should always be notified of an eviction and called in to stand by to prevent a breach of the peace.
> • If police advise that it is inappropriate to carry out an eviction, it should always be delayed until an agreed time.[133]

5.108   If the person using common law powers is subsequently prosecuted for wrongful use of those powers (see para 5.105 above), failure to follow the above guidance may be used in evidence against them.

5.109   It is also noted that Lord Denning stated that these powers were 'not to be recommended' to landowners due to the 'possible disturbance' which might be caused.[134]

Planning enforcement

Who can use it?

Local authorities

5.110   The Town and Country Planning Act (TCPA) 1990 enables local authorities to take enforcement action against unauthorised developments by the use of enforcement notices, stop notices or injunctions. Very often the Gypsies or Travellers on such encampments may also be trying to obtain planning permission. On other occasions, the Gypsies or Travellers may be on land with the consent of the owner but may not have the requisite planning permission. Action may be threatened by the local authority against the owner and/or the Gypsies and Travellers.[135] The existence of these powers does not preclude a potential public law challenge by way of judicial review by the Gypsies or Travellers.[136]

---

133   *Guidance on Managing Unauthorised Camping* at para 6.16.

134   *McPhail v Persons Unknown* [1973] 3 All ER 393 at 396.

135   For a full discussion of planning matters as they affect Gypsies and Travellers, see chapter 4 above.

136   And see the case of *R v Kerrier DC ex p Uzell Blythe* [1996] JPL 837, where Latham J (as he then was) applied the principles of the *Atkinson* case (see from para 5.111, below) to a situation involving planning enforcement powers.

Public law challenges[137]

Local authorities

5.111   In *R v Lincolnshire CC ex p Atkinson; Wealden DC ex p Wales and Stratford* (the *Atkinson* case),[138] Sedley J (as he then was) made it clear that local authorities, when considering the eviction of unauthorised encampments, ought to comply with DoE Circular 18/94, Welsh Office Circular 76/94 (hereafter DoE Circular 18/94).[139] Sedley J stated:

> Detailed analysis of [passages from the Circular] and debate about what legal force, if any, an advisory circular of this kind possesses has been made unnecessary by the realistic concession of counsel for both local authorities that whether or not they were spelt out in a departmental circular the matters mentioned ... would be material considerations in the public law sense that to overlook them in the exercise of a local authority's powers under sections 77 to 79 of the Act of 1994 would be to leave relevant matters out of account and so jeopardise the validity of any consequent step. The concession is rightly made because those considerations in the material paragraphs which are not statutory are considerations of common humanity, none of which can be properly ignored when dealing with one of the most fundamental human needs, the need for shelter with at least a modicum of security.[140]

5.112   DoE Circular 18/94 is, therefore, a vital tool for those advising on this area of the law. At paragraph 6 it states:

> While it is a matter for local discretion to decide whether it is appropriate to evict an unauthorised gypsy encampment, the Secretary of State believes that local authorities should consider using their powers to do so wherever the gypsies concerned are causing a level of nuisance which cannot be effectively controlled. They also consider that it would usually be legitimate for a local authority to exercise these powers wherever gypsies who are camped unlawfully refuse to move onto an authorised local authority site. Where there are no such sites, and the authority reaches the view that an unauthorised gypsy encampment is not causing a level of nuisance which cannot be effectively controlled, it should consider providing basic services, such as toilets, a refuse skip and a supply of drinking water at that site.

137 Public law challenges are taken by way of an application for judicial review. For full discussion of judicial review, see appendix A, below.

138 [1995] 8 Admin LR 529.

139 *Gypsy Sites Policy and Unauthorised Camping*, issued 23 November 1994 and amended 26 July 2000. See appendix B.

140 [1995] 8 Admin LR 529 at 535.

5.113   The *Atkinson* case made it clear that local authorities must have regard to humanitarian considerations (and this is emphasised later in the Circular, as we will see below). Paragraph 6 lays emphasis on the question of 'nuisance'. It follows that if the unauthorised encampment is situated on a disused piece of land and not causing any problems, the local authority may wish to consider 'toleration' of the encampment. Eviction may lead to the group of Gypsies or Travellers moving to a less appropriate, more high profile site. 'Toleration' might certainly be appropriate where the local authority cannot suggest an authorised permanent site, transit site or emergency stopping place that the Gypsies or Travellers could go to. On the other hand, if the encampment was in the town hall car park, there would need to be the most extreme welfare circumstances before a court might expect the local authority to hold back from eviction.

5.114   At paragraph 9 of the Circular it is stated:

> [Local authorities] should use [their] powers in a humane and compassionate way, taking account of the rights and needs of the gypsies concerned, the owners of the land in question, and the wider community whose lives may be affected by the situation.

5.115   Local authorities are also reminded of their obligations under Children Act 1989 Part III (regarding the welfare of 'children in need'), Housing Act 1985 Part III (now Housing Act 1996 Part VII, covering duties to homeless people), and concerning the provision of education for school-age children.[141] Local authorities should also bear in mind possible assistance from local health and/or welfare services.[142]

5.116   DoE Circular 18/94 is intended to give local authorities guidance on the use of CJPOA 1994 s77. Local authorities clearly need to carry out some form of enquiry process in order to gather the necessary information and then adopt a suitable method by which to analyse and consider such information. They will also need to be able to show that the decision-maker has proper delegated authority. For example, in a case involving remuneration for long-term foster carers,[143] the policy of the local authority was quashed, among other things, because the preparation of the policy had not been lawfully delegated to the officers who had, in fact, devised it. Solicitors or

141 DoE Circular 18/94 paras 10 and 11.
142 DoE Circular 18/94 para 13.
143 *R (L) v Manchester CC* [2001] EWHC Admin 707; [2002] 1 FLR 43, Munby J.

advisers assisting Gypsies or Travellers who are facing eviction from an unauthorised encampment by a local authority, should consider requesting details of who made the decision to evict and whether that person or persons had properly delegated powers to do so.

5.117   Following the *Atkinson* case, some local authorities sought to test whether the general thrust of DoE Circular 18/94 would apply to other methods of eviction and there followed a line of somewhat conflicting High Court judgments.[144] However, the position was clarified in October 1998 by the publication of the Department of the Environment, Transport and the Regions (DETR)/Home Office *Good Practice Guide, Managing Unauthorised Camping*.[145] This guidance was the result of research commissioned by the government from the University of Birmingham. The guidance made clear that local authorities should take into account welfare issues regardless of the method of eviction being contemplated. The guidance has now been superseded by the Office of the Deputy Prime Minister (ODPM) *Guidance on Managing Unauthorised Camping* (hereafter 'the ODPM Guidance').[146] Though the ODPM Guidance only applies to England it is argued, by analogy, that it should also be followed by local authorities and other public authorities in Wales. The Equality of Opportunity Committee of the National Assembly for Wales believes

144 *R v Kerrier DC ex p Uzell Blythe* [1996] JPL 837; *R v Brighton and Hove Council ex p Marmont* [1998] HLR 1046; *R v Hillingdon LBC ex p McDonagh* [1999] HLR 531; and *R v Leeds CC ex p Maloney* [1999] HLR 552. Broadly speaking, the judgments in *Uzell Blythe* and *Maloney* stated that Circular 18/94 (or, at least, the spirit of it) should apply to enforcement/eviction action other than just evictions under CJPOA 1994 s77, and the judgments in *Marmont* and *McDonagh* stated the contrary view, though it was at least accepted in those cases that there must be some reference to 'humanitarian considerations'.

145 This Guidance was amended in 2000. The fact that welfare enquiries should be carried out regardless of the type of eviction action was effectively confirmed in *R (Martin Ward) v Hillingdon LBC* [2001] LGR 457, where Stanley Burnton J at 460, stated: '[A] local authority considering exercising its powers to evict travellers ... from an unauthorised encampment must not act in an uninformed, precipitate and inconsiderate manner. It must make adequate enquiries to elicit relevant information, including the number, age, health and needs of the travellers concerned, and make its decision having properly taken that information into account. The guidance expressly envisages that there will be circumstances in which a local authority may properly decide not to evict travellers from an unauthorised encampment.'

146 The ODPM Guidance also resulted from further research by the University of Birmingham headed (as with the previous guidance) by Pat Niner of the Centre for Urban and Regional Studies. The Guidance came into effect on 27 February 2004. See appendix B.

that Welsh Office Circular 76/94[147] should apply in all eviction situations.[148]

5.118   The ODPM Guidance stresses the importance for local authorities of the information gathering process and the importance of strategies being put in place.[149] It will be important, therefore, for advisers to obtain copies of the relevant strategies on unauthorised camping from local authorities and police authorities in order to check that they have been followed.

5.119   The ODPM Guidance makes clear the government's emphasis on the need for site provision. At paragraph 4.2 it is stated:

> Site provision is an essential element in any strategy. In a context where the number of Gypsy caravans exceeds the number of authorised places where they can stop – which is the case in England – provision of suitable accommodation for Gypsies and Travellers must be seen as a vital part of an approach to dealing with unauthorised camping. Population increase and family growth among Gypsies and Travellers must also be considered.

5.120   With regard to Wales, the Equality of Opportunity Committee of the National Assembly for Wales has stated:

> Put bluntly, providing services to Gypsy-Travellers tends to be unpopular with the wider public, and given that there is no longer a requirement to provide sites, the issue is given a low priority. The service providers [including local authorities] were strongly in favour of a new national framework for sites, even a reintroduction of a duty to provide sites as the only way to make progress on this issue.[150]

5.121   The ODPM Guidance, at paragraph 4.3, continues:

> All local authorities should review the provision of sites for Gypsies and Travellers.

The lack of a clear and coherent written strategy in itself may be a factor in a potential public law challenge.

5.122   The ODPM Guidance also emphasises the importance of welfare enquiries and the need for public bodies to take account of considerations of common humanity.[151] However, the ODPM

---

147 The equivalent, in Wales, of DoE Circular 18/94.

148 *Review of Service Provision for Gypsies and Travellers* (National Assembly for Wales, 2003), paras 10.55 and 10.56.

149 See chapter 3 of the ODPM Guidance, 'Developing a Strategy for Unauthorised Camping'.

150 *Review of Service Provision for Gypsies and Travellers* (National Assembly for Wales May 2003) para 10.27.

151 See the ODPM Guidance, paras 5.7 to 5.10.

Guidance also makes it clear that the location of an encampment will be an important consideration. For example, at paragraph 5.4 it is stated:

> Unauthorised encampments are almost always, by definition, unlawful. However, while there are insufficient authorised sites, it is recognised that some unauthorised camping will continue. There are locations, however, where encampments will not be acceptable under any circumstances. Each encampment location must be considered on its merits against criteria such as health and safety considerations for the unauthorised campers, traffic hazard, public health risks, serious environmental damage, genuine nuisance to neighbours and proximity to other sensitive land-uses.

Thus, to take the extreme example of an encampment in the town hall car park, the location of the encampment, in such a case, may preclude any question of a public law challenge due to lack of enquiries.[152]

5.123   It will be important for local authorities to keep written records of the enquiry process and, for this purpose, pro formas might be used.[153] At paragraph 5.17 of the ODPM Guidance it is stated that:

> Reasonable attempts should be made to get information from unauthorised campers not present at the time of a visit. Other members of the group may sometimes be able to provide information. A letter or self-completion form may be left with clear instructions for its return (at no cost to the unauthorised camper). All such actions should be clearly recorded, and if there is still no response, this should be noted.

Usually Gypsies and Travellers will not be aware in advance of the time of a visit. More than one visit may therefore be required. Reliance on pro formas or self-completion forms may also be dependent on questions of literacy.

5.124   It is important, however, that the enquiry process is more than just a paper exercise. A proper decision-making process is required. Paragraph 5.20 of the ODPM Guidance states:

> Any welfare needs of unauthorised campers are a material consideration for local authorities when deciding whether to start eviction proceedings or to allow the encampment to remain longer. Welfare needs do not give

---

152 This is not to say that enquiries should not be made in such a case. However, if the Gypsies or Travellers are unlawfully encamped on a location such as the town hall car park, only the most extreme of personal circumstances might lead to a decision to 'tolerate' the encampment for a short period.

153 ODPM Guidance, para 5.14.

an open-ended 'right' for unauthorised campers to stay as long as they want in an area. For example, the presence of a pregnant woman or school age children does not, per se, mean that an encampment must remain indefinitely. To defer an eviction which is justified on other grounds, the need must be more immediate and/or of a fixed term.

The ODPM Guidance gives some specific examples of situations where good practice suggests that eviction should be delayed:

- advanced pregnancy – a period shortly before and after birth, longer on medical advice if there are complications;
- ill health – where a hospital appointment is booked; in-patient treatment for a close family member; a period during which a medical condition can be diagnosed, stabilised and a course of treatment started;
- educational needs – children in school if within four weeks of the end of term or if access to special education has been gained (this is not an exhaustive list).[154]

5.125   It is important for local authorities to identify who is responsible for taking decisions (as is also the case for the police).[155] A decision being taken by the wrong officer or employee may lead to a successful challenge.[156] As mentioned above,[157] the government stresses that it wants local authorities to follow a route that ultimately requires a court order.[158] If the local authority decide to 'tolerate' an encampment for the time being, they must take a 'management' role.[159] The Guidance makes clear that the same standards of behaviour should be expected of the occupants of an unauthorised encampment as might be expected of the settled community.[160] Examples of unacceptable behaviour are given such as over-large encampments, aggressive or threatening behaviour, failure to control dogs, persistent and disturbing noise, littering/fly-tipping, damage to property or criminal activity.[161]

5.126   If a Gypsy or Traveller has made a homeless application to a local authority relying on the case of *R (Margaret Price) v Carmarthenshire*

---

154 ODPM Guidance, Box 18 p31.
155 ODPM Guidance, para 5.22.
156 See para 5.116.
157 At para 5.106 above.
158 ODPM Guidance, para 6.5.
159 See ODPM Guidance, Chapter 7 'Managing Unauthorised Encampments'.
160 ODPM Guidance, para 7.1.
161 ODPM Guidance, para 7.3.

CC,[162] and is camping on a piece of the same local authority's land, then it can be argued that he or she should be allowed to remain there while the homelessness application is progressed, providing that he or she are not causing any nuisance or obstruction.

The police

5.127   The police must also take account of welfare considerations. Home Office Circular 45/94 states, in relation to CJPOA 1994 s61:

> The decision whether or not to issue a direction to leave is an operational one for the police alone to take in the light of all the circumstances of the particular case. But in making this decision, the senior officer at the scene may wish to take account of the personal circumstances of the trespassers; for example, the presence of elderly persons, invalids, pregnant women, children and other persons whose well-being may be jeopardised by a precipitate move.

5.128   This is reinforced by the Guidance on the CJPOA 1994 issued by the Association of Chief Police Officers (ACPO)[163] which states that welfare considerations *must* be taken into account. The ACPO Guidance makes reference to the case of *R v Metropolitan Police ex p Small*.[164] The ODPM Guidance sums up the case-law position thus:

> Case law (*Small*) has established that, while police officers do not have to undertake welfare enquiries as such, they must be aware of humanitarian considerations in reaching their decisions and must ensure that all decisions are proportionate. A decision may be taken to explicitly exclude individuals or families with serious welfare needs from a section 61 direction to leave.[165]

It is difficult to see how the police officers present can take account of humanitarian considerations without making some form of enquiry. However, it is suggested that it will be difficult to argue that the police have failed to comply with their duty if they request that

---

162 [2003] EWHC 42 Admin; March 2003 *Legal Action* 30. For full discussion of this case, see chapter 6 paras 6.51–6.58 below.

163 Latest edition August 2000.It should be noted that ACPO have recently indicated that this Guidance is to be withdrawn and they will, from now on, be relying on the Office of the Deputy Prime Minister (ODPM) Guidance on Managing Unauthorised Camping, issued February 2004.

164 Unreported leave application in the (as it then was) Crown Office List before Collins J, 27 August 1998.

165 ODPM Guidance, para 6.9.

the Gypsies or Travellers provide details of the existence of any welfare concerns and then take account of any relevant information when deciding whether to issue a removal direction.

5.129   The ODPM Guidance indicates that, where a local authority is involved, the police can probably rely on the enquiries conducted by the local authority.[166] Equally it can be argued that, if it is local authority land, the local authority ought to go through their correct processes before even considering police involvement.[167]

5.130   At paragraph 6.8, the ODPM Guidance provides some examples of factors which might prompt police eviction action:

- unacceptable behaviour by unauthorised campers at the encampment, including individual criminal activity, which cannot be controlled by means other than eviction;
- significant disruption to the life of the surrounding community;
- serious breaches of the peace or disorder caused by the encampment.

The same paragraph continues:

> Police forces/commands should not adopt blanket policies or presumptions either for or against the use of [CJPOA 1994] section 61.

It will be important for advisers to have a copy of the relevant police authority's policy on unauthorised encampments. Flagrant failure to follow written policies may also enable a public law challenge to be made.

5.131   The ACPO Guidance on CJPOA 1994 states:

> Local policies agreed between the police and the local authority should make clear the circumstances in which trespassers may be permitted to stay without eviction being started ... It may be felt that a trespass on one site is less damaging to the community than a trespass on a more sensitive site nearby.

The ACPO Guidance goes on to give its own examples of when the use of the power under CJPOA 1994 s61 might be appropriate:

> There will always be circumstances where it is not possible for an unauthorised encampment to be allowed to remain and prompt action will be required. Examples include problems of crime and disorder associated with the site, such as criminal damage, camping on unsuitable sites such as school playing fields, public or private car parks which deny amenities to local residents or which cause highway hazards.

---

166 ODPM Guidance, para 5.10.
167 See paras 5.34–5.35 and discussion of the *Fuller* case, above.

5.132   Police powers of eviction were first introduced in the Public Order Act (POA) 1986. It is clear from the debates during the passage of POA 1986 and CJPOA 1994 through parliament, that the Conservative government intended that the legislation would primarily be used to deal with incidents of 'mass trespass'[168] and this fact gives weight to the argument that police powers of eviction should not be used as a matter of course or following every request from a landowner or occupier of land.

Race relations legislation[169]

5.133   The ACPO Guidance on CJPOA 1994 states:

> Gypsies and Irish Travellers are recognised as racial groups for the purposes of public order and anti-discrimination legislation ... [O]fficers will need to be aware of the responsibilities placed upon *them* to provide the same standard of service as would be expected to those living in settled communities. This applies to all groups of travellers who should not, for example, be subjected to their vehicles being stopped and searched without good reason or required to produce their documents just because they are recognisably from traveller communities' (emphasis in text).

> Discriminatory use of the police powers of eviction may give grounds for a police complaint.[170]

Government departments and other public authorities

5.134   Up until recently, there was a long running debate about the extent to which other public bodies needed to have regard to considerations of common humanity before deciding to evict Gypsies and Travellers from their land. DoE Circular 18/94 states, at paragraph 8:

> Where gypsies are unlawfully encamped on government-owned land, it is for the local authority, with the agreement of the land-owning department, to take any necessary steps to ensure that the encampment does not constitute a hazard to public health. It will continue to be the

---

168 For example, during the passage of CJPOA 1994, the Home Secretary stated: 'Local communities should not have to put up with, or even fear the prospect of, mass invasions by those who selfishly gather, regardless of the rights of others.' *Hansard*, Commons, 11 January 1994, col 29.

169 For further discussion, see chapter 8 below.

170 See further, chapter 8 at paras 8.91–8.93 below.

policy of the Secretary of State that government departments should act in conformity with the advice that unauthorised encampments should not normally be allowed to continue where they are causing a level of nuisance which cannot be effectively controlled, particularly where local authority authorised sites are available. The National Assembly for Wales will act in the same way.

5.135   It has been argued that government departments also have a duty to make enquiries and to take into account humanitarian considerations and should not take eviction action in circumstances where an encampment on land that they own or occupy is not causing a nuisance

5.136   Over recent years there have been a series of cases involving the Forestry Commission.[171] The Forestry Commission practice, when they become aware of an unauthorised encampment, has been to write to the local authority to bring the encampment to their attention and to suggest that the authority may like to investigate whether there are any welfare concerns. The standard letter used invites the authority (or authorities) to revert to the Forestry Commission if they want to make any submissions about the encampment following on from any welfare enquiries.[172] The problem with this procedure, as has been pointed out over the years to the Forestry Commission by Gypsies' and Travellers' solicitors and advisers, is that the local authority concerned are, perhaps, unlikely to take a pro-active approach when the encampment is not on their own land. This may result in no welfare enquiries being carried out.

5.137   The ODPM Guidance appears to have now made the position clear:

> 5.7   ... The police and other public bodies who might be involved in dealing with unauthorised encampments do not have comparable duties [to local authorities] but must still, as public servants, show common humanity to those they meet.
>
> 5.8   The Human Rights Act (HRA) applies to all public bodies including local authorities (including town and parish councils), police, public bodies and the courts. With regard to eviction, the issue that must be determined is whether the interference with

---

171 Now part of the Department of the Environment, Food and Rural Affairs (DEFRA) but formerly part of the Ministry of Agriculture, Fisheries and Food (MAFF).

172 This approach was effectively approved in the case of *R v MAFF ex p Callaghan and others* [2000] HLR 8, though it should be pointed out that this was only a leave application.

Gypsy/Traveller family life and home is justified and proportionate. Any particular welfare needs experienced by unauthorised campers are material in reaching a balanced and proportionate decision. The human rights of members of the settled community are also material if any authority fails to act to curb nuisance from an encampment. Case law is still developing with regard to the sorts of welfare enquiries, which the courts consider necessary to properly take decisions in relation to actions against unauthorised encampments. Cases are testing the requirements under different powers, and the requirements placed on different agencies (authorities, police, and other public landowners). Very generally, court decisions to date suggest:

- All public authorities need to be able to demonstrate that they have taken into consideration any welfare needs of unauthorised campers prior to making a decision to evict.
- The courts recognise that the police and other public bodies have different resources and welfare duties from local authorities. Generally the extent and detail of appropriate enquiries is less for police and non-local authority 'public authorities' …

5.10 Because local authorities have appropriate skills and resources to enable them to make (or co-ordinate) welfare enquiries, it is considered good practice for local authorities to respond positively to requests for assistance in making enquiries from the police or other public bodies.

5.138 However, if a local authority does not respond effectively (or at all) to a request from the police or other public body regarding an unauthorised encampment, it seems clear that the kind of procedure previously adopted by the Forestry Commission will not be sufficient. Some kind of pro-active approach to making welfare enquiries will be required if, despite the guidance, a local authority does not assist. Thus it is suggested that police and other public bodies should adopt their own written procedures for dealing with unauthorised encampments.

5.139 It is further suggested that the above guidance applies equally not only to government departments, such as the Forestry Commission, the Highways Agency or the Ministry of Defence, but also to other public authorities such as Network Rail Infrastructure or the National Trust. Doubtless case law will elaborate on this area in due course.

Other matters

Width of possession orders

5.140   It has long been the practice of certain large landowners, when seeking a possession order against Gypsies or Travellers on an unauthorised encampment, to obtain an order not only covering the piece of land on which the encampment is situated but also covering other land in their ownership in the surrounding area. Recognition of this practice was to be found in the notes to the Civil Procedure Rules:

> Where a claimant, such as the Forestry Commission, owns a number of parcels of land in a particular area which are susceptible to unlawful occupation and is seeking possession in respect of one such parcel which is unlawfully occupied but apprehends that if the order is made the unlawful occupiers will move to one or more of the other parcels and seeks to include them in the possession order such other areas must be clearly defined ... The court can then include in the possession order those parcels to which on the evidence and the law the claimants are found to be entitled.[173]

5.141   It is now clear from the decision in the case of *Drury v Secretary of State for the Environment, Food and Rural Affairs*,[174] that the law as previously propounded in the notes to the Civil Procedure Rules is incorrect. Ms Drury and other Travellers were encamped on a piece of woodland owned by the Forestry Commission. The Forestry Commission obtained a possession order covering the piece of woodland in question but also 30 other pieces of woodland within a 20-mile radius of the encampment on the basis of an assertion made by the Forestry Commission that further unauthorised encampments would occur on other pieces of woodland in the area. The evidence adduced by the Forestry Commission in support of their assertion was minimal: reference was made to the fact that the registration plate on one of the vehicles involved in the current encampment was the same as the registration plate on a vehicle involved in an encampment on the same piece of woodland some five years previously and the fact that there had been a number of other unlawful encampments in the area over recent years (but no

---

173   *Civil Procedure* ('the White Book') 2003, Vol 1, p1748. Reference is also made to the Forestry Commission practice of seeking orders covering a 20-mile radius around the encampment.

174   [2004] EWCA Civ 200, April 2004 *Legal Action* 34.

evidence was provided that these other encampments involved the Travellers on the encampment that was the subject of the action in *Drury*).

5.142   The Court of Appeal quashed the possession order obtained for the other 30 pieces of woodland. Wilson J stated:

> [I]f a claimant entitled to an order for possession of a certain area of land contends that its occupants are likely to decamp to a separate area of land owned by him, the separate area should in my view be included in the order for possession if, but only if, he would have been entitled to an injunction quia timet[175] against the occupants in relation to the separate area ... It follows that the inclusion in a possession order of an area of land owned by the claimant which has not yet been occupied by the defendants should be exceptional. Although it would be foolish to be prescriptive about the nature of the necessary evidence, it seems safe to say that it will usually take the form either of an expression of intention to decamp to the other area or of a history of movement between the two areas from which a real danger of repetition can be inferred or ... of such propinquity and similarity between the two areas as to command the inference of a real danger of decampment from one to the other.[176]

5.143   Though this decision is to be welcomed it is suggested that it does not go far enough and that the legality of wide possession orders may require further consideration by the higher courts. Many advisers acting for Gypsies' and Travellers' consider that CPR Part 55 simply does not permit a court to grant possession for any land other than that on which an unauthorised encampment is situated. CPR Part 55 refers to the land *occupied*.[177] It should also be noted that an order covering other areas of land may encompass other Gypsies or Travellers who happen to be encamped on one of those other areas and who will, therefore, have no opportunity of putting their case forward. Nevertheless, for the moment, wide orders can be obtained but only following the production of very cogent evidence and only in exceptional circumstances.

5.144   If a claimant is seeking a wide possession order covering parcels of land other than the area of land where the encampment is situated, they will have to also properly identify those other areas of land. In other words, certainty as to the identification of all areas of land concerned is essential. In *Christchurch BC v Thomas*

---

175 In other words, an injunction in anticipation of an unlawful event or action. Such an injunction requires a very high level of cogent evidence.

176 [2004] EWCA Civ 200 at paras 20 and 21.

177 CPR PD 55 para 5.

McDonagh,[178] the borough council sought an order for possession of the car park where the Travellers were unlawfully encamped and for all other land in the borough council's ownership. The land, other than the car park, was not specified or described in the claim form or at court. At first instance, an order was made covering both the car park and all other land in the ownership of the borough council. On appeal in the county court the latter part of the order, with regard to all the other land, was quashed. The judge stated:

> The resulting order made by the court ... did not sufficiently identify the land to which it referred. It was suggested on behalf of Christchurch that the order could be amended to add to the order the words 'as shown on the terriers.'[179] This would not be sufficient to remedy the deficiency. It is unrealistic to expect travellers to be able to refer to records held by a local authority to discover whether land is owned by that authority.

The court also felt that the wider order originally obtained was 'disproportionate' having regard to the Human Rights Act 1998.

Injunctions

5.145 Occasionally local authorities will seek injunctions against Gypsies or Travellers who frequent their area and have no authorised place to stay. Sometimes the motivation for such an action by the local authority will be allegations of nuisance or anti-social behaviour made against the Gypsies or Travellers concerned. However, sometimes the motivation will be simply to try and prevent the Gypsies or Travellers stopping on any land in the area on the basis of frequency or number of unauthorised encampments by the group of Gypsies or Travellers in question. Such injunctions will be brought under the powers contained in Local Government Act 1972 s222.

5.146 It is suggested that such injunction actions may be susceptible to judicial review (though no definitive case law on the matter exists as yet with regard to unauthorised encampments).[180] In *Stoke-on-Trent CC v B&Q (Retail) Ltd*,[181] it was held that it must be established that

---

178 Bournemouth County Court (2002) 11 July, HHJ Mastin.

179 The local authority records of land in its ownership.

180 However, with regard to unauthorised developments (ie, where the Gypsies or Travellers have not obtained planning permission to reside on the land) there is very extensive case-law, culminating in the case of *South Buckinghamshire DC v Porter* [2003] UKHL 26. For full discussion of this case, see chapter 4 at paras 4.107–4.124 above.

181 [1984] 2 All ER 332.

the defendant is not merely infringing the law but that he or she is deliberately or flagrantly flouting it before an injunction will be granted. It is also suggested that such an order would be disproportionate in terms of article 8 of the European Convention on Human Rights, especially since a less severe form of action[182] could be taken. Moreover, local authorities who seek such orders will ignore the government's recommendations in the ODPM Guidance which states at paragraph 4.4:

> All local authorities experiencing unauthorised encampments should provide either transit sites or stopping places to cater for Gypsies and Travellers moving within or passing through their area.

It is suggested that local authorities should not be allowed to ignore this recommendation and similar recommendations contained within the ODPM Guidance by simply seeking to obtain injunctions banning certain groups of Gypsies or Travellers from their area.

Conclusion

5.147   The government position on unauthorised camping is made clear in the ODPM Guidance which at paragraph 4.2 states:

> In a context where the number of Gypsy caravans exceeds the number of authorised places where they can stop – which is the case in England – provision of suitable accommodation for Gypsies and Travellers must be seen as a vital part of an approach to dealing with unauthorised camping.

5.148   The sometimes dire effects on Gypsies and Travellers of the lack of sites (of all sorts, including transit and emergency stopping places) are well documented. For example, the report from the Equality of Opportunity Committee of the National Assembly for Wales stated:

> [S]ervice providers in the education and health fields both identified accommodation issues as one of the barriers to successful service provision in their area. Undoubtedly the lack of appropriate accommodation can be a significant barrier to education. Evictions from

---

182 Such as, in the case of anti-social behaviour, an anti-social behaviour order under the Crime and Disorder Act 1998, or, in the case of an unauthorised encampment, a possession order.

unauthorised sites can lead to a lack of continuity in education and discourage parents from seeking to register their children in the first place.[183]

5.149   The Institute for Public Policy Research (IPPR) has stated:

There is an unacceptable and persistent culture of linking anti-social behaviour and the accommodation needs of Travellers and Gypsies. Accommodation needs and anti-social behaviour are two completely separate issues and they must be dealt with as such, irrespective of the pressure, both political and social, to link the two. As was pointed out by many of those with whom we consulted ... this is not done with any other section of the community and would be considered racist under any other circumstances.[184]

5.150   It remains to be seen how the police deal with their new powers under Criminal Justice and Public Order Act (CJPOA) 1994 ss62A–E. Early indications are that police forces appreciate that these new powers cannot realistically be put into action until sufficient transit sites have been provided. In general, with regard to the CJPOA 1994 powers of eviction conferred on both the police and local authorities, the criminalisation of trespass[185] has often, due to the speed with which evictions can take place, precluded Gypsies and Travellers from effectively challenging such eviction actions where they believe that substantive defences or public law challenges may lie. This is especially the case with the police powers.

5.151   The law on how public bodies should deal with the conduct of welfare enquiries and the legality of wide possession orders is ripe for further development.

5.152   The following chapter looks at the homelessness legislation as it relates to Gypsies and Travellers. Where Gypsies or Travellers are on an unauthorised encampment on local authority land (where that encampment is not causing severe nuisance or disruption), and where the same Gypsies and Travellers have made a homeless application in the hope of obtaining an authorised pitch or piece of land,

---

183   *Review of Service Provision for Gypsies and Travellers* (National Assembly for Wales, 2003) para 12.21. For further discussion of this, in the context of the law relating to education and health, see chapter 7 at paras 7.11, 7.63–7.65 below.

184   H Crawley, *Moving Forward: the provision of accommodation for Travellers and Gypsies* (IPPR 2004) p13.

185   First brought in, in terms of police powers, by the Public Order Act 1986.

there is a forceful argument for allowing that encampment to remain where it is while the homelessness application is progressed.[186]

5.153   Campaigners for Gypsies and Travellers have called for the return of the duty to provide (or facilitate the provision of) sites. The Traveller Law Reform Coalition has stated:

> On a daily basis, Gypsies and Travellers without authorised stopping places are hounded from one place to another. Due to the repeal of the duty the number of pitches on official sites has actually declined with some sites being shut down altogether. Despite their opposition at the time of the 1994 Act, the Labour Government ... has singularly failed to redress this disastrous situation.[187]

---

186 For a full discussion of these issues, see chapter 6 para 6.93 below.
187 Traveller Law Reform Coalition, *Decent Homes for All* (pamphlet) 2004. For further discussion of future issues for Gypsy and Traveller law, see chapter 9.

CHAPTER 6

Homelessness as it relates to Gypsies and Travellers

continued overleaf

Homelessness legislation

Introduction

6.1   This chapter aims to highlight aspects of the homelessness legislation in England and Wales which are of specific interest to and importance for Gypsies and Travellers. However, some broad idea of the law in this area is required and the first part of this chapter aims to provide that.[1]

6.2   The relevant statutory provisions are to be found in the Housing Act 1996 Part VII, as amended by the Homelessness Act 2002.[2]

6.3   Housing Act (HA) 1996 places an obligation on local housing authorities to secure that suitable accommodation is available for a person who is:

- homeless;
- eligible for assistance;
- in priority need of accommodation;
- and who did not become homeless intentionally.

There are also other obligations imposed by HA 1996 which will be discussed further below.

6.4   There are three categories of person who are ineligible for assistance[3] (although they may still benefit from the general 'advice and information' duty):[4]

- 'persons from abroad', which means persons who are subject to immigration control under the Asylum and Immigration Act 1999, unless they are re-qualified by regulations;[5]
- those asylum-seekers, or dependants of asylum-seekers, who are not excluded as 'persons from abroad', but who will still be ineligible for assistance if they have accommodation in the

---

1   For a full coverage of homelessness, see Arden and Hunter, *Homelessness and Allocations* (Legal Action Group, Revised 6th edn, 2003).

2   For Scotland the relevant statute is the Housing (Scotland) Act 1987 as amended and for Northern Ireland reference should be made to the Housing (Northern Ireland) Order 1988.

3   The question of 'eligibility' can be a complex one and is beyond the scope of this book. For a full discussion of this issue see note 1 above.

4   HA 1996 s179.

5   HA 1996 s185(1) and (2).

United Kingdom, however temporary, which is available for their occupation;[6] and

- certain nationals of European Economic Area countries.[7]

This obviously may be of relevance to Roma from Eastern Europe. If an applicant is not within these categories, he or she will be 'eligible for assistance'.

Homelessness

6.5   HA 1996 s175 defines homelessness:

(1) A person is homeless if he has no accommodation available for his occupation, in the United Kingdom or elsewhere, which he –
   (a) is entitled to occupy by virtue of an interest in it or by virtue of an order of a court,
   (b) has an express or implied licence to occupy, or
   (c) occupies as a residence by virtue of any enactment or rule of law giving him the right to remain in occupation or restricting the right of another person to recover possession.

(2) A person is also homeless if he has accommodation but –
   (a) he cannot secure entry to it, or
   (b) it consists of a moveable structure, vehicle or vessel designed or adapted for human habitation and there is no place where he is entitled or permitted both to place it and reside in it.

(3) A person shall not be treated as having accommodation unless it is accommodation which it would be reasonable for him to continue to occupy.

(4) A person is threatened with homelessness if it is likely that he will become homeless within 28 days.

6.6   HA 1996 s175(2)(b) will be the most relevant provision for Gypsies and Travellers, though HA 1996 s175(3) may also be relevant for those Gypsies and Travellers that have left conventional housing.[8]

---

6 HA 1996 s186(1).

7 The European Economic Area encompasses the European Union (EU), plus Iceland, Norway and Liechtenstein. The homelessness regulations regarding eligibility are amended by the Allocation of Housing and Homelessness (Amendment) (England) Regulations 2004 SI No 1235, which are targeted at nationals of the eight EU Accession countries but introduce wider changes affecting persons from abroad not being persons subject to immigration control. The regulations do not cover Wales.

8 'Conventional housing' means bricks and mortar accommodation.

6.7 'Accommodation available for occupation' is defined by HA 1996 s176 thus:

> Accommodation shall be regarded as available for a person's occupation only if it is available for occupation by him together with –
> (a) any other person who normally resides with him as a member of his family, or
> (b) any other person who might reasonably be expected to reside with him.[9]

6.8 The phrase 'reasonable to continue to occupy' is defined by HA 1996 s177 as follows:

> (1) It is not reasonable for a person to continue to occupy accommodation if it is probable that this will lead to domestic violence or other violence against him, or against –
> (a) a person who normally resides with him as a member of his family, or
> (b) any other person who might reasonably be expected to reside with him.

Priority need

6.9 HA 1996 s189 deals with 'priority need for accommodation':

> (1) The following have a priority need for accommodation –
> (a) a pregnant woman or a person with whom she resides or might reasonably be expected to reside;
> (b) a person with whom dependent children reside or might reasonably be expected to reside;
> (c) a person who is vulnerable as a result of old age, mental illness or handicap or physical disability or other special reason, or with whom such a person resides or might reasonably be expected to reside;
> (d) a person who is homeless or threatened with homelessness as a result of an emergency such as flood, fire or other disaster.
> (2) The Secretary of State may by order –
> (a) specify further descriptions of persons as having a priority need for accommodation, and
> (b) amend or repeal any part of subsection (1).[10]

---

9 The question of extended Gypsy and Traveller families is discussed at para 6.71 below.

10 For a discussion of extended Gypsy and Traveller families, see para 6.71 below. 'Other special reason' is a category that may have specific relevance to single homeless Gypsies and Travellers, as discussed at paras 6.72–6.76 below.

6.10   In Wales, the HA 1996 s189(2)(a) power has been used to specify:[11]

    (i)   all those who are aged 18 or over, and under 21, if at any time while they were a child they were looked after, accommodated or fostered, or they are at particular risk of sexual or financial exploitation;

    (ii) all 16- and 17- year olds;

    (iii) those without dependent children who have been subject to domestic violence, who are at risk of such violence or would be if they returned home;

    (iv) those who formerly served in the regular armed forces and have been homeless since leaving those forces;

    (v) former prisoners who have been homeless since leaving custody, provided they have a local connection with the local housing authority.

6.11   In England, the section 189(2)(a) power has been used to specify:[12]

    (i)   all 16- and 17- year olds, provided they are not a relevant child (as defined by the Children Act (CA) 1989), or a child to whom the local authority owes a duty to provide accommodation under CA 1989 s20;

    (ii) any person who is aged 18 to 20, other than a relevant student,[13] who at any time after reaching the age of 16 but while still under 18 was, but is no longer, looked after, accommodated or fostered;

    (iii) those who are vulnerable because they have previously been looked after, accommodated or fostered;

    (iv) those who are vulnerable as a result of service in Her Majesty's regular armed forces;

    (v) those who are vulnerable as a result of having served a custodial sentence, having been committed for contempt of court or having been remanded in custody;

    (vi) those who are vulnerable because they have had to cease to occupy accommodation because of violence or threats of violence which are likely to be carried out.

---

11 Homeless Persons (Priority Need) (Wales) Order 2001 SI No 607.

12 Homelessness (Priority Need for Accommodation) (England) Order 2002 SI No 2051.

13 As defined by CA 1989 s24B(3).

Intentional homelessness

6.12 The phrase 'intentional homelessness' is defined in HA 1996 s191 as:

> (1) A person becomes homeless intentionally if he deliberately does or fails to do anything in consequence of which he ceases to occupy accommodation which is available for his occupation and which it would have been reasonable for him to continue to occupy.
>
> (2) For the purposes of subsection (1) an act or omission in good faith on the part of a person who was unaware of any relevant fact shall not be treated as deliberate.
>
> (3) A person shall be treated as becoming homeless intentionally if –
>
> > (a) he enters into an arrangement under which he is required to cease to occupy accommodation which it would have been reasonable for him to continue to occupy, and
> >
> > (b) the purpose of the arrangement is to enable him to become entitled to assistance under this Part,
>
> and there is no other good reason why he is homeless.

There is a similar definition to cover the situation of becoming threatened with homelessness intentionally.[14]

Local connection

6.13 A person has a local connection with the district of a local housing authority if he or she has a connection with it because:

- he or she is, or was, normally resident there of his or her own choice;
- he or she is employed there;
- of family associations; or
- of special circumstances.[15]

6.14 A person in the regular armed forces will not be considered as either employed in the district or as resident in the district.[16] A person is not resident in a district if he or she is detained under the authority of an Act of Parliament, for example, a prisoner or a patient in a mental hospital.[17] The secretary of state may specify other

---

14 HA 1996 s196.
15 HA 1996 s199(1).
16 HA 1996 s199(2) and (3)(a).
17 HA 1996 s199(3)(b).

circumstances when someone will not be treated as either resident or employed in a district but this power has not been used to-date.[18]

Preliminary duties

6.15   Where a local authority have reason to believe that an applicant may be homeless or threatened with homelessness, they shall make such enquiries as are necessary to see whether –

- he or she is eligible for assistance, and
- if so, what duty, if any, might be owed to him or her.[19]

6.16   On completion of their inquiries, the local authority must notify the applicant of their decision in writing and, if it is against the interests of the applicant, must also notify him or her of the reasons for that decision.[20] The notification should also tell the applicant about his or her right to request a review of the decision (within 21 days).[21] The Homelessness Code of Guidance[22] states, at paragraph 3.18:

> Wherever possible, housing authorities should aim to complete their inquiries, and notify the applicant, within 33 working days of accepting the duty to make inquiries under [HA 1996] s184.

6.17   The local authority may also make inquiries into whether the applicant has a local connection with the district of another local housing authority in England, Wales or Scotland.[23] If the local authority decide to make a local connection referral to another authority,[24] they shall still notify the applicant of this decision and of the reasons for it.[25]

6.18   The notice required to be given to the applicant, if not received by him or her, shall be treated as having been given to him or her if it is made available at the authority's office for a reasonable period

---

18 HA 1996 s199(5). The particular position of Gypsies and Travellers who may be moving around several districts or forced by frequent evictions to move around several districts, will be discussed at para 6.87 below.

19 HA 1996 s184(1).

20 HA 1996 s184(3) and (6).

21 HA 1996 s184(5).

22 See further at para 6.42 below.

23 HA 1996 s184(2).

24 See further at paras 6.13–6.14 above.

25 HA 1996 s184(4).

for collection by him or her.[26] In other words, the burden is on the applicant who does not receive the decision to go to the local authority's office and ask for it.

6.19 Enquiries might take some time to complete. Meanwhile, if the local housing authority has reason to believe that the applicant may be homeless, eligible for assistance and has a priority need, they have a duty to secure that accommodation is available for his or her occupation pending a decision as to what duty, if any, is owed to him or her.[27] The duty is placed on the authority to whom the applicant applies, regardless of any question about local connection.[28] The accommodation available must be available for occupation by the applicant together with any other person who normally resides with him or her as a family member or any other person who might reasonably be expected to reside with him or her.[29] The duty to provide interim accommodation will end once an applicant has been notified of the local authority's decision. However, if the applicant requests a review of the decision then the local authority has the power to provide interim accommodation pending that review.[30]

Principal duties

6.20 The principal duties that may be owed to an applicant by a local housing authority can be divided into limited duties and full duties.

Limited duties

6.21 If the authority are satisfied that the applicant is homeless and in priority need but that he or she is intentionally homeless, they shall secure that accommodation is available for his or her occupation for such period as they consider will give the applicant a reasonable opportunity of securing accommodation for his or her occupation and provide him or her with appropriate advice and assistance to try and locate such accommodation.[31] Such advice and assistance should

---

26 HA 1996 s184(6).
27 HA 1996 s188(1) and see paras 6.88–6.93 below, for a more detailed
    discussion on the interim accommodation duty and its relevance to homeless
    applications made by Gypsies and Travellers.
28 HA 1996 s188(2).
29 HA 1996 s176.
30 HA 1996 s188(3).
31 HA 1996 s190(2).

include information about the likely availability in the authority's district of types of accommodation appropriate to the applicant's housing needs.[32] This advice and assistance should be provided after the applicant's housing needs have been assessed.[33] In the case of Gypsies and Travellers, such information would presumably include details of local authority or private Gypsy/ Traveller sites in the district.

6.22   If the authority provides its own accommodation in order to comply with the above duty, it will not be secure unless and until the authority notifies the applicant otherwise under the allocation provisions.[34] If the authority fulfil their duty by arranging for accommodation with a private landlord, a tenancy granted in this way cannot be an assured tenancy before the end of the period of 12 months beginning with the date when the applicant was notified of the local authority's decision or the date of notification of the decision on review or appeal, unless during that period the landlord notifies the applicant otherwise.[35]

6.23   If the authority –

- are not satisfied that the applicant has a priority need, or
- are so satisfied but also conclude that he or she became threatened with homelessness intentionally,

they shall secure that he or she is provided (whether by the authority or by someone else) with advice and assistance in any attempts he or she may make to secure that accommodation does not cease to be available to him or her.[36] This advice and assistance should be provided after the applicant's housing needs have been assessed.[37] If homelessness does then occur, and the applicant is in priority need but intentionally homeless, a period of temporary accommodation[38] will then be available.

32   HA 1996 s190(5), inserted by HA 2002 Sch 1 para 10.
33   HA 1996 s190(4), inserted by HA 2002 Sch 1 para 10.
34   HA 1985 Sch 1 para 4, substituted by HA 1996 Sch 17 para 3. The allocation provisions under HA 1996 Part VI are outside the scope of this book – see further in Arden and Hunter *Homelessness and Allocations* (Legal Action Group, Revised 6th edn, 2003). No doubt, in terms of Gypsy sites under local authority control, there will usually be specific allocation policies that the local authority operates – see also chapter 3.
35   HA 1996 s209.
36   HA 1996 s195(5).
37   HA 1996 s195(6), inserted by HA 2002 Sch 1 para 14.
38   See para 6.21 above.

6.24   If the authority are satisfied that the applicant did not become homeless intentionally but are also satisfied that he or she is not in priority need, they may nevertheless secure that accommodation is available for occupation by the applicant.[39] If satisfied that he or she is threatened with homelessness but not intentionally, the authority may take reasonable steps to secure that accommodation does not cease to be available.[40]

6.25   Similarly, if the authority are satisfied that the applicant has a priority need and is threatened with homelessness, but not intentionally, they shall take reasonable steps to ensure that accommodation does not cease to be available for his or her occupation.[41] However this duty cannot affect the right of the authority to gain possession of its own accommodation, that is, it cannot be used as a defence by an individual.[42]

Full duties

6.26   Where a local authority are satisfied that an applicant is homeless, in priority need and not intentionally homeless, they shall secure that accommodation is available for occupation by the applicant.[43] The accommodation must also be available for any other family member who normally resides with him or her, or anyone else who might reasonably be expected to reside with him or her.[44]

6.27   A local housing authority may discharge this duty as follows –

- by securing that suitable accommodation provided by the authority is available,
- by securing that the applicant obtains suitable accommodation from some other person (which may include another local authority or a housing association), or
- by giving the applicant such advice and assistance as will secure that suitable accommodation is available from some other person.[45]

6.28   In deciding whether accommodation is 'suitable' for a person, the local housing authority shall have regard to certain provisions of HA

39 HA 1996 s192(3).
40 HA 1996 s195(9), inserted by HA 2002 s5(2).
41 HA 1996 s195(2).
42 HA 1996 s195(3).
43 HA 1996 s193(1) and (2).
44 HA 1996 s176 and see para 6.19 above.
45 HA 1996 s206(1).

1985 which relate to slum clearance, overcrowding and houses in multiple occupation.[46] The secretary of state can add to the definition of what is 'suitable'.[47] So far as reasonably practicable, the authority shall ensure that accommodation is available for the occupation of the applicant in their district.[48] If an applicant is placed in another area, the authority must give notice to the local housing authority with responsibility for that area; any such notice must contain certain specified details[49] and must be given in writing within two weeks of the accommodation being made available.[50]

6.29   Where a local authority provides its own accommodation in discharge of the duty, it is not secure.[51] This is not normally relevant to a Gypsy or Traveller seeking other than bricks and mortar accommodation, since occupants of local authority Gypsy or Traveller sites have minimal security of tenure.[52]

6.30   The 'full duty' owed to the applicant can be brought to an end if:

- the applicant, having been informed by the authority of the possible consequences of refusal and his or her right to request a review, refuses an offer of accommodation which the authority is satisfied is suitable for him or her and the authority then notify him or her that they consider that they have discharged their duty;
- the applicant ceases to be eligible for assistance;
- the applicant becomes homeless intentionally from the accommodation made available for his or her accommodation;
- the applicant accepts an offer under HA 1996 Part VI (the allocation provisions);
- the applicant accepts an offer of an assured (not an assured shorthold) tenancy from a private landlord;
- the applicant otherwise voluntarily ceases to occupy as his or her only or principal home the accommodation made available for his or her occupation;

46 HA 1996 s210(1).
47 HA 1996 s210(2). See the Homelessness (Suitability of Accommodation) Order 1996 SI No 3204 (in force 20 January 1997) and the Homelessness (Suitability of Accommodation) (England) Order 2003 SI No 3326 (in force 1 April 2004). For a full discussion of 'suitable accommodation' as it relates to Gypsies and Travellers, see paras 6.88–6.99 below.
48 HA 1996 s208(1).
49 HA 1996 s208(2) and (3).
50 HA 1996 s208(4).
51 HA 1985 Schedule 1 para 4.
52 See chapter 3 above.

- the applicant, having been informed of the possible consequences of refusal and his or her right to request a review of the suitability of the accommodation, refuses a final offer (which is defined as an offer 'made in writing' stating 'that it is a final offer for the purposes of [HA 1996 s193(7)]'[53]) and the authority is satisfied that the offer is suitable and that it is reasonable for the applicant to accept the offer;
- the applicant, in certain circumstances, accepts the offer of an assured shorthold tenancy from a private landlord.[54]

Local connection

6.31   The local connection provisions allow one local housing authority to transfer the responsibility of ensuring that accommodation becomes available to another authority where –

- the applicant was placed in accommodation in that area by another local housing authority in the first place,[55] or
- neither the applicant nor any person who might reasonably be expected to reside with him or her has a local connection with the district of the authority they are applying to, and the applicant or a person who might reasonably be expected to reside with him or her has a local connection with the district of another authority, and neither the applicant nor a person who might reasonably be expected to reside with him or her will run the risk of domestic violence in that other area.[56]

6.32   The definition of what amounts to 'local connection' is supplemented by the Local Authority Agreement, which is discussed in further detail at paras 6.85–6.87 below. The applicant can request a review of a local authority's decision that she or he has a local connection.[57] There is an arbitration system put in place to deal with disagreements between local authorities.[58] The arbitration decision itself can be subject to review and appeal.[59]

---

53 HA 1996 s193(7A).
54 HA 1996 s193(5)–(8). For fuller details see Arden and Hunter, *Homelessness and Allocations* (Legal Action Group, Revised 6th edn, 2003).
55 HA 1996 s198(4). See para 6.13 above.
56 HA 1996 s198(2).
57 HA 1996 s200(2).
58 HA 1996 s198(5).
59 HA 1996 s202(1)(d) and (e).

Protection of property

6.33   Where a local authority is or has been under a duty under HA 1996 ss188, 190, 193, 195 or 200,[60] it may also be under a duty to take reasonable steps to prevent the loss of an applicant's property, or prevent or mitigate damage to it.[61] An applicant's property includes the personal property of any person reasonably expected to reside with him or her.[62]

6.34   The duty arises where the local authority have reason to believe that there is a danger of loss of, or damage to, any personal property of an applicant by reason of his or her inability to protect it or deal with it, and no other suitable arrangements have been or are being made.[63]

6.35   In other circumstances, the local authority have a power to protect property.[64] The local authority, when agreeing to protect property under these provisions, can impose reasonable charges and conditions as to the disposal of property.[65] These provisions are not reviewable but could be subject to public law challenge by way of judicial review.[66]

6.36   These provisions might be most relevant to Gypsies and Travellers who have decided to seek conventional housing. For example, such applicants may require storage for their caravans pending the provision of suitable accommodation.

Homelessness strategies

6.37   The Homelessness Act (HA) 2002 imposed a new duty on local authorities to carry out a homelessness review and to formulate and publish a homelessness strategy based on the results of that review.[67]

6.38   A homelessness review means a review by a local authority of:

(a) the levels, and likely future levels, of homelessness in their district;

---

60 See paras 6.19–6.21, 6.24–6.27 and 6.32 above.
61 HA 1996 s211(2).
62 HA 1996 s211(5).
63 HA 1996 s211(1).
64 HA 1996 s211(3).
65 HA 1996 s211(4).
66 For a fuller discussion of judicial review, see appendix A below.
67 HA 2002 s1(1) and (3).

(b) the activities which are carried out for any purpose mentioned in paragraph 6.39 below (or which contribute to their achievement); and

(c) the resources available to the housing authority, the social services authority for their district, other public authorities, voluntary organisations and other persons for such activities.[68]

6.39 The purposes of the review are:

(a) preventing homelessness in the district of the authority;

(b) securing that accommodation is or will be available for people in the district who are or may become homeless;

(c) providing support for people in the district –
- who are or may become homeless; or
- who have been homeless and need support to prevent them becoming homeless again.[69]

6.40 A homelessness strategy is a strategy formulated by a local housing authority to deal with those matters mentioned in paragraph 6.39 above.[70]

6.41 Research by Lord Avebury[71] has shown that the majority of local authorities that had recorded unauthorised encampments in their district,[72] had failed to even mention Gypsies and Travellers in their review and strategy. It is difficult to see how local authorities can properly deal with applications from homeless Gypsies and Travellers if they have failed to even address those needs in their strategy. It is further suggested that the strategy should include an assessment of available land in the local authority area and the possibility of assistance from other public authorities, neighbouring local authorities or (where relevant) the county council.[73]

---

68 HA 2002 s2(1).

69 HA 2002 s2(2).

70 HA 2002 s3(1).

71 The peer who, as Eric Lubbock MP, sponsored the private members bill that became the Caravan Sites Act 1968. The research is available on Lord Avebury's own website www.btinternet.com/~ericavebury/-mm/Gypsies.htm. The research showed that, of 152 local authorities whose strategies were checked, 107 (70.4 %) did not mention Gypsies or Travellers.

72 According to the ODPM Gypsy Count figures.

73 See para 6.93 below.

Code of guidance

6.42   In the exercise of their functions under the homelessness provisions of HA 1996, local authorities are bound to have regard to such guidance as may from time to time be given by the secretary of state.[74] The secretary of state has issued a Code of Guidance.[75]

Reviews and appeals

6.43   Applicants have a statutory right to request an internal review[76] of any of the following decisions regarding:

- eligibility for assistance;
- referral to another authority under the local connection provisions;
- whether the conditions for local connection referral are met;
- what duty is owed following a local connection referral; or
- any decision about the suitability of accommodation offered in discharge of duty.

6.44   The right to a review does not include the right to a review of an earlier decision made following a review.[77] If the local authority in question have a procedure involving a further 'review' stage, it is important that the Gypsy or Traveller (or their adviser or solicitor) obtain confirmation that the previous decision no longer stands, otherwise, it will be necessary to appeal to the county court within the necessary time limit from the *original* review decision.[78]

6.45   Pending the outcome of the review, the local authority has a discretion to provide accommodation for the applicant.[79]

6.46   An appeal can be made to the county court if the applicant either:

- is dissatisfied with the outcome of the review; or
- has not been notified of the outcome within the time-limit prescribed.[80]

---

74 HA 1996 s182.
75 Homelessness Code of Guidance for Local Authorities.
76 HA 1996 s202.
77 HA 1996 s202(2).
78 *Demetri v Westminster CC* [2000] 1 WLR 772.
79 HA 1996 s188(3).
80 HA 1996 s204(1).

6.47   Appeal lies only on a point of law, whether arising from the original decision (if the local authority has failed to conclude the review within the time prescribed) or from the decision on review.[81]

6.48   Pending an appeal, the local authority has a discretion to provide accommodation for the applicant.[82] If the authority refuses or fails to do so, the applicant may also appeal that decision to the county court.[83]

6.49   The procedure to be adopted on review and on appeal to the county court are detailed in appendix A below.

Criminal offences

6.50   It is a criminal offence knowingly or recklessly to make a statement which is false in a material particular, or knowingly to withhold information which an authority has reasonably required in connection with the exercise of its functions under the homelessness legislation, with intent to induce an authority to believe that the person making the statement or withholding the information, or any other person, is entitled to accommodation or assistance.[84]

Effect of the homelessness legislation on Gypsies and Travellers

R (Margaret Price) v Carmarthenshire CC[85]

6.51   *Price* is the leading case on homeless Gypsies and Travellers. Mrs Price and her family are Irish Travellers and were homeless in terms of the legislation because they were living on an unauthorised encampment and did not have an authorised pitch for their caravans.[86] The family had been resorting to Carmarthenshire for several years and applied to the local authority for homeless persons accommodation. In 2001 Mrs Price had made an enquiry about conventional (that is, bricks and mortar) accommodation. When she

---

81   HA 1996 s204(1).
82   HA 1996 s204(4).
83   HA 1996 s204A.
84   HA 1996 s214(1).
85   [2003] EWHC 42 Admin; March 2003 *Legal Action* 30.
86   HA 1996 s175(2)(b) – see para 6.5 above.

made her subsequent homeless application to the local authority, Mrs Price explained that she had made her earlier enquiry purely because of pressure from a local authority officer and that she had had no intention of moving into conventional housing.

6.52   In the planning case of *Clarke v Secretary of State for the Environment Transport and the Regions,*[87] the High Court (later upheld by the Court of Appeal) had overturned the decision of a planning inspector who had refused planning permission to Mr Clarke, a Romani Gypsy, in circumstances where the inspector had taken into account a previous offer of settled accommodation that had been made to him by the local authority. Burton J, at first instance, stated that, if an 'aversion to conventional housing' were established then 'bricks and mortar, if offered, are unsuitable, just as would be the offer of a rat-infested barn.'[88]

6.53   In Mrs Price's case, the local authority had regard to the *Clarke* decision, but concluded from the facts of Mrs Price's case (including the fact that her mother, who had previously travelled, now lived in a bungalow due to ill health, and her sister, who travelled with her, had previously lived in settled accommodation for a short period of time) that she did not have a 'cultural aversion to conventional housing'. They offered her a house which she refused. They then sought to evict her from the piece of their own land where they had, until then, been 'tolerating' her encampment. Mrs Price sought judicial review of the local authority's decision.

6.54   In the High Court, Newman J quashed the decision to evict, stating:

> In order to meet the requirements and accord respect, something more than 'taking account' of an applicant's gypsy culture is required. As the court in *Chapman*[89] stated, respect includes the positive obligation to act so as to facilitate the gypsy way of life, without being under a duty to guarantee it to an applicant in any particular case.[90]

6.55   Newman J also found that, in seeking to respect her Gypsy way of life, the local authority's approach was flawed because it had given too much weight to the fact that she had seemingly been prepared to

87 *Clarke v Secretary of State for the Environment, Transport and the Regions and Tunbridge Wells BC* [2001] EWHC 800 Admin; [2002] JPL 552; July 2002 *Legal Action* 27. For full discussion of this case see chapter 4 at paras 4.80–4.85 above.
88 [2001] EWHC 800 Admin at para 34.
89 *Chapman v UK* [2001] 33 EHRR 399 and see chapter 2.
90 *R (Price) v Carmarthenshire CC* [2003] EWHC 42 Admin at para 19.

give it up to live in conventional housing in 2001 and had used this as sufficient reason for disregarding her Gypsy way of life altogether when considering her wishes. Equally he found that, had the local authority reached the conclusion that her cultural commitment to traditional life was so powerful as to present great difficulty in her living in conventional housing, the local authority was not bound by duty to find her a pitch, but her cultural commitment would have been a significant factor in considering how far the authority should go to facilitate her traditional way of life.

6.56   It is worth noting that the Code of Guidance[91] addresses the position of homeless Gypsies and Travellers under the heading 'Applicants who normally occupy moveable accommodation (eg, caravans, houseboats)':

> If a duty to secure accommodation arises in such cases, the housing authority are not required to make equivalent accommodation available (or provide a site or berth for the applicant's own accommodation), but they should consider whether such options are reasonably available, particularly where this would provide the most suitable solution to the applicant's accommodation needs. These circumstances will be particularly relevant in the case of gypsies and travellers, whose applications must be considered on the same basis as all other applicants. If no pitch or berth is available to enable them to resume occupation of their moveable home, it is open to the housing authority to discharge its homelessness obligations by arranging for some other form of suitable accommodation to be made available.[92]

6.57   It is suggested that the authors of the Code of Guidance have misunderstood the reality of the situation faced by most homeless Gypsies and Travellers: they will not have given up the occupation of their caravans or vehicles but will still be living in them on an unauthorised site, or on their own land without planning permission to do so.[93] It is also suggested that this part of the guidance does not correctly take account of the ruling in *Price* that, in certain circumstances, it is incumbent on the local authority to use their best endeavours to see if a pitch or land can be made available.

91 Homelessness Code of Guidance for Local Authorities.
92 Homelessness Code of Guidance, para 11.40.
93 For more detail on 'unauthorised developments', see chapter 4 above. It should be pointed out that a Gypsy or Traveller who has failed to get planning permission to reside on his on her own land, and who is facing enforcement action by the local authority, would also be entitled to make a homeless application.

6.58   There is no reason why houseboat dwellers might not be able to avail themselves of the court's decision in the *Price* case.

When is a Gypsy or Traveller regarded as being homeless?

6.59   A Gypsy or Traveller is homeless if there is no place where he or she is entitled or permitted to place his or her caravan or vehicle.[94] In this context, what do the words 'entitled' or 'permitted' mean?

6.60   In *R v Chiltern DC ex p Roberts et al*,[95] the applicants were Travelling Showpeople who had lost their winter accommodation. They were travelling in connection with their work during the summer months when they made their application. When travelling from fair to fair, they were permitted to stay on land provided by the organisers of the fairs. They were held not to be 'homeless' since, at the time of the applications, they were 'permitted' to stop in various places.

6.61   In *Smith v Wokingham DC*,[96] the applicants were parked in a caravan on land belonging to the county council. Though they had no express permission or licence, they had lived at this encampment for two and a half years. The county court judged decided that this amounted to 'permission' and, accordingly, that they were not homeless.

6.62   In *R (O'Donoghue) v Brighton and Hove CC*,[97] the applicant had been allowed to place her caravans on a piece of land owned by the local authority for a 'tolerated' period of 30 days. Once that period had ended, she made a homelessness application to the authority. The authority decided that she was not homeless and, therefore, that they did not, at that stage, owe her any duty to provide interim accommodation. No eviction action had yet been commenced by the local authority. In refusing permission to proceed with a judicial review application concerning the failure to provide interim accommodation, Jackson J held that the applicant had effectively been given implicit permission to remain before eviction action was commenced and that the judicial review application was premature.

94 HA 1996 s175(2)(b).
95 [1990] 23 HLR 387, QBD.
96 April 1980 *LAG Bulletin* 92, CC.
97 [2003] EWCA Civ 459.

When refusing permission to appeal that decision, the Court of Appeal agreed that the application for judicial review was premature because no eviction action had been taken but accepted that it was arguable that the applicant no longer had permission to remain on the land and that she was homeless at the time that she made her application.

6.63   As an alternative to challenging the failure to provide interim accommodation, by means of judicial review,[98] Ms O'Donoghue could have requested that the local authority conduct a review of its decision that she was not homeless.[99]

6.64   It has to be said that there is a lack of clear, authoritative case-law on this area. For example, it could be said that a Gypsy or Traveller who is allowed by a landowner to remain on their land for a period of time, with or without payment to the landowner of any fee or rent, is 'entitled' to remain there. However, if that occupation required planning permission, which it almost certainly would,[100] it could also be argued that the Gypsy or Traveller did not have 'permission' to remain there.

6.65   Following *O'Donoghue*, it is suggested that a challenge by way of judicial review (presumably because of a failure to provide interim accommodation following a homelessness application),[101] where no actual 'permission' had been given by the landowner or occupier of the land, would only be possible once some form of eviction action is commenced or eviction is effected. By way of contrast, an internal review (and, if that was unsuccessful, a county court appeal) could potentially be lodged in such a case, before any eviction action has been taken. However, the decision in *Smith v Wokingham DC* suggests that such an option may not be possible where the occupation of the land had continued for a long period of time, even if it did so without licence or consent.

Making a homeless application

6.66   Before any of these matters can be considered a (potentially) homeless Gypsy or Traveller has to make a homelessness application to a local authority.

---

98 See para 6.48 above, for the jurisdiction of the county court in respect of interim accommodation.

99 However, note that a failure to take any decision on the initial application would also have to be challenged, if at all, by means of judicial review.

100 See chapter 4.

101 See para 6.19 above.

6.67   Gypsies and Travellers can encounter considerable problems when first trying to make an application. Some authorities may try to simply put the person on the ordinary housing register. This is unlawful. A local authority that has reason to believe that an applicant may be homeless or threatened with homelessness must investigate the matter further and must accept and process an application from that applicant.[102] It is also, unfortunately, not uncommon to meet with local authorities who turn away homeless Gypsies or Travellers who have made applications because they have no pitches or sites to which they can direct them. This is unlawful for the same reason.

6.68   Many Gypsies and Travellers are illiterate or have trouble with literacy. As a consequence, they may encounter difficulties when making homelessness applications. It is important to remember that an application under the homelessness legislation does not have to be made in any particular form. In *Roberts,*[103] a letter from the applicants' solicitors, giving appropriate particulars in a schedule, was held to amount to an application. It is suggested that 'appropriate particulars' might include:

- details and dates of birth of the applicant and his or her family (if any);
- previous accommodation over, say, the last five years[104] – in many cases, the applicant will have been moving frequently from one unauthorised encampment to another and it is suggested that a general history of encampments, concentrating in particular on the districts or areas in which he or she had been residing would be sufficient;
- details of health problems if 'priority need' is in question;
- details of schools, colleges, and employment (to ensure that the local authority focus on the provision of suitable accommodation within a reasonable distance of such educational establishments and/or areas in which work is undertaken);
- details of local connections, including reference to other family members in the area (to address the issue of 'local connection');
- if the applicant has previously occupied conventional housing then the local authority should be told why that accommodation

102 HA 1996 s184(1) – and see para 6.15 above.
103 *R v Chiltern DC ex p Roberts et al* [1990] 23 HLR 387, QBD.
104 See the discussion of 'local connection' at paras 6.85–6.87 below.

was vacated (to address the question whether the applicant is intentionally homeless).[105]

6.69 Though a local authority may insist, as part of its own homelessness procedures, on an interview and/or the completion of an application form, the important point here is that a letter written by the applicant's advisers will be sufficient to ensure that the local authority investigates whether the applicant is eligible for assistance and whether it owes any duty to him or her, provided the letter contains sufficient information. Additionally, application forms that are used typically do not cater for the needs of Gypsies and Travellers. For example, there may be no optional box for indicating that the applicant requires an authorised site or pitch for their caravan or vehicle. It may be wise for a solicitor or adviser to assist their client in filling in such a form to ensure that no misunderstandings arise. The local authority to whom the application is made could be asked to send any application form to the adviser or solicitor so that they can assist their client in completing it.

6.70 If a local authority insists on a formal interview taking place where a Gypsy or Traveller has made a homeless application then it may be wise, if possible, for someone (for example, from a local Gypsy or Traveller support group) to accompany the applicant to the interview to ensure, once again, that the local authority processes the application correctly. Those advising Gypsies and Travellers have met with many instances where, for example, applicants have simply been turned away by local authorities without a formal application having been accepted or where it transpires that the local authority have processed the application on the basis that it is for conventional, 'bricks and mortar' accommodation when the applicants specifically requested a site for their caravans. Practical support for the applicant can, therefore, be very important.

6.71 Some Gypsy and Traveller families travel around as an extended family group. This is especially so with Irish Travellers.[106] If an extended family group has always travelled together, it could be argued that one application should be taken from the whole group

---

105 See paras 6.77–6.84 below.
106 See, for example, Michael McDonagh, 'Nomadism' in *Travellers: Citizens of Ireland* (The Parish of the Travelling People, Dublin, 2000) pp33–46.

rather than a series of applications from each 'household'. This argument is based on HA 1996 s176:

> Accommodation shall be regarded as available for a person's occupation only if it is available for occupation by him together with –
> (a) *any other person who normally resides with him as a member of his family* ... (emphasis added).

The Homelessness Code of Guidance does not refer to 'extended families'. There is, as yet, no case-law on this particular point.

Priority need[107]

6.72   In the case of *Myhill and Faith v Wealden DC*,[108] the applicants, who were single men, argued that they were 'vulnerable' for some 'other special reason' for the purposes of HA 1996 s189(1)(c) on the basis that:

- as Travellers they were statistically far more likely to be homeless than the general population – the government statistics presented to the court, which were not challenged by the local authority, indicated that whereas 1.2 per cent of settled households were homeless, 18 per cent (at that time) of Gypsies and Travellers were homeless;
- Gypsies and Travellers were much less likely to be able to find accommodation due to the acknowledged lack of sites;
- while on unauthorised encampments, Gypsies and Travellers faced possible criminal prosecution under Criminal Justice and Public Order Act 1994.

6.73   The county court judge rejected these arguments. He relied on the judgment of Hobhouse LJ in one of the leading cases on 'priority need', *R v Camden LBC ex p Pereira*:

> The Council must ask itself whether the applicant is, when homeless, less able to fend for himself than an ordinary homeless person so that injury or detriment to him will result when a less vulnerable person would be able to cope without harmful effects ...[109]

---

107 See paras 6.9–6.11 above for the details of the categories of 'priority need'.
108 [2004] EWCA Civ 224; April 2004 *Legal Action* 34; 23 November 2003, Tunbridge Wells County Court.
109 [1998] HLR 317 at 330.

6.74   In refusing permission to appeal to the Court of Appeal, Buxton LJ stated:

> The focus [in the above quote] is quite clearly on the ability of the individual to deal with the condition of homelessness, rather than on the question to which the statistics and oral arguments in this case go, of how likely it is that the persons when they become homeless will remain such.[110]

6.75   A person who is homeless or threatened with homelessness as a result of an emergency such as flood, fire or other disaster, is also in 'priority need'.[111] In the case of *Scott-Higgs v Brighton and Hove CC*,[112] the single applicant had been residing in his caravan on an unauthorised encampment. The local authority obtained a possession order against him but had not yet enforced the order when, after going out one day, he returned to find his caravan had disappeared (it was never established what happened to the caravan). He applied as a homeless person to the local authority for accommodation. He claimed that the loss of his caravan should mean that he was in priority need. The local authority found him not to be in priority need. The judge at first instance upheld this decision. On appeal, the Court of Appeal stated that the loss of one's caravan in such circumstances could come within the definition of 'flood, fire or other disaster' but that his homelessness was not *as a result* of this event. He was already homeless since he did not have an authorised place to pitch his caravan. He could not, therefore, be said to be in priority need. It should be noted that, if Mr Scott-Higgs had been on an authorised encampment (such as a licensee on a local authority site) and his caravan had disappeared, then he would have been in priority need. In other words, in such a situation, the loss of the caravan would have caused his homelessness.

6.76   In the absence of any duty to provide sites,[113] there remains a huge problem for homeless Gypsies and Travellers who (especially in the light of the *Myhill and Faith* case) are not considered to be in priority need.

---

110 *Myhill and Faith v Wealden DC* [2004] EWCA Civ 224 at para 5.
111 HA 1996 s189(1)(d).
112 [2003] 3 All ER 753, CA.
113 Repealed by the CJPOA 1994.

Intentional homelessness

6.77   A local authority will only conclude that a person is intentionally homeless if he or she has deliberately done or failed to do something in consequence of which he or she has ceased to occupy accommodation which is available for his or her occupation and which it would have been reasonable for him or her to continue to occupy.[114] Thus, it is clear that there must be a causal link between a person's deliberate act or omission and the loss of accommodation; a person can only be considered to be intentionally homeless if his or her deliberate act or omission caused the homelessness.

6.78   There have been a number of cases where the courts have had to consider whether the causal link or 'chain of causation' has been broken by an intervening event. For example, in *Din v Wandsworth LBC*,[115] the House of Lords held that the chain of causation will be broken in circumstances where a person has lived in 'settled accommodation'[116] for a period of time.

6.79   More recently, in *R v Harrow LBC ex p Fahia*,[117] the applicant had been found intentionally homeless and was placed in a guest-house where she remained for over a year. She was evicted from the guest house when her housing benefit was cut (through no fault of her own) and she could no longer afford the rent. The local authority did not accept that the period of time in the guest house amounted to 'settled accommodation'. However, the Court of Appeal allowed the homeless applicant's appeal. It held that events other than securing settled accommodation could break the chain of causation and ordered that the local authority reconsider whether the change in the applicant's entitlement to housing benefit amounted to such an event.

6.80   Similarly, in *R v Basingstoke and Deane DC ex p Bassett*,[118] the fact that the applicant had spent a period of time staying with her sister-in-law (which it was accepted the applicant might have been entitled to believe would continue but for her sister-in-law separating from her husband and leaving the accommodation) was held to break the chain of causation.

114 See para 6.12 above and HA 1996 s191(1).
115 [1983] 1 AC 657.
116 The question of what constitutes 'settled accommodation' has been considered by the courts in a number of cases. For further discussion see Arden and Hunter, *Homelessness and Allocations* (Legal Action Group, Revised 6th edn, 2003).
117 [1998] 1 WLR 1396.
118 [1983] HLR 125, QBD.

6.81   By way of contrast, in *R v Hackney LBC ex p Ajayi*,[119] the applicant had left accommodation in Nigeria to come to London. After staying with various friends for short periods, she moved in with another friend in January 1996, just as she discovered that she was pregnant. When the baby was born, her friend asked her to leave. It was held that the chain of causation had not been broken and that the decision that she was 'intentionally homeless' because of leaving the accommodation in Nigeria, was correct.

6.82   These cases indicate that it will very much be a matter of fact and degree, based on the circumstances of an individual case, as to whether the chain of causation has been broken.

6.83   It is not uncommon for homeless Gypsies and Travellers to have previously lived in 'bricks and mortar' accommodation for a period of time and the vast majority of New Travellers will, at one time or another, have lived in conventional housing.[120] When considering whether a Gypsy or Traveller is intentionally homeless a local authority will pay particular attention to any periods that he or she spent living in bricks and mortar to see whether the applicant ceased to occupy the accommodation as a result of a deliberate act or omission or whether he or she left such accommodation in circumstances where it was reasonable for him or her to continue to occupy it.

6.84   Where a Gypsy or Traveller has been found intentionally homeless because he or she left conventional housing, the solicitor or adviser assisting them on a review or appeal will have to examine the past history of accommodation carefully and avoid taking matters at face value. For example:

- if a Gypsy or Traveller leaves conventional housing because it transpires that he or she has a psychological aversion to 'bricks and mortar', it may not be possible to say that he or she left the accommodation and became homeless as a result of a deliberate act or omission and it can be argued that it was not reasonable for him or her to continue to occupy the accommodation – in such a case expert evidence from a psychologist or other relevant professionals should be obtained;

119 [1997] HLR 473, QBD.

120 The casework of the Travellers' Advice Team at the Community Law Partnership demonstrates that there are now adult New Travellers who were born on the road and have never lived in conventional housing, though they remain very much a minority of the New Traveller population – there are no official statistics available.

- if a New Traveller only ever lived in insecure accommodation (such as a 'squat') it may be argued that the accommodation did not amount to settled accommodation;
- a previous eviction from conventional housing may not have been the fault of the Gypsy or Traveller applicant, for example, it may have been because of housing benefit department errors which led to rent arrears in circumstances where the Gypsy or Traveller applicant did not realise that the problem could have been resolved without the need for eviction to take place.

Local connection

6.85   The statutory provisions relating to 'local connection'[121] are further explained in the guidance known as the Local Authority Agreement.[122] The guidance states that:

- 'normal residence' in an area should be residence for at least six months in the area during the previous 12 months, or for not less than three years during the previous five-year period;
- regarding employment in an area, it is recommended that confirmation should be obtained from the applicant's employer and it should be established that the employment is not of a casual nature;
- 'family associations' normally arise when an applicant or member of the household has parents, adult children or brothers or sisters who have been resident in the area for at least five years at the date of the application and the applicant indicates a wish to be near them. Only in exceptional circumstances would the residence of relatives other than those listed above be taken to establish a local connection. The residence of children in another area from that of their parents cannot be taken to be residence of their own choice and therefore does not constitute a local connection. However, a referral should not be made to another local authority on the grounds of family association if the applicant objects;
- there are special circumstances which the local authority considers give rise to a local connection in the area. The fact that an applicant seeks to return to an area where he or she was

---

121 See paras 6.13–6.14 above.
122 Guidelines for Local Authorities and Referees agreed by Association of London Government, Convention of Scottish Local Authorities, Local Government Association and the Welsh Local Government Association.

brought up or lived in the past may be grounds for finding a local connection.

6.86   The Local Authority Agreement also lists certain exceptions to the above categories:

- time spent in the service of the Regular Armed Forces;
- time spent in detention under the authority of an Act of Parliament (for example, prisons, mental hospitals);
- time spent as a result of an earlier homeless application, in accommodation secured by another local authority under the homelessness legislation within the last five years;
- time spent in hospital;
- time spent in an institution in which households are accepted only for a limited period (for example, refuges and rehabilitation centres).

It should be stressed that if a homeless applicant has a local connection with the area of the local authority to whom he or she applies, then a referral to another local authority will not be possible even if the applicant also has a local connection with that other authority's area.

6.87   The Local Authority Agreement is not a statute but is strong guidance and cannot be ignored. Nevertheless, it is suggested that the guidance should not be applied too rigidly by local authorities in the case of homeless Gypsies and Travellers and that their particular circumstances and the difficulties they face should also be taken into account. By way of example it is perhaps worth looking at the guidance on 'normal residence' and 'family associations':

- According to the guidance, a Gypsy or Traveller would have to have spent at least six months in the area during the last 12 months to have a local connection but it is suggested that a local authority should not apply the guidance too rigidly in the case of Gypsies or Travellers who have been frequently forced to move from one unauthorised encampment to another, particularly when eviction action taken by the local authority itself forced them to spend a period of time in a neighbouring local authority's area.
- The extended family is an essential part of Irish Traveller culture[123] and the list of relatives in the guidance, by which an

---

123 See, for example, Michael McDonagh, 'Nomadism', *Travellers: Citizens of Ireland* (The Parish of the Travelling People, Dublin, 2000) pp33–46.

applicant can establish a local connection with an area, may be too narrow in the case of an Irish Traveller.

Suitable interim accommodation[124]

6.88 It can be seen above that if a local authority have reason to believe that an applicant may be homeless, eligible for assistance and in priority need, they have a duty to secure that accommodation is available pending their final decision.[125] If, having conducted enquiries, the local authority decides that a full duty is not owed to the applicant,[126] then the local authority has a power to ensure that accommodation is available pending any review of that decision requested by the applicant.[127] If the original decision is upheld on review, the local authority, once again, then has a power to secure that accommodation is available pending a county court appeal.[128]

6.89 Interim accommodation must be suitable.[129] When deciding what is suitable, a local authority must have regard to the slum clearance, overcrowding and 'houses in multiple occupation' provisions of the Housing Act 1985. The case law and statutory instruments to date have almost entirely related to the provision of conventional housing. In England, the government has indicated that bed and breakfast accommodation is not to be regarded as suitable for an applicant with family commitments[130] where the accommodation is secured for:

- a homeless applicant pending final decision,[131]
- for a homeless applicant in priority need but intentionally homeless,[132]
- for an applicant who is owed the full duty to secure accommodation,[133]

---

124 See paras 6.51–6.65 above.
125 HA 1996 s188(1).
126 HA 1996 s184.
127 HA 1996 s188(3).
128 HA 1996 s204(4).
129 HA 1996 s210.
130 The Homelessness (Suitability of Accommodation) (England) Order 2003 SI No 3326 reg 3.
131 HA 1996 s188(1).
132 HA 1996 s190(2).
133 HA 1996 s193(2).

- for an applicant who is to be referred to another local authority under the local connection provisions,[134] or
- for an applicant who is threatened with homelessness.[135]

6.90   However, where no accommodation other than bed and breakfast is available for such an applicant and he or she occupies the bed and breakfast accommodation for a period, or a total of periods, not exceeding six weeks, then such accommodation will be considered 'suitable'.[136]

6.91   Accommodation outside the local authority's area may be suitable depending on the circumstances of the case. In deciding the question of suitability, the local authority must consider the individual needs of the applicant and his or her family, including those relating to work, education and health.[137] It will be important, therefore, that the homeless Gypsy or Traveller supplies the local authority with all relevant information with regard to work in the area, schools attended and whether this involves special educational needs, registration with a local general practitioner or attendance at a local hospital, the need for support from relatives or friends in the area and any other relevant matters.

6.92   The main question with regard to interim accommodation for a homeless Gypsy or Traveller who seeks an authorised pitch on which to place his or her caravans or vehicles, will be whether an offer of conventional, 'bricks and mortar' accommodation in the interim can be seen as being 'suitable'. In *R v Southampton CC ex p Ward*,[138] accommodation on a caravan site, described by a social worker as being in appalling condition, was nevertheless an adequate discharge of the interim duty, having regard to the family's express wish to live on a site. However, it should be noted that the draft guidance from the Office of the Deputy Prime Minister (ODPM) on the use of Criminal

---

134 HA 1996 s200(1).
135 HA 1996 s195(2).
136 The Homelessness (Suitability of Accommodation) (England) Order 2003 reg 4.
137 See, for example, *R v Newham LBC ex p Sacupima* [2001] HLR 2, CA, [2001] HLR 1,QBD.
138 [1984] HLR 114,QBD.

Justice and Public Order Act 1994 ss62A–E (with regard to police eviction powers from unauthorised encampments),[139] states:

> The meaning of *suitable pitch* is not defined in the legislation. Of course, it is for the courts to interpret legislation, but the secretary of state considers that a *suitable pitch* is one that provides basic amenities including water, toilets and waste disposal facilities. This could include an authorised transit site or stopping place' (emphasis in text).

6.93   The report by Niner, *Local Authority Gypsy/Traveller Sites in England*[140] indicated that, on the 324 local authority Gypsy sites recorded by the January 2002 Gypsy Count, there were only 307 transit pitches (there is no indication as to whether all those pitches would be deemed 'suitable' for the purposes of the ODPM draft guidance). Given the severe shortfall in suitable pitches, it is suggested that in cases where a homeless Gypsy or Traveller is camping on local authority land and the encampment is not causing any undue nuisance, then it would be reasonable for the local authority to permit him or her to remain on the land while his or her homelessness application is processed. Alternatively the local authority could seek to identify temporary sites, perhaps on disused or underused land[141] where facilities could be provided.[142] Indeed, a local authority's decision to proceed with the eviction from their own land of a homeless Gypsy or Traveller when the local authority had failed to comply with the duty to secure that accommodation is available pending their final decision could well result in a public law challenge by way of judicial review.[143]

The full duty to accommodate

6.94   There is conflicting case law on the question whether a local authority that has decided that they have a full duty to accommodate a homeless applicant under HA 1996 s193(2),[144] must comply with

---

139   See chapter 5 paras 5.45–5.65 above. Finalised guidance expected autumn 2004.

140   (ODPM, 2003).

141   This could include other public authority land or even private land.

142   By way of example, a tap could be installed for water, refuse collection services set up and portaloos provided.

143   As, indeed, occurred in the *Price* case itself. For a discussion of judicial review procedures, see appendix A, below.

144   See para 6.26, above.

the duty immediately. In *R v Southwark LBC ex p Anderson,*[145] Moses J stated:

> The statutory scheme under the Housing Act [1996] shows that there is no time limit within which a housing authority is obliged under the statute to comply with a duty to secure available accommodation for those who fall within section 193 ...[146]

By way of contrast, in *R v Newham LBC ex p Begum,*[147] Collins J held that the duties under the HA 1996 could not be deferred. It is suggested that Collins J's judgment is to be preferred; otherwise, there would be nothing to stop local authorities from delaying compliance with their statutory duty. However, Collins J also accepted that, where there were great difficulties in finding suitable accommodation, a court would not enforce the duty unreasonably provided the local authority was doing all that it could to comply with it.

6.95   Where a local authority are satisfied that a homeless Gypsy or Traveller has a sufficient degree of 'cultural aversion to conventional housing' such that they should use their best endeavours to seek a suitable pitch or site, it will be incumbent on that authority to show that they have taken all reasonable steps to do so.[148] Local authorities are no longer obliged to keep registers of disused or underused land. However, the National Land Use Database[149] may be of great assistance to a local authority, combined with their own knowledge of land in their area. Additionally, the Gypsy or Traveller applicant may have good local knowledge of the area and may be able to provide the local authority with suggestions as to pieces of land. It is also suggested that it will not be sufficient for the local authority simply to have regard to any vacant pitches on authorised sites in the area. If there are vacant pitches on a site, the local authority may also

---

145 [1998] HLR 96, QBD.

146 [1998] HLR 96, at 98.

147 *R v Newham LBC ex p Begum* [1999] HLR 808.

148 In *Codona v Mid-Bedfordshire DC* (2003) 20 November, Luton County Court, HHJ Farnworth, an argument that, where a Gypsy or Traveller has a cultural aversion to conventional housing, 'bricks and mortar' accommodation could never be suitable, was rejected. See Recent Developments in Gypsy and Traveller Law at pxi above.

149 A partnership project between ODPM, English Partnerships, the Improvement and Development Agency and Ordnance Survey. The National Land Use Database is not yet publicly accessible though the aim is that it should be in the future. However it can be accessed by local authorities. For more information, contact NLUD by e-mail at enquiries@nlud.org.uk.

have to have regard to the allocations policy for that particular site before offering a pitch to a homeless applicant.[150]

6.96   The ODPM Guidance[151] states:

> There must be close working between site managers and local authority ... dealing with unauthorised camping over allocations of pitches on sites. Site managers may be aware of issues around Gypsy/Traveller group and family compatibility, which must be taken into account when allocating pitches on residential sites.[152]

In other words, the question of 'compatibility' of groups or families will also be relevant to the issue of suitability. Another relevant matter may be the location of the accommodation and its distance from schools, employment and healthcare facilities.

6.97   Obviously, New Travellers who are homeless can also make homeless applications. When it comes to the duty to accommodate, it should be remembered that the central issue is 'suitability'. Therefore, in the case of New Travellers, they may not be able to show a *'cultural* aversion to conventional housing', but it should be sufficient if they can show an *'aversion* to conventional housing'. It should be remembered that many New Travellers have spent many years travelling and some were born on the road.

6.98   The vast majority of homeless Gypsies or Travellers will have their own caravan or living vehicle but will not have an authorised pitch where they can place it. If a Gypsy or Traveller no longer has his or her caravan or living vehicle,[153] it is arguable that the duty to secure that accommodation becomes available might include the provision of a suitable caravan or vehicle.[154]

6.99   Those advising homeless Gypsies or Travellers who are owed the duty to secure accommodation, may have to consider obtaining expert reports on the question of 'aversion to housing' (for example, from a psychologist or other medical practitioner) and/or from a planning consultant or land surveyor on the question of available land in an area. Those providing reports on the availability of land will have to have regard to the relevant development plans and DoE Circular 1/94 (Welsh Office 2/94) *Gypsy Sites and Planning.*[155]

---

150 See further the discussion on 'allocation' in chapter 3 paras 3.28–3.29 above.
151 *Guidance on Managing Unauthorised Camping* (ODPM, February 2004).
152 *Guidance on Managing Unauthorised Camping,* at para 4.8.
153 See the *Scott-Higgs* case above for an example at para 6.75.
154 This argument was raised in *Price* but was not referred to in the judgment.
155 For detailed discussion of these and other planning issues, see chapter 4 above.

Conclusion

6.100 Clearly, there are many issues regarding homeless applications made by Gypsies and Travellers that need resolving. For instance, precisely when can a Gypsy or Traveller be said to be homeless? When can the 'chain of causation' be broken with regard to a decision that a Gypsy or Traveller was intentionally homelessness? How will the local connection provisions be applied to Gypsies and Travellers? How far does a local authority need to go in seeking an authorised pitch for the homeless Gypsy or Traveller applicant? How should an application from a homeless New Traveller be processed?

6.101 For those Gypsies and Travellers who are in priority need and cannot afford to buy their own land and seek planning permission,[156] a homelessness application may be the only way to avoid a life of continual eviction and the dire consequences that such a life can have upon the health of their families and the education of their children. However, the legislation does not assist homeless Gypsies and Travellers who are not in priority need and the lack of a duty to provide sites for such people leaves them in a particularly vulnerable situation.[157]

---

156 See chapter 4.
157 See chapter 9, for a discussion of current campaigns and other issues for the future.

CHAPTER 7

Education and healthcare

Introduction

7.1   This chapter is designed to provide the reader with an overview of the law relating to education and healthcare in so far as it may affect the lives of Gypsies and Travellers and their children.

Education

7.2   Research conducted in 1996[1] and 1999[2] led the Office for Standards in Education (Ofsted) to report its view that Gypsy and Traveller pupils have the lowest level of attainment of any ethnic minority group and that they are most at risk in the education system. More recent research conducted by Ofsted revealed the fact that there were between 10,000 and 12,000 Gypsy and Traveller children of secondary school age that were not registered and did not attend school and led Ofsted to state in its report in 2003 that:

> The vast majority of Traveller pupils linger on the periphery of the education system. The situation has persisted for too long and the alarm bells rung in earlier reports have yet to be heeded.[3]

7.3   There are a number of reasons for the poor levels of attendance and achievement of Gypsy and Traveller pupils. Perhaps the most obvious reason stems from enforced mobility; children that live on unauthorised sites are bound to suffer considerable disruption to their schooling when their families are evicted and it is not surprising that those that are subject to numerous evictions are the least likely to attend school.[4]

7.4   When commenting on the poor levels of attendance Ofsted also noted the fact that Gypsy and Traveller children tend to come from very caring and protective families and that some parents fear that their children will be subjected to racist bullying at school and that schooling will lead to potential erosion of their community's moral

---

1 *The Education of Travelling Children: a survey of Educational Provision for Travelling Children* (Ofsted, 1996).
2 *Raising the Attainment of Minority Ethnic Pupils* (Ofsted, 1999).
3 *Provision and support for Traveller pupils* (Ofsted, 2003).
4 H Crawley, *Moving Forward: the provision of accommodation for Travellers and Gypsies* (The Institute for Public Policy Research, 2004) p33.

codes and values.[5] In addition, Ofsted noted that there is a very strong tradition of starting work in the family business at a young age within the Travelling community and that some Gypsy and Traveller parents regard the somewhat inflexible school curriculum as having little relevance to their traditional way of life.

The right to education

7.5 The Human Rights Act (HRA) 1998 came into force on 2 October 2000 and incorporates most of the European Convention on Human Rights (ECHR) into United Kingdom law. Of particular relevance to education is ECHR protocol 1 article 2 which provides that:

> No person shall be denied the right to education. In the exercise of any functions which it assumes in relation to education and to teaching, the state shall respect the right of parents to ensure such education and teaching in conformity with their own religious and philosophical convictions.

7.6 However, when the United Kingdom ratified the ECHR it entered the following reservation with regard to the second sentence of Protocol 1 article 2:

> ... in view of certain provisions of the Education Acts in the United Kingdom, the principle affirmed in the second sentence of article 2 is accepted by the United Kingdom only so far as it is compatible with the provision of efficient instruction and training, and the avoidance of unreasonable public expenditure.

7.7 Thus, it has been held that the general right to education comprises a number of rights (none of which is absolute):

   (i) a right of access to such educational establishments as exist;
   (ii) a right to effective (but not the most effective possible) education;
   (iii) a right to official recognition of academic qualifications ...

As regards the right to an effective education, for the right to education to be meaningful the quality of the education must reach a minimum standard.[6]

---

5 For more information on the culture and customs of Romani Gypsies and Irish Travellers, see: Vesey-Fitzgerald, *Gypsies of Britain* (Readers Union, 1973); Sheehan, ed, *Travellers: Citizens of Ireland* (The Parish of the Travelling People, Dublin, 2000).

6 *R (Holub and Holub) v Secretary of State for the Home Department* [2001] 1 WLR 1359. See also *Belgian Linguistics Case (No 2)* [1968] 1 EHRR 252 at 281, and *A v Head Teacher and Governors of Lord Grey School* [2003] 4 All ER 1317.

7.8   Local education authorities (LEAs) have a statutory duty to ensure that education is available for all children of compulsory school age (5- to 16- year-olds) in their area that is appropriate to their age, abilities, aptitudes and any special educational needs that they might possess.[7]

7.9   LEAs have a duty to have regard to the 'general principle that pupils are to be educated in accordance with the wishes of their parents, so far as this is compatible with the provision of efficient instruction and training and the avoidance of unreasonable expenditure'.[8] LEAs have a duty to respect parents' religious and philosophical convictions. 'Respect' means more than simply 'acknowledge' or 'take into account' such views but does not require LEAs to cater for all parents' convictions and parents do not have an absolute right to choose the manner in which their children are to be educated at school.[9]

7.10   LEAs also have a duty to give parents the opportunity to express a preference as to which school they wish their child to attend.[10] LEAs must comply with parental preference unless to do so would be prejudicial to efficient education or the efficient use of resources.[11] These duties are owed to all of the children residing in the area of a LEA, whether permanently or temporarily and must, therefore, apply to Gypsy and Traveller children residing with their families on unauthorised sites on a temporary basis.

7.11   Although Gypsy and Traveller children of school age have the same legal right to education as anyone else, it is difficult in practical terms for them to exercise that right without a permanent or legal place to stop. Most LEAs provide specialist Traveller educational support services to help Gypsy and Traveller pupils and parents to access education and to provide practical advice and support to schools admitting them. When a Gypsy or Traveller family with children of school age move into a new area, they should contact the local Traveller Education Support Service for assistance.

7 Education Act (EA) 1996 s14.

8 EA 1996 s9.

9 *The Belgian Linguistic Case (No 2)* [1968] 1 EHRR 252. But see also *Campbell and Cosans v United Kingdom* [1982] 4 EHRR 293, for an example of a case where there was found to be a breach of both the first and the second sentence of article 2 of the first protocol of the ECHR.

10 School Standards and Framework Act 1998 s86.

11 School Standards and Framework Act 1998 ss86(2), (3) and 87 and *R (B) v Head Teacher and Governing Body of Alperton Community School* [2001] EWHC 229 Admin; [2001] 1 ELR 359.

7.12   The National Association of Teachers of Travellers (NATT) produces an annual booklet listing the local Traveller Education Support Services, and can also provide information about books and other educational resources specifically for Gypsy and Traveller children.[12]

Admission to school

7.13   Gypsy and Traveller children should be admitted to schools on the same basis as any other children. However, some schools may still rely upon admissions policies that disadvantage Gypsy and Traveller children: for instance, an admissions policy which gives preference to children whose older brothers and sisters have already attended the school could be argued to unfairly disadvantage Gypsy and Traveller families who have recently moved into the area. Such a policy may be susceptible to legal challenge on grounds that it is discriminatory and/or unreasonable.

7.14   There is anecdotal evidence of some schools having refused admission to Gypsy and Traveller pupils, whether through racism, fear that school league tables will be affected, or that non-Travelling parents will resent such admission. In a report published in 2001 Ofsted noted that:

> ... a few schools in a small number of the LEAs inspected had expressed reservations to Traveller education services about taking on pupils from Traveller families, such schools [are] clearly failing to recognise their legal responsibilities.[13]

7.15   If it can be proved that a Gypsy or Traveller child has been refused admission on any such grounds then a claim brought under the Race Relations Act (RRA) 1976[14] and/or article 2 of protocol 1 (the right to education) combined with article 14 (the prohibition of discrimination) of the ECHR may be possible.

---

12 See appendix C for a list of useful organisations at Room 125, Cricket Road Centre, Cricket Road, Oxford, OX4 3DW; by telephone on 01865 428 089; or visit their website at www.natt.org.uk.

13 *Managing Support for the Attainment of Pupils from Minority Ethnic Groups,* (Ofsted, 2001).

14 As amended by the Race Relations (Amendment) Act 2000. See paras 7.46–7.51 below and chapter 8.

Attendance at school

7.16   Education Act (EA) 1996 s7 provides that:

> It shall be the duty of the parent of every child of compulsory school age to cause him to receive efficient full-time education suitable to his age, ability and aptitude and to any special educational needs he may have either by regular attendance at school or otherwise.

Failure to do so is an offence and can lead to prosecution.[15]

7.17   In *R v Secretary of State for Education and Science ex p Talmud Torah Madizikei Hedass School Trust*,[16] it was held that education is 'suitable' if it primarily equips a child for life in a community of which he or she is a member as long as it does not foreclose the child's option later to adopt some other form of life if he or she wishes to do so.

7.18   Schools must report all unauthorised absences and LEAs have a responsibility to prosecute parents in appropriate cases.[17]

7.19   If a child is not registered at a school and the LEA considers that the child is not receiving suitable education then it may issue a 'school attendance order' requiring the parent to register a child at a named school.[18] EA 1996 s443(1) provides that a parent who fails to comply with a school attendance order will be guilty of a criminal offence unless he or she can prove that the child is receiving suitable education out of school.

7.20   Where a child is registered at a school but fails to attend that school regularly, a LEA has the power to prosecute the parent. EA 1996 s444(1) provides that:

> If a child of compulsory school age who is a registered pupil at a school fails to attend regularly at the school, his parent is guilty of an offence.

7.21   A parent convicted of an offence under section 444 can be punished with a fine. The offence is one of 'strict liability' and parents cannot defend a prosecution by claiming that they had no knowledge of their child's non-attendance or by claiming that they had done all that they could reasonably be expected to do to ensure that their child attended school.[19]

---

15 EA 1996 s444 or s444(1A).
16 (1985) *Times* 12 April.
17 EA 1996 s446.
18 EA 1996 s437.
19 *Bath and North East Somerset DC v Warman* [1999] ELR 81 and *Crump v Gilmore* [1968] LGR 56.

7.22   EA 1996 s444(1A) provides that a parent will be guilty of a more serious offence and be liable to a fine or to imprisonment for a term not exceeding three months, if he or she knows that his or her child is failing to attend regularly at school and he or she fails without reasonable justification to cause the child to do so.[20]

7.23   It had been thought that the offence created by EA 1996 s444 might breach ECHR article 6(2)[21] because it is a strict liability offence which does not require proof of any knowledge or fault on the part of the parent. However, in the case of *Barnfather v Islington LBC and the Secretary of State for Education and Skills*,[22] it was held that section 444 did not engage article 6(2) and that the offence was compatible with the ECHR.

7.24   However, EA 1996 s444(3) does provide parents with a number of statutory excuses or defences to a prosecution brought under section 444(1). For example, a child will not be taken to have failed to attend regularly at school if he or she:

- has been given authorised leave of absence;
- was unable to attend due to sickness;
- did not attend school on any day of religious observance;
- was unable to attend because the school was not within walking distance and no suitable transport arrangements had been made by the LEA.[23]

7.25   More particularly, Gypsy and Traveller parents are protected from conviction for the non-attendance of their children at school where they can demonstrate, in accordance with the EA 1996 s444(6), that:

- they are engaged in a trade or business of such a nature that requires them to travel from place to place;
- the child has attended at a school as a registered pupil as regularly as the nature of that trade permits; and
- where the child has attained the age of six years, they have attended school for at least 200 half-day sessions during the preceding school year (September to July).

---

20 EA 1996 s444(1A), which was inserted by Criminal Justice and Court Services Act 2000 s72(1)(a) and (2).
21 ECHR article 6(2) provides that: 'Everyone charged with a criminal offence shall be presumed innocent until proved guilty according to law.'
22 [2003] ELR 263.
23 See paragraph 7.29 below.

7.26   However, there is some concern that this statutory exception may, in practice, deny Gypsy and Traveller children equality of access in education. For example, the authors of the Swann Report wrote:

> We are concerned that the specific provision ... although presumably intended originally to protect travelling parents from unreasonable prosecution for failing to send their children to school, may in practice serve to deprive travellers' children of equality of access to education; LEAs may see this provision in the Act as offering a convenient excuse for not enforcing school attendance for travellers' children, rather than, as we would wish, striving to achieve full time attendance by all school age children in their areas.[24]

More recently the Department for Education and Skills (DfES) has emphasised the fact that Gypsy and Traveller parents should not regard the 200 half-day sessions as the norm but should continue to comply with their legal duty to ensure that their children are receiving efficient, suitable full-time education even when not at school.[25]

7.27   To protect the continuity of learning for Gypsy and Traveller children, the DfES has introduced the concept of 'dual registration'. If parents inform their 'base' school or the Traveller Education Service that the family will be travelling and intend to return by a given time, the school may keep the child's place for them and record their absence as authorised. The child can then register at other schools while the family is travelling. Gypsy and Traveller parents can also take advantage of 'school-based distance learning' whereby teachers and the Traveller Education Service work together to provide pupils with a package of curriculum-based material to be taken away and studied by them while the family are travelling.

7.28   Before a LEA can prosecute a parent under either EA 1996 s443 or s444 it must first consider whether to apply to a family proceedings court for an 'education supervision order'.[26] Such an order will be made where a child 'is of compulsory school age and is not being properly educated',[27] or in other words, is not receiving a suitable education. Education supervision orders last 12 months but can be extended for up to three years. They are designed to ensure that both the parent and the child receive support and advice from a supervisor such as an education welfare officer or an educational social worker.

24 Committee of Inquiry into the Education of Children from Ethnic Minority Groups (1985) *Education for All* ('The Swann Report'), HMSO, paras 26–27.
25 *Aiming High: Raising the Achievement of Gypsy Traveller Pupils* (DfES, 2003).
26 EA 1996 s447.
27 Children Act 1989 s36.

Transport to school

7.29 EA 1996 s509 provides that LEAs have a duty to make appropriate arrangements to provide free transport for children to attend school unless the school is within walking distance, that is two miles (or three miles where the child is over eight years old). Alternatively, LEAs may 'as they think fit' provide funding for 'reasonable travelling expenses' for children for whom they have not made arrangements to provide free transport. As has already been noted, parents will have a defence to the charge of failing to send their children to school under EA 1996 s444(4) if the school at which their children are registered is not within walking distance and no suitable arrangements have been made by the LEA for their transportation to and from school.[28]

Special educational needs

7.30 A child has 'special educational needs', for the purposes of the EA 1996, if he or she has a 'learning difficulty' that requires special educational provision to be made.[29] A child will have a learning difficulty if he or she:

- has a significantly greater difficulty in learning than the majority of children of the same age;
- has a disability which either prevents or hinders him or her from making use of educational facilities of a kind generally provided for children of the same age in schools within the area of the LEA; or
- is under the age of five years and is, or would be, if special educational provision was not made, likely to fall within the above categories when over that age.[30]

7.31 LEAs have a duty to identify those children with special educational needs for whom it is responsible and to make special educational provision to address those needs.[31] Where a LEA is of the opinion that a child for whom it is responsible is, or probably is, a child with special educational needs, it must follow the procedure for the assessment of the needs of a child laid down by EA 1996 s323. If, in the light of such an assessment, it is necessary for a LEA to

---

28 See *George v Devon CC* [1988] 3 All ER 1002.

29 EA 1996 s312(1).

30 EA 1996 s312(2).

31 EA 1996 s321(1).

determine the special educational provision that is required to address the needs of a child found to have a learning difficulty, then it must make and maintain a statement of the child's special educational needs.[32] Having done so, the LEA must then arrange for the special educational provision specified in the statement to be made for the child.[33]

7.32   If a Gypsy or Traveller child has started school late or attended school irregularly, he or she may be judged to have special needs and parents should contact their local Traveller Education Service for advice and assistance on the decision-making process relating to the assessment of the special needs of their child.

Exclusion from school

7.33   In 1996 Ofsted found that Gypsy and Traveller children suffer a disproportionately high level of school exclusion.[34]

7.34   The Education Act (EA) 2002 s52 states that:

(1) The headteacher of a maintained school may exclude a pupil from the school for a fixed period or permanently.
(2) The teacher in charge of a pupil referral unit[35] may exclude a pupil from the unit for a fixed period or permanently.

7.35   EA 1996 s19(1) provides that:

Each local education authority shall make arrangements for the provision of suitable full-time or part-time education at school or otherwise than at school for those children of compulsory school age who, by reason of illness, exclusion from school or otherwise, may not for any period receive suitable education unless such arrangements are made for them.

LEAs are also required to have regard to the guidance in Circular 10/99 regarding the provision of education to those children who are

---

32 EA 1996 s324(1).

33 EA 1996 s324(5)(a)(i), *R v Secretary of State for Education and Science ex p E* [1992] 1 FLR 377 and *R v Harrow LBC ex p M* [1997] ELR 62.

34 *Report on the Education of Travelling Children* (Ofsted, 1996) and also see Department for Education and Employment (DfEE) Circular 10/99 *Social Inclusion: Pupil Support* and Circular 11/99 *Social Inclusion: the LEA role in Pupil Support.*

35 Any school established and maintained by a LEA which is not a 'community school' or a 'special school' but is specially organised to provide education for children who, by reason of illness, exclusion from school or otherwise, may not for any period receive suitable education will be known as a 'pupil referral unit': see EA 1996 s19(2).

out of school.[36] Where a Gypsy or Traveller parent has concerns regarding the provision of education to an excluded child he or she may wish to challenge the school or the LEA by bringing a claim for judicial review and/or damages.

7.36   The exclusion of a pupil from school will not violate ECHR protocol 1 article 2 (the right to education) unless the pupil is given no access to alternative educational facilities. Everything will depend upon the circumstances of the case and in *A v Head Teacher and Governors of Lord Grey School*,[37] Stanley Burnton J held that:

> [Article 2 of the first protocol] does not create a right to be educated in any particular institution or in any particular manner. Expulsion from a school of a pupil who has no access to alternative educational facilities, such as enrolment in another school or education through a pupil referral unit, may cause a breach [of article 2], and if so the school authority may be liable in damages; but if the pupil is able to have access to efficient education elsewhere, no breach of his Convention right will be involved. If the cause of the unavailability of alternative efficient education is the action or inaction of the local education authority, on whom duties are imposed [by EA 1996 ss13 and 19(1)], it will be the local education authority, rather than the school authority, that will have caused the infringement of the pupil's rights under [article 2].[38]

7.37   The DfES has published guidance on exclusions headed 'Improving behaviour and attendance: Guidance on exclusions from schools and pupil referral units' and it applies to any exclusion that takes place from 20 January 2003.[39] The Education (Pupil Exclusions and Appeals) (Maintained Schools) (England) Regulations 2002[40] also came into force on 20 January 2003 and set out the constitution and procedure for independent appeal panels to follow when considering whether a pupil should be excluded from school.

7.38   The guidance indicated that decision-makers needed only to be satisfied on the balance of probabilities that a pupil had committed an act that had been alleged against him or her. However, in the case of *R (S) v The Governors of YP School*,[41] the Court of Appeal made it clear that, in cases where an allegation against a pupil amounted to a crime, decision-makers had to be satisfied beyond

---

36 DfEE Circular 10/99 *Social Inclusion: Pupil Support*.
37 [2003] 4 All ER 1317 and see also *Yanasik v Turkey* [1993] 74 DR 98.
38 [2003] 4 All ER 1317 at p1337.
39 See www.teachernet.gov.uk and March 2003 *Legal Action* 10 for more information on the guidance.
40 SI No 3178.
41 [2003] EWCA Civ 1306.

reasonable doubt (the criminal standard of proof) that the pupil had committed the act that had been alleged.

7.39   As a consequence the DfES was forced to publish further 'interim guidance' that required decision-makers to apply the criminal standard of proof in such cases. When publishing the interim guidance the DfES stated it considered that the judgment in *R (S) v The Governors of YP School*[42] creates practical difficulties and indicated that the Secretary of State had made further regulations that will have the effect of requiring decision-makers on exclusions to apply the civil standard of proof (that is, the 'balance of probabilities'), in all cases of exclusion in the future.[43]

7.40   There is a duty on headteachers, teachers in charge of pupil referral units, governing bodies and independent appeal panels to have regard to the guidance and abide by the regulations and failure to do so may well give rise to a successful legal challenge.

7.41   Exclusion hearings conducted by governing bodies or independent appeal panels are also open to challenge on the basis that they have been conducted in breach of the rules of evidence and natural justice. For example, in *R v Governors of W School and West Sussex CC ex p K*,[44] the court held that the decision of the governing body to exclude K should be quashed on the basis that it had been unfair and procedurally flawed in circumstances where: K had been handicapped in the presentation of his defence; the 'evidence' included the verbal opinions of an anonymous police officer; and, only lip service had been paid to the standard of proof at the hearing.

7.42   However, it has been held that exclusion proceedings are not subject to ECHR article 6 (which guarantees the right to a fair trial in the determination of civil rights and obligations and criminal charges).[45] In the case of *R (B) v Head Teacher and Governing Body of Alperton Community School*,[46] several claimants sought judicial review of decisions regarding admission to and exclusion from schools and they alleged that certain provisions of the School Standards and Framework Act (SSFA) 1998 breached the ECHR. In the event, the court held that: as no private right to an education existed in English

---

42 [2003] EWCA Civ 1306.

43 See www.teachernet.gov.uk/wholeschool/behaviour/exclusionupdate for the interim guidance and March 2004 *Legal Action* 26 for more information on the future amendments to the guidance and the regulations.

44 [2001] ELR 311.

45 ECHR article 6(2) provides that: 'Everyone charged with a criminal offence shall be presumed innocent until proved guilty according to law.'

46 [2001] EWHC 229 Admin; [2001] 1 ELR 359.

law, ECHR article 6 was not applicable to independent appeal panel exclusion proceedings; and SSFA 1998 s87 did not breach ECHR protocol 1 article 2.[47]

7.43 Where an independent appeal panel upholds an appeal and quashes a decision to exclude a child from school, the child will be reinstated. However, reinstatement will not necessarily result in a return to mainstream classes.

7.44 In *L v Governors of J School*,[48] the House of Lords considered a case where a school had imposed terms and conditions on a child's reinstatement which required him to receive tuition in isolation from other pupils, prohibited him from socialising with his former classmates and restricted his movements in the school in circumstances where staff threatened strike action if the child returned to mainstream classes. By a majority, the House of Lords held that reinstatement (that is, the re-establishment of the 'school-pupil relationship') occurred when a school resumed responsibilities and obligations towards a pupil and that, on the facts of the case, the regime imposed by the school was sufficient to amount to reinstatement. When doing so, the House of Lords made it clear that a school must always act in good faith and that reinstatement must be genuine and not a sham. However, Lord Bingham expressed specific concern that the special arrangements failed to facilitate the child's actual re-integration into the school.[49]

7.45 If the child of a Gypsy or Traveller is threatened with exclusion then he or she should contact the local Traveller Education Service or the National Association of Teachers of Travellers for initial assistance but may also need to seek specialist legal advice.[50]

Racial discrimination

7.46 Romani Gypsies and Irish Travellers are recognised as members of separate racial groups under the Race Relations Act (RRA) 1976.[51] Although there is, as yet, no case law on the matter, it is suggested

47 See also *A v Headteacher and Governors of the Lord Grey School* [2003] 4 All ER 1317 and *Simpson v United Kingdom* [1989] 64 DR 188 for a similar decision in relation to special educational needs.
48 [2003] UKHL 9.
49 See also the case of *P v NASUWT* [2003] UKHL 8.
50 See appendix C for a full list of useful organisations.
51 See chapter 8 and the cases of *Commission for Racial Equality v Dutton* [1989] 1 QB 783 and *O'Leary v Allied Domecq* 29 August 2000, (CL950275–79) HHJ Goldstein, Central London County Court (unreported).

that Welsh and Scottish Travellers should also be recognised under RRA 1976 as separate racial groups.[52]

7.47   The RRA 1976 outlaws both direct and indirect racial discrimination in education. Specifically, RRA 1976 s17 provides that it is unlawful for a body in charge of an educational establishment to discriminate against a person:

(a) in the terms on which it offers to admit him to the establishment as a pupil;

(b) by refusing or deliberately omitting to accept an application for his admission to the establishment as a pupil; or

(c) where he is a pupil of the establishment –

   (i) in the way that it affords him access to any benefits, facilities or services, or by refusing or deliberately omitting to afford him access to them; or

   (ii) by excluding him from the establishment or subjecting him to any other detriment.

7.48   More generally, RRA 1976 s18 states that it is unlawful for a local education authority and other responsible bodies to discriminate in the performance of any of their other functions under the Education Acts, although there is an exception made in the case of establishments that afford persons of a particular racial group access to facilities or services to meet the special needs of that group with regard to their education, training or welfare or any ancillary benefits.[53]

7.49   If an ethnic Gypsy or Traveller parent believes that their child has been the subject of discrimination then legal advice should be sought. A claimant must notify the secretary of state before proceedings are commenced and a claim should be brought in the county court within six months of the alleged act of discrimination.

7.50   The RRA 1976 now imposes a statutory duty on public bodies including LEAs and schools to promote race equality.[54] Schools are now required to:

- prepare a written statement of their policies for promoting race equality and act upon them;

- assess the impact of their policies on pupils, staff and parents from different racial groups, in particular the impact on attainment levels of these pupils; and

52 So the points made in paragraphs 7.47–7.51 below may also apply with equal force to Scottish and Welsh Travellers.

53 RRA 1976 s35.

54 RRA 1976 s71 (as amended).

- monitor the operation of all the school's policies, in particular their impact on the attainment levels of pupils from different racial groups.[55]

7.51 Ofsted will inspect schools' compliance with their new duties as part of their regular inspections.

Bullying at school

7.52 In 1996 Ofsted found that Gypsy and Traveller children are often subject to bullying of a racist nature[56] and more recently the Scottish Traveller Education Project indicated that bullying is an endemic problem in schools in Scotland.[57]

7.53 Schools should have clear policies and strategies to deal with the prevention of bullying and the punishment of such behaviour. The fact that schools must now comply with the duty to promote racial equality should cause them to address bullying and racist behaviour directed against Romani Gypsies and Irish Travellers.

7.54 If a LEA or a school fails to respond to bullying against Gypsies and Irish Travellers at all, or as effectively as when such behaviour is directed against pupils from other ethnic minority groups, then it could be guilty of discrimination.[58] Alternatively, if a LEA or a school fails to take reasonable steps to investigate bullying behaviour and to prevent its recurrence, then it may be liable in negligence to pay a pupil damages for breach of its duty to take care of the pupil's health and safety.[59]

Disability discrimination

7.55 The Special Educational Needs and Disability Act (SENDA) 2001 amended the Disability Discrimination Act (DDA) 1995 so as to introduce the duty not to discriminate on grounds of disability in education. Schools are now prohibited from discriminating against

---

55 The Commission for Racial Equality (CRE) has published a useful document called *The duty to promote race equality: a guide for schools* available at www.cre.gov.uk.

56 *The Education of Travelling Children: a survey of Educational Provision for Travelling Children* (Ofsted, 1996).

57 See H Crawley, *Moving Forward: the provision of accommodation for Travellers and Gypsies* (The Institute for Public Policy Research, 2004) at p33.

58 See chapter 8.

59 See, for example, *Bradford-Smart v West Sussex CC* [2002] EWCA Civ 7.

disabled children in their admission arrangements, in the provision of education and associated services, and in relation to exclusions from school.[60]

Education otherwise than at school

7.56   Parents do have the option of educating their children at home. However, the education a child receives must be 'suitable education', that is efficient full-time education suitable to the child's age, ability and aptitude and any special educational needs he or she may have.[61]

7.57   The right to educate one's child at home is clearly in keeping with ECHR article 9 (the right to freedom of thought, conscience and religion) and article 10 (the right to freedom of expression), but must be balanced against the right of the child to receive an effective education. In 2001 Ofsted indicated that the lack of monitoring and support undertaken by LEAs of the education of children outside school is a matter of some concern:

> In about half of the LEAs in which services were inspected there was a growing trend among Traveller families to opt for education other than at school (that is, education at home), particularly in the secondary phase. Services responded with appropriate advice, but the practice on registration and monitoring varied significantly among LEAs. The lack of evaluative monitoring typified the poorest provision.[62]

7.58   Parents need only inform the LEA of their intention to provide the child with 'education otherwise than at school' if the child has been registered at a school. The National Curriculum need not be followed and formal testing is not required. However, LEAs may inspect education being provided at home in order to monitor and assess whether a child is receiving a 'suitable education'.[63]

7.59   If it appears to a LEA that a child of school age is not receiving suitable education at home it must serve the parents with a notice in writing requiring them to satisfy it that the child is receiving such

---

60 DDA 1995 s28A and see C Palmer et al, *Discrimination Law Handbook* (Legal Action Group, 2002) for a more detailed explanation of DDA 1995 in the education field.

61 EA 1996 s19.

62 *Managing Support for the Attainment of Pupils from Minority Ethnic Groups* (Ofsted, 2001); see also *Provision of support for Traveller pupils,* (Ofsted, 2003).

63 See *R v Surrey Quarter Sessions Appeal Committee ex p Tweedie* [1963] 61 LGR 464 and *R v Gwent CC ex p Perry* [1985] 129 Sol Jo 737.

education.[64] If the LEA is not satisfied by the parents that the child is receiving a suitable education then it must serve the parents with a 'school attendance order' requiring the parents to register the child at a named school.[65] It is a criminal offence to fail to comply with a school attendance order and a parent convicted by the magistrates' court is liable to pay a fine.[66]

Education of children under school age

7.60   LEAs also have a duty to secure sufficient provision in their area for nursery education.[67]

7.61   Children that have not had the benefit of any form of pre-school learning experience are at risk of underachievement when at school. Gypsy and Traveller parents with three- and four-year-old children should contact their LEA or local Traveller Education Service for details of the facilities available in their area and should make enquiries about local Sure Start programmes in order to gain access to affordable childcare and pre-school education.[68]

Raising the achievement of Gypsy and Traveller pupils

7.62   In 2003, the DfES published a guide to good practice on the education of Gypsy and Traveller children entitled *Aiming High: Raising the Achievement of Gypsy Traveller Pupils.*[69] If LEAs and schools follow the guidance, then it is hoped by the government that they will begin to address many of the issues identified in this chapter and raise the level of achievement of Gypsy and Traveller children within the education system, thus ensuring that they experience real equality of opportunity.

7.63   Nevertheless, it is difficult to see how much will change for those Gypsy and Traveller children still living on unauthorised sites under

64 EA 1996 s437(1).
65 EA 1996 s437(3).
66 EA 1996 s443.
67 SSFA 1998 s119.
68 More information on Sure Start programmes can be found on www.surestart.gov.uk. Parents may also wish to obtain a copy of the booklet *Early Years: Traveller Children Training at Home and School* published by Educational Services and North Yorkshire County Council.
69 It can be obtained from DfES Publications: by post at PO Box 5050, Sherwood Park, Annesley, Nottingham, NG15 0DJ; by telephone on 0845 6022260; or by email at dfes@prolog.uk.com, and by quoting the reference DfES/0443/2003.

the threat of constant eviction unless and until both local authorities and the courts place greater weight on their educational needs.[70]

7.64   In February 2004 the government published new *Guidance on Managing Unauthorised Camping*,[71] which stipulates that all public authorities need to be able to demonstrate that they have taken the welfare needs of unauthorised campers into consideration before making a decision to evict. The educational needs of children camping with their parents on an unauthorised site will clearly be relevant to such a decision.[72] Yet, as Ofsted stated in its 2003 report:[73]

> Many authorities have clear statements about the inclusion of all pupils in education. However, in too many authorities, the ways in which they deal with unauthorised encampments contradict the principles set out in their public statements on inclusion, educational entitlement and race equality. Such contradictions undermine relationships and inhibit the effectiveness of the Traveller Education Support Services and other agencies.

7.65   It is very important, therefore, that Gypsies and Travellers who are living with their children and wish to challenge a local authority's decision to evict them from an unauthorised encampment (by way of judicial review) should place great emphasis upon the educational needs of their children (highlighting any special educational needs) and, if the matter comes to court, ask that it subject the local authority's justification for eviction to close and careful scrutiny.

70 See *Basildon DC v Secretary of State for the Environment and Appelby*, 21 December 2001 (unreported), Admin Ct and chapter 2 para 2.64 above, for an example of a planning case where a court upheld the decision of the Secretary of State to grant planning permission for a Gypsy site in the Green Belt. In that case it was considered that the educational needs of the children living on the site clearly outweighed the objections based on conflicts with planning policy and the environmental harm caused by the development.
71 The Guidance was effective from 27 February 2004 and published by the Office of the Deputy Prime Minister (ODPM) and replaces the earlier guidance contained in *Managing Unauthorised Camping: A Good Practice Guide*, that had been published by the Department of Environment, Transport and the Regions and the Home Office in 1998 (and was amended in 2000). See also chapter 5 above.
72 See paragraph 5.20 of the Guidance.
73 *Provision and support for Traveller pupils* (Ofsted, 2003) at p5.

Healthcare

The right to healthcare

7.66 In effect, everyone has a right to healthcare provided by the National Health Service (NHS).[74] What this means in practice is that no hospital should ever turn away an individual who is in need of treatment. However, that does not mean that a patient is entitled to insist upon a particular type of treatment. A number of cases in which individuals have sought to challenge decisions taken by healthcare professions with regard to a patient's treatment and, more generally, with regard to the management and allocation of resources to fund certain types of treatment have been unsuccessful.[75]

NHS structure

7.67 The structure of the NHS has changed recently and a number of bodies have been created in an attempt to improve the provision of health and care services to the public.[76]

7.68 The Department of Health is responsible for:

- setting overall direction and leading transformation of the NHS and social care;
- setting national standards to improve quality of services;
- securing resources and making investment decisions to ensure that the NHS and social care are able to deliver services; and
- working with key partners (such as with Strategic Health Authorities, the Commission for Healthcare Improvement, the Commission for Social Care Inspection, the NHS Modernisation Agency and the Social Care Institute for Excellence) to ensure quality of services.

---

74 National Health Service Act (NHSA) 1977 ss1 and 3 and article 13 of the European Social Charter (1961, revised 1996).

75 See, eg, *R v Cambridge Health Authority, ex p B* [1995] 2 All ER 129, CA and compare with *R v North East Devon HA ex p Coughlan* [2000] 3 All ER 850; (1999) 2 CCLR 285, where a patient was given a 'legitimate expectation' that she would be entitled to reside in a particular home for life and the court concluded that the health authority's subsequent decision to close the home was unlawful.

76 This chapter explains the structure of the NHS in England – different organisational structures are in place in Wales, Scotland and Northern Ireland.

7.69   The Modernisation Agency has been created to support NHS clinicians and managers in their efforts to deliver improvements to their services. The best performing organisations will be rewarded with more power to make decisions at a local level. The Agency will also support NHS organisations where services are poor or failing – identifying problems and helping to get these organisations back on track.

7.70   In April 2002, 28 new Strategic Health Authorities (SHAs) were created to cover larger areas, to develop strategies for the NHS and to make sure their local NHS organisations were performing well. They are responsible for:

- developing plans for improving health services in their local area;
- making sure local health services are of a high quality and are performing well;
- increasing the capacity of local health services – so they can provide more services;
- making sure national priorities – for example, programmes for improving cancer services – are integrated into local health service plans.

They manage the NHS locally and are a key link between the Department of Health and the NHS.

7.71   There are also a number of Special Health Authorities which provide a health service to the whole of the country, not just to the local community; for example, the National Blood Authority.

7.72   Locally based Primary Care Trusts (PCTs) have also been created and given the role of running the NHS, improving health and managing health services in their areas.[77] They work with local authorities and other agencies that provide health and social care to make sure the community's needs are being met.

7.73   PCTs are now at the centre of the NHS and receive 75 per cent of the NHS budget. As they are local organisations, they are expected to be in the best position to understand the needs of their community, so that they can make sure that the organisations providing health and social care services are working effectively. For example, PCTs must ensure that there are enough services for people in their area and that they are accessible to patients. They are also responsible for ensuring that health and social care systems work together to the benefit of patients.

77 See NHSA 1997 s16A.

7.74 'Primary care' is the care provided by people such as general practitioners (GPs), opticians and pharmacists. NHS walk-in centres and NHS Direct,[78] are also providers of primary care. All those offering primary care are now managed by PCTs. If a medical or other problem cannot be resolved by a provider of primary care then it will be referred to a 'secondary care' specialist. NHS hospitals provide acute and specialist secondary care services. PCTs are responsible for assessing the health needs of the local community and decide which secondary care services to commission to meet the needs of the people within their areas.

7.75 Hospitals are managed by NHS Trusts, which are expected to ensure that hospitals provide high quality health care, and that they spend their money efficiently. They also decide on a strategy for how the hospital will develop, so that services can improve. Trusts employ most of the NHS workforce, including nurses, doctors, dentists, pharmacists, midwives and health visitors, as well as people doing jobs related to medicine and other non-medical staff.

Gypsy and Traveller health research

7.76 In 1995, the Minority Rights Group (MRG) identified the following particular concerns about the health of the Gypsy population:

- life expectancy of Gypsies is poor and significantly less than the sedentary population;
- the Gypsy birth rate is high and perinatal mortality, stillbirth mortality and infant mortality is significantly higher than the national average;
- there are numerous chronic illnesses suffered by Gypsies (for example, respiratory and digestive diseases, rheumatism);
- many Gypsies have an unbalanced diet, leading to deficiencies;
- smoking is very common among Gypsies;
- Gypsies have little, if any, dental care with access to such care being more difficult as a result of many dental practices opting out of the NHS.[79]

7.77 In 2001, a two-year study of the health of Gypsies and Travellers (funded by the Inequalities Programme, Department of Health) was begun by the Sheffield Adult Mental Health Collaborative Research

---

78 NHS Direct is a 24-hour telephone service and can be contacted on 0845 4647.

79 *Roma/Gypsies: A European Minority* (MRG 1995).

Group Project. Preliminary research by the Project has already shown that:

- Gypsies' and Travellers' health status is poorer than matched urban deprived residents in terms of perceived overall health;
- Gypsies and Travellers suffer significantly higher levels of anxiety and depression than those from comparison groups; and
- both statutory health service providers and members of the Gypsy and Traveller community reported difficulties in access to appropriate services.[80]

Access to healthcare

7.78   There are a number of reasons why Gypsies and Travellers experience difficulty in gaining access to all types of health provision.[81]

7.79   High up on the list is the fact that many Gypsies and Travellers are still subject to a life of continual eviction in circumstances where there are not enough suitable places for them to camp.

7.80   Perhaps not surprisingly, the bureaucracy associated with the NHS also causes many Gypsies and Travellers problems. The completion of forms and the provision of information, such as dates of birth and history of previous healthcare, required by the NHS, causes particular difficulties for illiterate Gypsies and Travellers.

7.81   There is a the duty on Primary Care Trusts and NHS Trusts to have 'due regard' to the need to eliminate discrimination in their provision of services and to promote equality of opportunity and good relations between persons of different racial groups.[82]

7.82   However, some Gypsies and Travellers do experience discrimination at the hands of healthcare professionals. For example, Gypsies and Travellers living on unauthorised encampments still find that there are some GP surgeries that are reluctant to register them because they do not have a permanent address.

---

80 It is anticipated that the results of the study will be published in late 2004.

81 For a comprehensive European report on the elimination of discrimination and the improvement of access to healthcare for Gypsy and Traveller women and their communities see *Breaking the Barriers – Romani Women and Access to Public Health Care* (Council of Europe, 2003).

82 RRA 1976 s71(1) and Sch 1A.

7.83   More generally, there seems to be a lack of cultural awareness on the part of many service providers that can lead to discrimination and prejudice.[83]

7.84   For all those reasons Gypsies and Travellers without a permanent base tend to visit casualty departments or NHS Walk-In centres when they have an accident or illness and, as a consequence, are liable to experience a lack of consistency in health care provision. As a result they may be unable to receive the information, advice, support and preventative healthcare that is available to other members of the community.

7.85   Where Gypsies and Travellers can expect to be able to stay in an area for more than a few weeks, it is obviously sensible for them to try to register with a local GP if they have any health problems that need attention. Lists of doctors should be available at main Post Offices or by contacting 'NHS Direct'.[84] Alternatively, information can be provided by health visitors or obtained from the National Association of Health Workers with Travellers.[85]

Mental health and care in the community

7.86   Mental health care can be provided by GPs and by other primary care services. More specialist care (such as counselling and other psychological therapies, community and family support) is available in the community and may be provided by local authorities' social services departments. Alternatively, an individual may be admitted to hospital for treatment.

7.87   Local authorities have a duty to prepare and publish plans for community care services in their areas.[86] The term 'community care services' covers a wide range of services including: the provision of accommodation for adults who are unable to care for themselves;[87] services for adults who are blind, deaf, dumb, or substantially and permanently handicapped by illness, injury or congenital disability, including the adaptation of homes and the provision of meals and

---

83 Derbyshire Gypsy Liaison Group (see appendix C for contact details) have published an information booklet for healthcare and other professionals on the culture and customs followed by Gypsies and Travellers called *A Better Road* (2003).

84 NHS Direct can be contacted on 0845 4647 and is available 24 hours a day.

85 See appendix C for contact details.

86 National Health Service and Community Care Act 1990 s46.

87 National Assistance Act (NAA) 1948 s21.

special equipment;[88] services promoting the welfare of elderly people;[89] non-residential services for pregnant women and mothers; home help and laundry facilities for households caring for a person who is ill, handicapped or pregnant;[90] and, after-care services for those people who have been detained in hospital under the Mental Health Act (MHA) 1983 and subsequently discharged.[91]

7.88   Local authorities also have an obligation[92] to assess the needs of anyone who appears to them possibly to be in need of community care services and to decide whether such services should be provided in the light of that assessment.[93]

Healthcare and the ECHR

7.89   The ECHR does not give individuals an express right to medical treatment. However, it is clear that there could be circumstances where the failure to provide such treatment or the withdrawal of services could amount to a breach of article 2 (the right to life) and/or article 3 (the prohibition of inhuman and degrading treatment) of the ECHR.[94] Likewise, negligent medical treatment could also engage articles 2 and 3.

7.90   Health authorities, special health authorities, NHS Trusts, other regulatory bodies and local authorities all have a duty as public bodies to comply with the provisions of the ECHR.[95]

Medical records, privacy and the ECHR

7.91   In the UK, individuals are entitled to obtain access to medical and health records. The Access to Medical Reports Act 1988 gives an individual the right to obtain disclosure of medical reports prepared about him or her for the purposes of employment or insurance (save in certain circumstances). The Access to Health Records Act 1990[96]

---

88 NAA 1948 s29 and Chronically Sick and Disabled Persons Act 1970 s1.

89 Health Services and Public Health Act 1968 s45.

90 NHSA 1977 s21 and Sch 8.

91 MHA 1983 s117.

92 National Health Service and Community Care Act 1990 s47.

93 See generally, Luke Clements, *Community Care and the Law* (Legal Action Group, 3rd edn, 2004).

94 See, for example, *D v United Kingdom* [1997] 24 EHRR 423.

95 HRA 1998 s6.

96 As amended by the Data Protection Act (DPA) 1998.

gave individuals a general right of access to medical records created after November 1991 (subject also to exceptions) but most of its provisions have been superseded by the Data Protection Act (DPA) 1998. The Access to Health Records Act 1990 is now only of any real relevance in cases where disclosure of the medical records of a deceased person is sought.

7.92 DPA 1998 gives individuals the right, on a written application, to be informed whether their personal data is being processed, and, if it is, then they can request a description of the data, the purpose for which it is being processed, and the people to whom it may be disclosed.[97] DPA 1998 also gives individuals the right to have the information communicated to them in an intelligible form.

7.93 DPA 1998 covers all 'accessible records' and, therefore, all social services and health records,[98] educational records,[99] and accessible public records including information held by a local housing authority and by a local social services authority for any purpose relating to the functions of the authority.[100]

7.94 The written request for information made to the person holding the data (the 'data controller') must provide such information as the data controller reasonably requires in order to identify the individual making the request and locate the information required.[101] The request must also be accompanied by the payment of a fee.[102] If a valid request has been made, then disclosure of the information required ought to be made promptly and in any event within 40 days.[103]

7.95 In practice these provisions entitle patients to a copy of their records together, if necessary, with an intelligible explanation of their contents.[104]

7.96 However, there are a number of exceptions to the duty to provide disclosure. For example, disclosure need not be provided of material that would be likely to prejudice criminal investigations, national security or ongoing health education and social work. Nor is there any obligation to disclose information if to do so would involve the

---

97 DPA 1998 s7(1)(a) and (b).
98 DPA 1998 s68 and Schs 11 and 12.
99 DPA 1998 Sch 11.
100 DPA 1998 Sch 12.
101 DPA 1998 s7.
102 Currently £10; see Data Protection (Subject Access) (Fees and Miscellaneous Provisions) Regulations 2000 SI No 191.
103 DPA 1998 s7.
104 DPA 1998 s8(2).

disclosure of material relating to another individual, unless that individual consents or it is considered by the data controller to be reasonable in the circumstances to comply with the request without that individual's consent.[105]

7.97   If disclosure is refused by a data controller, then an individual can apply to the county court or High Court for an order that the data controller complies with the request[106] or an application can be made to the Information Commissioner for enforcement action to be taken.[107]

7.98   In *Z v Finland*,[108] it was held that the collection of medical data and the maintenance of medical records fell within the sphere of private life protected by ECHR article 8. In addition, it was said that medical confidentiality was a 'vital principle' crucial to privacy and also to preserving confidence in the medical profession and the health services in general. As a consequence it was held that:

> ... any state measures compelling communication or disclosure of such information without the consent of the patient call for the most careful scrutiny ...[109]

7.99   Likewise, any decision taken by a public body to restrict the disclosure of an individual's medical reports will engage article 8 (right to respect for private and family life, home and correspondence) and it should be possible to challenge such a decision by way of judicial review where it can be said that the restriction is unreasonable or disproportionate.[110]

Environmental health

7.100   Another matter of great concern to Gypsies, Travellers and healthcare practitioners alike is the fact that there is a clear and undeniable link between the poor living environment and poor health of many Gypsies and Travellers.

7.101   One particular problem for those Gypsies and Travellers without an authorised site results from the lack of access to fresh water. A variety of health problems can result from the lack of water and poor

105 DPA 1998 s7(4).
106 DPA 1998 ss7(9), 10(4), 11(2), 12(8) and 15(1).
107 DPA 1998 ss40–44.
108 [1997] 25 EHRR 371.
109 [1997] 25 EHRR 371 at para 96.
110 See, eg, *Gaskin v United Kingdom* [1989] 12 EHRR 36.

sanitation including skin diseases, gastro-enteritis, hepatitis and other infections.

7.102 While there is no statutory duty on local authorities to enable the provision of water to unauthorised encampments, Department of Environment (DoE) Circular 18/94, (Welsh Office 76/94) *Gypsy Sites Policy and Unauthorised Camping,* advises local authorities to consider tolerating the presence of Gypsies and Travellers on temporary or unofficial sites and to examine ways of minimising the level of nuisance on such sites. Local authorities should be encouraged to comply with the advice in DoE Circular 18/94 by providing basic services such as toilets, a refuse skip and a supply of drinking water to those camped on unauthorised sites.[111]

7.103 Alternatively, it may be possible to persuade a local authority to provide water in circumstances where there are children 'in need' living on the site, that is, children who are unlikely to achieve or maintain, or to have the opportunity of achieving or maintaining, a reasonable standard of health or development, without the provision of services by a local authority, or children whose health is likely to be significantly impaired or further impaired without the provision of such services.[112]

7.104 It is not only those living on the roadside that suffer health problems associated with their environment. Many Gypsies and Travellers living on permanent sites may, paradoxically, experience even worse conditions and resultant health complaints. Permanent sites are often found in isolated and environmentally poor areas (by, or sometimes under, major roads or railways, and often near rubbish dumps, on former industrial sites or close to sewage plants) where health problems can stem from poor air quality, poor drainage and the contamination of land.[113]

7.105 Where an authorised site run by a private individual or body is in such a state that it is prejudicial to health or a nuisance, then a resident Gypsy or Traveller is entitled to make a complaint to the local authority. If the local authority is satisfied that a statutory nuisance exists, is likely to occur, or is likely to recur in its area then

---

111 In a report from the Chartered Institute of Environmental Health, *Travellers and Gypsies: An Alternative Strategy* (1995) it was stated that: 'Emergency and temporary unofficial encampments can threaten public health. Local authorities must mitigate against this by providing basic sanitation, wholesome water and by removing refuse'. See also the ODPM *Guidance on Managing Unauthorised Camping* (February 2004).

112 Children Act 1989 s17.

113 See also chapter 3.

it has a duty to serve an Abatement Notice[114] on the 'person' responsible. Contravention of, or failure to comply with, an Abatement Notice without reasonable excuse is a criminal offence.[115]

7.106   In a case where a local authority site is in such a state that it is prejudicial to health or a nuisance, then a resident Gypsy or Traveller is entitled to make a complaint to the magistrates' court and request that the statutory nuisance be brought to an end.[116] Failure to comply with such an order is a criminal offence.

Conclusion

7.107   In a report published in 2004, the Institute for Public Policy Research (IPPR) made the point that:

> Gypsy [and Traveller] communities continue to be over-represented in nearly all indices of deprivation and social exclusion and to experience widespread prejudice and discrimination. Significant change will be needed in order to make a real impact on the lives of the Travelling community. As with other socially excluded groups it is clear that suitable, good quality, well managed and regulated accommodation is the key to overcoming other social problems.[117]

7.108   While it is not possible to predict whether the government will take any meaningful steps to ensure that sufficient suitable sites are provided for Gypsies and Travellers, it is hoped that it will grasp the nettle and incorporate the proposals for change advocated by the CRE, the IPPR, and the Traveller Law Reform Coalition within forthcoming legislation.[118]

114 Environment Protection Act 1990 s80. See chapter 3 paras 3.42–3.44 above, for a full discussion of this issue and explanation of the various terms.

115 Environment Protection Act 1990 s80(4).

116 EPA 1990 s82.

117 H Crawley, *Moving Forward: the provision of accommodation for Travellers and Gypsies* (The Institute of Public Policy Research, 2004) p5.

118 See chapter 9 for further discussion of the issues for the future.

Race discrimination

continued overleaf

Introduction

8.1   Romani Gypsies have been resident in Great Britain since the 16th century, Irish Travellers since the 19th century, yet they remain one of the most disadvantaged racial groups in Britain. An estimated 12,000 pupils of secondary age are not in school;[1] life expectancy is a decade less for Gypsy and Traveller men than for other racial groups, and still less for Gypsy and Traveller women. A key contributor to their poor socio-economic condition is the fact that thousands of families have no lawful residence: they are routinely refused planning permission and face constant eviction or other enforcement action, including criminal proceedings, when trying to pursue their traditional way of life, living in their caravans.

8.2   Although race relations legislation has been in force in the UK since 1965 and has developed considerably to protect against increasingly subtle forms of discrimination, Gypsies and Travellers are still experiencing discrimination of the most overt kind: 'No blacks, no Irish, no dogs' signs[2] disappeared decades ago, but the 'No Travellers' signs, used intentionally to exclude Gypsies and Travellers, are still widespread indicating that discrimination against these groups remains the last 'respectable' form of racism in the UK.[3] This is supported by the findings of a recent Mori poll conducted in England[4] in which 34 per cent of respondents admitted to being personally prejudiced against Gypsies and Travellers. Trevor Phillips, Chair of the Commission for Racial Equality (CRE) has compared the situation of Gypsies and Travellers living in Great Britain with that of black people living in the American Deep South in the 1950s.

The legal framework

8.3   The Race Relations Act (RRA) 1976[5] makes it unlawful to discriminate on racial grounds in employment, education, housing

---

1 *Provision and Support for Traveller Pupils* (Ofsted, 2003), available at http://www.ofsted.gov.uk.

2 See, eg, the discussion by McVeigh 'Nick, Nack, Paddywhack: Anti-Irish racism and the racialisation of Irishness' in Lentin and McVeigh, eds *Racism and Anti-Racism in Ireland* (Beyond the Pale, 2002) pp136–152.

3 See, for example, Hawes and Perez *The Gypsy and the State: The Ethnic Cleansing of British Society* (The Polity Press, 1996) pp148–155.

4 *Profiles of Prejudice: The Nature of Prejudice in England* (Stonewall, 2003).

5 As amended by the Race Relations (Amendment) Act (RRAA) 2000.

and planning, the exercise of public functions and in the provision of goods, facilities and services.

8.4   The RRA 1976 defines four main forms of unlawful discrimination: direct discrimination; indirect discrimination; victimisation; and harassment. The definitions of indirect discrimination and harassment vary according to the context in which the discrimination or harassment takes place. This is because of new, improved definitions introduced in July 2003 by the European Community race directive, which provides protection against discrimination on grounds of race, ethnic or national origins, but not on grounds of colour or nationality, in the areas of employment, training and service provision.

Direct discrimination

8.5   Direct discrimination occurs when a person is treated less favourably on racial grounds than another person is or would be treated in the same or similar circumstances. No justification is acceptable for direct racial discrimination.

8.6   Discrimination rarely takes place openly and may not even be conscious. It will, therefore, usually be proved only as a matter of inference.

8.7   The RRA 1976 recognises that a person alleging unlawful racial discrimination may not be able to compare his or her treatment with that of another actual person. In these circumstances, the RRA 1976 permits the comparison to be made with a hypothetical person of a different racial group in a similar situation. The question to be asked is: how would a person from a different racial group be treated, in circumstances that are not identical but not too dissimilar?

8.8   In certain cases involving Gypsies and Travellers, particularly where they live on sites and they feel they have been discriminated against in the way accommodation or ancillary facilities are offered or managed, it may be difficult to find an appropriate comparator. A council tenant is unlikely to be accepted as a comparator because the nature of a caravan on a council site would be considered 'materially different' from a council house.

8.9   The case of *Smith and Smith v Cheltenham BC and others*[6] provides a clear example of direct discrimination against a Gypsy. The

---

6 *Smith and Smith v Cheltenham BC, Avery, Lambert, and Hogg*, 7 June 1999, (CN755478), (unreported), Bristol County Court, HHJ Rutherford.

applicant, a Gypsy woman, had hired the Pittville Pump Rooms from the council for a reception for her daughter's wedding, and paid a deposit on the booking. Further wedding arrangements were then made, including catering and the printing of invitations. As a result of several allegations of disorder in recent years, and rumours about the forthcoming wedding, the police became concerned that the wedding celebrations might involve public disorder and liaised with the council, including the manager of the venue, to voice these concerns. The council attached conditions to the hire of the venue, including a requirement that entry should be by ticket only, and that a further deposit should be paid. The claimant and her daughter were very upset and booked an alternative venue (where the event took place without incident). They subsequently brought an action against the council for breach of contract and discrimination in the provision of goods and services[7] and against individual police officers for knowingly aiding the council to discriminate.[8]

8.10 HHJ Rutherford found in their favour and awarded damages. He stated:

> I find that there is no foundation for the assertions of the police that the Gypsy problems of 1997 were linked to the Smith family. The truth is that as soon as the word 'Gypsy' appears assumptions are made that large numbers will descend and cause trouble.

8.11 However, the judge concluded that the police had not breached RRA 1976 because they had not knowingly aided the council in discriminating and were not involved in the council's decision.[9]

Indirect discrimination

8.12 RRA 1976 contains two definitions for indirect discrimination.

Grounds of 'colour and nationality'

8.13 Indirect discrimination occurs when a person applies a 'condition or requirement' which is apparently neutral but which is such that the proportion of people from a particular racial group who can comply with it is considerably smaller than the proportion of people from

---

7 RRA 1976 ss20 and 21.
8 RRA 1976 s33, which prohibits a person from knowingly aiding another to do an act in breach of RRA 1976.
9 The Court of Appeal upheld the decision of HHJ Rutherford: see *Hallam, Smith v Avery and Lambert* [2001] 1 WLR 655.

other groups who could comply, and which cannot be justified on non-racial grounds.[10]

Grounds of 'race or ethnic or national origins only'

8.14   Indirect discrimination also occurs when a 'provision, criterion or practice', which on the face of it has nothing to do with race, puts or would put people of a particular race or ethnic or national origin at a particular disadvantage compared with others, unless it can be shown that the provision, criterion or practice is a 'proportionate means of achieving a legitimate aim'.[11]

8.15   In practical terms this broader definition will now cover informal practices in addition to more formal requirements and it need not require statistical evidence of disadvantage. The aim of the provision must be justifiable and the provision, criterion or practice needs to be proportionate.

8.16   The concept of 'practice' may be defined as the customary ways in which an intention or policy is actually carried out. It may include attitudes and behaviour that could amount to discrimination through unwitting prejudice, ignorance, thoughtlessness and racist stereotyping.

8.17   It is important to note however that this broader definition only applies to certain provisions of the RRA 1976:

- Part II – discrimination in employment,
- ss17 to 18D – discrimination in education;
- s19B (discrimination by public bodies in all functions) – only in so far as such functions relate to any form of social security, health care, any other form of social protection and any form of social advantage;
- ss20 to 24 – goods, facilities and services, disposal or management of premises;
- ss26A and 26B – barristers and advocates;
- ss76 and 76A – government appointments;
- Part IV (other unlawful acts – discriminatory advertisements, instructions to discriminate, employer liability, aiding unlawful acts).

8.18   Notable exclusions from the broader definition of *indirect* discrimination are planning, regulatory and law enforcement functions.

---

10   RRA 1976 s1(1)(b).
11   RRA 1976 s1A (as amended by Race Relations Act 1976 (Amendment) Regulations 2003 SI No 1626 reg 3).

8.19   In *Commission for Racial Equality v Dutton*,[12] the Court of Appeal concluded that a 'no Traveller' sign displayed in a pub was an example of indirect discrimination. It does not *directly* discriminate against Gypsies, as it applies to a wider nomadic group, but as Nicholls LJ stated:

> Clearly the proportion of Gypsies who will satisfy the 'No Travellers' condition is considerably smaller than the proportion of non-gypsies ... a far higher proportion of gypsies are leading a nomadic way of life than the rest of the population in general or, more narrowly, than the rest of the population who might wish to resort to the Cat and Mutton [public house].[13]

Segregation

8.20   Segregating a person from others on racial grounds automatically means treating him or her less favourably, and constitutes unlawful direct discrimination.

Victimisation

8.21   This occurs when a person is treated less favourably than another because they have brought or are suspected of having brought legal proceedings under RRA 1976; or because they have given evidence or information on behalf of someone else's complaint under RRA 1976; or because they have complained of racial discrimination.

Harassment

8.22   A person harasses another on grounds of race or ethnic or national origin when his or her behaviour is unwanted, and when it has the purpose or effect of:

(a) violating the other person's dignity; or
(b) creating an intimidating, hostile, degrading, humiliating or offensive [working] environment for them.[14]

8.23   For a finding of harassment, it must be reasonable to believe that the behaviour in question would have such an effect, taking all the

---

12 [1989] 2 WLR 17, CA.
13 [1989] 2 WLR 17 at 29.
14 RRA 1976 s3A(1) (as amended by Race Relations Act 1976 (Amendment) Regulations 2003 reg 5).

circumstances into account, including the complainant's view of the behaviour.[15]

8.24   It would be necessary to show that the conduct had, or was intended to have, the effect of violating a person's dignity or creating a degrading, humiliating hostile, intimidating or offensive working environment for that person.[16]

8.25   Harassment on grounds of colour or nationality amounts to less favourable treatment and may constitute unlawful direct discrimination under RRA 1976.

8.26   So, for example, if an Irish Traveller was subjected to a campaign of racist comments and taunts from work colleagues, then he or she could make a complaint of harassment against the harassers and the employer who is liable for the acts of employees. The employer is not however liable for the acts of third parties.[17]

Unlawful advertisements

8.27   It is unlawful to publish, or to be responsible for publishing, an advertisement that indicates, or may reasonably be taken to indicate, an intention to discriminate unlawfully.[18] RRA 1976 applies to all forms of advertising, including internal circulars or newsletters announcing staff vacancies, and displays on notice boards or shop windows. This provision would apply to 'No Traveller' signs.

8.28   RRA 1976 allows a small number of exceptions where discrimination is not unlawful, for example, in the case of a lawful positive action training measure or a genuine occupational requirement or qualification. The advertisement should make it clear that the employer is making use of the exception.

8.29   Only the CRE has the power to bring legal action against the publication of an unlawful advertisement.

Instructions to discriminate

8.30   It is unlawful for a person who has authority over another person, or whose wishes that person customarily follows, to instruct him or her to discriminate unlawfully on racial grounds.[19]

---

15 RRA 1976 s3A(2).
16 RRA 1976 s3A(1).
17 *Pearce v Governing Body of Mayfield School* [2003] UKHL 24.
18 RRA 1976 s29.
19 RRA 1976 s30.

Pressure to discriminate

8.31   It is also unlawful to induce, or attempt to induce, a person to discriminate unlawfully on racial grounds.[20] The courts have expressed the view that 'inducement' may be no more than persuasion and that it does not necessarily entail a benefit or detriment.

Aiding an unlawful act

8.32   It is unlawful to knowingly aid another person to do an act made unlawful by the RRA 1976.[21]

Scope of RRA 1976

8.33   The RRA 1976 prohibits discrimination in a wide range of areas.

Employment[22]

8.34   It is unlawful for a person: to apply discriminatory recruitment or application procedures; to offer different terms and conditions to employees of different racial groups; to withhold a job offer on racial grounds; to discriminate in offering opportunities for promotion, transfer, or training; to discriminate in offering or withholding other benefits, facilities or services; or to dismiss someone on racial grounds.

Education[23]

8.35   Local education authorities and governing bodies are prohibited from discriminating against pupils on racial grounds: by admitting them on different terms to other pupils; by rejecting their application; by withholding benefits, facilities or services or offering such benefits on differential terms; by excluding them or subjecting them to any other detriment and from any other discriminatory act.

---

20 RRA 1976 s31.
21 RRA 1976 s33 and *Smith and Smith v Cheltenham BC*, 7 June 1999 (CN755478), Bristol County Court, HHJ Rutherford.
22 RRA 1976 s4.
23 RRA 1976 ss17 and 18.

Planning[25]

8.36   Local planning authorities are prohibited from discriminating against a person on racial grounds in carrying out their planning functions.[26] So, for example, discrimination would have occurred if a planning authority rejected an application for planning permission for a site where it could be proved that the decision was based on the fact that the applicant was an ethnic Gypsy or Traveller.

Public functions[27]

8.37   It is unlawful for any public authority,[28] including the police, to discriminate in carrying out any of its functions. For example, the discriminatory use of 'stop and search' powers by the police would be unlawful.

Goods, facilities or services[29]

8.38   It is unlawful for anyone who provides goods, facilities or services to the public, to refuse provision on racial grounds, or to provide a lesser standard of provision. This provision could be used, for example, where an electricity or water company refuses to provide services for ethnic Gypsies or Travellers living on a site, or provided sub-standard services on racial grounds. *Smith and Smith v Cheltenham BC*[30] is an example of the successful use of RRA 1976 ss20 and 21.

Housing[31]

8.39   It is unlawful for someone to discriminate in how they dispose of or manage premises, by refusing an application for the premises, or treating an applicant differently in relation to any list of persons in

25   RRA 1976 s19A.
26   In England and Wales 'planning functions' means functions under the Town and Country Planning Act 1990, the Planning (Listed Buildings and Conservation Areas) Act 1990, the Planning (Hazardous Substances) Act 1990 and any others which are prescribed.
27   RRA 1976 s19B.
28   In this section, 'public authority' includes any person certain of whose functions are functions of a public nature.
29   RRA 1976 s20.
30   7 June 1999 (CN755478), Bristol County Court, HHJ Rutherford (unreported) and see para 8.9 above.
31   RRA 1976 s21.

need of such premises. It is unlawful for someone to discriminate in how they manage the premises, how they give or withhold benefits or facilities, and to discriminate in the way that an eviction is carried out. This provision applies to site provision and management. So, for example, a Romani Gypsy or ethnic Traveller could bring a claim that a housing authority had discriminated against them when allocating council housing or pitches on an official site.

Discrimination by other bodies

8.40 Trade unions, employers' associations and professional and trade associations have a dual role as employers and providers of services specifically covered by RRA 1976. They are also responsible for making sure their representatives and members do not discriminate unlawfully, on racial grounds:

- in the way they admit members, or
- treat them, as colleagues, supervisors or subordinates.[32]

8.41 The Act also applies to membership clubs. It is unlawful for clubs and associations to discriminate on racial grounds in membership and the provision of benefits, facilities or services to members or by subjecting a member to any other detriment. This applies only to clubs and associations of 25 or more members and where admission is regulated by a constitution.[33]

8.42 RRA 1976 does not apply to racist newspaper articles or to racist broadcasts. However, where it is considered that an article or broadcast amounts to an 'incitement to racial hatred' then the police may prosecute the person(s) responsible for breaching the provisions of the Public Order Act 1986 which outlaw such acts. Any member of the public can refer such material to the police. Although the CRE has no legal powers to deal with such cases, it may refer matters to the police directly. In October 2003 the CRE referred the burning of an effigy of a Gypsy caravan in Firle, Sussex to the police.[34] The police subsequently launched an investigation and a number of people were arrested.

---

32 RRA 1976 s11.
33 RRA 1976 s25.
34 See chapter 1 para 1.1.

Racial groups – protection for Gypsies and Travellers

8.43　RRA 1976 protects all racial groups from discrimination. 'Racial group' means a group of persons defined by reference to colour, race, nationality or ethnic or national origins.

8.44　Romani Gypsies and Irish Travellers have been held to be 'ethnic' groups for the purpose of the RRA 1976. The criteria for determining whether a group constitutes an ethnic group is set out in the House of Lords judgment in the case of *Mandla (Sewa Singh) v Dowell Lee*.[35] The Lords held that to constitute an 'ethnic group' under RRA 1976 a group had to regard itself, and be regarded by others, as a distinct community by virtue of certain characteristics. Two essential factors are:

- a long shared history, of which the group is conscious as distinguishing it from other groups, and the memory of which it keeps alive;
- a cultural tradition of its own, including family and social customs and manners, often but not necessarily associated with religious observance.

8.45　Other relevant considerations which are likely to indicate, but not essential to define, a distinct ethnic group include:

- a common geographical origin or descent from a small number of common ancestors;
- a common language, not necessarily peculiar to that group;
- a common literature peculiar to the group;
- a common religion different from that of neighbouring groups or from the general community surrounding it;
- being a minority or being an oppressed or a dominant group within a larger community.

8.46　In *CRE v Dutton*,[36] the Court of Appeal found that Romani Gypsies were a minority with a long shared history, a common geographical origin and a cultural tradition of their own.

35　[1983] 2 AC 548.
36　[1989] 2 WLR 17, CA.

8.47   In *O'Leary v Allied Domecq*,[37] HHJ Goldstein reached a similar decision in respect of Irish Travellers. Although a county court judgment, it should be noted that, in Northern Ireland, Irish Travellers are explicitly protected from discrimination under Race Relations (Northern Ireland) Order 1997 article 5, and this makes it highly unlikely that their status as members of a separate ethnic group could be open to challenge again in the UK. As HHJ Goldstein said in *O'Leary*:

> ... if indeed it be the case, as the defence argue, that Irish travellers do not bring themselves within the definition of an ethnic social group under the Act, then we have a very strange anomaly that Irish travellers are protected in Ireland but not protected in England as a result of legislation by a British government.[38]

8.48   The distinct racial identity of Scottish Travellers, Welsh Travellers or other Travellers has yet to be considered by the courts although there was some recognition of Welsh Travellers in the observations made by Nicholls LJ in *Dutton*.[39]

8.49   It is unlikely, that New Travellers or other occupational Travellers would come within the definition of a racial group. In *O'Leary*,[40] HHJ Goldstein made it clear that the court's decision would not enable all Travellers to claim ethnic status, and that it should not be seen as 'opening the floodgates to endless applications from amorphous groups seeking to take advantage of this decision.' Furthermore, it was made clear by Stocker LJ in *CRE v Dutton*,[41] that a strong case would need to be made by others and that 'the fact alone that a group may comply with all or most of the relevant criteria does not establish that such a group is of ethnic origin'.

8.50   Even after hearing expert evidence, the courts may still reject an argument that a group constitutes a racial group. For example, in *Dawkins v Department of the Environment*,[42] the EAT held that Rastafarians were not an ethnic group because, although they share a common religion and meet some of the other criteria, it was

---

37 *O'Leary and others v Allied Domecq and others*, 29 August 2000 (Case No CL 950275–79), Central London County Court. Goldstein HHJ (unreported).
38 P *O'Leary and others v Allied Domecq and others* at page 26 of the judgment.
39 [1989] 2 WLR 17 at 27.
40 29 August 2000 (Case No CL 950275–79), Central London County Court at page 39 of the judgment.
41 [1989] 2 WLR 17 at 34.
42 [1993] IRLR 284.

considered that they do not have a sufficiently long shared history and that there was not enough to distinguish them from the rest of the African Caribbean community. The same arguments may apply to other Travelling groups.[43]

Ethnicity and the statutory definition of 'Gypsy'

8.51   Ethnic Gypsies and Travellers are protected from discrimination, whether or not they are nomadic. However, the 'statutory' definition of 'Gypsy' in planning law[44] requires that a person be of a 'nomadic habit of life'. It follows that a person can qualify as a 'statutory' Gypsy, but not be an ethnic Romani Gypsy or Traveller or, as the recent judgment in *Berry v The National Assembly of Wales and Wrexham CBC*[45] illustrates.[46]

8.52   Nomadism was discussed in the judgments in both *Dutton*[47] and *O'Leary*[48] and was a particularly relevant consideration in the latter case where it was a feature which distinguished Irish Travellers from other Irish people, who were already protected. HHJ Goldstein accepted that Irish Travellers were a racial group, but left a degree of uncertainty about the issue of nomadism and questioned the view of Nicholls LJ in *CRE v Dutton*:[49]

> It [nomadism] certainly is not as clear, with great respect to Lord Justice Nicholls as he then was, in his judgment in *Dutton* would have us believe. Academically the learned writers' papers will go on doubtlessly debating this for time to come.

8.53   Goldstein HHJ also quoted the words of Michael Ancram, former Secretary of State for Northern Ireland, who suggested that the

---

43 Those Travellers that are not recognised members of an ethnic group can still use ECHR article 14 to challenge discrimination in respect of any other rights that they enjoy under the Convention. See chapter 2 paras 2.9–2.11 above.

44 Caravan Sites and Control of Development Act 1960 s24(8) as amended by Criminal Justice and Public Order Act 1994 s80. See chapter 4 paras 4.38–4.55 above, for further discussion of this issue.

45 [2003] EWCA Civ 835.

46 See chapter 4.

47 [1989] 2 WLR 17, CA.

48 *O'Leary and others v Allied Domecq and others*, 29 August 2000 (Case No CL 950275–79), Central London County Court. Goldstein HHJ (unreported).

49 29 August 2000 (Case No CL950275–79), Central London County Court. Goldstein HHJ (unreported) at page 27 of the judgment.

definition of Irish Travellers in Northern Ireland is not dependent on nomadism:

> The fact that they [Irish Travellers] travel is obviously another element but it is only one element ... I am told that some 60 per cent of Irish Travellers are settled, while they might lose that element of travelling they still retain those other elements of separate ethnicity.[50]

Clearly a paradoxical situation would arise if a different interpretation was applied in Britain.

8.54 Some helpful observations have been made about the relationship between ethnicity and nomadism in other cases. For example, in *Horsham DC v Secretary of State for the Environment*,[51] McCullough J commented:

> Clearly there can, and indeed must, come a time when as a matter of fact the nomadic habit of life has been lost. When it is lost the gypsy is no longer a gypsy for the purposes of the Act [Caravan Sites Act 1968]. He remains, of course, a gypsy by descent, by culture, and by tradition, but that is not the issue ...

8.55 The point to stress here is that Gypsies and Travellers who constitute racial groups are protected by the RRA 1976 whether or not they travel. It is their separate group identity which makes them eligible for protection.

8.56 As was said in *CRE v Dutton* by Nicholls LJ:

> Have Gypsies now lost their separate, group identity so that they are no longer a community recognisable by ethnic origins within the meaning of the Act? ... The fact that some have been ... absorbed [into a larger group] and are indistinguishable from any ordinary member of the public is not sufficient in itself to establish loss of what [has been] referred to as 'an historically determined social identity in [the group's] own eyes and in the eyes of those outside the group.'[52]

Enforcing the RRA 1976

8.57 If a Gypsy or Traveller feels that he or she has been discriminated against directly or indirectly, or victimised or harassed in any of the areas covered by RRA 1976 on racial grounds, he or she can make a complaint of discrimination.

---

50 29 August 2000 (Case No CL950275–79), Central London County Court. Goldstein HHJ (unreported) at pages 24–25 of the judgment.
51 13 October 1989 (unreported) at pages 4–5 of the judgment.
52 [1989] 2 WLR 17 at 28.

Pursuing a complaint of discrimination

8.58   A complainant can seek assistance from a citizens advice bureau (CAB), a local Race Equality Council (which is an independent voluntary organisation which may be part-funded by the CRE), a solicitor or other suitable advice agency. He or she can also approach the CRE for advice and assistance. Arrangements can be made upon request for those who are unable to read or write and for applicants to provide information to the nearest Race Equality Council if travelling.

8.59   While the CRE has an obligation to consider all applications for assistance, it is not obliged to *grant* assistance in all cases and will only support those cases that meet the statutory criteria set out in RRA 1976 s66(1), that is those cases that:

- raise a question of principle, or
- are of such complexity that it would be unreasonable to expect the applicant to deal with the case unaided or by reason of any other special consideration.

Assistance could take the form of legal advice, assisting in a settlement, arranging and financing advice or assistance by a solicitor or counsel, or arranging and financing representation in litigation.

8.60   Cases involving racial discrimination in employment are heard in employment tribunals. Other racial discrimination cases are heard in county courts (in England and Wales).[53] In many cases it is advisable to settle a case before it gets to a full hearing, if the terms are acceptable to both parties or are the same or better than what would be granted by a court or tribunal. In practice, a significant proportion of all cases are settled on agreed terms. A settlement may take the form of an agreement to pay a sum of money or an apology and frequently contains an undertaking to work with the CRE to bring the respondent into compliance with the RRA 1976.

8.61   In employment cases, the services of the Advisory, Conciliation and Arbitration Service (ACAS) are automatically offered, to help the complainant reach a settlement. ACAS is an independent body set up to act as a go-between in disputes. There is no obligation to accept ACAS's advice, but if a settlement is reached through ACAS, the complaint cannot go to the tribunal and must be withdrawn. ACAS cannot assist with settling county or sheriff court cases.

---

53 Sheriff courts in Scotland.

8.62   If cases do reach hearings, then, in the case of employment tribunal cases, the tribunal can order compensation to be paid to the applicant. The amount may include a sum for lost earnings and benefits and a sum for injury to feelings. There is no ceiling to the amount a tribunal can award, although it will normally follow guidelines and precedents from previous cases. If the case is successful, the tribunal can also recommend that the employer take certain steps to enable the complainant to work without further discrimination.

8.63   If the case is not successful, the applicant will not automatically be ordered to pay the other side's legal costs, but the tribunal may make them pay if they think he or she acted unreasonably, frivolously or vexatiously in pursuing the case. An appeal against the tribunal's decision can be made to the Employment Appeal Tribunal, but only on a point of law. An appeal must be lodged within 42 days.

8.64   In the county court,[54] if the case is successful, the court can order compensation to be paid. The amount may include a sum to compensate the claimant for any losses and a sum for injury to feelings. There is no ceiling to the compensation that a court can award, but awards tend to be lower than those made by tribunals. If the case is withdrawn before trial or is ultimately unsuccessful, then the claimant will normally be ordered to pay the defendant's legal costs.

Obtaining information by using the questionnaire procedure

8.65   Where a person suspects that they have been subjected to unlawful discrimination or harassment, they may send a questionnaire to the person or body suspected of discriminating against them.[55] RRA 1976 s65(1) permits the secretary of state by order to prescribe the forms that may be used by the aggrieved person and the respondent. The Race Relations (Questions and Replies) Order 1977 permits an 'aggrieved' person to question a possible 'respondent on his reasons for doing any relevant act, or any other matter which is or may be relevant'. The order permits the use of forms 'to the like effect' with such variations as the circumstances may require.

54 Sheriff court in Scotland.
55 The time limits for the service of and replies to questionnaires can be found in the Race Relations (Questions and Replies) Order 1977 art 4 and Race Relations Act 1976 (Amendment) Regulations 2003 reg 47.

Failure to reply or evasive and equivocal replies

8.66   Where the aggrieved person questions the respondent, the question and any reply are admissible in evidence in any proceedings that are brought. Where a respondent deliberately and without reasonable excuse omits to reply, or is evasive or equivocal in their reply, RRA 1976 s65(2) permits a court or tribunal to draw any inference that it considers just and equitable, including an inference that the respondent committed an unlawful act.

Power of the courts or tribunals to draw inferences

8.67   The Race Relations Act 1976 (Amendment) Regulations 2003[56] amends RRA 1976 by inserting two new sections into the Act. RRA 1976 ss54A and 57ZA apply to complaints of discrimination on grounds of race or ethnic or national origins and to complaints of harassment brought before employment tribunals and the courts respectively and change the burden of proof in these cases. Previously the burden of proof was on the claimant to prove the allegation of discrimination. Since 19 July 2003 the burden of proof has shifted so that once the complainant has established the facts from which discrimination or harassment could be inferred, the burden of proof is on the respondent to show that they did not discriminate against the complainant.

8.68   An applicant (or claimant in the county court) can take advantage of the questionnaire procedure to obtain information that might assist them in establishing a prima facie case of discrimination before the tribunal (or court). Where a respondent fails to provide evidence to show that they did not discriminate against the complainant, the court or tribunal is directed to find against the respondent (or defendant).

8.69   As RRA 1976 ss54A and 57ZA apply to complaints of discrimination on grounds of race or ethnic or national origins and to complaints of harassment, the burden of proof used by the tribunals and courts will now vary according to the grounds of the alleged discrimination.

Grounds of race or ethnic or national origin

8.70   If an applicant or claimant can establish the facts from which a tribunal or court can infer that an act of racial discrimination or

56   Reg 41.

harassment on grounds of race or ethnic or national origin has occurred, the employer will have to prove that any difference in treatment was not due in any way to discrimination or harassment. If the explanation is inadequate or unsatisfactory, the tribunal or court must find that unlawful discrimination or harassment has occurred.

Grounds of colour or nationality

8.71   If the act of discrimination or harassment is on the grounds of colour or nationality, and the applicant or claimant establishes facts from which a tribunal or court could infer that he or she has suffered racial discrimination, the tribunal or court will ask the employer for an explanation. If the explanation is inadequate or unsatisfactory, the tribunal or court *may* find that discrimination has occurred.

Time limits for making a complaint

8.72   A discrimination complaint must be made within a fixed period of the discriminatory act occurring, or ceasing to occur. There are separate time limits for county court and tribunal proceedings. Generally, complaints made in the county court must be brought within six months (that is, no later than six months less one day) of the act of discrimination complained of.

8.73   However, in the case of complaints made under RRA 1976 s57(5) (against education authorities or certain educational bodies that are listed in the table in RRA 1976 s17) the claimant is required to first give notice of the claim to the secretary of state, and the complaint must be made to the county court within eight months of the act complained of.

8.74   Generally a complaint made to the employment tribunal must be lodged within three months (that is, no later than three months less one day) of the act of discrimination complained of.[57] Exceptionally, and only in very limited circumstances, the court or tribunal will consider a late application when 'just and equitable' to do so.[58]

---

57   See C Palmer et al, *Discrimination Law Handbook* (Legal Action Group, 2002) for further information on time limits and exceptions to the general rule.

58   RRA 1976 s68(6).

'No Traveller' signs and other discriminatory advertisements

8.75 Such cases do not require a 'victim', and while an individual can bring signs to the CRE's attention, only the CRE is empowered to take legal action.[59] The practice is to ask the respondent to remove the sign and seeking formal agreement that the act will not be repeated. Where necessary, proceedings may be brought under RRA 1976, as in the case of *CRE v Dutton*.[60]

Formal investigations

8.76 The CRE is also empowered to conduct formal investigations.[61] This may take the form of a 'general investigation', to look at a whole sector or area of practice, or a 'belief investigation'. The outcome of a general investigation is usually a series of recommendations which are not legally enforceable but which may significantly influence practice in the area under investigation. General investigations are less adversarial than 'belief investigations' and, although more akin to research, they are still viewed as an important legal enforcement tool. During a general investigation the CRE has the power to serve a notice requiring information, where it is authorised by the secretary of state.

8.77 A 'belief investigation' may only be undertaken where there is reasonable belief that discrimination has occurred or is occurring and the complaint is made by or about a specific named body or bodies. The power to compel disclosure of information is an automatic adjunct of a 'belief investigation'. If evidence of discrimination is discovered, the CRE can issue a legally enforceable non-discrimination notice, with which the body must comply, or face further legal challenge.[62] The non-discrimination notice requires the body to take steps to address the discriminatory practices or behaviour.

8.78 In 1980, the CRE conducted four named formal investigations into suspected unlawful discrimination against a Gypsy. These investigations examined allegations that certain residents of the

---

59   RRA 1976 s29.
60   [1989] 2 WLR 17, CA.
61   RRA 1976 s48.
62   RRA 1976 s60.

village of Brymbo (near Wrexham) had unlawfully sought to influence Wrexham Maelor BC to withhold council housing from an applicant because he was a Gypsy. Two of the investigations examined the conduct of local residents, one the conduct of a councillor, and the other the local community council.

8.79 One of the residents had organised a petition to the council asking them not to house the Gypsy family in question. The petition stated 'we do not approve of the gypsies coming to live in Brymbo' and further that 'should our objections be ignored we are prepared to take whatever action is appropriate to further our objections'. The resident in question was further quoted in the local newspaper saying 'the gypsies will move in here over our dead bodies'. Another named subject of investigation made similar comments to a TV reporter. Brymbo Community Council had written to the council following a committee meeting expressing their 'profound dismay at the intentions of Wrexham Maelor Borough Council's Housing Department, to house another family of itinerants in the Brymbo area'. These actions were deemed to be in breach of RRA 1976 s31 which prohibits the use of pressure to discriminate and of the four subjects of the investigation three were issued with non-discrimination notices. However, the CRE concluded that the councillor was not guilty of discrimination.

The race equality duty

8.80 The RRA 1976 (as amended) also places a positive legal obligation on over 40,000 public bodies,[63] including local authorities, police, schools, higher and further educational institutions, health bodies and central government to 'have due regard to the need to eliminate unlawful discrimination, to promote equality of opportunity and good relations between persons of different racial groups' in carrying out all their functions ('the race equality duty').[64]

8.81 It is obligatory for all such public bodies to comply with the race equality duty in all functions that have some relevance to race equality.

8.82 In order to assist bodies to better comply with the race equality duty, certain bodies have been given additional duties.[65] The main

---

63 Listed in RRA 1976 Sch 1A.
64 RRA 1976 s71.
65 The Race Relations Act 1976 (Statutory Duties) Order 2001 SI No 3438.

public authorities, including local authorities, police, health authorities and central government have specific duties to prepare and publish a race equality scheme ('the scheme'). In this scheme they are obliged to:

- list the functions and policies they have assessed as being relevant to race equality;
- set out arrangements for consulting on and assessing the impact of new and proposed policies on race equality;
- monitor the impact of existing policies on race equality;
- ensure public access to information and training staff on the duty.

In addition such bodies have a separate duty to monitor their employment practices.

8.83   Schools must comply with slightly different additional duties and must:

- publish a race equality policy instead of a scheme,
- assess and monitor the impact of their policies on pupils, staff and parents of different racial groups, in particular, the impact on the attainment levels of such pupils,
- also take reasonably practicable steps to publish annually the results of the school monitoring.

8.84   Some public authorities, such as parish councils, only have to comply with the racial equality duty and are not obliged to comply with the additional duties.

8.85   In order to help public bodies comply with their obligations, the CRE has published a Statutory Code of Practice,[66] and sector-specific guides. The Code is admissible as evidence in a court or tribunal.

How can the race equality duty be used in practice?

8.86   In essence the race equality duty, supported by the additional duties, requires public bodies to be pro-active about race equality. Rather than wait for cases of discrimination to be brought against them, public bodies are advised to collect data on all areas of their employment, service delivery and other functions, to analyse the results, to establish whether there is an adverse impact on certain racial groups, and where this cannot be justified within the wider policy aim, to make changes to mitigate this adverse impact. For example, if a local authority was

---

66 *Statutory Code of Practice on the Duty to Promote Race Equality* (CRE, 2002).

collecting data on user satisfaction of particular relevant services and analysing this by reference to racial groups, they may discover that a particular group or groups was dissatisfied with the services offered, or under-represented as users of particular services in comparison with local census data. The authority would need to look further into the reasons for this situation and make necessary changes if the reason could not be justified.

8.87   The race equality duty could bring major benefits for Gypsies and Travellers. If implemented effectively it would mean that all listed public bodies were actively monitoring their policies for adverse impact on all racial groups, including those policies generally affecting Gypsies and Travellers. If they found that Gypsies and Travellers were adversely affected, and this could not be justified within the wider goals of their policies, then they should change the policy. They should also be actively assessing the impact of any new or proposed policies and consulting Gypsies and Travellers. Consultation responses and impact assessments should be publicly available to Gypsies and Travellers. Public authority staff should also be trained on the race equality duty and any relevant parts of the additional duties.

8.88   The section below highlights what should be expected of various public authorities in relation to Gypsies and Travellers. It should be noted that the suggestions set out below are not all statutory requirements, but suggested good practice in order to ensure compliance with the race equality duty.

Local authorities

8.89   Where there are Gypsies and Travellers in their area, or where Gypsies and Travellers periodically enter their areas, local authorities should list functions of general or particular relevance to Gypsies and Travellers in their race equality schemes, and set out their arrangements for complying with the duty in respect of these functions. They should consult on and assess the impact of new policies and monitor existing policies that are likely to have a particular impact on Gypsies and Travellers. This might include policies relating to planning, planning enforcement, site provision, site management, eviction and homelessness.

8.90   Local authorities should also assess the impact of wider policies and practices on Gypsies and Travellers, for example housing allocation or satisfaction with and uptake of the range of public services. Local authorities should also consider how they are promoting good race relations between Gypsies and Travellers and the rest of the community, particularly in the context of planning enforcement and eviction. Authorities will need to consider relevant functions whether they are providing them directly, or securing services from external suppliers through contractual arrangements. If local authorities engage an external supplier to provide services on their behalf then they are still responsible for meeting the duty, even though the supplier has no direct positive legal obligation to do so. This means that the local authorities need to build race equality considerations into the procurement process to the extent necessary to ensure compliance with the duty. Of relevance to Gypsies and Travellers may be the securing of site managers, companies providing electricity and facilities to sites, or a private company employed to carry out planning enforcement or eviction.

Police

8.91   Policies adopted by the police for dealing with the management of unauthorised encampments and eviction will impact particularly on Gypsies and Travellers and each police force or authority will need to establish whether their policies have or could have an unjustifiably adverse impact on Gypsies and Travellers.

8.92   They will also be a need to examine more general policies to assess the impact that they have on Gypsies and Travellers. For example, if monitoring showed that Gypsies and Travellers were over-represented in records showing the ethnic status of those refused bail at the police station, then the police force would need to conduct a thorough examination of its policies on the grant of bail to see if there was any justification for the statistics. If there was no such justification then the police would be obliged to make necessary changes to its policies to mitigate the adverse impact of those policies on Gypsies and Travellers.

8.93   The police will also need to ensure that they comply with their duty to promote good race relations, particularly in the event of evictions or enforcement, where there may be issues of public order. It follows that the police will also need to take appropriate action when provided with complaints of incitement to racial hatred against Gypsies and Travellers.

Schools

8.94   Schools (and local education authorities) will need to consider how their policies, in particular those on exclusion and admission and those relating to attainment, affect Gypsy and Traveller pupils and whether changes could be made to promote equal opportunities for Gypsies and Travellers.

8.95   Schools will also need to consider how good race relations are promoted in the school environment, for example, by developing aspects of the curriculum which celebrate Gypsy and Traveller culture, or through strong leadership particularly where there may be unauthorised encampments in the local area, and hostility to such encampments. Teachers would need to ensure that they have adequate policies in place on racism and bullying and that complaints made by Gypsy and Traveller pupils are taken seriously.

Health bodies

8.96   Health bodies will need to consider how they are promoting equal opportunities for Gypsies and Travellers, how their staff are trained to be aware of the particular issues facing Gypsies and Travellers, and how their general policies could impact on Gypsies and Travellers. If, for example, they established that there were dispro-portionately low levels of registration or take-up of preven-tative healthcare by Gypsies and Travellers in comparison with other racial groups, changes should be considered to improve Gypsies' and Travellers' access to and uptake of healthcare.

Central government and devolved administrations

8.97   With their responsibilities for creating law and policy, and providing a leadership role for other public authorities, central government departments, the Scottish Parliament and Executive and the National Assembly for Wales all have a vital role to play through their race equality duty. Each department, and devolved body must, like other listed public bodies, produce a race equality scheme.

8.98   Government departments and devolved administrations, have an obligation to fulfil their duty in respect of their internal work, and the policies and strategies they produce. Policies and Green and White papers, are all within the scope of the RRA 1976 and arrangements should be made to consult on and assess the impact of those policies that are relevant to race equality. Government departments also have an important leadership role to play in assisting the bodies in their sector to comply with the duty.

Ethnic monitoring

8.99   The effective implementation of the race equality duty relies on ethnic monitoring – collecting ethnic data, analysing results, identifying disproportionalities and making changes where they cannot be justified. The CRE's advice on monitoring is that authorities should base their monitoring categories on the Census 2001 categories, but adapt their ethnic classification system to the particular local circumstances, so that it includes the particular ethnic groups they employ or serve. So, for example, Romani Gypsy and Irish Travellers could be included as a specific sub-category of 'white other'. However, with the exception of schools, the majority of authorities are not ethnically monitoring Gypsies and Travellers. This is reflected at the national level, including, crucially, the Census itself, meaning that authorities at the local level do not have a baseline against which to compare their own data.

8.100   Public authorities should be encouraged to collect more detailed local data where appropriate, and to ensure that where data is lacking, detailed consultation is used to ascertain the impact of policies. For consultation to be meaningful it has to be carried out in a way that actively engages the consultees in an appropriate way.

Sanctions for non-compliance with the race equality duty

8.101   The RRA 1976 contains no express provision for enforcement of the race equality duty. Instead, compliance with the race equality duty may be secured by way of judicial review in the High Court by a person who is directly affected or has sufficient interest, such as the CRE itself.[67] Additionally, the CRE may also use its formal investigation powers to secure compliance.

8.102   In relation to the specific duties, if the CRE is satisfied that a public authority is not complying with the specific duties (for example, because it has failed to produce a race equality scheme or has produced a scheme that it so poorly drafted that it could not properly assist the authority to comply with the race equality duty), then it may serve a 'compliance notice' on the authority.[68] The compliance notice shall require the public authority to comply with

---

67 For details of judicial review procedures, see appendix A below.
68 RRA 1976 s71(1)(d).

the duty and within 28 days to inform the CRE of the steps that it has taken, or is taking, to comply with the duty.

8.103   If the CRE is satisfied that a public authority is not complying with the specific duties, then it may also require the public authority to furnish additional information to verify compliance. Where an authority fails to comply with a compliance notice, the CRE has the power to apply to the county court[69] for an order to comply with the specific duty and/or for an order to furnish information.

8.104   There is, as yet, no case law relating to the race equality duty and concepts such as 'due regard' and the detailed requirements of the specific duties have not yet received judicial scrutiny. Public authorities will be given wide discretion in carrying out their statutory duties and while an authority would need to be able to prove that it had taken adequate steps to meet its race equality duty, and had not wilfully ignored evidence to the contrary, the reasons for the authority's failure to act, including the resources available to the authority, are likely to be taken into account.

Opportunities and recommendations for the future

Challenging discriminatory legislation

8.105   The RRA 1976 has rarely been used to challenge legislation, for example, planning, eviction and homelessness legislation. Indeed, there is no mechanism or procedure for pre-legislative scrutiny or audits of proposed legislation or for declara-tions of unlawfulness of primary legislation under RRA 1976.

8.106   The status of the RRA 1976 was affirmed in the case of *R v Cleveland CC ex p CRE*,[70] in which the Court of Appeal ruled that the provisions of the Education Act 1980, requiring local education authorities to comply with parental preferences in the allocation of school places took precedence over the RRA 1976, even though this enabled local education authorities to allow parents to choose schools on the basis of the racial or ethnic composition of their pupil populations.

8.107   RRA 1976 s41 was partially repealed in July 2003 by the Race Relations Act 1976 (Amendment) Regulations 2003.[71] RRA 1976 s41

---

69 Sheriff court in Scotland.

70 [1992] LGR 139, CA.

71 SI No 1626 reg 35.

(as amended) now provides that the exemption does not apply to an act which is unlawful on grounds of race or ethnic or national origins in the following regulated areas of activity: employment; education; public functions relating to social security, health care, social protection and social advantage; service provision; housing; and public appointments. However, planning functions covered by RRA 1976 s19A are not included and are still exempt.

8.108   The amendment does not provide for the RRA 1976 to take precedence over other legislation and there is no statutory requirement for all legislation to be interpreted in accordance with the principle of non-discrimination. However, it is arguable that the amendment provides a new opportunity to challenge the discriminatory impact of legislation and for the courts to undertake a balancing exercise between the objectives behind the RRA 1976 and the aims of the alleged discriminatory legislation. Thus, it is likely that there will be closer judicial scrutiny than before of the legitimate aims and the proportionality of the measures used to achieve those aims; though such scrutiny will always be subject to the courts showing due deference to the will of parliament.

The European Union race directive[72]

8.109   The Race Relations Act 1976 (Amendment) Regulations 2003[73] were designed to insert the provisions of the European Union (EU) Race Directive[74] into our domestic legislation. The Race Directive establishes the principle of equal treatment. It also requires EU member states to introduce legislation to outlaw discrimination on grounds of race and ethnic origin in the fields of employment and training, education, goods and services, including housing, social protection and social advantages.

8.110   Of particular interest is article 14 of the Race Directive which imposes an obligation on member states to take the necessary measures to ensure that:

- 'Any laws, regulations and administrative provisions contrary to the principle of equal treatment are abolished'; and

---

72 Directive No 2000/43/EC.

73 SI No 1626.

74 The Directive implementing the principle of equal treatment between persons irrespective of racial or ethnic origin adopted under article 13 of the European Communities Treaty.

- 'Any provisions contrary to the principle of equal treatment which are included in individual or collective contracts or agreements, internal rules or undertakings, rules governing profit-making or non-profit-making associations, and rules governing the independent professions and workers' and employers' organisations are or may be declared null and void or are amended.'

8.111　The partial repeal of RRA 1976 s41 was as a result of the Race Directive since it was considered to be inconsistent with the principle of equal treatment.

8.112　The Race Directive may be enforced by the European Commission against a member state upon complaint by another member state or in certain circumstances by a natural and legal person such as the CRE. Alternatively, judicial review may be brought in the British courts on the basis that legislative provisions contravene an EU Directive.[75] Again, the CRE may have standing to bring such proceedings, as might other organisations with sufficient interest.

8.113　This is new and untested territory and there has not yet been any such challenge in terms of the Race Directive. Nevertheless, article 14 of the Race Directive provides another useful opportunity for strategic litigation and there are certain areas of law, particularly those that have already been challenged for compatibility with the ECHR, that could be explored afresh under this provision if there was further evidence of discriminatory impact. Listed below are some of the laws that may be ripe for reconsideration:

- Caravan Sites Act 1968 – Gypsies and Travellers have minimal security of tenure on local authority sites. In the case of *Albert Smith v Barking and Dagenham LBC and Secretary of State for the Office of the Deputy Prime Minister,*[76] Albert Smith, a Romani Gypsy, sought a declaration that this legislation was incompatible with ECHR article 8 (the right to respect for private and family life and the home) and discriminated against him in breach of ECHR article 14. The High Court refused to issue such a declaration, since the provision was seen to be appropriate and justified to allow Gypsies and Travellers on local authority sites to

---

75　For details of judicial review procedures, see appendix A below.
76　[2002] EWHC 2400 Admin. See Recent Developments in Gypsy and Traveller Law at pxi above.

remain nomadic. However, the judge hearing the claim did suggest that the government should continue monitoring the present position to check whether there continued to be such justification for the difference in treatment in the future.[77]

- Mobile Homes Act 1983 s5 – which exempts Gypsies and Travellers living on local authority sites from an entitlement to security of tenure. In *Somerset CC v Isaacs and Secretary of State for Transport, Local Government and the Regions*,[78] Mr Isaacs, a Romani Gypsy, claimed that lack of security of tenure for Gypsies living on council sites breached his ECHR article 8 rights and discriminated against him in breach of ECHR article 14 in circumstances where caravan dwellers on private sites enjoyed security of tenure. However, it was held that there had been no breach of article 8, since 'any such safeguards detract from the flexibility that Parliament has decided is appropriate for exempted sites',[79] and the article 14 challenge was dismissed because the provision 'depends on the status of the site owner and local authority, and not on any personal quality of the licensee or tenant.'

- Town and Country Planning Act 1990 s183(4) – by which stop notices can prevent the use of land as a site for a caravan, but not the use of a building as a dwelling-house. This measure could apply disproportionately to ethnic Gypsies and Travellers, particularly with the current shortage of alternative accommodation for many Gypsies and Travellers.[80]

Other levers for change

8.114   The Framework Convention for the Protection of National Minorities represents another significant lever for change. This was drawn up within the Council of Europe by the Ad Hoc Committee for the Protection of National Minorities and adopted by the Committee of Ministers of the Council of Europe in 1994. It was

---

77 For a full discussion of this case (and the related case of *Isaacs*), see chapter 3 paras 3.13–3.24.

78 [2002] EWHC 1014 Admin. See Recent Developments in Gypsy and Traveller Law at p00 above.

79 See chapter 3 paras 3.16–3.17.

80 See Recent Developments in Gypsy and Traveller Law at pxi above.

opened for signature by the member states of the Council of Europe the following year. Non-member states may also be invited by the Committee of Ministers to become party to this instrument.

8.115 The Framework Convention is not the only instrument to be developed within the Council of Europe for the protection of national minorities, but it is the most comprehensive, and, importantly, it is the Council's first legally binding multilateral instrument devoted to the protection of national minorities in general.

8.116 The Framework Convention sets out principles to be respected, as well as goals to be achieved, by the signatories, in order to ensure the protection of persons belonging to national minorities, while fully respecting the principles of territorial integrity and political independence of states. The principles contained in the Framework Convention have to be implemented through national legislation and appropriate governmental policies. It is envisaged that the provisions can also be implemented through bilateral and multilateral treaties.

8.117 Certain articles of the Framework Convention are of particular importance to Gypsies and Travellers:

- Article 4 obliges state-parties to 'undertake to guarantee to persons belonging to national minorities the right of equality before the law and of equal protection of the law' and to 'undertake to adopt, where necessary, adequate measures in order to promote, in all areas of economic, social, political and cultural life, full and effective equality between persons belonging to a national minority and those belonging to the majority'.
- Article 5 obliges state-parties to 'undertake to promote the conditions necessary for persons belonging to national minorities to maintain and develop their culture, and to preserve the essential elements of their identity, namely their religion, language, traditions and cultural heritage'.
- Article 6 obliges state-parties to 'encourage a spirit of tolerance and intercultural dialogue and take effective measures to promote mutual respect and understanding and co-operation among all persons living on their territory, irrespective of those persons' ethnic, cultural, linguistic or religious identity, in particular in the fields of education, culture and the media', and also to 'take appropriate measures to protect persons who may be subject to threats or acts of discrimination, hostility or violence as a result of their ethnic, cultural, linguistic or religious identity'.

- Article 15 requires state-parties to 'create the conditions necessary for the effective participation of persons belonging to national minorities in cultural, social and economic life and in public affairs.'

8.118   As a signatory, the UK government is required to submit periodic reports containing full information on legislative and other measures taken to give effect to the principles of the Framework Convention. The UK's first report was submitted in July 1999. The report was made public and examined by the Advisory Committee to the Committee of Ministers which prepared an Opinion on the measures taken by the UK.

8.119   Significantly, in the first round of monitoring the Advisory Committee highlighted the need for more effort in the UK in bridging the socio-economic gap between the majority of the population and Gypsy/Roma and Irish Travellers (article 4) and the need for further steps to provide adequate stopping places for Gypsy/Roma and Irish Travellers (article 5).[81] The UK government must now consider how to meet these recommendations.

Conclusion

8.120   While the race equality legislation has developed considerably over the last 25–30 years, it has had relatively little impact on the discrimination that Gypsies and Travellers experience within our community. However, there is no doubt that the recent changes to the legislation have strengthened the provisions designed to combat racism and that it could be used in the future to bring significant improvements to the lives of Gypsies and Travellers. The CRE has produced a Strategy regarding Gypsies and Travellers[82] which calls for the implementation of the kind of measures discussed above and which is essential reading for all those involved in issues and areas of law concerning Gypsies and Travellers, and perhaps more importantly for Gypsies and Travellers themselves.

81   The opinion can be found on the Council of Europe website at www.humanrights.coe.int/minorities/Eng/FrameworkConvention/Advisory Committee/Opinions/Table.htm.

82   *Gypsies and Travellers: A strategy for the CRE, 2004–2007* (CRE, 2004).

CHAPTER 9

Conclusion

Conclusion

9.1   Throughout this book the authors have drawn attention to anticipated changes in legislation, 'grey areas' and legal issues that might arise in the future and those points will not be repeated here.

9.2   It is clear that the lack of provision of suitable sites for Gypsies and Travellers is the root cause of most, if not all, of the difficulties that they face living in Great Britain today.

9.3   When the duty to provide sites was repealed by the Criminal Justice and Public Order Act 1994, the government stressed the point that Gypsies and Travellers should be encouraged to provide their own accommodation. However, the fact is that many Gypsies and Travellers cannot afford to develop their own sites and those that can have been frustrated in their attempts to do so. It remains to be seen whether anticipated amendments to the planning legislation and changes to government planning guidance will lead to an increase in private site provision.

9.4   However, for those thousands of Gypsies and Travellers who remain on unauthorised, roadside encampments, and who cannot afford to buy their own land and attempt to set up a site, it has become abundantly clear that public site provision will be a necessity.

9.5   There have been a number of reports (some commissioned by the government itself) that have stressed the need to bring back some form of duty to provide or facilitate sites for Gypsies and Travellers.

9.6   For example, the Niner report on *Local Authority Gypsy/Traveller Sites in England*[1] concluded:

> It is clear that local authorities hold the key to site provision, either directly through public site provision or – perhaps even more importantly – indirectly through planning controls exercised by local planning authorities. A major conclusion of the research can be summed up in the words of one participant: 'make site provision easier for elected members to support than to object to.' The obvious way to do this, advocated by most participants, is to re-introduce some form of statutory duty on local authorities to provide or enable the provision of Gypsy/Traveller sites, and to provide funding from government towards that provision.[2]

9.7   Similarly, when the Traveller Law Reform Coalition (TLRC)[3] made submissions to the ODPM Gypsy and Traveller Sites Enquiry

---

1   (ODPM, 2003).
2   *Local Authority Gypsy/Traveller Sites in England,* at p222.
3   Now known as the Gypsy and Traveller Law Reform Coalition. See appendix C for contact deatails.

2004, it called for: the mainstreaming of the provision of Gypsy and Traveller sites within housing legislation; the return of the duty to provide or facilitate the provision of sites; changes to planning legislation and guidance to ensure that Gypsies and Travellers are enabled to set up their own sites in suitable locations; and a change to the definition of 'Gypsy' for the purposes of planning law.[4]

9.8   The TLRC is a coalition of Gypsies and Travellers, their support groups, professionals and other concerned individuals who are working together to persuade the government to introduce a statutory duty to provide or facilitate the provision of a broad range of accommodation for Gypsies and Travellers in accordance with proposals set out in the Traveller Law Reform Bill. The Bill was originally drafted by the Traveller Law Research Unit at Cardiff University and is now one of the main planks of the campaign for reform of the law being promoted by the TLRC. The Bill proposes (among other things) that: local authori-ties prepare plans showing how they will meet the needs of Gypsies and Travellers in their area; there be a reinstatement of a duty on certain local authorities to provide or facilitate the provision of sites; and that a Gypsy and Traveller Accommodation Commission be established.

9.9   The report of the Equality of Opportunity Committee of the National Assembly for Wales, *Review of Service Provision for Gypsies and Travellers*,[5] makes the following reference to the Traveller Law Reform Bill:[6]

> The Traveller Law Reform Bill represents another strand of policy development in this area, but one formulated outside government ... [The Bill] was launched on 31 January 2002 and a revised version reached the House of Commons on 10 July 2002, but fell before second reading. The Bill is an important reference point for any recommenda-tions on accommodation as it represents a consensus between a wide range of organisations.[7]

4 The TLRC have suggested (to the Housing Minister, Yvette Cooper MP, at an ODPM seminar on planning on 10 May 2004) that legislation and policy be expressed to cover 'Gypsies and Travellers' and that 'Gypsy' means an ethnic Romani Gypsy; 'Irish Traveller' means an ethnic Irish Traveller; 'Other Traveller' means a person of nomadic habit of life, whatever their race or origin. The TLRC have stated that they also hope that Scottish and Welsh Travellers will soon be recognised as ethnic groups for the purposes of the race relations legislation (and see further chapter 8).

5 (National Assembly for Wales, 2003).

6 Moved (unsuccessfully on both occasions) as a private members bill in 2002 and 2003.

7 *Review of Service Provision for Gypsies and Travellers* at p51.

9.10   At the time of writing the Housing Bill 2004 is before parliament. The first draft of the Bill was just designed to deal with settled accommodation[8] but the Commission for Racial Equality (CRE) is promoting amendments to the Bill on behalf of Gypsies and Travellers. One of these amendments proposes the return of some form of duty to either provide or facilitate the provision of sites and in its recently published four-year strategy,[9] the CRE stated:

> A consensus is emerging among all the parties concerned – the ODPM, non-governmental organisations, think tanks, local authorities, and the CRE – that the question of accommodation must take priority, as it is the key to progress in other areas, such as community relations, education and health.[10]

9.11   One of the aforementioned 'think tanks', the Institute for Public Policy Research (IPPR), has also recently published an influential report on this subject.[11] In its report the IPPR also drew attention to the fact that there is strong support for the reinstatement of a duty to provide sites for Gypsies and Travellers:

> Reinstating some sort of compulsion or statutory duty to provide or facilitate the provision of sites is viewed by many as fundamental in helping to tackle resistance from settled communities to local authorities meeting the needs of Traveller and Gypsy communities. Many believe that a statutory duty and central subsidy are needed to 'encourage' local authorities to make provision.[12]

The consensus of opinion on this issue is quite remarkable but has yet to bear fruit.

9.12   A number of prominent Gypsy and Traveller campaigners have been lobbying parliament and influential organisations on this issue for many years and have made a significant and positive contribution to the debate. One of the leading Gypsy campaigners, Len Smith, brings us back to where we began this book, with the Firle bonfire incident:

8 Apart from one proposed change to the provision of disabled facilities grants for Gypsies and Travellers on official sites – see chapter 3 para 3.46, for more details.
9 *Gypsies and Travellers: A strategy for the CRE, 2004–2007* (CRE, 2004).
10 *Gypsies and Travellers: A strategy for the CRE, 2004–2007* at p16.
11 Crawley, *Moving Forward: the provision of accommodation for Gypsies and Travellers* (IPPR, 2004).
12 *Moving Forward: the provision for accommodation for Gypsies and Travellers* at p40.

Despite the desperate shortage of sites (residential and transit) local authorities and the police continued to evict Travellers into the endless repetitive cycle of illegality. New police powers in 2003 contained in the Anti-Social Behaviour Act gave cause for worry that widened the chances of abuse of the system to achieve evictions. 2003 also saw the astonishing burning of Gypsy effigies at the Firle bonfire celebrations ... Happily there were also things to celebrate in 2003. The political movement is still in a forward direction, with slight, though increasing, recognition of the validity of our case from all quarters ... It is our fervent hope that ... the Government can bring forward policies that will end the current discriminatory and unequal state of affairs that is unsatisfactory to all concerned.[13]

---

13 *Moving Forward: the provision for accommodation for Gypsies and Travellers* at pp60–61.

APPENDICES

Procedure

In this appendix, the reader is given an outline of the procedure to be followed in respect of:

- judicial review;
- Town and Country Planning Act 1990 s288 applications;
- Town and Country Planning Act 1990 s289 appeals; and
- homeless reviews and appeals.

Judicial review

Public law challenges are taken by way of judicial review in the High Court (Administrative Court).[1]

Decisions of public bodies, such as local authorities, may be challenged on public law grounds in the courts on the basis that:

- the decision is so unreasonable that no reasonable public authority could have come to the decision (known as *Wednesbury* unreasonableness);[2]
- the public authority failed to take into account relevant material when reaching the decision;
- the public authority took into account irrelevant material when reaching the decision;
- in reaching the decision the public authority misdirected itself in law;
- the public authority fettered its discretion by adopting a blanket policy without regard to the facts of the individual case;
- the public authority breached its obligations under the Human Rights Act (HRA) 1998.

---

1 Judicial review is, itself, a complex matter and for full details see Manning, *Judicial Review: a practitioner's guide* (Legal Action Group, 2nd edn, 2004). It is also essential to have reference to Civil Procedure Rules (CPR) Part 54 (see *Civil Procedure* known as 'The White Book', (Sweet & Maxwell, 2004)).

2 An expression that derives from *Associated Provincial Picture Houses v Wednesbury Corporation* [1947] 2 All ER 680.

There is a pre-action protocol procedure for judicial review claims[3] which should be followed wherever it is possible to do so. Among other things, the protocol advises that a 'letter before claim' should be sent to the defendant which sets out the grounds for the claim and gives the defendant 14 days to reply. However, the protocol does not have to be followed if the matter is urgent, for example, in the case of an impending eviction.

A judicial review claim must be lodged promptly and, in any event, no later than three months after the date on which the grounds for making the claim (normally the decision of the public authority) arose.[4] The court can extend or abridge time but only exercise its discretion in cases where it is satisfied that there are very good reasons for doing so.[5] Any application for an extension or abridgement of time must be made in the claim form and should be supported by written evidence.[6]

A judicial review claim is commenced by filing two copies of a paginated and indexed bundle containing the following documents in the Administrative Court Office of the High Court[7]: a claim form (on Form N461); a witness statement attaching all relevant documents; a notice of issue of public funding certificate or undertaking to lodge the same (where relevant); a bundle of statutory instruments and guidance that are relevant to the claim; and a list of essential reading.[8] In addition a fee is payable.[9]

In urgent cases an application for a stay or injunction (for example, to prevent an imminent eviction taking place) should be made in the claim form and a draft order setting out the terms of the stay or injunction sought should also be filed. In addition an application should be made on Form N463 for the claim to be given urgent consideration by the Administrative Court.

Permission is required before the matter can proceed to a final hearing as a substantive application.[10] Normally, permission is dealt

3   See above, note 1. The White Book Volume 1.
4   CPR 54.5.
5   See CPR 54.5 and CPR 3.1(2)(a).
6   CPR Practice Direction (PD) 54 paras 5.6–5.7.
7   The vast majority of claims are filed with the Administrative Court Office at the Royal Courts of Justice, Strand, London WC2A 2LL. However, judicial review cases can be brought in the Administrative Court in Wales (Law Courts, Cathays Park, Cardiff, CF10 3PG) if the remedy sought involves a devolution issue arising out of the Government of Wales Act 1998 or an issue concerning the National Assembly for Wales, the Welsh executive or any Welsh public body. Where a claim in such a case is filed in the Administrative Court in London there is discretion to transfer the claim to Cardiff: see CPR PD 54.3.
8   For more detail see CPR 54.6 and CPR PD 54.
9   £30 at the time of writing.
10   CPR 54.4.

with on the papers (that is, without a hearing). However, the court may, in its discretion, order that a hearing take place. If permission is refused on the papers, the claimant has an automatic right to request renewal of the matter at an oral hearing.[11] Where an application for permission in a civil matter has been refused by a judge after an oral hearing the claimant may appeal to the Court of Appeal within seven days.[12]

If the defendant (public authority) wishes to take part in the proceedings then it must file an acknowledgement of service (Form N462) within 21 days of service of the sealed claim form[13] and then serve the acknowledgement of service on the claimant no later than seven days after it has been filed.

If permission is granted, an additional fee is payable[14] and the matter will then proceed to a final hearing. The claimant must file and serve a skeleton argument not less than 21 working days before the date of the hearing. The defendant must file and serve a skeleton argument in response at least 14 days before the hearing date.[15]

In civil matters the court's decision on a substantive application can be appealed with leave to the Court of Appeal, Civil Division.[16] In criminal matters any appeal must be made to the House of Lords. However, an appellant will not be able to appeal to the House of Lords without leave of the court below or the House of Lords itself, and leave will not be granted unless it is certified by the court below that a point of law of general public importance is involved in the decision and it appears to the court or to the House of Lords, as the case may be, that the point is one which ought to be considered by the House.[17]

Town and Country Planning Act 1990 s288 applications[18]

A 'person aggrieved', for example, a person who has been refused planning permission by a planning inspector or the First Secretary of State (or a local authority who unsuccessfully opposed the grant of planning permission at a planning inquiry), will have a statutory right to apply to the High Court (Administrative Court) for an order that the decision be quashed on grounds that the decision-maker erred in law.

11 In the case of a publicly funded claimant, the solicitor will have to be able to justify such a step, on the merits of the case, to the Legal Services Commission.

12 CPR 52.15.

13 CPR 54.8. The claimant must lodge a Certificate of Service upon serving the sealed claim form on the defendant.

14 £120 at the time of writing.

15 CPR PD 54 paras 15.1, 15.2 and 16.1.

16 CPR 52.3.

17 See Administration of Justice Act 1960 s1.

18 See also chapter 4 paras 4.91–4.94.

An application must be filed *within* six weeks of the date of the decision letter.[19] The time limit is absolute[20] and will not be extended even if the applicant had not and could not reasonably have been expected to have known of the decision within the six week period.[21]

Details of the procedure to be followed can be found in RSC Order 94.[22]

The application is made on a CPR Part 8 claim form. The claim form (and three copies for the court to seal) must be filed[23] together with the application fee[24] and a notice of issue of public funding certificate or undertaking to lodge the same (where relevant). It is important to note that the applicant must also serve the claim form on the solicitors acting for the First Secretary of State (the Treasury Solicitor), and the relevant local authority within the six week period.[25]

Any witness statement to be relied upon must be filed and served within 14 days of service of the claim form.[26] The respondents will then have 21 days from service of the applicant's witness statement(s) to file and serve witness evidence in response.[27]

The applicant must file and serve a skeleton argument at least 21 working days before the hearing date together with a trial bundle. The respondent must serve a skeleton argument in response at least 14 days before the hearing.

An unsuccessful party may appeal to the Court of Appeal with permission of the court below or the Court of Appeal itself. Permission to appeal will only be granted where:

• the court considers that the appeal would have a real prospect of success; or

19 Town and Country Planning Act 1990 s288(3). Time starts to run from the date of the decision, not the date when the decision is received: see *Griffiths v Secretary of State for the Environment* [1983] 1 All ER 439, HL. However, the actual date on which the decision is made is ignored when calculating whether the period of six weeks has expired: see *Okolo v Secretary of State for the Environment* [1997] 4 All ER 242. Thus, if an unsuccessful applicant wishes to challenge a decision made on a Monday, then he or she must file an application before midnight on the Monday six weeks later.

20 *Smith v East Elloe Rural DC* [1956] AC 736.

21 *R v Secretary of State for the Environment ex p Kent* [1988] 3 PLR 17; [1990] 1 PLR 128.

22 See above, note 1. The White Book, Volume 1.

23 The claim form should be filed with the Administrative Court office at the Royal Courts of Justice, Strand, London WC2A 2LL.

24 At the time of writing, £120.

25 CPR Sch 1, RSC Order 94 r 2(2). The Treasury Solicitor is based at Queen Anne's Chambers, 28 Broadway, London SW1H 9JS.

26 CPR Sch 1, RSC Order 94 r 3(2).

27 CPR Sch 1 RSC Order 94 r3(3).

• there is some other compelling reason why the appeal should be heard.[28]

Town and Country Planning Act 1990 s289 appeals[29]

A decision made in respect of an enforcement notice by a planning inspector or the First Secretary of State can be appealed by an unsuccessful appellant, an unsuccessful local authority or any other persons having an interest in the land to which the enforcement notice relates, on a point of law to the High Court (Administrative Court).

Permission (or leave) to appeal is required before a TCPA 1990 s289 appeal can proceed to a final hearing.[30]

An application for permission to appeal must be filed within 28 days of the date on the decision letter.[31] There is power to extend the time limit if there is a good reason to do so.[32] Any application for an extension of time should be made at the same time that the application is filed.

The appellant should file: an appellant's notice (Form N161) together with copies for the court and the respondents; a witness statement verifying any facts relied upon; a paginated bundle of documents including the decision letter and any particularly relevant evidence, and a list of essential reading.[33] In addition the appellant must file a notice of issue of public funding certificate or undertaking to lodge the same (where relevant).

A skeleton argument should be included in the appellant's notice or should follow within 14 days of the date on which it is filed.[34]

Sealed copies of the appellant's notice, witness statement and skeleton argument must then be served on: the solicitor acting for the First Secretary of State (the Treasury Solicitor); the local planning authority that served the enforcement notice, and any other person having an interest in the land to which the notice relates, within seven days of the date on which they were filed.[35]

An application fee is required and a further fee is payable if permission is granted.[36]

28   CPR 52.3(6).
29   See chapter 4 para 4.104.
30   TCPA 1990 s289(6).
31   CPR Sch 1, RSC Order 94 r12.
32   CPR 3.1(2).
33   See CPR PD 52 para 5.6 for a full list of all the documents that must be filed with an appellant's notice.
34   CPR Part 52.4.5.
35   CPR Part 52.4. The address of the Treasury Solicitor is Queen Anne's Chambers, 28 Broadway, London SW1H 9JS.
36   At the time of writing the application fee is £30 and the fee payable on grant of permission is £100.

If permission is refused there is no right of appeal against that decision.

If permission is granted and a respondent wishes to contest the appeal then a respondent's notice must be filed within 14 days of the service of notification of the grant of permission[37] and it must be served on the appellant and any other respondent within seven days of it being filed.

An unsuccessful party may only appeal to the Court of Appeal against a decision made after a substantive hearing if the Court of Appeal itself grants permission to do so. Permission will only be granted if the Court of Appeal considers that: the appeal would raise an important point of principle or practice; or there is some other compelling reason for the Court of Appeal to determine the appeal.[38]

Homeless reviews and appeals[39]

A request for a review should be made within 21 days of notification of a decision under Housing Act 1996 s184. The applicant must be told of the right to request a review in the letter of notification.[40] The local authority has power to extend time.[41] The current regulations on review procedures are contained in the Allocation of Housing and Homelessness (Review Procedures) Regulations 1999.[42] The regulations specify that the reviewing officer must be someone who was not involved in the original decision and who is senior to the original decision-maker.[43] Where necessary, the reviewing officer will need to undertake further inquiries before reaching a decision and may have to have regard to matters occurring after the original decision was taken.[44] An applicant should be given the opportunity of refuting matters on which the local authority seek to rely.[45]

The regulations[46] require a local authority to notify applicants of their decision within eight weeks of their request for a review. Where

37   CPR Part 52.5.

38   CPR Part 52.13.

39   See chapter 6 paras 6.43–6.49 for details of the grounds on which a review or appeal against a negative (for the applicant) decision can be taken. For further details on review and appeal procedures, see Arden and Hunter, *Homelessness and Allocations* (Legal Action Group, Revised 6th edn, 2003).

40   Housing Act (HA) 1996 s184(5).

41   HA 1996 s202(3).

42   SI No 71.

43   Allocation of Housing and Homelessness (Review Procedures) Regulations 1999 reg 2.

44   *Mohammed v Hammersmith and Fulham LBC* [2002] HLR 7, HL.

45   *Robinson v Brent LBC* [1998] HLR 1015, CA.

46   Allocation of Housing and Homelessness (Review Procedures) Regulations 1999 reg 9(1)(a).

the applicant is seeking to review a decision made by two local authorities that the conditions for a local connection referral are met, the relevant period is ten weeks.[47] The parties may agree a longer period and this may be very useful for applicants where further evidence is being sought.[48]

When assisting a Gypsy or Traveller in such a review, it will be important for any adviser or solicitor involved to request a copy of the local authority's homelessness file. This will be required so that the adviser or solicitor can consider the information that was available to the local authority when they took their decision.

There is a right of appeal to the county court: against a review decision on a point of law; or, if the local authority fails to carry out the review decision within the requisite time limit, against the original decision.[49] 'Point of law' includes not only matters of legal interpretation but also the full range of issues that would be the subject of an application to the High Court for judicial review (see above).

The appeal must be brought within 21 days of the applicant being notified of the decision on review, or when the applicant should have been notified.[50] The court has power to extend this time limit 'for good reason'.[51]

An appeal is lodged using Claim Form N161 and should be accompanied by a witness statement attaching all relevant documentation and a notice of issue of public funding certificate or undertaking to lodge the same (where relevant). For this and all subsequent procedures in running a county court homeless appeal, advisers and solicitors should have careful reference to CPR Part 52.

47   Allocation of Housing and Homelessness (Review Procedures) Regulations 1999 reg 9(1)(b).
48   Homelessness Code of Guidance, para 13.13.
49   HA 1996 s204(1).
50   HA 1996 s204(2).
51   HA 1996 s204(2A).

Statutes and guidance

CARAVAN SITES ACT 1968 (EXTRACTS)

Minimum length of notice

2   In any case where a residential contract is determinable by notice given by either party to the other, a notice so given shall be of no effect unless it is given not less than four weeks before the date on which it is to take effect.

Protection of occupiers against eviction and harassment

3(1)   Subject to the provisions of this section, a person shall be guilty of an offence under this section –

(a) if, during the subsistence of a residential contract, he unlawfully deprives the occupier of his occupation on the protected site of any caravan which the occupier is entitled by the contract to station and occupy, or to occupy, as his residence thereon;

(b) if, after the expiration or determination of a residential contract, he enforces, otherwise than by proceedings in the court, any right to exclude the occupier from the protected site or from any such caravan, or to remove or exclude any such caravan from the site;

(c) if, whether during the subsistence or after the expiration or determination of a residential contract, with intent to cause the occupier –

(i) to abandon the occupation of the caravan or remove it from the site, or

(ii) to refrain from exercising any right or pursuing any remedy in respect thereof,

he does acts calculated to interfere with the peace or comfort of the occupier or persons residing with him, or persistently withdraws or withholds services or facilities reasonably required for the occupation of the caravan as a residence on the site.

(2)   References in this section to the occupier include references to the person who was the occupier under a residential contract which has expired or been determined and, in the case of the death of the occupier (whether during the subsistence or after the expiration or determination of the contract), to any person then residing with the occupier being –

(a) the widow or widower of the occupier; or

(b) in default of a widow or widower so residing, any member of the occupier's family.

(3) A person guilty of an offence under this section shall, without prejudice to any liability or remedy to which he may be subject in civil proceedings, be liable on summary conviction [to a fine not exceeding level 5 on the standard scale] or to imprisonment for a term not exceeding six months, or to both.

(4) In proceedings for an offence under paragraph (a) or (b) of subsection (1) of this section it shall be a defence to prove that the accused believed, and had reasonable cause to believe, that the occupier of the caravan had ceased to reside on the site.

(5) Nothing in this section applies to the exercise by any person of a right to take possession of a caravan of which he is the owner, other than a right conferred by or arising on the expiration or determination of a residential contract, or to anything done pursuant to the order of any court.

Provision for suspension of eviction orders

4(1) If in proceedings by the owner of a protected site the court makes an order for enforcing in relation thereto any such right as is mentioned in paragraph (b) of subsection (1) of section 3 of this Act, the court may (without prejudice to any power apart from this section to postpone the operation or suspend the execution of an order, and subject to the following provisions of this section) suspend the enforcement of the order for such period not exceeding twelve months from the date of the order as the court thinks reasonable.

(2) Where the court by virtue of this section suspends the enforcement of an order, it may impose such terms and conditions, including conditions as to the payment of rent or other periodical payments or of arrears of such rent or payments, as the court thinks reasonable.

(3) The court may from time to time, on the application of either party, extend, reduce or terminate the period of suspension ordered by virtue of this section, or vary any terms or conditions imposed thereunder, but shall not extend the period of suspension for more than twelve months at a time.

(4) In considering whether or how to exercise its powers under this section, the court shall have regard to all the circumstances, and in particular to the questions –

(a) whether the occupier of the caravan has failed, whether before or after the expiration or determination of the relevant residential contract, to observe any terms or conditions of that contract, any conditions of the site licence, or any reasonable rules made by the owner for the management and conduct of the site or the maintenance of caravans thereon;

(b) whether the occupier has unreasonably refused an offer by the owner to renew the residential contract or make another such contract for a reasonable period and on reasonable terms;

(c) whether the occupier has failed to make reasonable efforts to obtain elsewhere other suitable accommodation for his caravan (or, as the case may be, another suitable caravan and accommodation for it).

(5)   Where the court makes such an order as is mentioned in subsection (1) of this section but suspends the enforcement of that order by virtue of this section, the court shall make no order for costs unless it appears to the court, having regard to the conduct of the owner or of the occupier, that there are special reasons for making such an order.

(6)   The court shall not suspend the enforcement of an order by virtue of this section in the following cases, namely –

(a) where the proceedings are taken by a local authority within the meaning of section 24 of the Caravan Sites and Control of Development Act 1960;

(b) where no site licence under Part I of that Act is in force in respect of the site;

and where a site licence in respect of the site is expressed to expire at the end of a specified period, the period for which enforcement may be suspended by virtue of this section shall not extend beyond the expiration of the licence.

TOWN AND COUNTRY PLANNING ACT 1990 (EXTRACTS)

Status of development plans

54A   Where, in making any determination under the planning Acts, regard is to be had to the development plan, the determination shall be made in accordance with the plan unless material considerations indicate otherwise.

Meaning of 'development' and 'new development'

55(1)   Subject to the following provisions of this section, in this Act, except where the context otherwise requires, 'development,' means the carrying out of building, engineering, mining or other operations in, on, over or under land, or the making of any material change in the use of any buildings or other land.

(1A)   For the purposes of this Act 'building operations' includes –

(a) demolition of buildings;

(b) rebuilding;

(c) structural alterations of or additions to buildings; and

(d) other operations normally undertaken by a person carrying on business as a builder.

(2)   The following operations or uses of land shall not be taken for the purposes of this Act to involve development of the land –

(a) the carrying out for the maintenance, improvement or other alteration of any building of works which –

(i) affect only the interior of the building, or

(ii) do not materially affect the external appearance of the building,

and are not works for making good war damage or works begun after 5th December 1968 for the alteration of a building by providing additional space in it underground;

(b) the carrying out on land within the boundaries of a road by a local highway authority of any works required for the maintenance or improvement of the road but, in the case of any such works which are not exclusively for the maintenance of the road, not including any works which may have significant adverse effects on the environment;

(c) the carrying out by a local authority or statutory undertakers of any works for the purpose of inspecting, repairing or renewing any sewers, mains, pipes, cables or other apparatus, including the breaking open of any street or other land for that purpose;

(d) the use of any buildings or other land within the curtilage of a dwellinghouse for any purpose incidental to the enjoyment of the dwellinghouse as such;

(e) the use of any land for the purposes of agriculture or forestry (including afforestation) and the use for any of those purposes of any building occupied together with land so used;

(f) in the case of buildings or other land which are used for a purpose of any class specified in an order made by the Secretary of State under this section, the use of the buildings or other land or, subject to the provisions of the order, of any part of the buildings or the other land, for any other purpose of the same class;

(g) the demolition of any description of building specified in a direction given by the Secretary of State to local planning authorities generally or to a particular local planning authority.

(3) For the avoidance of doubt it is hereby declared that for the purposes of this section –

(a) the use as two or more separate dwellinghouses of any building previously used as a single dwellinghouse involves a material change in the use of the building and of each part of it which is so used;

(b) the deposit of refuse or waste materials on land involves a material change in its use, notwithstanding that the land is comprised in a site already used for that purpose, if –

(i) the superficial area of the deposit is extended, or

(ii) the height of the deposit is extended and exceeds the level of the land adjoining the site.

(4) For the purposes of this Act mining operations include –

(a) the removal of material of any description –

(i) from a mineral-working deposit;

(ii) from a deposit of pulverised fuel ash or other furnace ash or clinker; or

(iii) from a deposit of iron, steel or other metallic slags; and

(b)   the extraction of minerals from a disused railway embankment.

(4A)   Where the placing or assembly of any tank in any part of any inland waters for the purpose of fish farming there would not, apart from this subsection, involve development of the land below, this Act shall have effect as if the tank resulted from carrying out engineering operations over that land; and in this subsection –

'fish farming' means the breeding, rearing or keeping of fish or shellfish (which includes any kind of crustacean and mollusc);

'inland waters' means waters which do not form part of the sea or of any creek, bay or estuary or of any river as far as the tide flows; and

'tank' includes any cage and any other structure for use in fish farming.

(5)   Without prejudice to any regulations made under the provisions of this Act relating to the control of advertisements, the use for the display of advertisements of any external part of a building which is not normally used for that purpose shall be treated for the purposes of this section as involving a material change in the use of that part of the building.

(6)   *Repealed.]*

Form and content of applications for planning permission

62   Any application to a local planning authority for planning permission –

(a)   shall be made in such manner as may be prescribed by regulations under this Act; and

(b)   shall include such particulars and be verified by such evidence as may be required by the regulations or by directions given by the local planning authority under them.

Determination of applications: general considerations

70(1)   Where an application is made to a local planning authority for planning permission –

(a)   subject to sections 91 and 92, they may grant planning permission, either unconditionally or subject to such conditions as they think fit; or

(b)   they may refuse planning permission.

(2)   In dealing with such an application the authority shall have regard to the provisions of the development plan, so far as material to the application, and to any other material considerations.

(3)   Subsection (1) has effect subject to section 65 and to the following provisions of this Act, to sections 66, 67, 72 and 73 of the Planning (Listed Buildings and Conservation Areas) Act 1990 and to section 15 of the Health Services Act 1976.

Power of local planning authority to decline to determine applications

70A(1) A local planning authority may decline to determine an application for planning permission for the development of any land if –

(a) within the period of two years ending with the date on which the application is received, the Secretary of State has refused a similar application referred to him under section 77 or has dismissed an appeal against the refusal of a similar application; and

(b) in the opinion of the authority there has been no significant change since the refusal or, as the case may be, dismissal mentioned in paragraph (a) in the development plan, so far as material to the application, or in any other material considerations.

(2) For the purposes of this section an application for planning permission for the development of any land shall only be taken to be similar to a later application if the development and the land to which the applications relate are in the opinion of the local planning authority the same or substantially the same.

(3) The reference in subsection (1)(a) to an appeal against the refusal of an application includes an appeal under section 78(2) in respect of an application.

(Right to appeal against planning decisions and failure to take such decisions

78(1) Where a local planning authority –

(a) refuse an application for planning permission or grant it subject to conditions;

(b) refuse an application for any consent, agreement or approval of that authority required by a condition imposed on a grant of planning permission or grant it subject to conditions; or

(c) refuse an application for any approval of that authority required under a development order or grant it subject to conditions,

the applicant may by notice appeal to the Secretary of State.

(2) A person who has made such an application may also appeal to the Secretary of State if the local planning authority have done none of the following –

(a) given notice to the applicant of their decision on the application;

(aa) given notice to the applicant that they have exercised their power under section 70A to decline to determine the application;

(b) given notice to him that the application has been referred to the Secretary of State in accordance with directions given under section 77,

within such period as may be prescribed by the development order or within such extended period as may at any time be agreed upon in writing between the applicant and the authority.

(3)   Any appeal under this section shall be made by notice served within such time and in such manner as may be prescribed by a development order.

(4)   The time prescribed for the service of such a notice must not be less than –

(a) 28 days from the date of notification of the decision; or

(b) in the case of an appeal under subsection (2), 28 days from the end of the period prescribed as mentioned in subsection (2) or, as the case may be, the extended period mentioned in that subsection.

(5)   For the purposes of the application of sections 79(1), 253(2)(c), 266(1)(b) and 288(10)(b) in relation to an appeal under subsection (2), it shall be assumed that the authority decided to refuse the application in question.

Time limits

171B(1) Where there has been a breach of planning control consisting in the carrying out without planning permission of building, engineering, mining or other operations in, on, over or under land, no enforcement action may be taken after the end of the period of four years beginning with the date on which the operations were substantially completed.

(2)   Where there has been a breach of planning control consisting in the change of use of any building to use as a single dwellinghouse, no enforcement action may be taken after the end of the period of four years beginning with the date of the breach.

(3)   In the case of any other breach of planning control, no enforcement action may be taken after the end of the period of ten years beginning with the date of the breach.

(4)   The preceding subsections do not prevent –

(a) the service of a breach of condition notice in respect of any breach of planning control if an enforcement notice in respect of the breach is in effect; or

(b) taking further enforcement action in respect of any breach of planning control if, during the period of four years ending with that action being taken, the local planning authority have taken or purported to take enforcement action in respect of that breach.

Issue of enforcement notice

172(1) The local planning authority may issue a notice (in this Act referred to as an 'enforcement notice') where it appears to them –

(a) that there has been a breach of planning control; and

(b) that it is expedient to issue the notice, having regard to the provisions of the development plan and to any other material considerations.

(2)   A copy of an enforcement notice shall be served –

    (a)   on the owner and on the occupier of the land to which it relates; and

    (b)   on any other person having an interest in the land, being an interest which, in the opinion of the authority, is materially affected by the notice.

(3)   The service of the notice shall take place –

    (a)   not more than twenty-eight days after its date of issue; and

    (b)   not less than twenty-eight days before the date specified in it as the date on which it is to take effect.

Contents and effect of notice

173(1)   An enforcement notice shall state –

    (a)   the matters which appear to the local planning authority to constitute the breach of planning control; and

    (b)   the paragraph of section 171A(1) within which, in the opinion of the authority, the breach falls.

(2)   A notice complies with subsection (1)(a) if it enables any person on whom a copy of it is served to know what those matters are.

(3)   An enforcement notice shall specify the steps which the authority require to be taken, or the activities which the authority require to cease, in order to achieve, wholly or partly, any of the following purposes.

(4)   Those purposes are –

    (a)   remedying the breach by making any development comply with the terms (including conditions and limitations) of any planning permission which has been granted in respect of the land, by discontinuing any use of the land or by restoring the land to its condition before the breach took place; or

    (b)   remedying any injury to amenity which has been caused by the breach.

(5)   An enforcement notice may, for example, require –

    (a)   the alteration or removal of any buildings or works;

    (b)   the carrying out of any building or other operations;

    (c)   any activity on the land not to be carried on except to the extent specified in the notice; or

    (d)   the contour of a deposit of refuse or waste materials on land to be modified by altering the gradient or gradients of its sides.

(6)   Where an enforcement notice is issued in respect of a breach of planning control consisting of demolition of a building, the notice may require the construction of a building (in this section referred to as a 'replacement building') which, subject to subsection (7), is as similar as possible to the demolished building.

(7)   A replacement building –

    (a)   must comply with any requirement imposed by any enactment applicable to the construction of buildings;

(b)   may differ from the demolished building in any respect which, if the demolished building had been altered in that respect, would not have constituted a breach of planning control;

(c)   must comply with any regulations made for the purposes of this subsection (including regulations modifying paragraphs (a) and (b)).

(8)   An enforcement notice shall specify the date on which it is to take effect and, subject to sections 175(4) and 289(4A), shall take effect on that date.

(9)   An enforcement notice shall specify the period at the end of which any steps are required to have been taken or any activities are required to have ceased and may specify different periods for different steps or activities; and, where different periods apply to different steps or activities, references in this Part to the period for compliance with an enforcement notice, in relation to any step or activity, are to the period at the end of which the step is required to have been taken or the activity is required to have ceased.

(10)   An enforcement notice shall specify such additional matters as may be prescribed, and regulations may require every copy of an enforcement notice served under section 172 to be accompanied by an explanatory note giving prescribed information as to the right of appeal under section 174.

(11)   Where –

(a)   an enforcement notice in respect of any breach of planning control could have required any buildings or works to be removed or any activity to cease, but does not do so; and

(b)   all the requirements of the notice have been complied with,

then, so far as the notice did not so require, planning permission shall be treated as having been granted by virtue of section 73A in respect of development consisting of the construction of the buildings or works or, as the case may be, the carrying out of the activities.

(12)   Where –

(a)   an enforcement notice requires the construction of a replacement building; and

(b)   all the requirements of the notice with respect to that construction have been complied with,

planning permission shall be treated as having been granted by virtue of section 73A in respect of development consisting of that construction.

Appeal against enforcement notice

174(1)   A person having an interest in the land to which an enforcement notice relates or a relevant occupier may appeal to the Secretary of State against the notice, whether or not a copy of it has been served on him.

(2)   An appeal may be brought on any of the following grounds –

    (a)   that, in respect of any breach of planning control which may be constituted by the matters stated in the notice, planning permission ought to be granted or, as the case may be, the condition or limitation concerned ought to be discharged;

    (b)   that those matters have not occurred;

    (c)   that those matters (if they occurred) do not constitute a breach of planning control;

    (d)   that, at the date when the notice was issued, no enforcement action could be taken in respect of any breach of planning control which may be constituted by those matters;

    (e)   that copies of the enforcement notice were not served as required by section 172;

    (f)   that the steps required by the notice to be taken, or the activities required by the notice to cease, exceed what is necessary to remedy any breach of planning control which may be constituted by those matters or, as the case may be, to remedy any injury to amenity which has been caused by any such breach;

    (g)   that any period specified in the notice in accordance with section 173(9) falls short of what should reasonably be allowed.

(3)   An appeal under this section shall be made either –

    (a)   by giving written notice of the appeal to the Secretary of State before the date specified in the enforcement notice as the date on which it is to take effect; or

    (b)   by sending such notice to him in a properly addressed and pre-paid letter posted to him at such time that, in the ordinary course of post, it would be delivered to him before that date; or

    (c)   by sending such notice to him using electronic communications at such time that, in the ordinary course of transmission, it would be delivered to him before that date.

(4)   A person who gives notice under subsection (3) shall submit to the Secretary of State, either when giving the notice or within the prescribed time, a statement in writing –

    (a)   specifying the grounds on which he is appealing against the enforcement notice; and

    (b)   giving such further information as may be prescribed.

(5)   If, where more than one ground is specified in that statement, the appellant does not give information required under subsection (4)(b) in relation to each of those grounds within the prescribed time, the Secretary of State may determine the appeal without considering any ground as to which the appellant has failed to give such information within that time.

(6)   In this section 'relevant occupier' means a person who –

    (a)   on the date on which the enforcement notice is issued occupies the land to which the notice relates by virtue of a licence; and

    (b)   continues so to occupy the land when the appeal is brought.

Execution and cost of works required by enforcement notice

178(1)   Where any steps required by an enforcement notice to be taken are not taken within the period for compliance with the notice, the local planning authority may –

(a)   enter the land and take the steps; and

(b)   recover from the person who is then the owner of the land any expenses reasonably incurred by them in doing so.

(2)   Where a copy of an enforcement notice has been served in respect of any breach of planning control –

(a)   any expenses incurred by the owner or occupier of any land for the purpose of complying with the notice, and

(b)   any sums paid by the owner of any land under subsection (1) in respect of expenses incurred by the local planning authority in taking steps required by such a notice to be taken,

shall be deemed to be incurred or paid for the use and at the request of the person by whom the breach of planning control was committed.

(3)   Regulations made under this Act may provide that –

(a)   section 276 of the Public Health Act 1936, (power of local authorities to sell materials removed in executing works under that Act subject to accounting for the proceeds of sale);

(b)   section 289 of that Act (power to require the occupier of any premises to permit works to be executed by the owner of the premises); and

(c)   section 294 of that Act (limit on liability of persons holding premises as agents or trustees in respect of the expenses recoverable under that Act),

shall apply, subject to such adaptations and modifications as may be specified in the regulations, in relation to any steps required to be taken by an enforcement notice.

(4)   Regulations under subsection (3) applying section 289 of the Public Health Act 1936 may include adaptations and modifications for the purpose of giving the owner of land to which an enforcement notice relates the right, as against all other persons interested in the land, to comply with the requirements of the enforcement notice.

(5)   Regulations under subsection (3) may also provide for the charging on the land of any expenses recoverable by a local planning authority under subsection (1).

(6)   Any person who wilfully obstructs a person acting in the exercise of powers under subsection (1) shall be guilty of an offence and liable on summary conviction to a fine not exceeding level 3 on the standard scale.

Offence where enforcement notice not complied with

179(1)   Where, at any time after the end of the period for compliance with an enforcement notice, any step required by the notice to be taken has not been taken or any activity required by the notice to cease is being carried on, the person who is then the owner of the land is in breach of the notice.

(2)   Where the owner of the land is in breach of an enforcement notice he shall be guilty of an offence.

(3)   In proceedings against any person for an offence under subsection (2), it shall be a defence for him to show that he did everything he could be expected to do to secure compliance with the notice.

(4)   A person who has control of or an interest in the land to which an enforcement notice relates (other than the owner) must not carry on any activity which is required by the notice to cease or cause or permit such an activity to be carried on.

(5)   A person who, at any time after the end of the period for compliance with the notice, contravenes subsection (4) shall be guilty of an offence.

(6)   An offence under subsection (2) or (5) may be charged by reference to any day or longer period of time and a person may be convicted of a second or subsequent offence under the subsection in question by reference to any period of time following the preceding conviction for such an offence.

(7)   Where –

(a)   a person charged with an offence under this section has not been served with a copy of the enforcement notice; and

(b)   the notice is not contained in the appropriate register kept under section 188,

it shall be a defence for him to show that he was not aware of the existence of the notice.

(8)   A person guilty of an offence under this section shall be liable –

(a)   on summary conviction, to a fine not exceeding £20,000; and

(b)   on conviction on indictment, to a fine.

(9)   In determining the amount of any fine to be imposed on a person convicted of an offence under this section, the court shall in particular have regard to any financial benefit which has accrued or appears likely to accrue to him in consequence of the offence.

Injunctions restraining breaches of planning control

187B(1) Where a local planning authority consider it necessary or expedient for any actual or apprehended breach of planning control to be restrained by injunction, they may apply to the court for an injunction, whether or not they have exercised or are proposing to exercise any of their other powers under this Part.

(2)   On an application under subsection (1) the court may grant such an injunction as the court thinks appropriate for the purpose of restraining the breach.

(3)   Rules of court may provide for such an injunction to be issued against a person whose identity is unknown.

(4)   In this section 'the court' means the High Court or the county court.

Proceedings for questioning the validity of other orders, decisions and directions

288(1) If any person –

    (a) is aggrieved by any order to which this section applies and wishes to question the validity of that order on the grounds –

        (i) that the order is not within the powers of this Act, or

        (ii) that any of the relevant requirements have not been complied with in relation to that order; or

    (b) is aggrieved by any action on the part of the Secretary of State to which this section applies and wishes to question the validity of that action on the grounds –

        (i) that the action is not within the powers of this Act, or

        (ii) that any of the relevant requirements have not been complied with in relation to that action,

    he may make an application to the High Court under this section.

(2) Without prejudice to subsection (1), if the authority directly concerned with any order to which this section applies, or with any action on the part of the Secretary of State to which this section applies, wish to question the validity of that order or action on any of the grounds mentioned in subsection (1), the authority may make an application to the High Court under this section.

(3) An application under this section must be made within six weeks from the date on which the order is confirmed (or, in the case of an order under section 97 which takes effect under section 99 without confirmation, the date on which it takes effect) or, as the case may be, the date on which the action is taken.

(4) This section applies to any such order as is mentioned in subsection (2) of section 284 and to any such action on the part of the Secretary of State as is mentioned in subsection (3) of that section.

(5) On any application under this section the High Court –

    (a) may, subject to subsection (6), by interim order suspend the operation of the order or action, the validity of which is questioned by the application, until the final determination of the proceedings;

    (b) if satisfied that the order or action in question is not within the powers of this Act, or that the interests of the applicant have been substantially prejudiced by a failure to comply with any of the relevant requirements in relation to it, may quash that order or action.

(6) Paragraph (a) of subsection (5) shall not apply to applications questioning the validity of tree preservation orders.

(7) In relation to a tree preservation order, or to an order made in pursuance of section 221(5), the powers conferred on the High Court by subsection (5) shall be exercisable by way of quashing or (where applicable) suspending the operation of the order either in whole or in part, as the court may determine.

(8)   References in this section to the confirmation of an order include the confirmation of an order subject to modifications as well as the confirmation of an order in the form in which it was made.

(9)   In this section 'the relevant requirements', in relation to any order or action to which this section applies, means any requirements of this Act or of the Tribunals and Inquiries Act 1992, or of any order, regulations or rules made under this Act or under that Act which are applicable to that order or action.

(10)   Any reference in this section to the authority directly concerned with any order or action to which this section applies –

(a) in relation to any such decision as is mentioned in section 284(3)(f), is a reference to the council on whom the notice in question was served and, in a case where the Secretary of State has modified such a notice, wholly or in part, by substituting another local authority or statutory undertakers for that council, includes a reference to that local authority or those statutory undertakers;

(b) in any other case, is a reference to the authority who made the order in question or made the decision or served the notice to which the proceedings in question relate, or who referred the matter to the Secretary of State, or, where the order or notice in question was made or served by him, the authority named in the order or notice.

Appeals to High Court relating to enforcement notices and notices under section 207

289(1) Where the Secretary of State gives a decision in proceedings on an appeal under Part VII against an enforcement notice the appellant or the local planning authority or any other person having an interest in the land to which the notice relates may, according as rules of court may provide, either appeal to the High Court against the decision on a point of law or require the Secretary of State to state and sign a case for the opinion of the High Court.

(2)   Where the Secretary of State gives a decision in proceedings on an appeal under Part VIII against a notice under section 207, the appellant or the local planning authority or any person (other than the appellant) on whom the notice was served may, according as rules of court may provide, either appeal to the High Court against the decision on a point of law or require the Secretary of State to state and sign a case for the opinion of the High Court.

(3)   At any stage of the proceedings on any such appeal as is mentioned in subsection (1), the Secretary of State may state any question of law arising in the course of the proceedings in the form of a special case for the decision of the High Court.

(4)   A decision of the High Court on a case stated by virtue of subsection (3) shall be deemed to be a judgment of the court within the meaning of section 16 of the Supreme Court Act 1981 (jurisdiction of the Court

of Appeal to hear and determine appeals from any judgment of the High Court).

(4A)   In proceedings brought by virtue of this section in respect of an enforcement notice, the High Court or, as the case may be, the Court of Appeal may, on such terms if any as the Court thinks fit (which may include terms requiring the local planning authority to give an undertaking as to damages or any other matter), order that the notice shall have effect, or have effect to such extent as may be specified in the order, pending the final determination of those proceedings and any re-hearing and determination by the Secretary of State.

(4B)   Where proceedings are brought by virtue of this section in respect of any notice under section 207, the notice shall be of no effect pending the final determination of those proceedings and any re-hearing and determination by the Secretary of State.

(5)   In relation to any proceedings in the High Court or the Court of Appeal brought by virtue of this section the power to make rules of court shall include power to make rules –

(a) prescribing the powers of the High Court or the Court of Appeal with respect to the remitting of the matter with the opinion or direction of the court for re-hearing and determination by the Secretary of State; and

(b) providing for the Secretary of State, either generally or in such circumstances as may be prescribed by the rules, to be treated as a party to any such proceedings and to be entitled to appear and to be heard accordingly.

(5A)   Rules of court may also provide for the High Court or, as the case may be, the Court of Appeal to give directions as to the exercise, until such proceedings in respect of an enforcement notice are finally concluded and any re-hearing and determination by the Secretary of State has taken place, of any other powers in respect of the matters to which such a notice relates.

(6)   No proceedings in the High Court shall be brought by virtue of this section except with the leave of that Court and no appeal to the Court of Appeal shall be so brought except with the leave of the Court of Appeal or of the High Court.

(7)   In this section 'decision' includes a direction or order, and references to the giving of a decision shall be construed accordingly.

CRIMINAL JUSTICE AND PUBLIC ORDER ACT 1994 (EXTRACTS)

PART V: PUBLIC ORDER: COLLECTIVE TRESPASS OR NUISANCE ON LAND

POWERS TO REMOVE TRESPASSERS ON LAND

Power to remove trespassers on land

61(1)   If the senior police officer present at the scene reasonably believes that two or more persons are trespassing on land and are present there with the common purpose of residing there for any period, that reasonable steps have been taken by or on behalf of the occupier to ask them to leave and –

(a)   that any of those persons has caused damage to the land or to property on the land or used threatening, abusive or insulting words or behaviour towards the occupier, a member of his family or an employee or agent of his, or

(b)   that those persons have between them six or more vehicles on the land,

he may direct those persons, or any of them, to leave the land and to remove any vehicles or other property they have with them on the land.

(2)   Where the persons in question are reasonably believed by the senior police officer to be persons who were not originally trespassers but have become trespassers on the land, the officer must reasonably believe that the other conditions specified in subsection (1) are satisfied after those persons became trespassers before he can exercise the power conferred by that subsection.

(3)   A direction under subsection (1) above, if not communicated to the persons referred to in subsection (1) by the police officer giving the direction, may be communicated to them by any constable at the scene.

(4)   If a person knowing that a direction under subsection (1) above has been given which applies to him –

(a)   fails to leave the land as soon as reasonably practicable, or

(b)   having left again enters the land as a trespasser within the period of three months beginning with the day on which the direction was given,

he commits an offence and is liable on summary conviction to imprisonment for a term not exceeding 51 weeks or a fine not exceeding level 4 on the standard scale, or both.

(4A)   Where, as respects Scotland, the reason why these persons have become trespassers is that they have ceased to be entitled to exercise access rights by virtue of –

(a)   their having formed the common purpose mentioned in subsection (1) above; or

(b) one or more of the conditions specified in paragraphs (a) and (b) of that subsection having been satisfied,

the circumstances constituting that reason shall be treated, for the purposes of subsection (4) above, as having also occurred after these persons became trespassers.

(4B) In subsection (4A) above 'access rights' has the meaning given by the Land Reform (Scotland) Act 2003.

(5) A constable in uniform who reasonably suspects that a person is committing an offence under this section may arrest him without a warrant.

(6) In proceedings for an offence under this section it is a defence for the accused to show –

(a) that he was not trespassing on the land, or

(b) that he had a reasonable excuse for failing to leave the land as soon as reasonably practicable or, as the case may be, for again entering the land as a trespasser.

(7) In its application in England and Wales to common land this section has effect as if in the preceding subsections of it –

(a) references to trespassing or trespassers were references to acts and persons doing acts which constitute either a trespass as against the occupier or an infringement of the commoners' rights; and

(b) references to 'the occupier' included the commoners or any of them or, in the case of common land to which the public has access, the local authority as well as any commoner.

(8) Subsection (7) above does not –

(a) require action by more than one occupier; or

(b) constitute persons trespassers as against any commoner or the local authority if they are permitted to be there by the other occupier.

(9) In this section –

'common land' means common land as defined in section 22 of the Commons Registration Act 1965;

'commoner' means a person with rights of common as defined in section 22 of the Commons Registration Act 1965;

'land' does not include –

(a) buildings other than –

(i) agricultural buildings within the meaning of, in England and Wales, paragraphs 3 to 8 of Schedule 5 to the Local Government Finance Act 1988 or, in Scotland, section 7(2) of the Valuation and Rating (Scotland) Act 1956, or

(ii) scheduled monuments within the meaning of the Ancient Monuments and Archaeological Areas Act 1979;

(b) land forming part of –

(i) a highway unless it falls within the classifications in section 54 of the Wildlife and Countryside Act 1981 (footpath, bridleway or byway open to all traffic or road used as a public path) it is a footpath, bridleway or byway open to all traffic within the meaning of Part III of the Wildlife and Countryside Act 1981, is a restricted byway within the meaning of Part II of the Countryside and Rights of Way Act 2000 or is a cycle track under the Highways Act 1980 or the Cycle Tracks Act 1984; or

(ii) a road within the meaning of the Roads (Scotland) Act 1984 unless it falls within the definitions in section 151(2)(a)(ii) or (b) (footpaths and cycle tracks) of that Act or is a bridleway within the meaning of section 47 of the Countryside (Scotland) Act 1967;

'the local authority', in relation to common land, means any local authority which has powers in relation to the land under section 9 of the Commons Registration Act 1965;

'occupier' (and in subsection (8) 'the other occupier') means –

(a) in England and Wales, the person entitled to possession of the land by virtue of an estate or interest held by him; and

(b) in Scotland, the person lawfully entitled to natural possession of the land;

'property', in relation to damage to property on land, means –

(a) in England and Wales, property within the meaning of section 10(1) of the Criminal Damage Act 1971; and

(b) in Scotland, either –

(i) heritable property other than land; or

(ii) corporeal moveable property,

and 'damage' includes the deposit of any substance capable of polluting the land;

'trespass' means, in the application of this section –

(a) in England and Wales, subject to the extensions effected by subsection (7) above, trespass as against the occupier of the land;

(b) in Scotland, entering, or as the case may be remaining on, land without lawful authority and without the occupier's consent; and

'trespassing' and 'trespasser' shall be construed accordingly;

'vehicle' includes –

(a) any vehicle, whether or not it is in a fit state for use on roads, and includes any chassis or body, with or without wheels, appearing to have formed part of such a vehicle, and any load carried by, and anything attached to, such a vehicle; and

(b) a caravan as defined in section 29(1) of the Caravan Sites and Control of Development Act 1960;

and a person may be regarded for the purposes of this section as having a purpose of residing in a place notwithstanding that he has a home elsewhere.

Supplementary powers of seizure

62(1) If a direction has been given under section 61 and a constable reasonably suspects that any person to whom the direction applies has, without reasonable excuse –

(a) failed to remove any vehicle on the land which appears to the constable to belong to him or to be in his possession or under his control; or

(b) entered the land as a trespasser with a vehicle within the period of three months beginning with the day on which the direction was given,

the constable may seize and remove that vehicle.

(2) In this section, 'trespasser' and 'vehicle' have the same meaning as in section 61.

Power to remove trespassers: alternative site available

62A(1) If the senior police officer present at a scene reasonably believes that the conditions in subsection (2) are satisfied in relation to a person and land, he may direct the person –

(a) to leave the land;

(b) to remove any vehicle and other property he has with him on the land.

(2) The conditions are –

(a) that the person and one or more others ('the trespassers') are trespassing on the land;

(b) that the trespassers have between them at least one vehicle on the land;

(c) that the trespassers are present on the land with the common purpose of residing there for any period;

(d) if it appears to the officer that the person has one or more caravans in his possession or under his control on the land, that there is a suitable pitch on a relevant caravan site for that caravan or each of those caravans;

(e) that the occupier of the land or a person acting on his behalf has asked the police to remove the trespassers from the land.

(3) A direction under subsection (1) may be communicated to the person to whom it applies by any constable at the scene.

(4) Subsection (5) applies if –

(a) a police officer proposes to give a direction under subsection (1) in relation to a person and land, and

(b) it appears to him that the person has one or more caravans in his possession or under his control on the land.

(5) The officer must consult every local authority within whose area the land is situated as to whether there is a suitable pitch for the caravan or each of the caravans on a relevant caravan site which is situated in the local authority's area.

(6) In this section –

'caravan' and 'caravan site' have the same meanings as in Part 1 of the

Caravan Sites and Control of Development Act 1960;

'relevant caravan site' means a caravan site which is –

(a) situated in the area of a local authority within whose area the land is situated, and

(b) managed by a relevant site manager;

'relevant site manager' means –

(a) a local authority within whose area the land is situated;

(b) a registered social landlord;

'registered social landlord' means a body registered as a social landlord under Chapter 1 of Part 1 of the Housing Act 1996.

(7) The Secretary of State may by order amend the definition of 'relevant site manager' in subsection (6) by adding a person or description of person.

(8) An order under subsection (7) must be made by statutory instrument and is subject to annulment in pursuance of a resolution of either House of Parliament.

Failure to comply with direction under section 62A: offences

62B(1) A person commits an offence if he knows that a direction under section 62A(1) has been given which applies to him and –

(a) he fails to leave the relevant land as soon as reasonably practicable, or

(b) he enters any land in the area of the relevant local authority as a trespasser before the end of the relevant period with the intention of residing there.

(2) The relevant period is the period of 3 months starting with the day on which the direction is given.

(3) A person guilty of an offence under this section is liable on summary conviction to imprisonment for a term not exceeding 51 weeks or a fine not exceeding level 4 on the standard scale or both.

(4) A constable in uniform who reasonably suspects that a person is committing an offence under this section may arrest him without a warrant.

(5) In proceedings for an offence under this section it is a defence for the accused to show –

(a) that he was not trespassing on the land in respect of which he is alleged to have committed the offence, or

(b) that he had a reasonable excuse –

(i) for failing to leave the relevant land as soon as reasonably practicable, or

(ii) for entering land in the area of the relevant local authority as a trespasser with the intention of residing there, or

(c) that, at the time the direction was given, he was under the age of 18 years and was residing with his parent or guardian.

Failure to comply with direction under section 62A: seizure

62C(1) This section applies if a direction has been given under section 62A(1) and a constable reasonably suspects that a person to whom the direction applies has, without reasonable excuse –

   (a) failed to remove any vehicle on the relevant land which appears to the constable to belong to him or to be in his possession or under his control; or

   (b) entered any land in the area of the relevant local authority as a trespasser with a vehicle before the end of the relevant period with the intention of residing there.

(2) The relevant period is the period of 3 months starting with the day on which the direction is given.

(3) The constable may seize and remove the vehicle.

Common land: modifications

62D(1) In their application to common land sections 62A to 62C have effect with these modifications.

(2) References to trespassing and trespassers have effect as if they were references to acts, and persons doing acts, which constitute –

   (a) a trespass as against the occupier, or

   (b) an infringement of the commoners' rights.

(3) References to the occupier –

   (a) in the case of land to which the public has access, include the local authority and any commoner;

   (b) in any other case, include the commoners or any of them.

(4) Subsection (1) does not –

   (a) require action by more than one occupier, or

   (b) constitute persons trespassers as against any commoner or the local authority if they are permitted to be there by the other occupier.

(5) In this section 'common land', 'commoner' and 'the local authority' have the meanings given by section 61.

Sections 62A to 62D: interpretation

62E(1) Subsections (2) to (8) apply for the interpretation of sections 62A to 62D and this section.

(2) 'Land' does not include buildings other than –

   (a) agricultural buildings within the meaning of paragraphs 3 to 8 of Schedule 5 to the Local Government Finance Act 1988, or

   (b) scheduled monuments within the meaning of the Ancient Monuments and Archaeological Areas Act 1979.

(3) 'Local authority' means –

   (a) in Greater London, a London borough or the Common Council of the City of London;

   (b) in England outside Greater London, a county council, a district council or the Council of the Isles of Scilly;

(c) in Wales, a county council or a county borough council.
(4) 'Occupier', 'trespass', 'trespassing' and 'trespasser' have the meanings given by section 61 in relation to England and Wales.
(5) 'The relevant land' means the land in respect of which a direction under section 62A(1) is given.
(6) 'The relevant local authority' means –
(a) if the relevant land is situated in the area of more than one local authority (but is not in the Isles of Scilly), the district council or county borough council within whose area the relevant land is situated;
(b) if the relevant land is situated in the Isles of Scilly, the Council of the Isles of Scilly;
(c) in any other case, the local authority within whose area the relevant land is situated.
(7) 'Vehicle' has the meaning given by section 61.
(8) A person may be regarded as having a purpose of residing in a place even if he has a home elsewhere.

POWERS TO REMOVE UNAUTHORISED CAMPERS

Power of local authority to direct unauthorised campers to leave land

77(1) If it appears to a local authority that persons are for the time being residing in a vehicle or vehicles within that authority's area –
(a) on any land forming part of a highway;
(b) on any other unoccupied land; or
(c) on any occupied land without the consent of the occupier,
the authority may give a direction that those persons and any others with them are to leave the land and remove the vehicle or vehicles and any other property they have with them on the land.
(2) Notice of a direction under subsection (1) must be served on the persons to whom the direction applies, but it shall be sufficient for this purpose for the direction to specify the land and (except where the direction applies to only one person) to be addressed to all occupants of the vehicles on the land, without naming them.
(3) If a person knowing that a direction under subsection (1) above has been given which applies to him –
(a) fails, as soon as practicable, to leave the land or remove from the land any vehicle or other property which is the subject of the direction, or
(b) having removed any such vehicle or property again enters the land with a vehicle within the period of three months beginning with the day on which the direction was given,
he commits an offence and is liable on summary conviction to a fine not exceeding level 3 on the standard scale.

(4)   A direction under subsection (1) operates to require persons who re-enter the land within the said period with vehicles or other property to leave and remove the vehicles or other property as it operates in relation to the persons and vehicles or other property on the land when the direction was given.

(5)   In proceedings for an offence under this section it is a defence for the accused to show that his failure to leave or to remove the vehicle or other property as soon as practicable or his re-entry with a vehicle was due to illness, mechanical breakdown or other immediate emergency.

(6)   In this section –

'land' means land in the open air;

'local authority' means –

(a)   in Greater London, a London borough or the Common Council of the City of London;

(b)   in England outside Greater London, a county council, a district council or the Council of the Isles of Scilly;

(c)   in Wales, a county council or a county borough council;

'occupier' means the person entitled to possession of the land by virtue of an estate or interest held by him;

'vehicle' includes –

(a)   any vehicle, whether or not it is in a fit state for use on roads, and includes any body, with or without wheels, appearing to have formed part of such a vehicle, and any load carried by, and anything attached to, such a vehicle; and

(b)   a caravan as defined in section 29(1) of the Caravan Sites and Control of Development Act 1960;

and a person may be regarded for the purposes of this section as residing on any land notwithstanding that he has a home elsewhere.

(7)   Until 1st April 1996, in this section 'local authority' means, in Wales, a county council or a district council.

Orders for removal of persons and their vehicles unlawfully on land

78(1)   A magistrates' court may, on a complaint made by a local authority, if satisfied that persons and vehicles in which they are residing are present on land within that authority's area in contravention of a direction given under section 77, make an order requiring the removal of any vehicle or other property which is so present on the land and any person residing in it.

(2)   An order under this section may authorise the local authority to take such steps as are reasonably necessary to ensure that the order is complied with and, in particular, may authorise the authority, by its officers and servants –

(a)   to enter upon the land specified in the order; and

(b)   to take, in relation to any vehicle or property to be removed in pursuance of the order, such steps for securing entry and rendering it suitable for removal as may be so specified.

(3)   The local authority shall not enter upon any occupied land unless they have given to the owner and occupier at least 24 hours' notice of their intention to do so, or unless after reasonable inquiries they are unable to ascertain their names and addresses.

(4)   A person who wilfully obstructs any person in the exercise of any power conferred on him by an order under this section commits an offence and is liable on summary conviction to a fine not exceeding level 3 on the standard scale.

(5)   Where a complaint is made under this section, a summons issued by the court requiring the person or persons to whom it is directed to appear before the court to answer to the complaint may be directed –
(a)   to the occupant of a particular vehicle on the land in question; or
(b)   to all occupants of vehicles on the land in question, without naming him or them.

(6)   Section 55(2) of the Magistrates' Courts Act 1980 (warrant for arrest of defendant failing to appear) does not apply to proceedings on a complaint made under this section.

(7)   Section 77(6) of this Act applies also for the interpretation of this section.

Provisions as to directions under section 77 and orders under section 78

79(1)   The following provisions apply in relation to the service of notice of a direction under section 77 and of a summons under section 78, referred to in those provisions as a 'relevant document'.

(2)   Where it is impracticable to serve a relevant document on a person named in it, the document shall be treated as duly served on him if a copy of it is fixed in a prominent place to the vehicle concerned; and where a relevant document is directed to the unnamed occupants of vehicles, it shall be treated as duly served on those occupants if a copy of it is fixed in a prominent place to every vehicle on the land in question at the time when service is thus effected.

(3)   A local authority shall take such steps as may be reasonably practicable to secure that a copy of any relevant document is displayed on the land in question (otherwise than by being fixed to a vehicle) in a manner designed to ensure that it is likely to be seen by any person camping on the land.

(4)   Notice of any relevant document shall be given by the local authority to the owner of the land in question and to any occupier of that land unless, after reasonable inquiries, the authority is unable to ascertain the name and address of the owner or occupier; and the owner of any such land and any occupier of such land shall be entitled to appear and to be heard in the proceedings.

(5)   Section 77(6) applies also for the interpretation of this section.

Repeal of certain provisions relating to gipsy sites

80(1), (2) ...

(3)   The repeal by subsection (1) above of section 8 of the said Act of 1968 shall not affect the validity of directions given under subsection (3)(a) of that section; and in the case of directions under subsection (3)(c), the council may elect either to withdraw the application or request the Secretary of State to determine the application and if they so request the application shall be treated as referred to him under section 77 of the Town and Country Planning Act 1990.

(4)   The repeal by subsection (1) above of the definition of 'gipsies' in section 16 of the said Act of 1968 shall not affect the interpretation of that word in the definition of 'protected site' in section 5(1) of the Mobile Homes Act 1983 or in any document embodying the terms of any planning permission granted under the Town and Country Planning Act 1990 before the commencement of this section.

(5)   ... so far as it extends to England and Wales except for the purposes of applications for grant received by the Secretary of State before the commencement of this section.

HUMAN RIGHTS ACT 1998

INTRODUCTION

The Convention Rights

1(1)   In this Act 'the Convention rights' means the rights and fundamental freedoms set out in –
(a) Articles 2 to 12 and 14 of the Convention,
(b) Articles 1 to 3 of the First Protocol, and
(c) Articles 1 and 2 of the Sixth Protocol,
as read with Articles 16 to 18 of the Convention.

(2)   Those Articles are to have effect for the purposes of this Act subject to any designated derogation or reservation (as to which see sections 14 and 15).

(3)   The Articles are set out in Schedule 1.

(4)   The Secretary of State may by order make such amendments to this Act as he considers appropriate to reflect the effect, in relation to the United Kingdom, of a protocol.

(5)   In subsection (4) 'protocol' means a protocol to the Convention –
(a) which the United Kingdom has ratified; or
(b) which the United Kingdom has signed with a view to ratification.

(6)   No amendment may be made by an order under subsection (4) so as to come into force before the protocol concerned is in force in relation to the United Kingdom.

Interpretation of Convention rights

2(1)   A court or tribunal determining a question which has arisen in connection with a Convention right must take into account any –

(a) judgment, decision, declaration or advisory opinion of the European Court of Human Rights,

(b) opinion of the Commission given in a report adopted under Article 31 of the Convention,

(c) decision of the Commission in connection with Article 26 or 27(2) of the Convention, or

(d) decision of the Committee of Ministers taken under Article 46 of the Convention,

whenever made or given, so far as, in the opinion of the court or tribunal, it is relevant to the proceedings in which that question has arisen.

(2)   Evidence of any judgment, decision, declaration or opinion of which account may have to be taken under this section is to be given in proceedings before any court or tribunal in such manner as may be provided by rules.

(3)   In this section 'rules' means rules of court or, in the case of proceedings before a tribunal, rules made for the purposes of this section –

(a) by the Lord Chancellor or the Secretary of State, in relation to any proceedings outside Scotland;

(b) by the Secretary of State, in relation to proceedings in Scotland; or

(c) by a Northern Ireland department, in relation to proceedings before a tribunal in Northern Ireland –

(i) which deals with transferred matters; and

(ii) for which no rules made under paragraph (a) are in force.

LEGISLATION

Interpretation of legislation

3(1)   So far as it is possible to do so, primary legislation and subordinate legislation must be read and given effect in a way which is compatible with the Convention rights.

(2)   This section –

(a) applies to primary legislation and subordinate legislation whenever enacted;

(b) does not affect the validity, continuing operation or enforcement of any incompatible primary legislation; and

(c) does not affect the validity, continuing operation or enforcement of any incompatible subordinate legislation if (disregarding any possibility of revocation) primary legislation prevents removal of the incompatibility.

Declaration of incompatibility

4(1)   Subsection (2) applies in any proceedings in which a court determines whether a provision of primary legislation is compatible with a Convention right.

(2)   If the court is satisfied that the provision is incompatible with a Convention right, it may make a declaration of that incompatibility.

(3)   Subsection (4) applies in any proceedings in which a court determines whether a provision of subordinate legislation, made in the exercise of a power conferred by primary legislation, is compatible with a Convention right.

(4)   If the court is satisfied –

    (a)   that the provision is incompatible with a Convention right, and

    (b)   that (disregarding any possibility of revocation) the primary legislation concerned prevents removal of the incompatibility,

    it may make a declaration of that incompatibility.

(5)   In this section 'court' means –

    (a)   the House of Lords;

    (b)   the Judicial Committee of the Privy Council;

    (c)   the Courts-Martial Appeal Court;

    (d)   in Scotland, the High Court of Justiciary sitting otherwise than as a trial court or the Court of Session;

    (e)   in England and Wales or Northern Ireland, the High Court or the Court of Appeal.

(6)   A declaration under this section ('a declaration of incompatibility') –

    (a)   does not affect the validity, continuing operation or enforcement of the provision in respect of which it is given; and

    (b)   is not binding on the parties to the proceedings in which it is made.

Right of Crown to intervene

5(1)   Where a court is considering whether to make a declaration of incompatibility, the Crown is entitled to notice in accordance with rules of court.

(2)   In any case to which subsection (1) applies –

    (a)   a Minister of the Crown (or a person nominated by him),

    (b)   a member of the Scottish Executive,

    (c)   a Northern Ireland Minister,

    (d)   a Northern Ireland department,

    is entitled, on giving notice in accordance with rules of court, to be joined as a party to the proceedings.

(3)   Notice under subsection (2) may be given at any time during the proceedings.

(4)   A person who has been made a party to criminal proceedings (other than in Scotland) as the result of a notice under subsection (2) may,

with leave, appeal to the House of Lords against any declaration of incompatibility made in the proceedings.

(5) In subsection (4) –

'criminal proceedings' includes all proceedings before the Courts-Martial Appeal Court; and

'leave' means leave granted by the court making the declaration of incompatibility or by the House of Lords.

PUBLIC AUTHORITIES

Acts of public authorities

6(1) It is unlawful for a public authority to act in a way which is incompatible with a Convention right.

(2) Subsection (1) does not apply to an act if –

   (a) as the result of one or more provisions of primary legislation, the authority could not have acted differently; or

   (b) in the case of one or more provisions of, or made under, primary legislation which cannot be read or given effect in a way which is compatible with the Convention rights, the authority was acting so as to give effect to or enforce those provisions.

(3) In this section 'public authority' includes –

   (a) a court or tribunal, and

   (b) any person certain of whose functions are functions of a public nature,

but does not include either House of Parliament or a person exercising functions in connection with proceedings in Parliament.

(4) In subsection (3) 'Parliament' does not include the House of Lords in its judicial capacity.

(5) In relation to a particular act, a person is not a public authority by virtue only of subsection (3)(b) if the nature of the act is private.

(6) 'An act' includes a failure to act but does not include a failure to –

   (a) introduce in, or lay before, Parliament a proposal for legislation; or

   (b) make any primary legislation or remedial order.

Proceedings

7(1) A person who claims that a public authority has acted (or proposes to act) in a way which is made unlawful by section 6(1) may –

   (a) bring proceedings against the authority under this Act in the appropriate court or tribunal, or

   (b) rely on the Convention right or rights concerned in any legal proceedings,

but only if he is (or would be) a victim of the unlawful act.

(2) In subsection (1)(a) 'appropriate court or tribunal' means such court or tribunal as may be determined in accordance with rules; and

proceedings against an authority include a counterclaim or similar proceeding.

(3)　If the proceedings are brought on an application for judicial review, the applicant is to be taken to have a sufficient interest in relation to the unlawful act only if he is, or would be, a victim of that act.

(4)　If the proceedings are made by way of a petition for judicial review in Scotland, the applicant shall be taken to have title and interest to sue in relation to the unlawful act only if he is, or would be, a victim of that act.

(5)　Proceedings under subsection (1)(a) must be brought before the end of –

(a)　the period of one year beginning with the date on which the act complained of took place; or

(b)　such longer period as the court or tribunal considers equitable having regard to all the circumstances,

but that is subject to any rule imposing a stricter time limit in relation to the procedure in question.

(6)　In subsection (1)(b) 'legal proceedings' includes –

(a)　proceedings brought by or at the instigation of a public authority; and

(b)　an appeal against the decision of a court or tribunal.

(7)　For the purposes of this section, a person is a victim of an unlawful act only if he would be a victim for the purposes of Article 34 of the Convention if proceedings were brought in the European Court of Human Rights in respect of that act.

(8)　Nothing in this Act creates a criminal offence.

(9)　In this section 'rules' means –

(a)　in relation to proceedings before a court or tribunal outside Scotland, rules made by the Lord Chancellor or the Secretary of State for the purposes of this section or rules of court,

(b)　in relation to proceedings before a court or tribunal in Scotland, rules made by the Secretary of State for those purposes,

(c)　in relation to proceedings before a tribunal in Northern Ireland –

(i)　which deals with transferred matters; and

(ii) for which no rules made under paragraph (a) are in force,

rules made by a Northern Ireland department for those purposes,

and includes provision made by order under section 1 of the Courts and Legal Services Act 1990.

(10)　In making rules, regard must be had to section 9.

(11)　The Minister who has power to make rules in relation to a particular tribunal may, to the extent he considers it necessary to ensure that the tribunal can provide an appropriate remedy in relation to an act (or proposed act) of a public authority which is (or would be) unlawful as a result of section 6(1), by order add to –

(a)　the relief or remedies which the tribunal may grant; or

(b)　the grounds on which it may grant any of them.

(12)   An order made under subsection (11) may contain such incidental, supplemental, consequential or transitional provision as the Minister making it considers appropriate.

(13)   'The Minister' includes the Northern Ireland department concerned.

Judicial remedies

8(1)   In relation to any act (or proposed act) of a public authority which the court finds is (or would be) unlawful, it may grant such relief or remedy, or make such order, within its powers as it considers just and appropriate.

(2)   But damages may be awarded only by a court which has power to award damages, or to order the payment of compensation, in civil proceedings.

(3)   No award of damages is to be made unless, taking account of all the circumstances of the case, including –

(a)   any other relief or remedy granted, or order made, in relation to the act in question (by that or any other court), and

(b)   the consequences of any decision (of that or any other court) in respect of that act,

the court is satisfied that the award is necessary to afford just satisfaction to the person in whose favour it is made.

(4)   In determining –

(a)   whether to award damages, or

(b)   the amount of an award,

the court must take into account the principles applied by the European Court of Human Rights in relation to the award of compensation under Article 41 of the Convention.

(5)   A public authority against which damages are awarded is to be treated –

(a)   in Scotland, for the purposes of section 3 of the Law Reform (Miscellaneous Provisions) (Scotland) Act 1940 as if the award were made in an action of damages in which the authority has been found liable in respect of loss or damage to the person to whom the award is made;

(b)   for the purposes of the Civil Liability (Contribution) Act 1978 as liable in respect of damage suffered by the person to whom the award is made.

(6)   In this section –

'court' includes a tribunal;

'damages' means damages for an unlawful act of a public authority; and

'unlawful' means unlawful under section 6(1).

Judicial acts

9(1) Proceedings under section 7(1)(a) in respect of a judicial act may be brought only –

(a) by exercising a right of appeal;

(b) on an application (in Scotland a petition) for judicial review; or

(c) in such other forum as may be prescribed by rules.

(2) That does not affect any rule of law which prevents a court from being the subject of judicial review.

(3) In proceedings under this Act in respect of a judicial act done in good faith, damages may not be awarded otherwise than to compensate a person to the extent required by Article 5(5) of the Convention.

(4) An award of damages permitted by subsection (3) is to be made against the Crown; but no award may be made unless the appropriate person, if not a party to the proceedings, is joined.

(5) In this section –

'appropriate person' means the Minister responsible for the court concerned, or a person or government department nominated by him;

'court' includes a tribunal;

'judge' includes a member of a tribunal, a justice of the peace and a clerk or other officer entitled to exercise the jurisdiction of a court;

'judicial act' means a judicial act of a court and includes an act done on the instructions, or on behalf, of a judge; and

'rules' has the same meaning as in section 7(9).

REMEDIAL ACTION

Power to take remedial action

10(1) This section applies if –

(a) a provision of legislation has been declared under section 4 to be incompatible with a Convention right and, if an appeal lies –

(i) all persons who may appeal have stated in writing that they do not intend to do so;

(ii) the time for bringing an appeal has expired and no appeal has been brought within that time; or

(iii) an appeal brought within that time has been determined or abandoned; or

(b) it appears to a Minister of the Crown or Her Majesty in Council that, having regard to a finding of the European Court of Human Rights made after the coming into force of this section in proceedings against the United Kingdom, a provision of legislation is incompatible with an obligation of the United Kingdom arising from the Convention.

(2) If a Minister of the Crown considers that there are compelling reasons for proceeding under this section, he may by order make

such amendments to the legislation as he considers necessary to remove the incompatibility.

(3) If, in the case of subordinate legislation, a Minister of the Crown considers –

(a) that it is necessary to amend the primary legislation under which the subordinate legislation in question was made, in order to enable the incompatibility to be removed, and

(b) that there are compelling reasons for proceeding under this section,

he may by order make such amendments to the primary legislation as he considers necessary.

(4) This section also applies where the provision in question is in subordinate legislation and has been quashed, or declared invalid, by reason of incompatibility with a Convention right and the Minister proposes to proceed under paragraph 2(b) of Schedule 2.

(5) If the legislation is an Order in Council, the power conferred by subsection (2) or (3) is exercisable by Her Majesty in Council.

(6) In this section 'legislation' does not include a Measure of the Church Assembly or of the General Synod of the Church of England.

(7) Schedule 2 makes further provision about remedial orders.

OTHER RIGHTS AND PROCEEDINGS

Safeguard for existing human rights

11 A person's reliance on a Convention right does not restrict –

(a) any other right or freedom conferred on him by or under any law having effect in any part of the United Kingdom; or

(b) his right to make any claim or bring any proceedings which he could make or bring apart from sections 7 to 9.

Freedom of expression

12(1) This section applies if a court is considering whether to grant any relief which, if granted, might affect the exercise of the Convention right to freedom of expression.

(2) If the person against whom the application for relief is made ('the respondent') is neither present nor represented, no such relief is to be granted unless the court is satisfied –

(a) that the applicant has taken all practicable steps to notify the respondent; or

(b) that there are compelling reasons why the respondent should not be notified.

(3) No such relief is to be granted so as to restrain publication before trial unless the court is satisfied that the applicant is likely to establish that publication should not be allowed.

(4) The court must have particular regard to the importance of the Convention right to freedom of expression and, where the proceed-

ings relate to material which the respondent claims, or which appears to the court, to be journalistic, literary or artistic material (or to conduct connected with such material), to –

(a) the extent to which –

  (i) the material has, or is about to, become available to the public; or

  (ii) it is, or would be, in the public interest for the material to be published;

(b) any relevant privacy code.

(5) In this section –

'court' includes a tribunal; and

'relief' includes any remedy or order (other than in criminal proceedings).

Freedom of thought, conscience and religion

13(1) If a court's determination of any question arising under this Act might affect the exercise by a religious organisation (itself or its members collectively) of the Convention right to freedom of thought, conscience and religion, it must have particular regard to the importance of that right.

(2) In this section 'court' includes a tribunal.

DEROGATIONS AND RESERVATIONS

Derogations

14(1) In this Act 'designated derogation' means any derogation by the United Kingdom from an Article of the Convention, or of any protocol to the Convention, which is designated for the purposes of this Act in an order made by the Secretary of State.

[(2) *Repealed.*]

(3) If a designated derogation is amended or replaced it ceases to be a designated derogation.

(4) But subsection (3) does not prevent the Secretary of State from exercising his power under subsection (1) to make a fresh designation order in respect of the Article concerned.

(5) The Secretary of State must by order make such amendments to Schedule 3 as he considers appropriate to reflect –

(a) any designation order; or

(b) the effect of subsection (3).

(6) A designation order may be made in anticipation of the making by the United Kingdom of a proposed derogation.

Reservations

15(1) In this Act 'designated reservation' means –

(a) the United Kingdom's reservation to Article 2 of the First Protocol to the Convention; and

(b) any other reservation by the United Kingdom to an Article of the

Convention, or of any protocol to the Convention, which is designated for the purposes of this Act in an order made by the Secretary of State.

(2)   The text of the reservation referred to in subsection (1)(a) is set out in Part II of Schedule 3.

(3)   If a designated reservation is withdrawn wholly or in part it ceases to be a designated reservation.

(4)   But subsection (3) does not prevent the Secretary of State from exercising his power under subsection (1)(b) to make a fresh designation order in respect of the Article concerned.

(5)   The Secretary of State must by order make such amendments to this Act as he considers appropriate to reflect –
        (a)   any designation order; or
        (b)   the effect of subsection (3).

Period for which designated derogations have effect

16(1)   If it has not already been withdrawn by the United Kingdom, a designated derogation ceases to have effect for the purposes of this Act in the case of any other derogation, at the end of the period of five years beginning with the date on which the order designating it was made.

(2)   At any time before the period –
        (a)   fixed by subsection (1), or
        (b)   extended by an order under this subsection,
        comes to an end, the Secretary of State may by order extend it by a further period of five years.

(3)   An order under section 14(1) ceases to have effect at the end of the period for consideration, unless a resolution has been passed by each House approving the order.

(4)   Subsection (3) does not affect –
        (a)   anything done in reliance on the order; or
        (b)   the power to make a fresh order under section 14(1).

(5)   In subsection (3) 'period for consideration' means the period of forty days beginning with the day on which the order was made.

(6)   In calculating the period for consideration, no account is to be taken of any time during which –
        (a)   Parliament is dissolved or prorogued; or
        (b)   both Houses are adjourned for more than four days.

(7)   If a designated derogation is withdrawn by the United Kingdom, the Secretary of State must by order make such amendments to this Act as he considers are required to reflect that withdrawal.

Periodic review of designated reservations

17(1)   The appropriate Minister must review the designated reservation referred to in section 15(1)(a) –
        (a)   before the end of the period of five years beginning with the date on which section 1(2) came into force; and

(b)   if that designation is still in force, before the end of the period of five years beginning with the date on which the last report relating to it was laid under subsection (3).

(2)   The appropriate Minister must review each of the other designated reservations (if any) –

(a)   before the end of the period of five years beginning with the date on which the order designating the reservation first came into force; and

(b)   if the designation is still in force, before the end of the period of five years beginning with the date on which the last report relating to it was laid under subsection (3).

(3)   The Minister conducting a review under this section must prepare a report on the result of the review and lay a copy of it before each House of Parliament.

Appointment to European Court of Human Rights

18(1)   In this section 'judicial office' means the office of –

(a)   Lord Justice of Appeal, Justice of the High Court or Circuit judge, in England and Wales;

(b)   judge of the Court of Session or sheriff, in Scotland;

(c)   Lord Justice of Appeal, judge of the High Court or county court judge, in Northern Ireland.

(2)   The holder of a judicial office may become a judge of the European Court of Human Rights ('the Court') without being required to relinquish his office.

(3)   But he is not required to perform the duties of his judicial office while he is a judge of the Court.

(4)   In respect of any period during which he is a judge of the Court –

(a)   a Lord Justice of Appeal or Justice of the High Court is not to count as a judge of the relevant court for the purposes of section 2(1) or 4(1) of the Supreme Court Act 1981 (maximum number of judges) nor as a judge of the Supreme Court for the purposes of section 12(1) to (6) of that Act (salaries, etc);

(b)   a judge of the Court of Session is not to count as a judge of that court for the purposes of section 1(1) of the Court of Session Act 1988 (maximum number of judges) or of section 9(1)(c) of the Administration of Justice Act 1973 ('the 1973 Act') (salaries, etc);

(c)   a Lord Justice of Appeal or judge of the High Court in Northern Ireland is not to count as a judge of the relevant court for the purposes of section 2(1) or 3(1) of the Judicature (Northern Ireland) Act 1978 (maximum number of judges) nor as a judge of the Supreme Court of Northern Ireland for the purposes of section 9(1)(d) of the 1973 Act (salaries, etc);

(d)   a Circuit judge is not to count as such for the purposes of section 18 of the Courts Act 1971 (salaries, etc);

(e)   a sheriff is not to count as such for the purposes of section 14 of the Sheriff Courts (Scotland) Act 1907 (salaries, etc);

  (f) a county court judge of Northern Ireland is not to count as such for the purposes of section 106 of the County Courts Act Northern Ireland) 1959 (salaries, etc).

(5) If a sheriff principal is appointed a judge of the Court, section 11(1) of the Sheriff Courts (Scotland) Act 1971 (temporary appointment of sheriff principal) applies, while he holds that appointment, as if his office is vacant.

(6) Schedule 4 makes provision about judicial pensions in relation to the holder of a judicial office who serves as a judge of the Court.

(7) The Lord Chancellor or the Secretary of State may by order make such transitional provision (including, in particular, provision for a temporary increase in the maximum number of judges) as he considers appropriate in relation to any holder of a judicial office who has completed his service as a judge of the Court.

PARLIAMENTARY PROCEDURE

Statements of compatibility

19(1) A Minister of the Crown in charge of a Bill in either House of Parliament must, before Second Reading of the Bill –

  (a) make a statement to the effect that in his view the provisions of the Bill are compatible with the Convention rights ('a statement of compatibility'); or

  (b) make a statement to the effect that although he is unable to make a statement of compatibility the government nevertheless wishes the House to proceed with the Bill.

(2) The statement must be in writing and be published in such manner as the Minister making it considers appropriate.

SUPPLEMENTAL

Orders, etc, under this Act

20(1) Any power of a Minister of the Crown to make an order under this Act is exercisable by statutory instrument.

(2) The power of the Lord Chancellor or the Secretary of State to make rules (other than rules of court) under section 2(3) or 7(9) is exercisable by statutory instrument.

(3) Any statutory instrument made under section 14, 15 or 16(7) must be laid before Parliament.

(4) No order may be made by the Lord Chancellor or the Secretary of State under section 1(4), 7(11) or 16(2) unless a draft of the order has been laid before, and approved by, each House of Parliament.

(5) Any statutory instrument made under section 18(7) or Schedule 4, or to which subsection (2) applies, shall be subject to annulment in pursuance of a resolution of either House of Parliament.

(6)   The power of a Northern Ireland department to make –
       (a) rules under section 2(3)(c) or 7(9)(c), or
       (b) an order under section 7(11),
       is exercisable by statutory rule for the purposes of the Statutory Rules
       (Northern Ireland) Order 1979.

(7)   Any rules made under section 2(3)(c) or 7(9)(c) shall be subject to
       negative resolution; and section 41(6) of the Interpretation Act
       Northern Ireland) 1954 (meaning of 'subject to negative resolution')
       shall apply as if the power to make the rules were conferred by an Act
       of the Northern Ireland Assembly.

(8)   No order may be made by a Northern Ireland department under
       section 7(11) unless a draft of the order has been laid before, and
       approved by, the Northern Ireland Assembly.

Interpretation, etc

21(1) In this Act –
       'amend' includes repeal and apply (with or without modifications);
       'the appropriate Minister' means the Minister of the Crown having
       charge of the appropriate authorised government department (within
       the meaning of the Crown Proceedings Act 1947);
       'the Commission' means the European Commission of Human
       Rights;
       'the Convention' means the Convention for the Protection of Human
       Rights and Fundamental Freedoms, agreed by the Council of Europe
       at Rome on 4th November 1950 as it has effect for the time being in
       relation to the United Kingdom;
       'declaration of incompatibility' means a declaration under section 4;
       'Minister of the Crown' has the same meaning as in the Ministers of
       the Crown Act 1975;
       'Northern Ireland Minister' includes the First Minister and the
       deputy First Minister in Northern Ireland;
       'primary legislation' means any –
       (a) public general Act;
       (b) local and personal Act;
       (c) private Act;
       (d) Measure of the Church Assembly;
       (e) Measure of the General Synod of the Church of England;
       (f) Order in Council –
             (i) made in exercise of Her Majesty's Royal Prerogative;
             (ii) made under section 38(1)(a) of the Northern Ireland
                 Constitution Act 1973 or the corresponding provision of the
                 Northern Ireland Act 1998; or
             (iii) amending an Act of a kind mentioned in paragraph (a), (b) or
                 (c);
                 and includes an order or other instrument made under
                 primary legislation (otherwise than by the National Assembly

for Wales, a member of the Scottish Executive, a Northern Ireland Minister or a Northern Ireland department) to the extent to which it operates to bring one or more provisions of that legislation into force or amends any primary legislation;

'the First Protocol' means the protocol to the Convention agreed at Paris on 20th March 1952;

'the Sixth Protocol' means the protocol to the Convention agreed at Strasbourg on 28th April 1983;

'the Eleventh Protocol' means the protocol to the Convention (restructuring the control machinery established by the Convention) agreed at Strasbourg on 11th May 1994;

'remedial order' means an order under section 10;

'subordinate legislation' means any –

(a) Order in Council other than one –

  (i) made in exercise of Her Majesty's Royal Prerogative;

  (ii) made under section 38(1)(a) of the Northern Ireland Constitution Act 1973 or the corresponding provision of the Northern Ireland Act 1998; or

  (iii) amending an Act of a kind mentioned in the definition of primary legislation;

(b) Act of the Scottish Parliament;

(c) Act of the Parliament of Northern Ireland;

(d) Measure of the Assembly established under section 1 of the Northern Ireland Assembly Act 1973;

(e) Act of the Northern Ireland Assembly;

(f) order, rules, regulations, scheme, warrant, byelaw or other instrument made under primary legislation (except to the extent to which it operates to bring one or more provisions of that legislation into force or amends any primary legislation);

(g) order, rules, regulations, scheme, warrant, byelaw or other instrument made under legislation mentioned in paragraph (b), (c), (d) or (e) or made under an Order in Council applying only to Northern Ireland;

(h) order, rules, regulations, scheme, warrant, byelaw or other instrument made by a member of the Scottish Executive, a Northern Ireland Minister or a Northern Ireland department in exercise of prerogative or other executive functions of Her Majesty which are exercisable by such a person on behalf of Her Majesty;

'transferred matters' has the same meaning as in the Northern Ireland Act 1998; and

'tribunal' means any tribunal in which legal proceedings may be brought.

(2) The references in paragraphs (b) and (c) of section 2(1) to Articles are to Articles of the Convention as they had effect immediately before the coming into force of the Eleventh Protocol.

(3) The reference in paragraph (d) of section 2(1) to Article 46 includes a

reference to Articles 32 and 54 of the Convention as they had effect immediately before the coming into force of the Eleventh Protocol.

(4)   The references in section 2(1) to a report or decision of the Commission or a decision of the Committee of Ministers include references to a report or decision made as provided by paragraphs 3, 4 and 6 of Article 5 of the Eleventh Protocol (transitional provisions).

(5)   Any liability under the Army Act 1955, the Air Force Act 1955 or the Naval Discipline Act 1957 to suffer death for an offence is replaced by a liability to imprisonment for life or any less punishment authorised by those Acts; and those Acts shall accordingly have effect with the necessary modifications.

Short title, commencement, application and extent

22(1)   This Act may be cited as the Human Rights Act 1998.

(2)   Sections 18, 20 and 21(5) and this section come into force on the passing of this Act.

(3)   The other provisions of this Act come into force on such day as the Secretary of State may by order appoint; and different days may be appointed for different purposes.

(4)   Paragraph (b) of subsection (1) of section 7 applies to proceedings brought by or at the instigation of a public authority whenever the act in question took place; but otherwise that subsection does not apply to an act taking place before the coming into force of that section.

(5)   This Act binds the Crown.

(6)   This Act extends to Northern Ireland.

(7)   Section 21(5), so far as it relates to any provision contained in the Army Act 1955, the Air Force Act 1955 or the Naval Discipline Act 1957, extends to any place to which that provision extends.

SCHEDULE 1: THE ARTICLES

PART I: THE CONVENTION: RIGHTS AND FREEDOMS

Article 2: Right to life

1   Everyone's right to life shall be protected by law. No one shall be deprived of his life intentionally save in the execution of a sentence of a court following his conviction of a crime for which this penalty is provided by law.

2   Deprivation of life shall not be regarded as inflicted in contravention of this Article when it results from the use of force which is no more than absolutely necessary:

(a)   in defence of any person from unlawful violence;

(b)   in order to effect a lawful arrest or to prevent the escape of a person lawfully detained;

(c)   in action lawfully taken for the purpose of quelling a riot or insurrection.

Article 3: Prohibition of torture

No one shall be subjected to torture or to inhuman or degrading treatment or punishment.

Article 4: Prohibition of slavery and forced labour

1   No one shall be held in slavery or servitude.

2   No one shall be required to perform forced or compulsory labour.

3   For the purpose of this Article the term 'forced or compulsory labour' shall not include:

(a)   any work required to be done in the ordinary course of detention imposed according to the provisions of Article 5 of this Convention or during conditional release from such detention;

(b)   any service of a military character or, in case of conscientious objectors in countries where they are recognised, service exacted instead of compulsory military service;

(c)   any service exacted in case of an emergency or calamity threatening the life or well-being of the community;

(d)   any work or service which forms part of normal civic obligations.

Article 5: Right to liberty and security

1   Everyone has the right to liberty and security of person. No one shall be deprived of his liberty save in the following cases and in accordance with a procedure prescribed by law:

(a)   the lawful detention of a person after conviction by a competent court;

(b)   the lawful arrest or detention of a person for non-compliance with the lawful order of a court or in order to secure the fulfilment of any obligation prescribed by law;

(c)   the lawful arrest or detention of a person effected for the purpose of bringing him before the competent legal authority on reasonable suspicion of having committed an offence or when it is reasonably considered necessary to prevent his committing an offence or fleeing after having done so;

(d)   the detention of a minor by lawful order for the purpose of educational supervision or his lawful detention for the purpose of bringing him before the competent legal authority;

(e)   the lawful detention of persons for the prevention of the spreading of infectious diseases, of persons of unsound mind, alcoholics or drug addicts or vagrants;

(f)   the lawful arrest or detention of a person to prevent his effecting an unauthorised entry into the country or of a person against whom action is being taken with a view to deportation or extradition.

2   Everyone who is arrested shall be informed promptly, in a language which he understands, of the reasons for his arrest and of any charge against him.

3   Everyone arrested or detained in accordance with the provisions of paragraph 1(c) of this Article shall be brought promptly before a judge or other officer authorised by law to exercise judicial power and shall be entitled to trial within a reasonable time or to release pending trial. Release may be conditioned by guarantees to appear for trial.

4   Everyone who is deprived of his liberty by arrest or detention shall be entitled to take proceedings by which the lawfulness of his detention shall be decided speedily by a court and his release ordered if the detention is not lawful.

5   Everyone who has been the victim of arrest or detention in contravention of the provisions of this Article shall have an enforceable right to compensation.

Article 6: Right to a fair trial

1   In the determination of his civil rights and obligations or of any criminal charge against him, everyone is entitled to a fair and public hearing within a reasonable time by an independent and impartial tribunal established by law. Judgment shall be pronounced publicly but the press and public may be excluded from all or part of the trial in the interest of morals, public order or national security in a democratic society, where the interests of juveniles or the protection of the private life of the parties so require, or to the extent strictly necessary in the opinion of the court in special circumstances where publicity would prejudice the interests of justice.

2   Everyone charged with a criminal offence shall be presumed innocent until proved guilty according to law.

3   Everyone charged with a criminal offence has the following minimum rights:

(a)   to be informed promptly, in a language which he understands and in detail, of the nature and cause of the accusation against him;

(b)   to have adequate time and facilities for the preparation of his defence;

(c)   to defend himself in person or through legal assistance of his own choosing or, if he has not sufficient means to pay for legal assistance, to be given it free when the interests of justice so require;

(d)   to examine or have examined witnesses against him and to obtain the attendance and examination of witnesses on his behalf under the same conditions as witnesses against him;

(e)   to have the free assistance of an interpreter if he cannot understand or speak the language used in court.

Article 7: No punishment without law

1   No one shall be held guilty of any criminal offence on account of any act or omission which did not constitute a criminal offence under national or international law at the time when it was committed. Nor

shall a heavier penalty be imposed than the one that was applicable at the time the criminal offence was committed.

2   This Article shall not prejudice the trial and punishment of any person for any act or omission which, at the time when it was committed, was criminal according to the general principles of law recognised by civilised nations.

Article 8: Right to respect for private and family life

1   Everyone has the right to respect for his private and family life, his home and his correspondence.

2   There shall be no interference by a public authority with the exercise of this right except such as is in accordance with the law and is necessary in a democratic society in the interests of national security, public safety or the economic well-being of the country, for the prevention of disorder or crime, for the protection of health or morals, or for the protection of the rights and freedoms of others.

Article 9: Freedom of thought, conscience and religion

1   Everyone has the right to freedom of thought, conscience and religion; this right includes freedom to change his religion or belief and freedom, either alone or in community with others and in public or private, to manifest his religion or belief, in worship, teaching, practice and observance.

2   Freedom to manifest one's religion or beliefs shall be subject only to such limitations as are prescribed by law and are necessary in a democratic society in the interests of public safety, for the protection of public order, health or morals, or for the protection of the rights and freedoms of others.

Article 10: Freedom of expression

1   Everyone has the right to freedom of expression. This right shall include freedom to hold opinions and to receive and impart information and ideas without interference by public authority and regardless of frontiers. This Article shall not prevent States from requiring the licensing of broadcasting, television or cinema enterprises.

2   The exercise of these freedoms, since it carries with it duties and responsibilities, may be subject to such formalities, conditions, restrictions or penalties as are prescribed by law and are necessary in a democratic society, in the interests of national security, territorial integrity or public safety, for the prevention of disorder or crime, for the protection of health or morals, for the protection of the reputation or rights of others, for preventing the disclosure of information received in confidence, or for maintaining the authority and impartiality of the judiciary.

Article 11: Freedom of assembly and association

1   Everyone has the right to freedom of peaceful assembly and to freedom of association with others, including the right to form and to join trade unions for the protection of his interests.

2   No restrictions shall be placed on the exercise of these rights other than such as are prescribed by law and are necessary in a democratic society in the interests of national security or public safety, for the prevention of disorder or crime, for the protection of health or morals or for the protection of the rights and freedoms of others. This Article shall not prevent the imposition of lawful restrictions on the exercise of these rights by members of the armed forces, of the police or of the administration of the State.

Article 12: Right to marry
Men and women of marriageable age have the right to marry and to found a family, according to the national laws governing the exercise of this right.

Article 14: Prohibition of discrimination
The enjoyment of the rights and freedoms set forth in this Convention shall be secured without discrimination on any ground such as sex, race, colour, language, religion, political or other opinion, national or social origin, association with a national minority, property, birth or other status.

Article 16: Restrictions on political activity of aliens
Nothing in Articles 10, 11 and 14 shall be regarded as preventing the High Contracting Parties from imposing restrictions on the political activity of aliens.

Article 17: Prohibition of abuse of rights
Nothing in this Convention may be interpreted as implying for any State, group or person any right to engage in any activity or perform any act aimed at the destruction of any of the rights and freedoms set forth herein or at their limitation to a greater extent than is provided for in the Convention.

Article 18: Limitation on use of restrictions on rights
The restrictions permitted under this Convention to the said rights and freedoms shall not be applied for any purpose other than those for which they have been prescribed.

PART II: THE FIRST PROTOCOL

Article 1: Protection of property
Every natural or legal person is entitled to the peaceful enjoyment of his possessions. No one shall be deprived of his possessions except in the public interest and subject to the conditions provided for by law and by the general principles of international law.

The preceding provisions shall not, however, in any way impair the right of a State to enforce such laws as it deems necessary to control the use of property in accordance with the general interest or to secure the payment of taxes or other contributions or penalties.

Article 2: Right to education

No person shall be denied the right to education. In the exercise of any functions which it assumes in relation to education and to teaching, the State shall respect the right of parents to ensure such education and teaching in conformity with their own religious and philosophical convictions.

Article 3: Right to free elections

The High Contracting Parties undertake to hold free elections at reasonable intervals by secret ballot, under conditions which will ensure the free expression of the opinion of the people in the choice of the legislature.

PART III: THE SIXTH PROTOCOL

Article 1: Abolition of the death penalty

The death penalty shall be abolished. No one shall be condemned to such penalty or executed.

Article 2: Death penalty in time of war

A State may make provision in its law for the death penalty in respect of acts committed in time of war or of imminent threat of war; such penalty shall be applied only in the instances laid down in the law and in accordance with its provisions. The State shall communicate to the Secretary General of the Council of Europe the relevant provisions of that law.

SCHEDULE 2: REMEDIAL ORDERS

Orders

1(1)   A remedial order may –

      (a) contain such incidental, supplemental, consequential or transitional provision as the person making it considers appropriate;

      (b) be made so as to have effect from a date earlier than that on which it is made;

      (c) make provision for the delegation of specific functions;

      (d) make different provision for different cases.

    (2)   The power conferred by sub-paragraph (1)(a) includes –

      (a) power to amend primary legislation (including primary legislation other than that which contains the incompatible provision); and

      (b) power to amend or revoke subordinate legislation (including subordinate legislation other than that which contains the incompatible provision).

    (3)   A remedial order may be made so as to have the same extent as the legislation which it affects.

(4)   No person is to be guilty of an offence solely as a result of the retrospective effect of a remedial order.

Procedure

2   No remedial order may be made unless –

(a)   a draft of the order has been approved by a resolution of each House of Parliament made after the end of the period of 60 days beginning with the day on which the draft was laid; or

(b)   it is declared in the order that it appears to the person making it that, because of the urgency of the matter, it is necessary to make the order without a draft being so approved.

Orders laid in draft

3(1)   No draft may be laid under paragraph 2(a) unless –

(a)   the person proposing to make the order has laid before Parliament a document which contains a draft of the proposed order and the required information; and

(b)   the period of 60 days, beginning with the day on which the document required by this sub-paragraph was laid, has ended.

(2)   If representations have been made during that period, the draft laid under paragraph 2(a) must be accompanied by a statement containing –

(a)   a summary of the representations; and

(b)   if, as a result of the representations, the proposed order has been changed, details of the changes.

Urgent cases

4(1)   If a remedial order ('the original order') is made without being approved in draft, the person making it must lay it before Parliament, accompanied by the required information, after it is made.

(2)   If representations have been made during the period of 60 days beginning with the day on which the original order was made, the person making it must (after the end of that period) lay before Parliament a statement containing –

(a)   a summary of the representations; and

(b)   if, as a result of the representations, he considers it appropriate to make changes to the original order, details of the changes.

(3)   If sub-paragraph (2)(b) applies, the person making the statement must –

(a)   make a further remedial order replacing the original order; and

(b)   lay the replacement order before Parliament.

(4)   If, at the end of the period of 120 days beginning with the day on which the original order was made, a resolution has not been passed by each House approving the original or replacement order, the order ceases to have effect (but without that affecting anything previously done under either order or the power to make a fresh remedial order).

Definitions

5   In this Schedule –

'representations' means representations about a remedial order (or proposed remedial order) made to the person making (or proposing to make) it and includes any relevant Parliamentary report or resolution; and

'required information' means –

(a) an explanation of the incompatibility which the order (or proposed order) seeks to remove, including particulars of the relevant declaration, finding or order; and

(b) a statement of the reasons for proceeding under section 10 and for making an order in those terms.

Calculating periods

6   In calculating any period for the purposes of this Schedule, no account is to be taken of any time during which –

(a) Parliament is dissolved or prorogued; or

(b) both Houses are adjourned for more than four days.

7(1)   This paragraph applies in relation to –

(a) any remedial order made, and any draft of such an order proposed to be made –

    (i) by the Scottish Ministers; or

    (ii) within devolved competence (within the meaning of the Scotland Act 1998) by Her Majesty in Council; and

(b) any document or statement to be laid in connection with such an order (or proposed order).

(2)   This Schedule has effect in relation to any such order (or proposed order), document or statement subject to the following modifications.

(3)   Any reference to Parliament, each House of Parliament or both Houses of Parliament shall be construed as a reference to the Scottish Parliament.

(4)   Paragraph 6 does not apply and instead, in calculating any period for the purposes of this Schedule, no account is to be taken of any time during which the Scottish Parliament is dissolved or is in recess for more than four days.

SCHEDULE 3: RESERVATION

[PART I: DEROGATION repealed by SI 2001 No 1216]

PART II: RESERVATION

At the time of signing the present (First) Protocol, I declare that, in view of certain provisions of the Education Acts in the United Kingdom, the principle affirmed in the second sentence of Article 2 is accepted by the United Kingdom only so far as it is compatible with the provision of efficient instruction and training, and the avoidance of unreasonable public expenditure.

Dated 20 March 1952. Made by the United Kingdom Permanent Representative to the Council of Europe.

SCHEDULE 4: JUDICIAL PENSIONS

Duty to make orders about pensions

1(1)   The appropriate Minister must by order make provision with respect to pensions payable to or in respect of any holder of a judicial office who serves as an ECHR judge.

(2)   A pensions order must include such provision as the Minister making it considers is necessary to secure that –

(a)   an ECHR judge who was, immediately before his appointment as an ECHR judge, a member of a judicial pension scheme is entitled to remain as a member of that scheme;

(b)   the terms on which he remains a member of the scheme are those which would have been applicable had he not been appointed as an ECHR judge; and

(c)   entitlement to benefits payable in accordance with the scheme continues to be determined as if, while serving as an ECHR judge, his salary was that which would (but for section 18(4)) have been payable to him in respect of his continuing service as the holder of his judicial office.

Contributions

2   A pensions order may, in particular, make provision –

(a)   for any contributions which are payable by a person who remains a member of a scheme as a result of the order, and which would otherwise be payable by deduction from his salary, to be made otherwise than by deduction from his salary as an ECHR judge; and

(b)   for such contributions to be collected in such manner as may be determined by the administrators of the scheme.

Amendments of other enactments

3   A pensions order may amend any provision of, or made under, a pensions Act in such manner and to such extent as the Minister making the order considers necessary or expedient to ensure the proper administration of any scheme to which it relates.

Definitions

4   In this Schedule –

'appropriate Minister' means –

(a)   in relation to any judicial office whose jurisdiction is exercisable exclusively in relation to Scotland, the Secretary of State; and

(b) otherwise, the Lord Chancellor;

'ECHR judge' means the holder of a judicial office who is serving as a judge of the Court;

'judicial pension scheme' means a scheme established by and in accordance with a pensions Act;

'pensions Act' means –

(a) the County Courts Act Northern Ireland) 1959;

(b) the Sheriffs' Pensions (Scotland) Act 1961;

(c) the Judicial Pensions Act 1981; or

(d) the Judicial Pensions and Retirement Act 1993; and

'pensions order' means an order made under paragraph 1.

GYPSY SITES AND PLANNING (DoE CIRCULAR 1/94)

Introduction

1   This Circular revises guidance on the planning aspects of sites for caravans which provide accommodation for gypsies. It applies equally to local authorities' own sites and to applications for planning permission from gypsies themselves or from others wishing to develop land for use as a gypsy caravan site. The Circular comes into effect immediately. Its main intentions are:

- to provide that the planning system recognises the need for accommodation consistent with gypsies' nomadic lifestyle;
- to reflect the importance of the plan-led nature of the planning system in relation to gypsy site provision, in the light of the Planning and Compensation Act 1991 ('the 1991 Act'); and
- to withdraw the previous guidance indicating that it may be necessary to accept the establishment of gypsy sites in protected areas, including Green Belts.

2   This Circular does not affect the advice given generally in other Departmental Circulars and Planning Policy Guidance Notes (PPGs). Those which may be of particular relevance are:

- PPG 1 ('General Policy and Principles');
- PPG 2 ('Green Belts');
- PPG 7 ('The Countryside and the Rural Economy');
- PPG 12 ('Development Plans and Regional Planning Guidance') and PPG 12 (Wales) ('Development Plans and Strategic Planning Guidance in Wales');
- Draft PPG 13 ('Transport');
- PPG 16 and PPG 16 (Wales) ('Archaeology and Planning');
- PPG 18 ('Enforcing Planning Control');
- PPG (forthcoming) ('Nature Conservation');
- DoE Circular 1/92 (WO 1/92) ('Planning Controls over Sites of Special Scientific Interest'); and

- DoE Circular 28/77 (WO 51/77), subject to the cancellations made by this Circular (see paragraph 34).

3   The Government announced on 31 March 1993 its intention to introduce legislation to reform the Caravan Sites Act 1968 ('the 1968 Act') when Parliamentary time is available. In particular, the Government proposes to repeal the statutory duty of local authorities to provide accommodation on caravan sites for gypsies residing in or resorting to their areas. Local authorities would continue to have discretionary powers to provide such sites under the Caravan Sites and Control of Development Act 1960 ('the 1960 Act'). The Government also proposes to repeal the Secretary of State's powers to 'designate' an area of a local authority (for example, on the grounds that provision for gypsies in its area was adequate); to repeal his powers to direct an authority to provide more local authority sites; and to repeal his powers to pay grant to authorities for the provision of sites. Provisions implementing these proposals were included in the Criminal Justice and Public Order Bill, introduced on 17 December 1993.

4   The proposed repeal of local authorities' duty to provide gypsy sites is expected to lead to more applications for private gypsy sites. The Government recognises that many gypsies would prefer to find and buy their own sites to develop and manage. More private sites should release pitches on local authority sites for gypsies most in need of public provision.

5   'Gypsies' are defined in section 16 of the 1968 Act as 'persons of nomadic habit of life, whatever their race or origin'. References to gypsies in this Circular are references to gypsies in that sense. The term does not include members of an organised group of travelling show people or circus people, travelling together as such. Planning advice relating to travelling showpeople is given in DoE Circular 22/91 (WO 78/91).

6   Gypsies make up a tiny proportion of the population of England and Wales, but their land-use requirements need to be met. Many gypsies are sel-femployed people, sometimes occupied in scrap and scrap-metal dealing, laying tarmacadam, seasonal agricultural work, casual labouring, and other employment associated with their itinerant lifestyle. The gypsy community also includes groups of long-distance travellers who nowadays earn their living mainly from trades such as furniture dealing, carpet selling and other related occupations. Local planning authorities need to be aware of the accommodation and occupational needs of gypsies, having regard to their statutory duties, including those in respect of homelessness under Part III of the Housing Act 1985.

Development plans

7   At an early stage in the preparation of structure plans, local plans, and unitary development plans ('development plans'), it will be important

for local planning authorities to be ready to discuss gypsies' accommodation needs with the gypsies themselves, their representative bodies and local support groups. A list of some relevant addresses is given in Annex A. Other important sources of advice are County Council Gypsy Liaison Officers. Planning departments may need to consult other departments and agencies with an interest, particularly highways authorities.

8 In preparing or amending their development plans, local planning authorities should indicate how they have taken account of their duty under the 1968 Act to make adequate provision for gypsies residing in or resorting to their areas. They should set out their land-use policies and proposals for fulfilling that statutory duty, for as long as it remains.

9 After the proposed repeal of this duty, local planning authorities should continue to indicate the regard they have had to meeting gypsies' accommodation needs. Repeal of the statutory duty will make it all the more important that local planning authorities make adequate gypsy site provision in their development plans, through appropriate use of locational and/or criteria-based policies. Structure plans and Part I of unitary development plans should continue to set out broad strategic policies, and provide a general framework for site provision. Local plans and Part II of unitary development plans should continue to provide detailed policies.

10 It is important that policies for gypsy site provision are set out clearly in development plans to avoid any potential for disagreements with the settled population which might otherwise arise because of inappropriate location or inadequate explanation of proposed development. With such policies in place in plans, there will be more certainty for all concerned when planning applications are determined by local planning authorities or appeals are considered by the Secretary of State.

Provision and location of sites

11 In deciding what level of provision is necessary, it is essential for authorities to have up-to-date information and to maintain records of trends through regular counts, particularly where the gypsy population varies appreciably. When preparing their development plans, authorities should take into consideration the number of gypsy caravans in their areas, particularly the six-monthly counts by local authorities, which are collected and published by the Department of the Environment and the Welsh Office. This information will also help determine the geographical distribution of caravans, and different needs between summer and winter months. Authorities should also consider making full use of the registers of unused and under-used land owned by public bodies as an aid to identifying suitable locations. Vacant land or surplus local authority land may be appropriate. Locations awaiting development in the future may also be suitable for a limited period.

12   Local plans and Part II of unitary development plans should wherever possible identify locations suitable for gypsy sites, whether local authority or private sites. Where this is not possible, they should set out clear, realistic criteria for suitable locations, as a basis for site provision policies. They should also identify existing sites which have planning permission, whether occupied or not, and should make a quantitative assessment of the amount of accommodation required. A tradition of sites occupied by gypsies and the demonstration of a local need will help authorities to make proposals for sites in suitable locations.

13   As a rule it will not be appropriate to make provision for gypsy sites in areas of open land where development is severely restricted, for example, Areas of Outstanding Natural Beauty, Sites of Special Scientific Interest, and other protected areas. Gypsy sites are not regarded as being among those uses of land which are normally appropriate in Green Belts. Green Belt land should therefore not be allocated for gypsy sites in development plans. PPG 2 gives guidance on Green Belt policy.

14   In deciding where to provide for gypsy sites, local planning authorities might, for example, consider locations outside existing settlements, but within a reasonable distance of local services and facilities, eg, shops, hospitals and schools. Sites on the outskirts of built-up areas may be appropriate, provided that care is taken to avoid encroachment on the open countryside. Many sites may be found in rural or semi-rural settings, but care needs to be taken to ensure consistency with agricultural and countryside policies, including those set out in PPG 7 on the protection of the best and most versatile agricultural land.

15   Sites, whether public or private, should be identified having regard to highways considerations; this may be achieved through early contact with Regional Operating Units of the Department of Transport, or, in Wales, the Welsh Office Highways Directorate. Guidance on access is given in draft PPG 13 ('Transport'). In setting their policies, local planning authorities should have regard to the potential for noise and other disturbance from the movement of vehicles to and from the site, the stationing of vehicles on the site, and on-site business activities.

16   Many gypsies prefer to run their businesses from the site on which their caravans are stationed. Local planning authorities should, wherever possible, identify in their development plans gypsy sites suitable for mixed residential and business uses, having regard to the safety of the occupants and their children. If mixed sites are not practicable, authorities should consider the scope for identifying separate sites for residential and for business purposes in close proximity to one another. Some sites or parts of sites unsuitable for residence might be suitable for parking vehicles or storing materials.

Site characteristics and services

17   Given the variety of occupations in which gypsies are engaged, there is no simple profile of an ideal gypsy site, but there are a number of

characteristics which may help local planning authorities to identify appropriate sites, whether publicly or privately owned. Three main types of site are referred to here for guidance: (1) sites for settled occupation; (2) temporary stopping places; and (3) transit sites. Even families who settle on sites may travel periodically, especially during the summer months, so there is often a need for transit sites for gypsies who are passing through a particular area.

18 Descriptions of various kinds of site are given for illustrative purposes in Annex B. For all kinds of site, consideration must be given to vehicular access from the public highway, as well as provision for parking, turning and servicing on site, and road safety for occupants and visitors. Landscaping and planting with trees and shrubs will help sites blend into their surroundings, give structure and privacy, and maintain visual amenity.

19 Private sites for settled occupation are generally small, accommodating pitches for individual or extended families without on-site business activities. Small sites can often be less obtrusive. Temporary stopping places and transit sites might also be small, except on routes frequented by those gypsy groups which travel in large numbers.

Applications

20 In order to encourage private site provision, local planning authorities should offer advice and practical help with planning procedures to gypsies who wish to acquire their own land for development. Wherever possible, gypsies should be encouraged to consult authorities on planning matters before buying land on which they intend to camp and for which planning permission would be required. Pre-application discussions are particularly important to avoid misunderstanding. The aim should be as far as possible to help gypsies to help themselves, to allow them to secure the kind of sites they need, and thus help avoid breaches of planning control. In particular, questions of road access, the availability of services, potential conflict with statutory undertakers or agricultural interests, and any significant environmental impacts should be resolved at the earliest opportunity.

21 Where a development plan contains policies relevant to a proposal for a gypsy site, authorities must determine the planning application in accordance with the plan unless material considerations indicate otherwise. If the plan is not relevant, applications should be determined in the light of all material considerations. **Authorities should recognise that they may receive applications from gypsies without local connections which could not reasonably have been foreseen in their development plan policies. Authorities should not refuse private applications on the grounds that they consider public provision in the area to be adequate, or because alternative accommodation is available elsewhere on the authorities own sites.**

22 As with any other planning applications, proposals for gypsy sites should continue to be determined solely in relation to land-use

factors. Whilst gypsy sites might be acceptable in some rural locations, the granting of permission must be consistent with agricultural, archaeological, countryside, environmental, and Green Belt policies (see paragraphs 2, 13 and 14, above). The aim should always be to secure provision appropriate to gypsies' accommodation needs while protecting amenity.

23   The appropriate use of *planning conditions* can enable some development proposals to proceed where it might otherwise be necessary to refuse permission. Conditions should be imposed only where they are necessary, relevant to planning and to the development to be permitted, enforceable, precise and reasonable in all other respects. General advice on the use of conditions is given in DoE Circular 1/85 (WO 1/85). A number of measures may be introduced to overcome planning objections to particular proposals. These might include ensuring adequate landscaping, and limiting which parts of a site may be used for business operations, in order to minimise the visual impact and limit the effect of noise. In certain circumstances, conditions might also be appropriate to specify the maximum number of days for which gypsy caravans might be permitted to stay on a transit site.

24   In some cases, for example where the applicants themselves propose to use a site for only a limited time, or where land is to be redeveloped on some occasion in the future, it may be appropriate to impose a condition allowing use for only a specified period. But unless such circumstances prevail, permission should generally be given for an indefinite period.

25   Where an authority's planning objectives cannot be achieved by imposing a planning condition (because, for example, they relate to development, roads or buildings other than those covered by the planning application), it may be appropriate to enter into a *planning obligation* under section 106 of the Town and Country Planning Act 1990 ('the 1990 Act') (as substituted by section 12 of the 1991 Act). Advice on the use of such obligations is given in DoE Circular 16/91 (WO 53/91) ('Planning Obligations').

Enforcement

26   If planning permission is required but not obtained for a gypsy site and the local planning authority are considering possible enforcement action, they should be guided by the policy advice in PPG 18 ('Enforcing Planning Control'). Local planning authorities should regard gypsies in the same manner as small businesses when considering possible enforcement action. The existence or absence of policies for gypsy sites in development plans could constitute a material consideration in matters of enforcement.

27   Local planning authorities have a range of enforcement powers available to them where the breach of planning control is sufficiently serious to justify taking action. Two powers may be particularly appropriate. *First*, the amended 'stop notice' provisions, in section 183 of the 1990 Act, now enable the authority: to serve a stop notice

at the same time as the related enforcement notice; and, where circumstances justify it, to bring a stop notice into immediate effect; and to prohibit the use of any of the land specified in the enforcement notice for a residential caravan site. *Second*, the authority may apply for an injunction, in the High Court or County Court, to restrain an actual or apprehended breach of planning control, under section 187B of the 1990 Act. An injunction can be sought irrespective of whether the identity of the person is known. Detailed guidance about these two powers is given in Annexes 3 and 4, respectively, to DoE Circular 21/91 (WO 76/91).

28   Once an enforcement notice has taken effect in relation to land specified in it, the local planning authority now have improved powers (in the amended section 178 of the 1990 Act) to enter the land and carry out the requirements of the notice themselves, in default of the owner or occupier. The authority may also recover from the person who is then the owner of the land any expenses they reasonably incur in taking remedial action themselves. Guidance about these powers is given in paragraphs 49 to 51 of Annex 2 to DoE Circular 21/91 (WO 76/91).

Caravan use not requiring a planning application

29   Some kinds of activity will not fall within the definition of 'development' in section 55 of the 1990 Act, and will not therefore require planning permission. Any gypsy living in a dwellinghouse will not require planning permission to use a caravan within the curtilage of the dwellinghouse, provided that the purpose is incidental to the enjoyment of the dwellinghouse as such. A caravan within the curtilage of a dwellinghouse may have a number of ancillary uses for which planning permission would not be required. For example, it could be used for additional living accommodation, provided that it remained part of the same planning unit as the dwellinghouse and the unit remained in single family occupation.

Permitted development

30   There are a number of circumstances in which gypsies, like any other users of the planning system, may carry out development for which a general permission is granted by the Town and Country Planning General Development Order 1988 ('the GDO'). Such development does not require a planning application. Types of permitted development are specified in Schedule 2 to the GDO. Some types which may benefit gypsies are described below.

31   The provision on land of caravans required temporarily in connection with and for the duration of permitted operations (other than mining) being carried out on, in, under or over that land, or on adjoining land-which might include, for example, agricultural or building work-is permitted development (Class A of Part 4 of Schedule 2 to the GDO).

32   The use of land for caravans may be permitted development in some of the cases, specified in Schedule I to the 1960 Act, where a site licence is not required (Class A of Part 5 of Schedule 2 to the GDO).

Such cases include

- the use of land as a caravan site for up to 28 days a year for (a) a single caravan staying no more than two nights at any time on sites of less than five acres; and (b) for up to three caravans on larger sites;
- the use of agricultural or forestry land as a temporary caravan site for accommodation used in connection with seasonal working on that land; and
- the use of a caravan site of land forming part of, or adjoining, land where permitted building or engineering operations are being carried out, where accommodation is for people employed in connection with the operations.

Licensing

33   Under the 1960 Act, a caravan site, whether or not it is for gypsies, is likely to need a site licence. The district or borough council is responsible for issuing the site licence and must do so once planning permission is granted. The licence will contain conditions which specify how a particular site should be regulated and equipped, in the interests of health, safety and amenity. Details of the licensing conditions may be discussed while the application for planning permission is being considered, so that the licence can be issued as soon as permission is granted.

Cancellations

34   Paragraphs 4, 5, 32 and 44-94 (inclusive) of the Appendix to, and the Annex of, DoE Circular 28/77 (WO 51/77); the response to recommendation 4.13(d) in DoE Circular 57/78 (WO 97/78); paragraph 7 of Annex D to PPG 12; and paragraph 4 of Annex D to PPG 12 (Wales); and remaining paragraphs 11 to 14 of Development Control Policy Note 8 ('Caravan sites') are hereby cancelled.

Financial and manpower implications

35   This Circular repeats and revises existing guidance. Its contents are not expected to have significant manpower or resource implications for local planning authorities in advance of proposed legislative changes repealing the authorities' duty to provide gypsy sites. Planning applications will continue to attract planning application fees.

Richard Jones, *Assistant Secretary*
H R Bollington, *Assistant Secretay*

Annex A – Select list of relevant organisations

Advisory Council for the Education of Romany and Other Travellers (ACERT): General Secretary: Mrs M Whiffin, Moot House, The Stow, Harlow CM20 3AG. Tel: 0279 418666

British Romani Union: General Secretary: Mr A Tadley, The Reservation, Hever Road, Edenbridge, Kent TN8 5DJ. Tel: 0732 866139

Consortium of Romany and Traveller Groups: c/o Miss J Day, Shelter, Third Floor, Sterling House, Fairfax Street, Bristol BS1 3HY. Tel: 0594 564529

Gypsy Council for Education, Culture, Welfare and Civil Rights: President: Mr P Mercer, 3 The Travellers' Site, Oxney Road, Peterborough PEl 5NX. Tel: 0733 347112. Chair: Mr C Smith, 10 Main Road, Hart Road Caravan Site, Thundersley, Benfleet, Essex SS7 3QH. Tel: 0268 774977

National Association of Teachers of Travellers: Co-ordinator: Ruth Dewhirst, c/o Braybrook Professional Centre, Amos Lane, Wednesfield, West Midlands WV11 1ND. Tel: 0902 305989

National Gypsy Council: President: Mr H Smith, Greenacres Caravan Park, Hapsford, Helsby, Warrington WA6 0JS. Tel: 0928 723138

National Romani Rights Association: President: Mr E Frankham, 8 Reid Way, King's Lynn, Norfolk PE30 2LL. Tel: 0553 775172

The Romany Guild: General Secretary: Mr T Lee, The Caravan Site, 50–56 Temple Mills Lane, London E15 2ER. Tel: 081 5557214

Romany Institute: Dr Kendrick, 61 Blenheim Crescent, London W11 2EG. Tel: 071 7272916

Society of Travelling People: Mr T B O'Doherty, 7 Upper Wortley Road, Leeds, West Yorkshire LE12 4LB. Tel: 0532 63803

Annex B – Characteristics of sites (for illustrative purposes only)

1 The ideal sites for long-term use will have access from properly surfaced roads. Individual pitches might have hardstandings for existing caravans, and additional parking space for extra caravans, cars and lorries, where necessary. There may need to be working spaces, and areas for clothes-drying and other domestic purposes, and a safe playing area for children. A reasonable level of services would be expected, including electricity and drinking water supplies, washing facilities, sewage disposal, and regular refuse collections. Each pitch would have access to its own drinking water supply and sanitation. Suitable means of marking site boundaries would include

fencing or natural vegetation such as hedges or trees. Spare capacity would enable the accommodation of visiting families passing through an area or attending family events.

2   The better temporary stopping places will have a hard-surfaced entrance or access road, hardstanding for caravans and vehicles, a convenient drinking water supply, a means of sewage disposal, and a refuse collection point. A typical site might have an impassable barrier such as hedging or an embankment to delineate its boundaries.

3   For transit sites, some provision to minimise impact and avoid health hazards should include a refuse collection point, access to a drinking water supply, and sewage disposal. A drained and stable surface, particularly at entrances and where vehicles and caravans are likely to be parked, might also be desirable.

GYPSY SITES POLICY AND UNAUTHORISED CAMPING (DoE CIRCULAR 18/94)

Introduction

1   This Circular offers guidance on the provisions in sections 77 to 80 of the Criminal Justice and Public Order Act 1994 ('the 1994 Act') which affect gypsies and unauthorised campers. The Act received Royal Assent on 3 November 1994, and sections 77 to 80 came into force on the same day.

Definition of 'gipsies'

2   Section 24 of the Caravan Sites and Control of Development Act 1960 ('the 1960 Act'), as amended by section 80 of the 1994 Act, provides that 'gipsies':

> 'means persons of nomadic habit of life, whatever their race or origin, but does not include members of an organised group of travelling showmen, or of persons engaged in travelling circuses, travelling together as such'.

3   The courts have recently clarified the definition of the word 'gipsies' in section 16 of the Caravan Sites Act 1968 ('the 1968 Act'), which was repealed by section 80 of the 1994 Act. In *R v South Hams District Council, ex parte Gibb* and two other applications – *The Times*, 8 June 1994; *The Independent*, 15 June 1994 – the Court of Appeal held that 'gipsies' meant persons who wandered or travelled for the purpose of making or seeking their livelihood, and did not include persons who moved from place to place without any connection between their movement and their means of livelihood. All references to 'gypsies' in this Circular are references to 'gipsies' in this sense.

Powers to control unauthorised camping

4   Section 77 of the 1994 Act empowers a local authority[1] to direct persons residing unlawfully in vehicles within the area of that local authority on highway land, other unoccupied land or occupied land without the consent of the occupier to leave the land and remove their vehicles and any other property they have with them on the land. It is an offence for a person, knowing that such a direction has been given to him, to fail to comply with it as soon as practicable. It is also an offence for a person so directed to re-enter the land concerned with a vehicle within three months of the date of the direction. In any proceedings brought for an offence, it is a defence for an accused person to show that his failure to comply with a direction or his re-entry of land was due to mechanical breakdown, illness or other immediate emergency. If a person who has been directed to leave does so as soon as practicable, and does not re-enter the land within three months of the date of the direction, no offence is committed.

5   Section 78 of the 1994 Act provides that a magistrates' court may, on a complaint by a local authority, make an order requiring the removal from land of any vehicle and property and any person residing in it, and authorising an authority to enter the land and remove the vehicle and property. It is an offence for a person wilfully to obstruct any person authorised to carry out the order. This power is modelled closely on the power that was available to authorities for areas designated under the 1968 Act, although it should be noted that sections 77 and 78 apply to any unauthorised camper, not just to gypsies.

Policy towards unauthorised encampments of gypsies

6   Whilst it is a matter for local discretion to decide whether it is appropriate to evict an unauthorised Gypsy encampment, the Secretary of State believes that local authorities should consider using their powers to do so wherever the Gypsies concerned are causing a level of nuisance which cannot be effectively controlled. They also consider that it would usually be legitimate for a local authority to exercise these powers wherever Gypsies who are camped unlawfully refuse to move onto an authorised local authority site. Where there are no such sites, and the authority reaches the view than an unauthorised Gypsy encampment is not causing a level of nuisance which cannot be effectively controlled, it should consider providing basic services, such as toilets, a refuse skip and a supply of drinking water at the site.

7   Local authorities should also try to identify possible emergency stopping places, as close as possible to the transit routes used by

1   In England, a county council, a district council, a London borough council, the Common Council of the City of London and the Council of the Isles of Scilly; and in Wales, a county council or district council until 1 April 1996 (and a county council or county borough council thereafter).

Gypsies, where Gypsy families would be allowed to camp for short periods. Authorities should consider providing basic services on these temporary sites.

8   Where Gypsies are unlawfully camped on Government-owned land, it is for the local authority, with the agreement of the land-owning Department, to take any necessary steps to ensure that the encampment does not constitute a hazard to public health. It will continue to be the policy of the Secretary of State that Government Department should act in conformity with the advice that unauthorised encampments should not normally be allowed to continue where they are causing a level of nuisance which cannot be effectively controlled. The National Assembly for Wales will act in the same way.

9   The Secretary of State continues to consider that local authorities should not use their powers to evict Gypsies needlessly. He considers that local should use their powers in a humane and compassionate way, taking account of the rights and needs of the Gypsies concerned, the owners of land in question, and the wider community whose lives may be affected by the situation.[2]

Local authorities' obligations under other legislation

10   Social services departments and local housing authorities are reminded of their obligations under Part III of the Children Act 1989 (Local Authority Support for Children and Families); and Part III of the Housing Act 1985 (Housing the Homeless). The Secretaries of State expect authorities to take careful account of these obligations when taking decisions about the future maintenance of authorised gypsy caravan sites and the eviction of persons from unauthorised sites.

11   Local education authorities should bear in mind their statutory duty to make appropriate educational provision available for all school-age children in their area, whether resident temporarily or permanently. As noted in paragraph 33 of Circular 11/88 and paragraph 9 of Circular 11/92 from the Department for Education (formerly the Department of Education and Science) and paragraph 6 of the annex (revised annually) to Welsh Office Circular 52/90, this duty embraces traveller children. Local education authorities should take careful account of the effects of an eviction on the education of children already enrolled, or in the process of being enrolled, at a school. Where an authority decides to proceed with an eviction, and any families concerned move elsewhere in the same area, alternative educational arrangements must be made in accordance with the requirements of the law appropriate to the children's ages, abilities and aptitudes.

2   Paras 6–9 above were inserted by an unnumbered DETR circular dated 26 June 2000.

12   The Secretaries of State also expect local authorities who decide to proceed with evictions to liaise with other local authorities who may have statutory responsibilities to discharge in respect of those persons who are being evicted.

13   Local authorities should also bear in mind that families camped unlawfully on land may need or may be receiving assistance from local health or welfare services. When they have decided to proceed with an eviction, they should liaise with the relevant statutory agencies, particularly where pregnant women or newly-born children are involved, to ensure that those agencies are not prevented from fulfilling their obligations towards these persons.

Repeal of Part II of the Caravan Sites Act 1968

14   Section 80(1) of the 1994 Act repeals:

(a) the duty of local authorities to provide and manage sites (sections 6 and 7 of the 1968 Act);

(b) the requirement for a county council to consult the relevant district council before adopting a proposal to acquire or appropriate land for such a site (section 8);

(c) the Secretary of State's powers to direct a local authority to provide a site (section 9) and to designate the area of a local authority (section 12); and

(d) the powers for a designated authority to deal with unauthorised camping (sections 10 and 11).

15   Section 80(2) of the 1994 Act amends section 24 of the 1960 Act so as to allow a local authority to provide working space on gypsy caravan sites. Section 80(4) of the 1994 Act ensures that the repeal of the definition of the word 'gipsies' in section 16 of the 1968 Act does not affect the interpretation of that word in the definition of a 'protected site' in section 5(1) of the Mobile Homes Act 1983, or in any document embodying planning permission granted under the Town and Country Planning Act 1990 before 3 November 1994.

16   Section 80(3) of the 1994 Act makes transitional arrangements for those cases where the Secretary of State has issued a direction under section 8(3)(a) of the 1968 Act to a local authority to abandon a proposal for a gypsy caravan site, or under section 8(3)(c) of the 1968 Act to make an application to him for planning permission.

17   Directions under section 8(3)(a) of the 1968 Act will remain valid; directions under section 8(3)(b) and (c) of the 1968 Act will cease to have effect. However, where a local authority has made an application for planning permission to the Secretary of State before 3 November 1994, they may elect either to withdraw that application or to request the Secretary of State to determine it. In the latter case, the application would be treated as having been referred to the Secretary of State under section 77 of the Town and Country Planning Act 1990. Local authorities with outstanding directions under section 8(3)(c) of the 1968 Act, may, therefore, wish to notify their decision to the relevant Government Office for their region, or to the Welsh Office.

18   Section 80(5) of the 1994 Act repeals the power of the Secretaries of
        State for the Environment and for Wales to pay grant to local
        authorities in respect of capital expenditure for gypsy caravan sites
        under section 70 of the Local Government, Planning and Land Act
        1980, except for the purposes of applications for grant received by the
        Secretaries of State before 3 November 1994. The repeal of section 70
        does not apply to Scotland.

Future management of local authority gypsy caravan sites

19   Section 7 of the 1968 Act made provision for a sharing of functions
        between county councils and non-metropolitan district councils:
        county councils were required to acquire or appropriate land, set
        charges for the use of sites and contribute towards the costs incurred
        by district councils in managing the sites. District councils were
        required to provide and manage the site. The majority of public sites
        in non-metropolitan districts are owned by county councils and
        managed by district councils.

20   The Secretaries of State consider that the repeal of section 7 of the
        1968 Act removes from district councils the delegation to manage
        sites on land owned by county councils. County councils become
        responsible for managing these sites by virtue of section 24 of the
        1960 Act. Nonetheless, the Secretaries of State consider that
        authorities have adequate powers to make suitable arrangements for
        the maintenance and management of sites depending on local
        circumstances. In particular, section 101 of the Local Government Act
        1972 empowers a local authority to arrange for the discharge of its
        functions by another local authority. Such an arrangement would
        enable a district council to continue to manage a site and the county
        council to contribute towards their expenses.

21   The Secretaries of State consider it important that authorities should
        maintain their existing gypsy caravan sites, or should make suitable
        arrangements for their maintenance by leasing them to other persons
        who are willing and able to maintain them.

22   The Secretaries of State also expect authorities to continue to consider
        whether it is appropriate to provide further permanent caravan sites
        for gypsies in their areas. Section 24 of the 1960 Act enables county
        councils, district councils and London borough councils to establish
        and manage sites or to lease them to another person and, as amended
        by section 80(2) of the 1994 Act, to provide working space on gypsy
        caravan sites.

'Gypsy sites and planning'

23   Local authorities are reminded of the advice in Department of the
        Environment (DoE) Circular 1/94 (Welsh Office (WO) Circular 2/94),
        'Gypsy Sites and Planning', dealing with the planning aspects of sites
        for gypsy caravans.

Bi-annual counts of gypsy caravans

24   The Department of the Environment and the Welsh Office intend to continue to ask local authorities to provide data for the compilation of the biannual counts of gypsy caravans in England and Wales on the same basis as at present.

Cancellations

25   DoE Circular 28/77 (WO Circular 51/77), DoE Circular 57/78 (WO Circular 97/78), and paragraphs 19 to 23 and Annex 2 of DoE Circular 8/81 (WO Circular 13/81) are now cancelled. DoE Circular 11/79 (WO Circular 11/79) is also cancelled, apart from Annex A which lists the capital costs of gypsy caravan site provision which are eligible for grant.

Financial and manpower implications

26   This Circular advises local authorities of the repeal of their duty to provide gypsy caravan sites and of the introduction of new discretionary powers to control unauthorised camping. Its contents are considered unlikely to have any net manpower or resource implications for local authorities.

Contact points

27   Any enquiries on the contents of this Circular may be referred to the following contact points:

in England

R J Netto, Homelessness Policy Division, Department of the Environment, Room N13/08, 2 Marsham Street, London SW1P 3EB. Telephone: 0171 276 4708; or

Ms L Patrick, Homelessness Policy Division, Department of the Environment, Room N13/10, 2 Marsham Street, London SW1P 3EB. Telephone: 0171 276 3244.

in Wales

Mrs R Douglas, Planning Division, Welsh Office, Room GO40, Cathays Park, Cardiff CF1 3NQ. Telephone: 0222 823476.

The Chief Executive
County Councils in England and Wales
District Councils in England and Wales
London Borough Councils
Council of the Isles of Scilly
The Town Clerk, City of London

ODPM GUIDANCE ON MANAGING UNAUTHORISED CAMPING

1. Introduction

Background to the Guidance

1.1 *Managing Unauthorised Camping: A Good Practice Guide* was first issued by DETR and the Home Office in 1998 and has influenced the approaches adopted by local authorities, police and others. There have been a number of developments since 1998, which together have led to a need to re-examine and revise this guidance.

1.2 Relevant developments since the issue of the previous guidance in 1998 include:

- Amendments to DETR Circular 18/94 and to Chapter 5 of the *Good Practice Guide* were issued in July 2000. The amendments dealt with advice about 'toleration' of encampments and made clear that there will always be some circumstances where an unauthorised encampment cannot be allowed to remain and where prompt action is required.

- The Association of Chief Police Officers (ACPO) issued guidance to its members on Collective Trespass or Nuisance on Land (including unauthorised camping) in 1996, 1999 and again in August 2000 in parallel with the DETR/Home Office *Guide*.

- In 2001 the results of research monitoring the impact of the DETR/Home Office *Good Practice Guide* were published. The report, by Edinburgh College of Art/Heriot-Watt University in conjunction with the Universities of Bristol and Cardiff, concludes that the *Guide* has been fairly influential in how local authorities and police forces tackle unauthorised camping. The research also highlights some perceived inadequacies and gaps in the guidance which this new Guidance aims to address. (See Annex C for a summary of the main findings.)

- The Human Rights Act 1998 (HRA) came into force in October 2000, incorporating the European Convention on Human Rights into British law.

- The Act means that all eviction and enforcement decisions made by public authorities must be 'proportionate'. Potential challenge under the HRA means that all decision-making must be fully recorded and evidenced to withstand scrutiny (see 5.7-5.9 and Annex D).

- The Race Relations (Amendment) Act 2000 has extended responsibilities given by the Race Relations Act 1976. Public authorities - including local authorities and the police - have a general duty to eliminate unlawful discrimination, promote equality of opportunity and good race relations in carrying out their functions. The 2000 Act also gives public bodies specific duties. Both Gypsies and Irish Travellers are now recognised as ethnic minorities against whom discrimination is unlawful. (See Annex D for more details.) In October 2003, the Commission for Racial Equality published a consultation draft entitled *Gypsies and Traveller - A Strategy 2003-2006* which sets out the Commissions own proposed role. It will be finalised during early 2004.

- A new £17 million Gypsy Sites Refurbishment Grant (GSRG) challenge fund was established with funding made available for three years from 2001/2. GSRG meets 75% of approved refurbishment costs for local authority Gypsy sites, with the aim of raising standards and helping to keep existing sites available for use - in part to help reduce the disruption of unauthorised camping. In its third year (2002/3) GSRG was extended to provide 100% funding for provision of transit and stopping place sites on a pilot basis. A further sum of £16 million has been announced for two further years of GSRG support (2004-6) for both site refurbishment and transit site and stopping place provision.

- The *National Policing Plan 2003-2006* identifies that the primary objective for the police service for the Plan's three-year duration is to deliver improved police performance and greater public reassurance with particular regard to four priorities including tackling anti-social behaviour and disorder.

Guidance on Managing Unauthorised Camping

- In March 2003, the Government published a White Paper *Respect and Responsibility*, which sets out the stand to be taken against anti-social behaviour. Communities, public services and authorities will be empowered to tackle anti-social behaviour. In return everyone is expected to play their part in setting and enforcing proper standards of behaviour. This guidance should be read in the context of that agenda.

- The Anti-social Behaviour Act 2003 includes measures to tackle anti-social behaviour, littering and fly-tipping. Part 7 introduces a new police power to evict unauthorised campers (see 6.12-6.13).

1.3 The Guidance has been produced against this developing background:

- In July 2002, the Office of the Deputy Prime Minister (ODPM) and the Home Office issued a joint press release outlining the Government's new approach to tackling unauthorised camping and signalling its intention to introduce stronger police powers to move on unauthorised encampments provided there was adequate site provision; these enhanced powers have now been provided in Part 7 of the Anti-social Behaviour Act 2003.

- In December 2002, the Government set out, and consulted upon, its broad policy towards unauthorised camping in a *Draft Framework Guide on Managing Unauthorised Gypsy/Traveller Encampments*. Central to the approach is the view that the use of stronger enforcement powers and adequate site provision must be linked.

- *Managing Unauthorised Camping Operational Guidance* was issued as a consultation paper by ODPM and the Home Office in April 2003 (closing date 23 May 2003). The consultation paper was sent to 1,500 organisations and a total of 87 responses were received from a wide range of organisations and individuals.

- Following consultation on the *Draft Framework Guide* and the *Operational Guidance*, it was decided that it would be clearer and less confusing to combine the two documents. The current Guidance therefore reflects the Government's broad policy towards unauthorised camping and incorporates comments received through consultation on both documents.

- As noted above, Part 7 of the Anti-social Behaviour Act 2003 introduces a new police power to evict unauthorised campers. ODPM and the Home Office will consult on guidance on the operation of these new powers in early 2004. Once finalised, it is intended that this will be incorporated into Chapter 6 of the current *Guidance on Managing Unauthorised Encampments* in the section on 'Powers Available to the Police'.

Aims of this Guidance

1.4 This Guidance takes account of all the changes outlined above. Its overall objective is to assist local authorities, police and others to tackle unauthorised camping to minimise the disruption it can cause. In doing this, it aims:

- To help strike an appropriate balance between the needs and legitimate expectations of members of the settled community, local businesses and other landowners, and Gypsies and Travellers.

- To set out recommended courses of action which all local authorities and police forces should follow to provide an effective response to unauthorised camping in their areas.

- To encourage a more consistent approach across the country, building on current good practice and sharing experience.

- To be practical yet creative in the face of a difficult reality.

- To show how to engage the settled and Gypsy/Traveller communities in order to achieve 'buy in' to the strategy, which is vital to ensure effective delivery.

Guidance on Managing Unauthorised Camping

1.5 The Guidance is primarily aimed at local authorities and police who share responsibility for managing unauthorised camping, but will also be relevant to all bodies likely to be involved in partnership approaches. While the Guidance is advisory, local authorities and police are strongly advised to bear it mind when devising and implementing their approaches, and are reminded that the courts may consider it as a material consideration in eviction or other enforcement decisions.

Use of Terms

1.6 Certain terms, conventions and abbreviations are used throughout the Guidance, and these are summarised in Box 1. A distinction is made between 'unauthorised camping' (a form of trespass) and 'unauthorised development' (a form of development of land without planning consent). This distinction is important because it affects the enforcement powers, which can be used. While paragraphs 6.20 to 6.24 refer specifically to planning enforcement powers available for dealing with 'unauthorised developments'; most of this Guidance deals with managing 'unauthorised encampments'.

Box 1 : Terms and abbreviations used in the Guidance

Gypsies and Travellers: used as a generic term to denote the whole population of those groups, families and individuals who subscribe to Gypsy/Traveller culture and/or lifestyle. The term encompasses ethnic Gypsies and Travellers and those who fall within the legal definition of a 'Gypsy' (s24 of the Caravan Sites and Control of Development Act 1960 as amended by s80 of the Criminal Justice and Public order Act 1994).

Unauthorised campers: people living on unauthorised encampments.

Unauthorised encampments: term restricted to encampments of caravans and/or other vehicles on land without the landowner or occupier's consent and constituting trespass.

Unauthorised development: Gypsy sites are among the types of development, which require planning permission. This term is used where such development is carried out on land with the agreement of the landowner, but without the appropriate planning permission.

Unauthorised sites: term used in Chapter 2 when describing findings from the Gypsy caravan count which include both unauthorised encampments and unauthorised development.

Sites or Gypsy/Traveller sites: term generally restricted to authorised sites with relevant planning consents (includes sites owned by local authorities and private owners).

Occupier of land: term used in its legal sense as 'the person entitled to possession of the land by virtue of an estate or interest held by him'. This might include a landowner, tenant or licensee but **not** unauthorised campers temporarily in 'occupation' of the land without any legal estate or interest.

ABCs : Acceptable Behaviour Contracts

ACPO : Association of Chief Police Officers

ASB : anti-social behaviour

ASBOs : Anti-Social Behaviour Orders

CJPOA : Criminal Justice and Public Order Act 1994

GSRG : Gypsy Sites Refurbishment Grant

HRA : Human Rights Act 1998

LPA : Local Planning Authority

ODPM : Office of the Deputy Prime Minister

PPG : Planning Policy Guidance Note

RSL : registered social landlord

TCPA : Town and Country Planning Act 1990

1.7 In the course of consultation on this Guidance a number of policy documents and leaflets were submitted as examples of current practice. Some of these are referred to in boxes at various points throughout the Guidance. Rather than reproducing submitted items in full or in part, the titles and author organisations are referred to and can be contacted by those who are interested. No more than five examples have been included under any heading. Chapter 9 provides useful references to other material referred to in this Guidance together with details of how they might be accessed.

Guidance on Managing Unauthorised Camping

2. Context

2.1 Gypsies and Travellers are a part of British life, and have been so for many centuries. They make up a very small minority within the wider population. Some Gypsies and Travellers live in caravans or other vehicles and follow a lifestyle, which is nomadic or semi-nomadic, in that it involves travel during at least part of the year.

2.2 At present there are more Gypsy/Traveller caravans in circulation than there are 'authorised' legal places for them to stop. At any one time there are around 3,500 Gypsy/Traveller caravans on unauthorised sites in England. Hardly any of these could be accommodated on existing authorised sites specifically provided for Gypsies and Travellers.

2.3 Unauthorised encampments vary enormously

- in size : from a couple of vehicles to groups with over 100 caravans

- in location : from the hidden away and unobtrusive to neighbours, to the highly visible and intrusive

- in behaviour of unauthorised campers : from those where no-one on the encampment causes any nuisance to others, to those where many cause nuisance

- in impact on the land : from groups who leave a camping area tidier than they found it, to those who leave the land damaged and with mountains of fly-tipped trade waste and domestic refuse

Numbers and Scale

2.4 Local authorities carry out the twice-yearly Gypsy caravan count for ODPM. It gives an indication of the numbers of Gypsy caravans on authorised (public and private) and unauthorised sites on set dates in January and July. While the counts may not be completely accurate - not least because of the technical problems of counting all Gypsy caravans over a large area - they provide local authorities with useful information about the accommodation needs of Gypsies who reside in or resort to their areas on the count dates. They also provide authorities; the Planning Inspectorate and the Secretary of State with some of the background information required when planning matters (development plans, planning applications, appeals and enforcement actions) are being considered.

2.5 The count has been carried out for over twenty years. Over this period the total number of Gypsy caravans has increased by some 70% while the number on unauthorised sites has decreased by between 500 to 1,000 from 4,600 (as counted in July 1979) thanks to the growth of private and public authorised site provision as well as movement of Gypsies and Travellers into housing.

2.6 In July 2003, about 14,700 Gypsy caravans were counted, of which 3,979 were on unauthorised sites. This latter figure can be split between 2,315 caravans on unauthorised encampments and 1,664 on Gypsy-owned land, which are likely to represent unauthorised developments. July counts consistently reveal higher numbers of Gypsy caravans on unauthorised sites. Over the past few years, on average, there have been about 800 more Gypsy caravans on unauthorised sites across England in July than in January, reflecting a seasonal element in travelling patterns.

2.7 Geographically, the counts consistently show highest numbers of Gypsy caravans on unauthorised sites in Eastern, Southeast and Southwest regions. Some local authorities, for example South Gloucestershire and some districts in Cambridgeshire and Norfolk, consistently have large numbers on unauthorised sites. Very generally, the patterns reflect traditional areas of resort for Gypsies and Travellers and - importantly - work opportunities for Gypsies and Travellers involved in various contracting (eg aspects of the building trade, garden and tree work), trading (eg carpets and furniture) and seasonal agricultural work.

2.8 There are three main Gypsy/Traveller groupings in England: traditional English (Romany) Gypsies, traditional Irish Travellers, and New Travellers. The first two groupings are accepted as ethnic minorities for the purposes of race relations legislation. There are smaller numbers of Welsh Gypsies and Scottish Travellers. The different groupings have different economic, social, cultural and lifestyle characteristics. While there are many examples of peaceful co-existence of Gypsy/Traveller groups, mixing can sometimes lead to friction.

Recent Research

2.9 Research for ODPM on the provision and condition of local authority Gypsy/Traveller sites in England was carried out by the Centre for Urban and Regional Studies at the University of Birmingham. A summary report was published in October 2002, and the full report in July 2003. The research made the following points.

- There is some evidence of a trend towards greater 'settlement' among some Gypsy/Traveller groups. However, other individuals and families have no desire to 'settle' and will continue to travel actively. Other more 'settled' Gypsies and Travellers - or their children - may take up active travelling when personal or family circumstances allow it. Some Gypsies and Travellers will continue to travel for the foreseeable future.

- In order to accommodate the desire for nomadism, between 2,000 and 2,500 additional authorised transit/mobility pitches were estimated to be needed before 2007. At present there are only about 500 transit pitches provided on authorised local authority and private sites.

- The research also estimated a requirement for up to 2,500 further pitches on residential sites for Gypsies and Travellers, which could be provided either by local authorities or Gypsies and Travellers themselves.

- Gypsies and Travellers, police and local authority personnel acknowledged to the researchers the existence of a minority of 'problem families' among the Travelling community who - whether on sites or on the roadside - are associated with criminal and anti-social behaviour, damage to property and fly-tipping. 'Problem families' cause problems for the majority law-abiding Gypsies and Travellers who also fear that this very visible minority disproportionately affects settled community images and stereotypes of the Travelling community as a whole.

2.10 The general context and recent research suggest:

- While unauthorised camping is much more significant in some areas, almost any local authority is at risk of encampment and should be prepared to deal with encampment.

- Unauthorised encampments vary widely. Local authorities, police and others dealing with unauthorised camping therefore need to be prepared to react to individual circumstances.

- Getting to know local travelling patterns and groups is critical to building a sound strategy. Getting to know individuals and building trust at a personal level with regular Gypsy and Traveller visitors can prevent problems developing.

- The nature of travelling and unauthorised encampment means it cannot be sensibly seen as a purely local phenomenon. An eviction in one area may have the effect of merely pushing the encampment over a local boundary for another authority to deal with. Local authorities and police forces should work together across boundaries to assess needs and determine strategies in response to unauthorised camping over the wider area. At a minimum, authorities should work together at county level, ideally at regional or sub-regional level.

- Good preparation and planning can minimise the disruption of unauthorised encampments. For this, sound intelligence and good networking is essential between local authorities and police forces in an area to keep everyone informed of Gypsy/Traveller groups and their movements. At the least, neighbouring authorities and other agencies that offer services for Gypsies and Travellers should always be informed when a large encampment is to be evicted.

3. Developing a Strategy for Unauthorised Camping

3.1 It is often impossible to predict just where and when an unauthorised encampment will occur. However, a purely reactive response to encampments as they arise is likely to be both inefficient and ineffective. Local authorities, police forces and other bodies need to be clear how they will respond to an encampment, who will take the lead, who else will be involved and under what circumstances.

3.2 To be effective this information should be clearly set out in an unauthorised encampments strategy and protocol. The strategy must be developed through consultation with all key stakeholders if it is to be effective; and it must seek to balance the rights and responsibilities of the travelling and settled communities.

Objectives of an Unauthorised Camping Strategy

3.3 The key objectives in a strategy for unauthorised encampments should include:

- Being able to plan ahead to minimise problems and to avoid the need to deal with everything on a crisis basis.

- Ensuring that the needs and legitimate expectations of all parties - Gypsies and Travellers, landowners and the settled community - are considered.

- Setting a framework within which clear, consistent and appropriate decisions can be made on unauthorised encampments to minimise disruption.

- Linking the approach to unauthorised camping firmly to other strategies and policies affecting Gypsies and Travellers (site provision, planning, health, education, housing etc).

- Directly involving all those with an interest in the process of developing the strategy so as to achieve maximum 'buy-in' and ownership.

- Reaching - as far as is possible - agreement so that all relevant parties will sign up to the strategy and its implementation.

- Clarifying roles and responsibilities so all parties to the strategy know who will do what in different circumstances, within the realistic limits of what is possible and allowing some flexibility for individual stakeholders.

- Ensuring that policies and approaches reflect the human rights of both the settled and travelling communities, and are compliant with race relations legislation including new requirements actively to promote equality of opportunity and good race relations.

- Ensuring the prevention of anti-social behaviour and effective enforcement against perpetrators.

3.4 Each local strategy will have its own objectives. Possible objectives are illustrated in Box 2.

Guidance on Managing Unauthorised Camping

Box 2 : Objectives of a Local Policy on Gypsy and Traveller Issues

The objectives of the policy are:

- To balance the rights and needs of resident communities with those of Gypsies and Travellers.

- To manage unauthorised encampments in an efficient and effective way taking account of the potential level of nuisance for local residents and the rights and responsibilities of Gypsies and Travellers.

- To work with partners in other authorities, the voluntary sector and the Police to address issues of social exclusion amongst Gypsy and Traveller communities.

Formulating the Strategy

Taking the Lead

3.5 It is appropriate that local authorities take the lead in formulating the strategy, and have responsibility for overseeing and monitoring its implementation, and for ensuring that the process is driven forward and does not become bogged down in inter-organisational wrangles and unacceptable delays. In areas of two-tier local government there should be clear agreement whether the county or district council will take the lead; both are clearly key players. Greater consistency and a wider perspective may be achieved where county councils take the lead.

3.6 The process of producing a strategy involves a number of key stages (see Box 3), which must be planned out and timetabled at the start. A named officer of the local authority should undertake this essential task, with the task fully recognised in his/her job description. It would be appropriate for the lead officer to be familiar with Gypsy and Traveller communities and their needs, and able to call on other experienced officers with skills suited to each stage of strategy development.

Guidance on Managing Unauthorised Camping

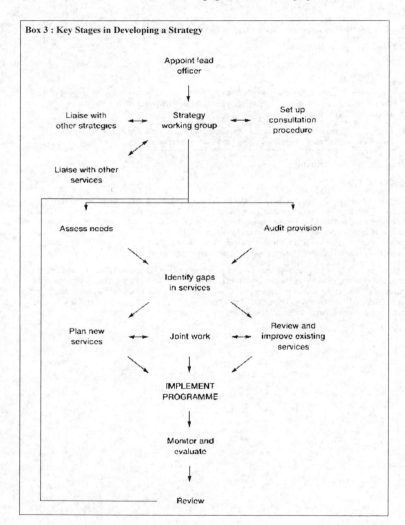

Box 3 : Key Stages in Developing a Strategy

Appoint lead officer

Liaise with other strategies ← → Strategy working group ← → Set up consultation procedure

Liaise with other services

Assess needs

Audit provision

Identify gaps in services

Plan new services ← → Joint work ← → Review and improve existing services

IMPLEMENT PROGRAMME

Monitor and evaluate

Review

Who Should be Involved?

3.7 While local authorities take the lead, it is essential that many others are involved in the process and are willing to sign up to the strategy when it is agreed and published. Generating commitment among participants is an important part of the strategy building process.

3.8 Annex E shows the stakeholders - including Gypsies and Travellers - who might be involved in the strategy process and the ways in which they might be engaged. Key players should be closely involved, perhaps within a working party or steering group charged with moving the strategy process forward. Focus groups or consultative meetings could be used to engage other stakeholders. A designated local authority officer should be given overall responsibility for seeing the process through; he or she must have sufficient seniority to negotiate commitment from partners.

Box 4 : Consultation and Involvement in Developing a Strategy

Dorset County Council consulted widely on a Gypsy and Traveller Issues Report. Following this consultation a County Council Member Policy and Scrutiny Review Panel was formed which met nine times and heard evidence from a wide range of people including district council officers, county council officers concerned with education and children, police, groups representing Traveller views and a solicitor. One meeting was a site visit to residential site, an unauthorised encampment and to meet a farmer and residents neighbouring another unauthorised encampment.

West Sussex County Council adopted its strategy for Gypsies and Travellers in West Sussex following extensive consultation with interested parties and stakeholders. Bodies consulted included: district, town and parish councils, other local authorities, the police, business interests, landowners and farmers, residents' associations, organisations representing Gypsies, and members of the public.

Elements to be Included in the Strategy

3.9 There are ten essential elements to be thought through in any strategy for dealing with unauthorised camping:

- The legislative background for the strategy (this is summarised in Annex D which also deals more fully with human rights and race equality issues).

- Local information and data on which the strategy is based (see 3.10 and 3.11).

- Arrangements and protocols for sharing information (see 3.12).

- The approach to be taken on site provision (see Chapter 4).

- The policy to be followed when unauthorised encampments arise, setting out clearly the alternative courses of action to be taken and the circumstances which determine that action (see Chapter 5).

- Working arrangements and protocols for the involvement of different agencies (see 3.13-3.21).

- Resources for the strategy and constraints within which partners operate (see 3.22-3.24).

- Arrangements for communicating the strategy widely (see 3.25-3.28).

- Arrangements for monitoring the strategy and ensuring that it remains appropriate and is effective in practice, and meets race equality objectives (see 3.29-3.30).

- Involvement of other parts of the local authority, for example planning, education and social services, to ensure that there is a coherent authority-wide holistic approach to Gypsies/Travellers. In two-tier authorities this will involve both county and district councils (see 3.31).

Local Information for the Strategy

3.10 The starting point for a local strategy must be sound information on the characteristics and cultures of Gypsies and Travellers who reside in and resort to the area. Such information might include numbers, family structures, economic activity, travelling patterns, accommodation needs,

Guidance on Managing Unauthorised Camping

health and education needs. Information on Gypsy/Traveller culture is relevant in helping to develop an effective strategy, which will actually work.

3.11 Gypsy caravan counts provide a starting point. Other potential sources of information include monitoring of unauthorised encampments, planning applications and education records. Box 5 provides examples of Gypsy/Traveller needs assessments, which have used information from a range of sources.

Box 5 : Examples of assessments of Gypsy/Traveller accommodation needs

Assessments of accommodation needs have been made by:

LB Southwark

Derbyshire (through the Derbyshire Gypsy Liaison Group)

Wychavon

Sevenoaks District Council (through the PPG 3 housing needs assessment process)

In addition to information from the caravan count and other secondary sources, these also drew on experience of local professionals and research with local Gypsies and Travellers through interviews and discussions. Detailed references are in Chapter 9.

Fenland District Council has undertaken a one-year information gathering exercise, which has involved Gypsies and Travellers on all local authority and private sites and on the roadside. This identified travelling routes and reasons for coming to the District and highlighted Gypsy/Traveller expectations on health and welfare and led to wider understanding of needs.

Sharing Information

3.12 Sharing information at county and sub-regional level can help particularly when looking at travelling patterns and considering site provision. Where information is shared between partner agencies working together, protocols may be developed to deal with issues of professional confidentiality and data protection. Arrangements will already have been made for sharing information in relation to crime and disorder matters between partners in Crime and Disorder Partnerships.

Working Arrangements and Protocols - Towards Implementation

3.13 A strategy needs to spell out working arrangements. The local authority should be the lead agency in managing unauthorised camping in its area, and the strategic working arrangements should reflect this. The lead authority might, by agreement, be either the county or the district council in two-tier areas. There will be circumstances - which should be spelled out clearly - when other agencies will take the lead, for example the police may lead in the use of Criminal Justice and Public Order Act (CJPOA) s61 where urgent action is needed.

3.14 Named officers should be identified in each local authority and police basic command unit with clear responsibility for dealing with unauthorised camping. These officers need to be at a level, which enables them to take on the ground operational and enforcement decisions. It is important that all key stakeholders - including Gypsies and Travellers, elected members, members of the public and other local authority/police officers - know who these officers are. The information could be made available through the local authority web pages and in leaflets provided to the settled and travelling communities.

3.15 The responsible officer in a local authority should establish procedures for reporting to and informing elected members about encampments. It is particularly important that local members (and parish councils in areas where they exist) are kept closely in touch with action affecting encampments in their wards. They can provide a valuable channel for communication between local authority officers and members of the public as a supplement to direct contacts. It is important that elected members are fully aware of the legislative background, local strategies and policies on managing unauthorised encampments including, for example, their race relations responsibilities.

3.16 Other organisations, departments and sections likely to be involved in dealing with unauthorised encampments and in providing services to Gypsies and Travellers should be identified. These are likely to include Traveller Education Services, social services, environmental health, housing and health services. It may be appropriate to include the RSPCA where unauthorised campers are known to have horses, dogs or other animals. Where trading activities are a cause for concern, trading standards officers, Inland Revenue and Customs and Excise officers might also be included. Lists should be compiled of named contact officers in each stakeholder body with full contact details including telephone, fax and e-mail addresses; these lists must be kept up-to-date as people change jobs or responsibilities.

3.17 Responsibilities within the strategy for dealing with unauthorised camping must be recognised within the job descriptions and workloads of all these officers. While calls on their time will be variable and responsive to the number and nature of encampments arising, it is important to think through cover arrangements for their release from other duties when needed. Over time it should be possible to build up an estimate of the likely demands on their time.

3.18 Regular liaison meetings involving officers in all stakeholder organisations encourage good personal and working relationships to develop. People respond more easily to requests from people they know and trust. Liaison meetings provide an opportunity to discuss current issues and concerns and to review on-the-ground working arrangements in the light of experience.

Box 6 : Examples of Liaison Groups

Bedfordshire County Council set up a multi-agency forum in January 2002, which has commissioned independent research on Traveller community needs.

Kent Unauthorised Encampments Monitoring and Liaison Groups, between them, include representatives of all three tiers of local government, the police, health and Gypsy organisations.

Wiltshire County Council has set up a Gypsy and Traveller Officers' Liaison Group comprising officers from all departments actively involved in managing unauthorised camping; The Group's membership may be widened in the future to include police, health services, district council housing officers and certain voluntary agencies. The County Council has also established a Residents' Consultation Group for residents of its semi-permanent Gypsy sites in the county.

3.19 In some areas working relationships have been further cemented by joint training events where officers from different organisations, with different perspectives and professional interests learn together. Training should be balanced in coverage and include human rights, equalities and race relations. In some places Gypsies and Travellers have been directly involved in providing training to local authority and police personnel.

Guidance on Managing Unauthorised Camping

Box 7 : Examples of Joint Training

Derbyshire Gypsy Liaison Group has been extensively involved in training with the police. In conjunction with **Derbyshire Constabulary** they have produced inter-agency interactive training exercises and facilitation notes on unauthorised encampments.

Fenland District Council runs training for all members of their local strategic partnership, Primary Care Trust, police, fire and rescue and voluntary organisations. This aims to explain the culture and traditions of Gypsy people. A freelance Gypsy journalist is central to the training and explains how public bodies can better work with the media over Gypsy issues.

West Sussex County Council has reached agreement at county level with **Sussex Police** on the way training should be approached. The County Council is encouraging relevant local authority staff in each district to get together with district police commanders to agree local implementation plans.

3.20 In many areas across the country working arrangements between relevant bodies have been formalised into protocols or service level agreements. These set out the respective responsibilities of signatories, lines of command and communication, and may include performance targets.

- Protocols commonly involve local authorities (county and district councils in two-tier local government areas) and police.

- Protocols or service level agreements may also be relevant between lead local authority departments and education, health and welfare departments involved in making welfare enquiries at encampments. Such agreements set out the means of communication to be followed and provide targets for response times.

Box 8 : Examples of Protocols between Local Authorities and Police

Derbyshire: Good practice guide for unauthorised encampments: Joint protocol between Derbyshire County Council, Derbyshire Gypsy Liaison Group, Derbyshire Constabulary and the NHS.

Devon: Joint Policy and Practice Guidelines relating to people of nomadic lifestyle residing in or resorting to Devon: Devon County Council and Devon & Cornwall Constabulary.

Essex: A joint protocol for managing unauthorised encampments in Harlow: Essex County Council, Harlow District Council and Essex Police.

Kent: Kent protocol on the management of unauthorised encampments: Kent County Council, district and unitary councils, Kent County Constabulary.

Leicestershire: The Code of Practice for Travellers in Leicestershire, Leicester and Rutland: county council, district and unitary councils and Leicestershire Constabulary.

Wiltshire: Wiltshire County Council and Wiltshire Constabulary are currently developing a protocol for managing unauthorised camping incidents. This builds upon a successful Inter-Departmental protocol already in place within the County Council, which includes, amongst other sensitive issues, a Disclosure Statement, which addresses data protection and information sharing constraints.

3.21 In a few areas (for example Milton Keynes) arrangements for joint working between the local authority and police are still closer in a jointly staffed 'unit'. Advocates refer to the consistency of approach possible through true joint working; it avoids unnecessary duplication of effort; it means that there is less possibility of people being referred backwards and forwards between organisations. In such a structure it is important that reporting lines and accountability arrangements are carefully thought through.

Box 9 : Joint Working

Northamptonshire: A Countywide Traveller Unit has been established jointly funded by district councils, the county council, police and primary care trust, with a contribution from the Northamptonshire Chamber. Police and health workers are seconded to the Unit.

Resources

3.22 The Government believes that spending to achieve the pro-active approach towards site provision and managing unauthorised camping as set out here represents better value for money than the current position. Spending now on site provision should reduce the costs of dealing with unauthorised camping.

3.23 Local authorities and police should seek to apply Best Value principles to their strategy for dealing with unauthorised camping. Box 10 sets out some of the actions, which might be helpful in an area with extensive and/or frequent unauthorised encampments.

Box 10 : An Application of Best Value Principle to Dealing with Unauthorised Camping

Best Value principles suggest that local authorities and the police should:

- Identify what they are spending at present on dealing with unauthorised camping. Few organisations keep accurate records, which accurately identify all the costs involved in unauthorised camping, for example responding to complaints from the public.

- Estimate the costs borne by others, including local businesses and landowners. It may not be possible always to arrive at a monetary value, but attempting it ensures that wider implications of actions are clearer.

- Consider the indirect costs of unauthorised encampments in terms of, for example, additional costs to health and education services and others involved in fostering the greater social inclusion of Gypsies and Travellers.

- Compare these with the possible costs and benefits of taking a more pro-active approach to site provision and managing unauthorised camping on a partnership basis.

3.24 At present not all authorities have a budget for dealing with unauthorised camping, and staffing responsibilities are sometimes vague. Good practice suggests that all authorities should have a formal budget, based on past experience and best intelligence on future needs.

Communicating the Strategy

3.25 The strategy for unauthorised camping should be published and widely disseminated to local businesses, landowners, local residents, and Gypsies and Travellers. Objectives in publishing and publicising the strategy include:

- Making clear what can be achieved and over what time scales so as to mould realistic expectations among both the settled and Gypsy/Traveller communities.

- Making clear who is responsible for what elements of the strategy and its implementation. For example, it is appropriate that all members of the public should contact the police directly over matters involving crime associated with unauthorised encampments and that Gypsies and Travellers are encouraged to do so. The local authority might be the appropriate point of contact for other issues. This means listing names, telephone numbers and addresses.

Guidance on Managing Unauthorised Camping

3.26 A number of local authorities already provide information leaflets and/or have material on their web-sites dealing with unauthorised camping. Use of web-sites to provide information on local policy accords well with the Government's local e-government strategy.

Box 11 : Example of Information Leaflet on Unauthorised Camping

In **Bedfordshire**, the county council, district councils, Bedfordshire Police and the Bedford & Luton Community NHS Trust have jointly produced a leaflet *Travellers and the Law*.

Kent Unauthorised Encampments Working Group has produced a leaflet *Unauthorised Encampment : a document to answer your frequently asked questions.*

Suffolk County Council has produced a leaflet Unlawful Traveller Encampments in Suffolk, which is largely based on questions and answers.

Telford Borough Council has leaflets primarily intended to provide information to members of the public and landowners; these are also available on its web-site.

3.27 A 'communications strategy' is itself an important element in the strategy towards unauthorised encampments. A positive and co-ordinated approach to managing communication is an important element of a comprehensive strategy. Many bodies are likely to be involved in dealing with unauthorised encampments and other Gypsy/Traveller matters. A key aim of this strategy is to assure the travelling and settled community that effective action is being taken where necessary.

3.28 Deciding a co-ordinated approach to media briefings will reduce confusion and the possibility of conflicting accounts. The Commission for Racial Equality has issued Guidance to journalists on *Travellers, Gypsies and the media* which local authorities may find useful in encouraging a positive, or at least neutral, local press coverage for local encampments and other Gypsy/Traveller issues.

Monitoring the Strategy

3.29 It is important to monitor the strategy as it is implemented and review the need for change in the light of that monitoring.

- Monitoring arrangements need to be planned and resourced from the beginning. It would be appropriate for the local authority, as lead agency, to take responsibility, perhaps reporting back to a steering group including representatives of other key agencies.

- Obviously monitoring should identify progress towards meeting the objectives of the strategy. Protocols and other arrangements for partnership working are other obvious areas to be monitored and reviewed. In all cases, monitoring should identify areas, which have worked well and less well in order to learn from the process in recasting the strategy and/or its implementation.

- Above all, monitoring is required to ensure that the strategy leads to action on the ground. The strategy should not be merely a paper exercise.

3.30 Sound information is essential to monitoring. The Government sees great merit in encouraging local authorities, along with their police partners, to develop improved standard records of unauthorised encampments. As a minimum, information should be collected and monitored on the location of encampments, the number of caravans/vehicles involved and the duration of each encampment. Standardisation of information would allow aggregated data to be assembled across a county or region and would facilitate the exchange of data about unauthorised encampments between different areas. A review of the national Gypsy counts system has been undertaken and an amended system is to be introduced shortly.

Guidance on Managing Unauthorised Camping

A Holistic Approach

3.31 Unauthorised camping does not exist in a vacuum. Developing a strategic approach towards managing unauthorised camping provides an opportunity for local authorities and others to consider policies towards Gypsies and Travellers in a holistic manner, if they have not already done so. Relevant policy areas are land use planning (including development planning, planning control and enforcement), housing and homelessness, environmental health, health and education. Many general strategic approaches to dealing with local issues, crime and social exclusion are also very relevant and might refer to Gypsies and Travellers. Under-pinning all such work is policy on diversity, equality and human rights - not just towards Gypsies and Travellers, but towards the whole population of a local authority area.

Box 12 : Example of Contents of a Policy on Gypsy and Traveller Issues

The Dorset County Council Gypsy and Traveller Policy 2003 is comprehensive in coverage. Its sections are:

1. Introduction

2. Objectives

3. Travelling patterns in Dorset

4. Policies on site Provision and the management of unauthorised encampments

5. Site protection

6. Land use planning

7. Housing

8. Education, health and welfare

9. Making decisions on unauthorised encampments

10. Provision of services for encampments

11. Keeping people informed

12. Strategic background and joint working arrangements

13. Staff and other resource issues

Guidance on Managing Unauthorised Camping

Box 13 : Strategies and Partnerships Relevant to Gypsies and Travellers

- Local strategic partnerships and community strategies
- Community Cohesion Policies
- Supporting People
- Homelessness Strategies
- Children and Young People's Partnerships
- Sure Start and Early Years
- Connexions
- Primary Care Group Trust commissioning plans
- Crime and Disorder Reduction Strategies
- Race Equality Schemes
- Anti-poverty strategies
- Local Agenda 21 strategies

In **Devon** there are examples of holistic working:

- *Travellers Making Connexions : A good practice guide for multi-agency work*, Connexions Cornwall & Devon and Devon County Council
- The Health Forum Social Inclusion Task Group has identified Travellers in Devon as a group where inequalities in health exist alongside other service provision issues. A Traveller Forum has been formed with a wide membership including Travellers. A report is being finalised addressing *Travellers Wellbeing.*

---

4. Site Provision and Unauthorised Camping

4.1 Local authorities do not have a duty to provide sites for Gypsies. They do, however, have the power to do so (under s24 of the Caravan Sites and Control of Development Act 1960). Circulars 1/94 and 18/94 both encourage authorities to consider the need for site provision. Local Planning Authorities essentially control the creation of new public and private authorised sites through development plan policies and development control.

A Range of Accommodation

4.2 Site provision is an essential element in any strategy. In a context where the number of Gypsy caravans exceeds the number of authorised places where they can stop - which is the case in England - provision of suitable accommodation for Gypsies and Travellers must be seen as a vital part of an approach to dealing with unauthorised camping. Population increase and family growth among Gypsies and Travellers must also be considered.

4.3 All local authorities should review the provision of sites for Gypsies and Travellers. Site provision can be provided publicly or privately and take a variety of forms:

- Residential sites provide long-term settled accommodation. Most current local authority site provision is residential. Many private sites also provide long-term accommodation for individual families on an owner-occupier basis or commercially.

- Transit sites are also provided both by local authorities and private owners, though much less frequently. Transit sites, with varying levels of amenities, provide for Gypsies and Travellers who want to stay for a period of up to about three months in an area.

- Less formal stopping places are also rare. These would be identified areas of land to which Gypsies and Travellers could be directed when they come to an area, and where they could stop for a short time - perhaps up to a month.

- Emergency stopping places would be locations where families have stopped which are judged suitable for a short stay. Facilities might be temporarily provided at such locations.

4.4 All local authorities experiencing unauthorised encampments should provide either transit sites or stopping places to cater for Gypsies and Travellers moving within or passing through their area. This might be done on a collaborative basis between neighbouring authorities. Some provision could be made by private individuals at no cost to the local authority.

4.5 Gypsies and Travellers should be involved in site planning and design to ensure that sites are well used and are safe and appropriate to the cultures and lifestyles of Gypsy and Traveller families, including children.

Site Provision and Land Use Planning

4.6 The Government's policy on Gypsy sites and planning is set out in DoE Circular 1/94 and it provides for a flexible approach. The Circular puts Gypsies on the same footing in planning law as everyone else whilst recognising their special circumstances. It is designed to ensure that applications for Gypsy caravan sites are treated in the same way as any other form of development. It places emphasis on assessing the need for Gypsy site provision (also stressed in *Planning Policy Guidance (PPG) 3: Housing*, para 13). Local authorities should identify suitable locations for Gypsy sites in their development plans wherever possible (re-iterated in *PPG 12: Development Plans*, para 4.14). Failing this they should identify clear and realistic criteria for suitable locations as a basis for their site provision policies. Local authorities should encourage Gypsies to consult with them on planning matters before buying land on which they intend to camp and for which planning permission would be required.

Guidance on Managing Unauthorised Camping

4.7 Instances of unauthorised camping may be reduced if local planning authorities follow the advice in DoE Circular 1/94 which encourages them to identify suitable sites in their local plans wherever possible for Gypsies to buy and to settle (see 4.6).

■   Sites on traditional routes are likely to be well used and sustainable. It may be easier to gain acceptance for sites in areas where Gypsies and Travellers traditionally stop and are a known part of the local community.

■   Sites, which are screened from view, may be deemed suitable by Gypsies and Travellers as well as by the settled community.

■   Granting temporary planning permissions for sites in a planned sequence might make provision more acceptable to the settled community. This is particularly appropriate for stopping places where little fixed infrastructure may be involved. Temporary sites could be provided in advance of longer-term development proposals.

Authorised Sites and Managing Unauthorised Camping

4.8 If authorised sites are to contribute effectively to reducing the disruption caused by some unauthorised camping, site management and management of unauthorised camping must be integrated. At the least:

■   Local authority and police officers dealing with unauthorised encampments should have information about vacancies on local authority sites within their area, and ideally in neighbouring areas. Ideally, local authority officers should also be prepared to assist unauthorised campers without local accommodation to find places on privately-owned sites and in permanent housing if this is requested.

■   There must be close working between site managers and local authority and police officers dealing with unauthorised camping over allocations of pitches on sites. Site managers may be aware of issues around Gypsy/Traveller group and family compatibility, which must be taken into account when allocating pitches on residential sites.

■   More specifically, where police are seeking to use the new powers under s62A of the Criminal Justice and Public Order Act 1994 (inserted by the Anti-social Behaviour Act 2003), a police officer must consult the local authorities in whose area the encamped land lies about the availability of suitable pitches on relevant sites. ODPM and the Home Office will be consulting in detailed guidance on the use of these powers, which will then be incorporated into a revised version of this Guidance.

■   Transit sites and stopping places must be managed to prevent Gypsies and Travellers staying longer than the maximum permitted stay. Site turnover must be maintained if such sites are to continue to cater for Gypsies and Travellers with a nomadic lifestyle. Reluctance to move from transit sites and stopping places may indicate a need for further residential site provision.

Site Protection

4.9 Protection of land, which is vulnerable to unauthorised encampment, is a valid part of a strategy, but should not be the sole strategy. Some authorities have undertaken protection works on their own land and/or have advised private landowners how best to secure their land.

■   Site protection work is not cheap. A risk assessment should be carried out before investing, including consideration of risks of encampment, nuisance arising from encampment on that land, and cost of effectively protecting the site.

Guidance on Managing Unauthorised Camping

- Site protection and continuing development of open land can have the effect of forcing Gypsies and Travellers to camp in prominent and still more unsuitable places including farmland and other private land, prompting complaints from the landowner. Site protection must only be considered alongside the creation of permanent sites, transit sites and stopping places to ensure that there are places for Gypsies and Travellers to stop without causing disruption.

5. Making Decisions on Unauthorised Encampments

5.1 This chapter deals with some of the considerations to be borne in mind by local authorities, police and others when making decisions about how to deal with unauthorised encampments as they occur. Its aim is to help:

- To make clear, consistent and appropriate decisions on unauthorised encampments.

- To ensure that a balance is struck between the needs of all parties.

- To ensure that decisions taken will withstand challenge.

5.2 Sections below cover the policy statement; carrying out welfare enquiries; and reaching decisions.

A Policy Statement

5.3 It is important that the local authority produces a policy statement, which includes:

- A statement of which travelling people the policy relates to. Many policies relate to **all** travelling groups including non-traditional Travellers since the issues raised by encampments are similar and the education, welfare and homelessness duties owed are identical.

- Identification of the action to be considered in respect of land not owned by the local authority (see 6.17).

- The responsibilities of different authorities and agencies. The statement should set out which authority will act in specified circumstances where county and district councils, and sometimes other agencies including national ones, share responsibilities (for example on highways), and the circumstances in which the police might take the lead.

- The alternative courses of action to be taken. This should set out clearly the circumstances in which eviction processes would be instigated and the circumstances in which an encampment might remain for a period under regular review.

- The characteristics of encampment sites, which would normally trigger rapid eviction proceedings (see 5.4-5.6).

- The standards of behaviour expected from unauthorised campers on encampments (see 7.3).

- The circumstances in which an authority might provide rubbish storage and collection services, water supply or toilets to an encampment (see 7.15).

Box 14 : Examples of Policy Statements and Procedures Guides

Adur District Council: Policy and guidance: Travellers and unauthorised encampments.

Dorset County Council: Dealing with unauthorised camping: procedure.

Leicestershire County Council : Policy and Administration Procedure statement in relation to unauthorised encampments by Gypsies and Travellers

Suffolk County Council : Unlawful Traveller encampments in Suffolk : a strategy

Wiltshire County Council: Policy statement in relation to unauthorised Gypsy and Traveller encampments.

Guidance on Managing Unauthorised Camping

Unacceptable Encampment Locations

5.4 Unauthorised encampments are almost always, by definition, unlawful. However, while there are insufficient authorised sites, it is recognised that some unauthorised camping will continue. There are locations, however, where encampment will not be acceptable under any circumstances. Each encampment location must be considered on its merits against criteria such as health and safety considerations for the unauthorised campers, traffic hazard, public health risks, serious environmental damage, genuine nuisance to neighbours and proximity to other sensitive land-uses. The list in Box 15 of sites where an unauthorised encampment would not normally be acceptable is illustrative only and is not intended to be exhaustive.

Box 15 : Some Examples of Types of Site where Unauthorised Camping would Normally be Unacceptable

- A Site of Special Scientific Interest (SSSI) where an encampment endangers a sensitive environment or wildlife

- School car park or playing fields (especially in term time)

- An urban park

- Car parks, including hospital, supermarket or leisure facility car parks

- An industrial estate

- Recreation ground and public playing fields

- A site where pollution from vehicles or dumping could damage ground water or water courses

- A derelict area with toxic waste or other serious ground pollution

- A village green or other open area within a residential area

- The verge of a busy road where fast traffic is a danger to unauthorised campers' children

---

5.5 Wherever possible, local authorities and/or police should seek to prevent Gypsies and Travellers from establishing an encampment in an unacceptable location. Where this proves impossible, they should attempt to encourage the unauthorised campers to move to an authorised site where available. Identification of possible 'acceptable' sites could assist local authorities and the police in the management of unauthorised encampments in circumstances where there are no available pitches on authorised sites. If the unauthorised campers refuse to move from an unacceptable location, eviction processes (including appropriate welfare enquiries) should be commenced.

5.6 To be effective, such an approach requires a very swift response from the local authority and/or police. Ideally, initial contact should be made within 24 hours of the encampment being established.

Welfare Enquiries

Requirements to Make Welfare Enquiries

5.7 Local authorities may have obligations towards unauthorised campers under other legislation (mainly regarding children, homelessness and education). Authorities should liaise with other local authorities; health and welfare services who might have responsibilities towards the families of unauthorised campers. Some form of effective welfare enquiry is necessary to identify whether needs exist which might trigger these duties or necessitate the involvement of other sectors, including the voluntary sector, to help resolve issues. The police and other public bodies who might be involved in dealing with unauthorised encampments do not have comparable duties but must still, as public servants, show common humanity to those they meet.

5.8 The Human Rights Act (HRA) applies to all public authorities including local authorities (including town and parish councils), police, public bodies and the courts. With regard to eviction, the issue that must be determined is whether the interference with Gypsy/Traveller family life and home is justified and proportionate. Any particular welfare needs experienced by unauthorised campers are material in reaching a balanced and proportionate decision. The human rights of members of the settled community are also material if an authority fails to act to curb nuisance from an encampment.

5.9 Case law is still developing with regard to the sorts of welfare enquiries, which the courts consider necessary to properly taken decisions in relation to actions against unauthorised encampments. Cases are testing the requirements under different powers, and the requirements placed on different agencies (authorities, police, and other public landowners). Very generally, court decisions to date suggest:

- All public authorities need to be able to demonstrate that they have taken into consideration any welfare needs of unauthorised campers prior to making a decision to evict.

- The courts recognise that the police and other public bodies have different resources and welfare duties from local authorities. Generally the extent and detail of appropriate enquiries is less for police and non-local authority 'public authorities'.

- In the case of local authorities, the onus of making welfare enquiries appears to be greater when using Criminal Justice and Public Order Act 1994 s77, where the use of the section can result in criminal sanctions, than when using landowners' civil powers against trespass. Local authorities should, however, make thorough welfare enquiries whatever powers they intend to use.

5.10 Because local authorities have appropriate skills and resources to enable them to make (or to co-ordinate) welfare enquiries, it is considered good practice for local authorities to respond positively to requests for assistance in making enquiries from the police or other public bodies.

Procedures for Making Enquiries

5.11 Speed of response is key to managing unauthorised encampments so as to minimise disruption. There should be a recognised system, which ensures that all reports of new encampments reach the lead officer as quickly as possible. Passing on information rapidly should be part of protocols and joint working arrangements between agencies/departments (see 3.20). Staff on local authority switchboards and at call centres should know how to handle calls from the public and to whom they should be referred. Police call handlers require similar briefing and information that might take the form of frequently asked questions (FAQs) based on mutually agreed policies.

5.12 Ideally, an initial visit should be made to a new encampment within 24 hours of the authority becoming aware of it unless the location is very unobtrusive or remote. An encampment should always be visited very rapidly if initial reports indicate exceptional problems. The initial visit is the first step in making decisions about, and effectively managing, unauthorised encampments. It has several functions:

- To check the accuracy of initial reports/complaints of an encampment, and to gather basic information on its location and size. This information enables issues such as land ownership to be checked.

- Where an encampment location is likely to prove unacceptable (see 5.4-5.5), officers at the initial visit might try to encourage the unauthorised campers to move to an authorised site where a place is available, or to a less immediately unacceptable location chosen by the unauthorised campers themselves.

- To collect basic information from the unauthorised campers about the families and vehicles involved, and about past and intended future movement, anticipated length of stay and reasons for stay.

- To collect initial information from unauthorised campers on any perceived welfare, health or educational needs. Such information is the starting point for liaison with other relevant departments. Where school-age children are present, the Traveller Education Service should be notified. Similarly social services or health authorities should be notified where there seem to be social, welfare or health needs to be further assessed and met.

- The initial visit should note the state of the encampment - how well it is kept, any damage, rubbish accumulation and so on. This will provide baseline information from which subsequent changes can be monitored. Photographs can provide a useful record of potential health and safety issues; people should not be photographed without their express consent.

- Officers at an initial visit can also note any features of the encampment or its location that is likely to be particularly problematic or which might affect future decisions.

- The initial visit is also an opportunity for giving information to unauthorised campers about:

  □ the standard of behaviour expected of them. Where a Code of Expected Behaviour has been developed (see 7.3 et seq), copies should be provided and, where necessary in the event of any reading difficulties, be clearly explained to avoid misunderstanding;

  □ what is going to happen next, what procedures the authority or police are likely to follow and what this means for the unauthorised campers; and

  □ names and addresses of local services and sources of advice likely to be useful to the unauthorised campers. Information ideally should include locations of housing providers, health, education and social services, and waste disposal facilities.

Box 16 : Examples of Information Leaflets Provided to Gypsies and Travellers

Information leaflets for Gypsies and Travellers normally set out the main policy approach adopted by the local authority, a code of expected behaviour and useful contact addresses for services and advice.

Devon County Council: On the Road - Guidelines for people of a nomadic lifestyle

Dorset County Council: Notice to Travellers

Essex County Council: Guidance notes for Gypsy/Travellers in Essex

Suffolk County Council: Notice to Travellers on unauthorised camp sites

---

5.13 Welfare enquiries should always be carried out as swiftly as possible where the initial visit indicates that the unauthorised campers may have serious unmet health or welfare needs or where it seems likely that the encampment will lead to serious disruption or nuisance.

5.14 It is vital that all information given and received during visits and enquiries is clearly recorded. This is helpful to the local authority, especially if different officers are involved at a later date. It will also form the basis of an audit trail for subsequent decisions in case of challenge. Pro formas have been developed by many authorities (see Box 17) to collect and record this initial information. Some authorities and police forces have developed scoring matrices as an aid to assessing risk and decision making.

Guidance on Managing Unauthorised Camping

Box 17 : Example of a Pro-Forma used to Record Data on Encampments

Adur District Council: Welfare checks for Travellers

Coventry City Council: Traveller enquiry form, and Form for guidance of authorising officer

Devon County Council: Unauthorised occupation notification, and Personal circumstances questionnaire

Devon & Cornwall Constabulary: Checklist and record of action taken by officers attending alleged trespass on land

Leicestershire County Council: Unauthorised occupation Social Assessment Report

---

5.15 Information gathered in the course of visits and enquiries is subject to data protection legislation. Authorities should make clear the purposes for which information is being collected and give assurances about how it will be used and to whom it might be passed. Chapter 9 provides reference to the web-site of the Information Commissioner for guidance on data protection issues.

5.16 Local authorities have no powers to insist that information be given. Some information may be confidential and require the unauthorised camper to give consent to follow up, for example, medical records. A sensitive approach is necessary, and authorities should always bear in mind issues of confidentiality and data protection. Where information is refused, the fact that questions were asked and not answered should be clearly recorded to avoid any subsequent claim for failure to take some relevant consideration into account. If unauthorised campers give reasons for not responding, these should also be noted. Unauthorised campers should be informed of any possible consequences of not providing information when requested. If they want to provide information through another person they trust, they should be able to do so provided that arrangements can be made quickly.

5.17 Reasonable attempts should be made to get information from unauthorised campers not present at the time of a visit. Other members of the group may sometimes be able to provide information. A letter or self-completion form may be left with clear instructions for its return (at no cost to the unauthorised camper). All such actions should be clearly recorded, and if there is still no response, this should be noted.

5.18 When visiting and managing unauthorised encampments, local authorities and police should adopt the same legal and careful health and safety procedures and practices as they apply to any other activity they are engaged in.

Reaching Decisions

5.19 Decisions about what action to take in connection with an unauthorised encampment must be made in the light of information gathered. Decisions must always be:

- 'Lawful' - that is in line with local policy and procedures, taking into account relevant considerations and not taking into account the irrelevant.

- 'Reasonable' in the legal sense of not being perverse or irrational in the light of the evidence available.

- 'Balanced' in that they take account of the rights and needs of both the settled community and Gypsies and Travellers.

- 'Proportionate' - what is proportionate will vary according to the precise circumstances of each encampment, including the nature of the location and the behaviour and needs of the unauthorised campers.

Guidance on Managing Unauthorised Camping

Making Decisions

5.20 Any welfare needs of unauthorised campers are a material consideration for local authorities when deciding whether to start eviction proceedings or to allow the encampment to remain longer. Welfare needs do not give an open-ended 'right' for unauthorised campers to stay as long as they want in an area. For example, the presence of a pregnant woman or school age children does not, per se, mean that an encampment must remain indefinitely. To defer an eviction which is justified on other grounds, the need must be more immediate and/or of a fixed term. Box 18 gives some examples of welfare needs to be considered by local authorities, although the list is not intended to be exhaustive and all cases must be judged on their individual merits. Good practice suggests that eviction should be delayed while such acute welfare needs exist and are being met; during this period the encampment should be pro-actively managed (see Chapter 7).

Box 18 : Some Examples of Welfare Needs to be Considered in Eviction Decisions

Advanced pregnancy: a period shortly before and after birth in normal circumstances; longer on medical advice if there are complications.

Ill health: indicators might include a hospital appointment booked; in-patient treatment of a close family member; period during which a condition can be diagnosed, stabilised and a course of treatment started.

Educational needs: children in school if within 4 weeks of the end of term or if access to special education has been gained.

5.21 In some circumstances it may be appropriate to exclude a single person or family with welfare need from eviction action taken against the larger group. However, this must always be sensitively handled to ensure that an individual is not isolated and unsupported, leading to still greater need. In practice, groups may prefer to move on together. It is important that the appropriate authority follows up identified welfare needs whether or not the encampment is moved on.

Arrangements for Making Decisions

5.22 Responsibility for taking decisions must be clearly identified within the authority's (and/or police) policies and procedures, whether delegated to officers or retained by elected members.

5.23 Some authorities have established special procedures for reaching decisions, for example:

- Structures which ensure that decisions are taken by officers who have not been directly involved in site visits or contact with unauthorised campers. It is argued that this increases the consistency, logic and objectivity of decisions. Since all evidence is presented to the 'authorising officer' in writing such a procedure ensures that there is a clear record of the decision and the issues considered.

- Some authorities have arrangements for joint site visits and/or case conferences for reaching decisions on 'difficult' cases. Such procedures ensure that all parties are represented and have the opportunity to influence the decision. Case conferences could include representatives of the unauthorised campers and the local settled community, although there would need to be clear 'rules' for making decisions in the absence of consensus.

5.24 It is important that decisions to pro-actively manage encampments for a period are kept under review. Circumstances can change quickly, for example if newcomers join the encampment and swell its size unacceptably or if behaviour deteriorates.

Recording Decisions

5.25 All decisions (including any decision to allow an encampment to remain for a period) must be fully recorded and documented. Any damage and nuisance should be charted in writing; a

Guidance on Managing Unauthorised Camping

photographic or video record might also be taken in support. Records should also be kept of all complaints received about the encampment, with comments as to their validity. Information passed to unauthorised campers should be recorded, along with offers of assistance made - for example help with a housing application, offer of a pitch on an authorised site - and the response. Similarly it would be good practice to record the fact that an encampment was unproblematic and did **not** cause nuisance or damage. Any complaints received, including any from Gypsy/Traveller unauthorised campers, should be recorded.

5.26 Records can provide valuable information on the number and nature of unauthorised encampments in an area and which sites are particularly prone to encampment. This information is useful in assessing the need for further site provision, site protection priorities and in setting budgets and appropriate staffing levels. It provides material on which a risk-based response to encampments could be developed drawing on past experience relating to the site or the group/family involved. Standard minimum information, to be collected in all areas, as suggested in paragraph 3.30, would facilitate information sharing and better planning.

6. Resorting to Eviction

6.1 This chapter covers the eviction process itself. Once a decision to evict an unauthorised encampment has been properly taken, the aims should be:

■ To act quickly and efficiently.

■ To use powers most appropriate to the circumstances.

■ To reduce scope for challenge through the courts by ensuring that policies and procedures are properly followed so as to reduce cost and delay.

6.2 The first three sections relate to eviction powers available to local authorities, police and other landowners. The final section in the chapter (6.20-6.24) deals with local planning authority powers to enforce against unauthorised development (ie Gypsies and Travellers 'developing' land as a caravan site without planning consent).

Powers Available to Local Authorities

6.3 Many encampments are dealt with through negotiation. Where this fails, local authorities have two main sets of powers to tackle unauthorised encampments:

■ A landowner (including a local authority) can obtain a possession order in the civil courts requiring the removal of trespassers from property, including land. Under the Civil Procedures Rules Part 55 the claim must be issued in the County Court in whose jurisdiction the property or land is situated. Exceptionally the claim may be issued in the High Court if there is substantial risk of public disturbance or of serious harm to persons or property which properly require immediate determination.

■ The Criminal Justice and Public Order Act 1994 (CJPOA) gives local authorities in England and Wales powers to make directions to leave land being used by itinerant groups (s77). It is an offence to fail to comply with such a direction. In proceedings for an offence under this section, it is a defence for the accused to show that his failure to leave or to remove the vehicle or other property as soon as practicable, or his re-entry with a vehicle, was due to illness, mechanical breakdown or other immediate emergency. If the direction to leave is not complied with, the local authority can apply to magistrates' court for an order requiring the removal of vehicles and any occupants from the land (s78).

6.4 Box 19 summarises some of the main features of the two sets of powers, highlighting differences and similarities.

Box 19 : Some Features of Civil and Criminal Justice and Public Order Act Powers for Local Authorities

Civil Powers	CJPOA ss77 and 78
Only on land in LA ownership	On private as well as LA land where encampment is without the consent of the occupier of the land
Possession orders are effective against anyone on the land, not necessarily those resident when the notice was first served	Only effective against people directed to leave. All newcomers must be served with directions to leave

Guidance on Managing Unauthorised Camping

Civil orders can cover wide geographical areas where a real threat of further encampment can be demonstrated	It is an offence for unauthorised campers to return within three months to land they have been directed to leave; only applies to the same individuals
There is no defence to an action for trespass (other than showing non-trespass)	It is a defence for the accused to show that his failure to leave or to remove the vehicle or other property as soon as practicable, or his re-entry with a vehicle, was due to illness, mechanical breakdown or other immediate emergency
No criminalising effect	Can have the effect of criminalising Gypsy/Traveller unauthorised campers who fail to move when directed to leave, a factor taken seriously by the courts. In practice, authorities normally proceed against the unauthorised campers by way of complaint for an order requiring them to remove their vehicles from the land, and not for the criminal offence of contravening a direction to leave the land.
County court bailiffs can be used; their services must be paid for and may lead to delay in enforcement. . It is recommended that the police attend such evictions in order to prevent a breach of the peace	Responsibility for eviction lies with the local authority. Officers or agents of the local authority may use reasonable force to evict. It is recommended that the police attend such evictions in order to prevent a breach of the peace
Often seen as safe and relatively straightforward	Potentially quicker than civil powers, but greater risk of being effectively contested

Local authorities have responsibilities to make welfare enquiries when reaching eviction decisions, to take into account considerations of common humanity, and to honour the other statutory duties they may have towards the unauthorised campers
Unauthorised campers can attend and be represented at the court hearing
Decisions can be similarly challenged by means of judicial review on the grounds that they have been reached improperly

6.5 Other legal measures may be available to local authorities:

- The Government believes that local authorities should always follow a route which requires a court order. As local authorities and public bodies, authorities must have regard to considerations of common humanity or other statutory duties, and must ensure that the human rights of unauthorised campers are safeguarded.

- Local highways authorities have powers to evict unauthorised campers from highway land in certain circumstances under the Highways Acts. Section 143 of the Highways Act 1980 requires unauthorised campers to be given 28 days notice to leave, and its use may be unsuitable where rapid eviction is called for.

- Local bylaws may have provisions for evicting unauthorised campers from car parks, parks or other public areas.

Guidance on Managing Unauthorised Camping

Powers Available to the Police

6.6 Powers are available to the police under the Criminal Justice and Public Order Act 1994 ss61-62E.

Criminal Justice and Public Order Act 1994 Section 61

6.7 Under s61 of the CJPOA, the police have discretionary powers to direct trespassers to leave land. The senior police officer present can direct trespassers to leave if reasonable steps have been taken by or on behalf of the landowner/occupier to ask them to leave and there are two or more people intending to reside on the land. Any one of three further conditions must be met:

- if any of those persons has caused damage to the land or to property on the land; or

- used threatening, abusive or insulting words or behaviour towards the occupier, a member of his family or an employee or agent of his; or

- those persons have between them six or more vehicles on the land.

Section 61 cannot be used on land on the highway (with limited specific exclusions listed by s61 (9)(b)). It is an offence to fail to leave the land as soon as reasonably practicable or to enter the land again as a trespasser within three months of the date the direction was given.

6.8 The current ACPO guidance notes that there can be no blanket policies, but refers to some of the circumstances in which it might be appropriate to use s61 against an encampment.

- The statutory conditions must obviously be met (see 6.7). Case law (*Fuller*) has determined that any notice period given to unauthorised campers must have expired before s61 can be used. In other words, the unauthorised campers must clearly have failed to respond to requests from or on behalf of the legal occupier of the land to leave before the police can act. Some police forces have streamlined this process by drawing up standard documents which, when signed by the owner/occupier of the land, give the police authority to act as their agents in dealing with the encampment.

- The fact that a landowner initially allows an encampment to remain does not preclude subsequent police action so long as it is clear that reasonable steps have since been taken by the landowner/occupier to get the unauthorised campers to move, and that they have failed to do so.

- The fact that a local authority has started to make welfare enquiries cannot be taken as an indication that the encampment is being allowed to remain since this is an essential precondition for eviction action.

- The decision to use s61 is an operational one. Its early use should always be considered where it is likely to be a proportionate response, and especially where there is evidence of:

  □ unacceptable behaviour by unauthorised campers at the encampment, including individual criminal activity, which cannot be controlled by means other than eviction;

  □ significant disruption to the life of the surrounding community;

  □ serious breaches of the peace or disorder caused by the encampment.

- Where triggers such as the above are experienced, good practice suggests that police should be prepared to act as long as the statutory conditions are met. Police forces/commands should not adopt blanket policies or presumptions either for or against the use of s61.

6.9 Home Office Circular 45/1994 says 'The decision whether or not to issue a direction to leave is an operational one for the police alone to take in the light of all of the circumstances of the particular case. But in making his decision the senior officer at the scene may wish to take account of the personal circumstances of the trespassers; for example, the presence of elderly persons, invalids, pregnant women, children and other persons whose well-being may be jeopardised by a precipitate move.' Case law (*Small*) has established that, while police officers do not have to undertake welfare

Guidance on Managing Unauthorised Camping

enquiries as such, they must be aware of humanitarian considerations in reaching their decisions and must ensure that all decisions are proportionate. A decision may be taken to explicitly exclude individuals or families with serious welfare needs from a s61 direction to leave.

6.10 Above all, s61 should be used within the framework of a jointly agreed strategy for managing unauthorised camping (see Chapter 3). Local authorities, police and other stakeholders should agree the sorts of circumstances in which s61 might be considered appropriate. It is also important that s61 should be used consistently within a local area.

Box 20 : Example of a Local Agreement for the Use of Section 61

The joint protocol on unauthorised encampments within the Borough of Northampton between **Northampton Borough Council** and **Northamptonshire Police** includes a local agreement for the use of s61. It specifies exceptional circumstances in which the police may be requested by the Council or choose themselves to consider using their powers under s61.

6.11 Regular exchange of monitoring information on unauthorised encampments between police and local authority personnel is important. In particular, each party should keep the other informed about decisions taken and progress.

Criminal Justice and Public Order Act 1994 Section 62A to 62E

6.12 Sections 67 to 71 of the Anti-social Behaviour Act 2003 insert sections 62A to 62E into the Criminal Justice and Public Order Act 1994 (CJPOA). The legislation provides the police with a power to direct trespassers to leave land and to remove any vehicles and other property from the land, where there is a suitable pitch available on a caravan site elsewhere in the local authority area. Where a direction has been given to a person, it is an offence for that person to enter any land in the local authority as a trespasser within three months of the direction being given.

6.13 This power will be enacted on 27 February 2004 and ODPM and the Home Office are consulting separately on draft guidance for its implementation in practice. Once guidance on the use of s62 is finalised, it will be incorporated into this Guidance.

Powers Available to Other Landowners

6.14 Several government bodies are major landowners and their land may be subject to unauthorised encampment - examples include the Forestry Commission and the Highways Agency. Public bodies should ask local authorities to assist with welfare enquires and local authorities should be prepared to help with these.

6.15 Private landowners may obtain a possession order through the civil courts requiring the removal of trespassers from their land, using Civil Procedures Rules Part 55 in the county court. Private landowners have no welfare responsibilities towards Gypsies and Travellers and would not be expected to take unauthorised campers' needs into account when deciding to evict.

6.16 Some private landowners seek to avoid the expense and costs of going to court by using common law rights to recover land from trespassers using 'reasonable force' as necessary. Such action is lawful, and some firms of bailiffs have carried out many evictions effectively and without trouble. Good practice guidelines for common law evictions would seek to ensure that no more than necessary 'reasonable force' is used and might include:

■ Police should always be notified of an eviction and called in to stand by to prevent a breach of the peace.

■ If police advise that it is inappropriate to carry out an eviction, it should always be delayed until an agreed time.

Guidance on Managing Unauthorised Camping

6.17 There is a role for local authorities and police in managing unauthorised camping on private land.

- As a minimum, local authorities should inform private landowners about their rights to recover land from trespassers, through the courts or using common law powers; authorities should not offer legal advice to landowners but rather refer them to Citizens' Advice Bureaux or solicitors. Authorities should remind landowners about the importance of using reputable bailiffs and only 'reasonable force'.

- Within the overall strategy for managing unauthorised camping, the local authority might consider acting more directly against encampments when requested by a private landowner, particularly if the police are not prepared to use s61 to evict the encampment.

- Police should take action if any criminal offences are perpetrated during eviction action by bailiffs or private firms.

Some Procedural Points

6.18 This guidance is not concerned with detailed procedures involved in court actions for eviction. Some pointers to good practice for local authorities were noted in *Managing Unauthorised Camping: A Good Practice Guide* issued in 1998 and are still valid:

- Both main sets of powers for taking eviction action involve their own detailed procedures for serving notices, entering cases into court, providing statements (civil powers) or witnesses (CJPOA) for evidence and so on. There is advantage in drawing up a detailed procedures guide as a checklist that everything is done properly and no necessary action missed. Losing an eviction action through an avoidable mistake is a waste of resources, and threatens the credibility of the authority.

- In drawing up detailed procedures, the close involvement of a legal officer is essential. Day-to-day liaison for legal advice while dealing with a specific encampment is also desirable to avoid omissions and to ensure the most effective case for eviction is built.

- Most authorities will probably use in-house legal expertise for preparation and court work. In some circumstances it may be desirable to use an external solicitor, which can be cost-effective where a local solicitor has special expertise.

- Good relations should be built with court officials to ensure a speedy service and to ensure that particularly urgent cases can be given priority when needed. The leaflet *Getting the best out of the court system: Claims for possession* issued by DTLR, the Court Service and the Welsh Assembly stresses the importance of establishing links with local courts. It is, of course, essential to establish what paperwork the courts will require and to ensure that it is always provided. It is also desirable to develop fast-track in-house processes to fit around court workings.

- It is important to be able to show that directions have been properly served if cases are to succeed at court. This normally means either personal service on the occupiers of each vehicle and/or attaching a copy of the direction to each caravan as well as posting the direction on the site. A verbal explanation of the direction should be given wherever possible as a supplement to the written documents to cater for possible reading difficulties.

- It is usual to proceed against unnamed persons occupying the land. This is specifically allowed in the CJPOA and may be the only practical course where unauthorised campers are unwilling to give their names. Getting comprehensive information on vehicles is important for identification purposes.

- Most authorities will probably think it appropriate to use council personnel to serve notices and so on. Where external bailiffs or other agents are employed, the authority must be satisfied that their behaviour is at all times lawful and in accord with human rights and race relations requirements.

Guidance on Managing Unauthorised Camping

- Serving directions, and site visits in general, can raise issues of personal safety for officers involved. Sensible precautions should be taken to avoid confrontation and personal danger. In certain circumstances, a police presence may be appropriate while notices are served.

- Local authorities have discretion to set notice periods beyond the legal minimum. For example, the direction to leave served under the CJPOA can require unauthorised campers to leave in 24 hours, 48 hours or a longer period. Decisions about the length of notice given should be taken in the light of the circumstances of each encampment, with a view to being more generous where problems are not extreme.

Preparing for Eviction

6.19 Eviction proceedings should not be commenced unless the authority is able to go the whole way to forced eviction if necessary.

- Every effort should be made to avoid forced eviction.

- Many encampments include children, who will find forced eviction especially stressful and frightening. All authority and other personnel involved in an eviction should remember this and seek to ensure that their actions have the least possible harmful effect on children.

- Authorities should think, in general terms at least, about options for forced eviction. Plans should be formulated on such matters as which personnel would be involved and which towing contractors would be used. An in-principle agreement should be reached with the police about where towed vehicles would be put.

- Other services should be alerted prior to a forced eviction. This should include warning social services (who may need to provide temporary care for children in the rare cases where parents are arrested and held in custody), Traveller Education Services and homelessness officers, and could also involve finding accommodation for horses and dogs.

- Many authorities do not employ council staff in forced evictions. Where bailiffs or other agencies and contractors are employed, a code of expected behaviour should be drawn up. This code must recognise that private bodies have a local authority's human rights and race relations responsibilities while acting as their agent.

- A senior local authority officer should always attend forced evictions to ensure that all agents follow codes of behaviour. The officer should attempt to encourage the unauthorised campers to move voluntarily wherever possible.

- Police should be involved at a very early stage in planning a forced eviction. They will be able to advise on personal safety issues. In addition, forced evictions could have implications for traffic management and the like.

- Elected members and other local stakeholders should be notified in advance of forced eviction. It is also appropriate routinely to inform neighbouring local authorities and police areas since the displaced unauthorised campers may look for other encampment sites locally.

- The respective roles of the local authority, police and other agencies in forced eviction should be clearly established in the local strategy for managing unauthorised camping. Since this is an area where good practice is hard to establish, it is particularly important that all agencies should monitor and evaluate local instances of eviction and learn from that experience.

Enforcing against Unauthorised Development

6.20 Where Gypsies and Travellers (or anyone else) buy land and develop it as a caravan site without planning consent, any enforcement must be through the planning system; the powers described above against trespass cannot be used.

Guidance on Managing Unauthorised Camping

6.21 A breach of planning control is not in itself an offence; enforcement is a matter for the discretion of the local planning authority. Decisions to enforce must be made on planning grounds. Some key factors may include whether the breach of control unacceptably affects public amenity, highway safety, the Green Belt, public landscape, or the existing use of land or buildings meriting protection in the public interest. The action taken should be proportionate to the breach.

6.22 The current enforcement regime provides a mix of powers with which to deal with breaches of planning control in a controlled but flexible manner. The main powers are summarised in Box 21.

Box 21 : Main Planning Enforcement Powers to be used against Unauthorised Development

The discretionary powers available to local planning authorities (LPAs) were set out in the Planning and Compensation Act 1991 which amended the Town and Country Planning Act 1990 (TCPA 1990). Section references below refer to the TCPA 1990 as amended.

Planning contravention notice (s171C): This may be used where it appears that there may have been a breach of planning control and the LPA requires information about the activities on the land or to find out more about the nature of the recipient's interest in the land.

Enforcement notice (s172): This requires steps to be taken to remedy the specified breach within a given period. There is a right of appeal to the Secretary of State against an enforcement notice. If the notice is upheld, failure to comply is an offence with a maximum penalty on conviction of £20,000 (unlimited in the Crown Court).

Stop notice (ss183-184): This has the effect of immediately stopping any activity which contravenes planning control; an enforcement notice must also be served. There is no right of appeal to a stop notice, but compensation may be payable if an appeal against the associated enforcement notice is allowed on legal grounds. If a stop notice is contravened the resulting offence can be prosecuted in the Magistrates' Court with a maximum penalty on conviction of £20,000 (unlimited in the Crown Court).

Breach of condition notice (s187A): Where there is a failure to comply with any condition or limitation imposed on a grant of planning permission this procedure provides a fast-track enforcement option to secure compliance with no statutory right of appeal to the Secretary of State.

Injunctions (s187b): The LPA is able to seek an injunction in the High Court or County Court to restrain any actual or expected breach of planning control. It is not necessary to serve an enforcement notice prior to applying for an injunction.

Direct action (s178): Where any steps required by an enforcement notice are not taken within the compliance period, the LPA may enter the land and take the required steps and recover reasonable costs incurred in doing so. The whole enforcement process must have been completed before direct action is possible.

Compulsory purchase (s226 (1)(b)): With the authorisation of the Secretary of State, an LPA may compulsorily acquire any land in their area 'for a purpose which it is necessary to achieve in the interests of the proper planning of an area in which the land is situated'. There is scope for objection and a public local inquiry. This has been successfully used against unauthorised development in order to restore land to its lawful use for agriculture.

6.23 Case law has determined that all enforcement measures must be proportionate in the context of the Human Rights Act, and in particular the Gypsy/Traveller's rights under Article 8. Guidance on using planning enforcement powers is available in Circular 10/97, Planning Policy Guidance 18: *Enforcing Planning Control* and *Enforcing Planning Control: Good Practice Guide for Local Planning Authorities.*

Guidance on Managing Unauthorised Camping

6.24 The planning enforcement system in England is currently being reviewed. One of the issues being considered is whether local authority enforcement powers are effective or whether more are needed to tackle breaches of planning control. Revised guidance to local authorities is also being considered. An announcement about the review is expected in 2004.

7. Managing Unauthorised Encampments

7.1 Although unauthorised camping is unlawful, it is likely to continue while there are insufficient spaces to accommodate Gypsies and Travellers on authorised sites. While more places are being provided it is vital that local authorities, with their police and other partners, pro-actively manage encampments to minimise the disruption caused. The principles involved are:

- To enforce the same standards of behaviour by unauthorised campers as are expected of the settled community.

- To respond rapidly to any deterioration of behaviour and growing disruption from an encampment.

- To facilitate access to services for Gypsy/Travellers on encampments.

- To keep all parties informed of decisions and actions.

7.2 The chapter also covers the special issue of dealing with mass gatherings by Gypsies and Travellers (7.30-7.37).

Behaviour at Encampments

7.3 Many local authorities (see Box 22) have drawn up Codes for Gypsy/Traveller unauthorised campers, detailing both locational and behaviour expectations. 'Acceptable behaviour' codes might include some or all of the following items:

- Small scale encampments, which can be accommodated with less disruption.

- No aggressive and threatening behaviour towards local authority and/or police officers or members of the public.

- Dogs and other animals to be kept under control.

- No persistent noise which disturbs others, especially at night, for example from work on the camp, vehicles, generators, dogs or music.

- Keeping the encampment site clean and tidy, avoiding littering and/or fly tipping on or near the site.

- No damage either to the site encamped or the surrounding area or nearby property.

- No criminal activity on the part of unauthorised campers.

Box 22 : Examples of Codes of Expected Behaviour
The code for Travellers in **Essex**
Guidance notes for Travellers in **Leicestershire, Leicester City** *and* **Rutland**

7.4 In drawing up a Code of Expected Behaviour, local authorities should consult Gypsies and Travellers, local businesses and other landowners and other members of the settled community. The objective should be to reach consensus on behaviour standards which it is appropriate to require, and which are sensitive to cultural differences between the Travelling and settled communities.

7.5 As noted above, a basic principle in establishing a Code of Expected Behaviour is applying the same standards as would be applied to members of the settled community. In this context it is important to consider 'individual' and 'group' behaviour and responsibilities. In the settled community, a whole street or estate would not be evicted because of the criminal or anti-social behaviour of one person or household. Wherever possible, police and local authorities should seek to enforce appropriately against a troublemaker rather than automatically evicting an encampment as a whole.

7.6 It is also important to identify and take action against unacceptable behaviour towards encampments by members of the settled community. Harassment of, and violence against, Gypsy/Traveller unauthorised campers are quite unacceptable. Local authorities and police, as public bodies, have responsibilities under the Race Relations (Amendment) Act 2000 to promote good race relations.

7.7 Tackling unacceptable behaviour of whatever sort requires - as outlined in Chapter 5 - rapid response, regular monitoring and determination to take appropriate enforcement action as necessary.

Dealing with Crime and Anti-Social Behaviour

7.8 Some encampments are associated with criminal and anti-social behaviour. The Government is clear that criminal and anti-social behaviour is not acceptable from unauthorised campers, just as it is not acceptable from members of the settled community. The White Paper *Respect and Responsibility* sets out the stand to be taken against anti-social behaviour. Measures provided (see 7.11-7.12 and Box 23) empower communities, public services and authorities to tackle anti-social behaviour. In return the Government expects everyone to play their part in setting and enforcing proper standards of behaviour. This Guidance should be read in the context of that agenda.

7.9 Dealing with any criminal behaviour on the part of unauthorised campers is properly the responsibility of the police. Other enforcement agencies may be involved depending on the nature of the crime, including Trading Standards Officers, Inland Revenue and Customs and Excise enforcement officers where there are indications of fraudulent trading, tax or excise evasion. A co-ordinated approach to enforcement is the key.

7.10 No group should be above the law. Where action is justified, there should be no blanket presumption against enforcing against members of the Travelling community on grounds of expediency. Where law enforcement agencies demonstrate a commitment to taking action where appropriate and are clearly determined to tackle crime, it is probable that some Gypsy/Traveller unauthorised campers will avoid that locality and some may amend their behaviour. A pro-active approach taken in one area may increase unauthorised camping in an adjoining area where a less active approach is taken. Consistency of approach is desirable.

7.11 Anti-social behaviour (see Box 23) can also arise at some unauthorised encampments. Both police and local authorities have a role here. Under the Police Reform Act 2002, the Government introduced improved measures for tackling anti-social behaviour including allowing Anti-Social Behaviour Orders (ASBOs) to be made following conviction for a criminal offence as well as on application to the civil magistrate's court, and allowing ASBOs to prohibit specified acts of anti-social behaviour across any geographical area up to and including the whole of England and Wales. This should help counter displacement of anti-social behaviour. Orders can also be made in the county court where the defendant is the principal party in related proceedings such as possession proceedings or eviction notices where the persons to be evicted from the area are named individuals. These changes were accompanied by Home Office guidance published in November. The white paper *Respect and Responsibility* strengthens the changes described above and outlines new measures which are to be introduced. The Anti-Social Behaviour Act 2003 will introduce further relevant changes to ASBOs, allowing Housing Action Trusts and county councils to apply for ASBOs, enabling persons to be joined to county court proceedings to seek an order against them and empowering local authorities to prosecute ASBO breaches.

7.12 It is important that local authorities and police seriously consider the possibility of using ASBOs against unauthorised campers and/or negotiating Acceptable Behaviour Contracts (see Box 23). The use of either measure would represent an opportunity to discuss behaviour with unauthorised campers, defining with and for them what is and is not acceptable.

Box 23 : Tackling Anti-Social Behaviour

The Crime and Disorder Act 1998 introduced Anti-Social Behaviour Orders (ASBOs) to tackle persistent anti-social behaviour (ASB). The scope of the orders was extended by the Police Reform Act 2002, which was accompanied by Home Office guidance on ASBOs and ABCs. Further improvements to the functioning of ASBOs were made in the Anti-Social Behaviour Act 2003.

ASB: is defined in the Crime and Disorder Act 1998 s1 as behaving in *'a manner that caused or was likely to cause harassment, alarm or distress to one or more persons not of the same household'*

ASBOs: are available to local authorities, police (including the British Transport Police) and Registered Social Landlords (RSLs') by application at a magistrates' court or on conviction in criminal proceedings. Orders are available in the county court where the person is the Defendant in related proceedings. Interim orders can also be obtained. From early 2004 Housing Action Trusts and county councils will also be able to apply for ASBOs, and persons will be able to be joined to county court proceedings where their anti-social behaviour is relevant to the principal reason for seeking an order against them. To obtain an ASBO it is necessary to show that the person(s) concerned have acted in an anti-social manner and an order is necessary to protect others from further anti-social acts by the individual(s). The rules of evidence are civil but a standard of proof equivalent to the criminal standard (beyond reasonable doubt) should be applied. The order must be negative, prohibiting the individual(s) from specified actions (which can include a general prohibition of acting in an anti-social manner) in specified areas which can be any defined part of or the whole of England and Wales. Breach of an ASBO is a criminal offence and has to be proved to the criminal standard of evidence beyond reasonable doubt. Conviction for breach carries the normal maximum sentence in the Magistrates' Court (6 months in prison, a fine or both) and five years and/or a fine in the Crown Court.

Acceptable Behaviour Contracts: have been developed, initially by Islington Council, as an informal way of dealing with low-level ASB and nipping it in the bud. They can be used with adults and young people and are tenure-neutral although they have been used mainly against teenagers in social rented housing. The perpetrator is interviewed by a council officer in the presence of parents and police, and is asked to sign a 'contract' agreeing not to engage in specified anti-social acts. The ABC principles might be adapted for use in relation to Gypsies/Travellers and unauthorised encampments. An ABC is not legally binding but it can be cited in proceedings such as for an ASBO at a later date.

Other measures: are available which can be used against specific forms of ASB, including:

- Environmental Protection Act 1990 where a problem is judged prejudicial to health or a statutory nuisance - normally enforced by the local authority environmental health department

- Noise Act 1996 - normally enforced by the local authority environmental health department

- Protection from Harassment Act 1997 - if ASB or unauthorised camper behaviour constitutes harassment, police could prosecute under this Act, or the person to whom harassment has occurred may claim damages and an injunction

- Public Order Act 1986

- Criminal Damage Act 1971

Guidance on Managing Unauthorised Camping

7.13 Measures to tackle crime and ASB must be set within a strategic framework. Dealing with any criminal and anti-social behaviour associated with unauthorised encampments should be considered by local Crime and Disorder Reduction Partnerships as part of their mandatory strategies (see Box 24).

Box 24 : Crime and Disorder Prevention Partnerships

The Crime and Disorder Act 1998 requires the police and local authorities - together with police authorities, health authorities and probation committees - to work together, in partnership with other agencies, to develop and implement a strategy for reducing crime and disorder in each district and unitary local authority area. County councils are to be involved in all strategies within their area. The Act also requires local authorities to have regard to crime and disorder when considering all other matters.

Police and local authorities (and other partners) must follow a three year cycle:

- Conduct and publish an audit of local crime and disorder problems, taking into account the views of those who live and work in the area

- Determine priorities for action

- Devise and publish a strategy which tackles these priority problems, including objectives and targets

- Monitor progress, fine tuning the strategy as required

Dealing with Waste and Fly-tipping

7.14 Accumulations of rubbish and waste - including human waste, domestic and trade refuse - represent one of the most common problems associated with unauthorised encampments. Accumulations can be visually unpleasant, smelly, hazardous and costly to clear up. Preventing a build up of waste and/or removing it is a central element in a policy of pro-active management of encampments.

Preventing Waste

7.15 Local authorities have an important role in preventing accumulation of waste by ensuring that unauthorised campers keep encampments clean and tidy:

- Many authorities provide supplies of plastic sacks and arrange regular collection of bagged refuse. This can work well with unauthorised campers who want to conform to a Code of Expected Behaviour, and will reduce the costs of cleaning up after the encampment has left. Regular removal of domestic refuse should deter tipping by members of the settled community.

- Some groups of Gypsies and Travellers are willing to use skips for domestic waste. Again, provision and removal may be cost-effective if the alternative is a build-up of refuse acting as a magnet for other fly tipping by members of the settled community. Local authorities should check that skips would be used before providing them. It is good practice to seek to recover costs from the unauthorised campers.

- One of the common complaints about unauthorised encampments is of people urinating and defecating in public. Public defecation is a difficult and sensitive issue. The practice is a nuisance and a health hazard. However, Gypsies and Travellers have strict cultural codes about hygiene and consider it unclean to use toilet facilities in a caravan or to share facilities. When managing encampments local authorities should liaise with unauthorised campers. They should make plain that public defecation is not acceptable behaviour, and discuss what form of toilet provision the local authority can assist with to prevent it and any arrangements for payment for the service.

Guidance on Managing Unauthorised Camping

7.16 Regular monitoring visits to encampments should reinforce messages about keeping the site clean and tidy. Unauthorised campers need to realise that, under a pro-active approach to managing unauthorised encampments, failure to keep the site clean and tidy in breach of a Code of Expected Behaviour is likely to lead to rapid eviction. Some local authorities, which have adopted such an approach and shown a determination to encourage acceptable behaviour, have found that behaviour of unauthorised campers has improved; in some instances groups which previously left encampment sites in very poor condition are now much tidier. This is extremely cost-effective in reducing the need to spend large sums on cleaning up.

Enforcement Action

7.17 Dealing with illicit waste disposal and fly tipping is difficult - whether the culprits are Gypsy/Traveller unauthorised campers or members of the settled community. Local authorities, police and the Environment Agency all have roles to play and co-ordinated action is necessary. Gypsy/Traveller unauthorised campers should be clearly informed that everyone who produces, treats, carries or disposes of controlled waste has a 'duty of care' under s34 of the Environment Protection Act 1990. Licensed carriers should take trade waste to appropriately licensed facilities in accordance with this duty of care. Information leaflets provided to unauthorised campers should identify nearby licensed waste facilities.

7.18 Enforcement measures are available (see Box 25). Collecting sufficient evidence for successful prosecution requires - as with the measures for countering crime and ASB outlined above - determination and partnership working from the agencies involved. The case study in Box 26 shows that action can succeed.

Box 25 : Measures for Enforcing against Pollution, Littering and Fly-tipping

Water Resources Act 1991 (as amended by the Environment Act 1995) gives the Environment Agency powers to prosecute those found illegally depositing waste into controlled waters and causing a pollution offence.

Environmental Protection Act 1990 makes fly-tipping a criminal offence with a maximum penalty of a £20,000 fine and/or imprisonment up to 6 months (unlimited fine or imprisonment of up to 5 years if convicted at a Crown Court). The Government has asked the Environment Agency to vigorously prosecute any person found to be illegally disposing of waste, where they have evidence. The waste collection authority and the Environment Agency may remove fly-tipped waste and recover costs from those responsible for causing the offence. The Environment Agency has set up an emergency telephone hotline (0800 807060) for members of the public to notify them of fly tipping (and water pollution incidents). The National Fly-Tipping Prevention Group includes a number of national organisations.

Environment Protection Act 1990 (Part III) gives local authorities powers to act against statutory nuisances (prejudicial to health or a nuisance). Local authorities can serve an abatement notice, which can be appealed. Failure to comply with an abatement notice is an offence.

Anti-social Behaviour Act 2003 extends the range of powers available to local authorities for dealing with fly tipping, for instance, by giving them powers to stop, search and seize vehicles suspected of being used for fly tipping and to investigate incidents.

Guidance on Managing Unauthorised Camping

Box 26 : A Case Study of Action against Fly-tipping

Officers from the Environment Agency met officers of Leicestershire Constabulary in December 2002 to discuss a strategy for dealing with illegal tipping by Travellers near the M50/M1 interchange. On 13 January 2003, the police contacted the Environment Agency to confirm that their officers had witnessed the deposit of around 3 tonnes of soil amongst other waste on the site. The offender was unable to satisfactorily respond to accusations of illegal tipping lodged by the police and they were able to arrest him under Police and Criminal Evidence Act 1984 powers. An Agency officer assisted the police in the interview process and provided the police with specimen charges.

The offender was subsequently bailed to appear at a later date to answer the charges lodged against him. He appeared at Loughborough Magistrates' Court and pleaded guilty to one charge of depositing waste without the benefit of a waste management licence, contrary to s33 (1)(a) of the Environmental Protection Act 1990. He was fined £250 and ordered to pay £65 costs.

7.19 Regular site monitoring is essential if evidence is to be gathered for successful enforcement. Environmental health authorities, police and the Environment Agency need to work closely together. Surveillance to identify individuals responsible for fly tipping is likely to be resource-intensive. Covert surveillance is now governed by the Regulation of Investigatory Powers Act 2000; the Home Office has issued guidance on the use of CCTV in relation to both the Human Rights and Data Protection Acts.

Rapid Clear-up

7.20 Whilst the measures outlined above may help reduce the accumulation of rubbish, cleaning up will still be needed after some encampments.

- Sites should be cleared as soon as possible after they are vacated.

- Where appropriate, responsibilities must be agreed between county and district councils for site clearance so that there is no delay due to uncertainty or dispute. Joint arrangements - including some apportionment of costs - must be set out in a joint agreement or protocol specifying speed of response.

- Some refuse left may need special care in collection and disposal, including hazardous industrial waste, excreta and drug-related waste. Contractors should be warned accordingly.

Recording Information

7.21 The state of the site on departure and the clean-up cost are relevant factors to record in the encampment log. A group's previous behaviour may well inform the approach adopted if they visit the area again. If the sharing of standard information becomes more common, poor behaviour in one area may in future also inform the approach adopted in another area.

Facilitating Access to Services

7.22 It is an important objective of a pro-active approach to managing encampments that Gypsy/Traveller unauthorised campers are enabled to access health, welfare and education services during the period of their stay. It is in everyone's interests that Gypsy/Traveller children are encouraged and enabled to complete their education. Arranging access to services will be easier when unauthorised campers conform to a Code of Expected Behaviour and may be permitted to stay longer. Local authorities should facilitate access to services and act as main contact point for specialist service providers. Information from the welfare enquiries will indicate what services are required.

Guidance on Managing Unauthorised Camping

A Robust Approach to Eviction

7.23 A pro-active approach to managing unauthorised camping involves keeping encampments under review. Police and local authorities should be prepared to review eviction decisions as circumstances change since the balance of interests will change as well. While a decision to evict might not have been 'proportionate' initially, experience of disruption to the settled community, crime or anti-social behaviour may justify eviction at a later date. The fact that an encampment has been permitted to remain for a period does not preclude eviction proceedings - whether by the local authority or police using s61 - being started at a later date provided proper procedures are followed.

Keeping People Informed

7.24 As noted in Chapter 3, communications and publicity arrangements are an important element in any strategy for managing unauthorised camping. It is important that other agencies/departments, Gypsies and Travellers, elected members and members of the settled community are kept informed about what is happening and what can be expected to happen with encampments.

7.25 An agreed communications strategy between partner organisations in an area should determine which agency will lead on providing information. Normally this should be the local authority in its role as lead agency in dealing with unauthorised camping. Communications with the press and members of the public should be co-ordinated and consistent to avoid confusion. One aim of a communications strategy should be to increase understanding and tolerance between the settled and travelling communities in line with duties to promote good race relations placed on local authorities and police by the Race Relations (Amendment) Act 2000.

7.26 Gypsy/Traveller unauthorised campers should always be clearly informed about what is expected of them and what is going to happen. Information should normally be by word of mouth as well as written to avoid communication problems because of any reading difficulties. Contact and communication should be at least weekly.

7.27 Any encampment is likely to be of concern to local residents and businesses. Elected members should be regularly briefed on encampments in their wards; they can pass information on to their constituents. In addition, the local authority should provide information to local residents, and especially to complainants, using resources of the internet and e-mail where appropriate.

7.28 Special arrangements may be appropriate for large and/or high profile encampments. In addition to the measures described above, these might include:

- Regular press briefings.

- Well-publicised advice lines for Gypsies and Travellers and other members of the public to ring for information.

- A special leaflet or newsletter to be distributed locally explaining background, events and plans for dealing with the encampment.

- Links to regularly updated information through the council's web-site. Police and other agencies likely to be approached for information should include hyperlink connections to information on local authority web pages.

7.29 Such measures will obviously be costly in staff time. However, in the case of a major encampment local authorities and police will have to deal with complaints and queries anyway, and planning will make this easier. Being pro-active in this way should reduce scope for rumour and misinformation, and confusion. It could provide opportunities to manage the message to avoid unnecessarily negative coverage and reduce inter-community tension. It could also be helpful in gathering evidence for fly-tipping or other ASB which could be used in enforcement action.

Guidance on Managing Unauthorised Camping

Dealing with Mass Gatherings

7.30 Gatherings, which bring families together for a short period of time for weddings, funerals or traditional fairs and other events, are an important element of Gypsy/Traveller culture. These traditional gatherings must always be handled sensitively and with respect.

7.31 In the past few years a number of other mass gatherings of Gypsies and Travellers have occurred, when several hundred vehicles and people have met up and camped for a period, as at Great Yarmouth (December 1999) and Bournemouth (December 2001).

7.32 Mass gatherings are not spontaneous events but are to some extent planned by those taking part. The Government believes that it is not acceptable for large numbers of Gypsies and Travellers (or anyone else) to turn up in an area and cause severe disruption. The Government also recognises that there are large gatherings which are part of the Gypsy and Traveller tradition such as Appleby Fair in Cumbria.

7.33 The responsibility for managing lawful gathering should lie with the Gypsies and Travellers themselves. Gypsies and Travellers, ideally, should provide advance notice of a mass gathering, and should themselves make arrangements for water, refuse and hygiene services. At the very least, Gypsy/Traveller 'leaders' at a gathering should be prepared to negotiate with local authority and police officers and to act in a co-operative manner so as to minimise disruption.

7.34 Local authorities and police can make advance plans for dealing with such mass gatherings (including those where 'leaders' do not co-operate fully):

■   It would be appropriate to include handling a major gathering and encampment of Gypsies and Travellers within the local emergency plan and local Crime and Disorder Plans.

■   In emergency plans, local authorities should think ahead about how they might prepare emergency accommodation, negotiate with farmers for the use of their fields, identify supplies of portable toilets, water supply, waste disposal etc. The authority's Chief Emergency Planning Officer might become involved in preparing and co-ordinating plans.

■   Close joint working between local authority personnel and police is key to managing mass gatherings. Dealing with hundreds of people and vehicles is likely to be beyond the resources of a single authority or police area. Local authorities and police have come together for joint planning at regional level in some parts of the country following recent experiences in order to be able to rapidly mobilise resources on a sufficient scale.

■   Joint planning should extend to sharing information and intelligence aimed at anticipating the size and location of gatherings.

7.35 Section 14A of the Public Order Act 1986 provides for the prevention of 'trespassory assemblies', and s14 provides for the imposition of conditions on all assemblies. Section 14C of the Public Order Act 1986 creates a power for police to turn people away from trespassory assemblies when a banning order is in force. Box 27 gives more details. Acting to ban a mass gathering under these powers clearly requires close co-operation and agreement between the local police and local authority. This can only be contemplated when advance intelligence of the gathering is available sufficiently long in advance to allow the various procedures to be followed and approvals to be sought. Enforcing such a ban - if agreed by the Secretary of State - will obviously have major staffing implications.

Guidance on Managing Unauthorised Camping

Box 27 : Preventing Trespassory Assemblies

Public Order Act 1986 s14A

A public assembly is a gathering of 20 or more people on land in the open air. A Chief Police Officer may take steps to prohibit such an assembly, provided that:

- The assembly must be on land to which the public has no right of access or limited right of access   **AND**

- The assembly is likely to be held without the permission of the owner/occupier of the land or to conduct itself in a way as to exceed the limits of any permission or limits the public's right of access   **AND**

- May result in serious disruption to life of the community.

If these conditions are fulfilled the Chief Officer may apply to the District Council for an order preventing trespassory assemblies for a specific period. This order may only be granted with the permission of the Secretary of State for the Home Department. The order may ban assemblies for up to 4 days within a radius of 5 miles. The order may be renewed.

It is an offence to organise such an assembly knowing that it as been prohibited, or to take part knowing it has been prohibited.

Public Order Act 1986 s14C

Creates a power for police to turn people away who are travelling towards trespassory assemblies. It is operative within the area covered by the banning order. A person who fails to comply is liable to arrest.

Public Order Act 1986 s14

A senior police officer is able to impose conditions on public assemblies. The officer may impose conditions if s/he reasonably believe that the assembly may result in:

- Serious public disorder   **OR**

- Serious damage to property   **OR**

- Serious disruption to the life of the community.

These conditions, which must be in writing, may be in regard to location, duration and maximum numbers attending. It is an offence to knowingly organise a public assembly in breach of the conditions, or to take part knowingly. These offences carry a statutory power of arrest.

7.36 When an illegal mass gathering is anticipated and likely to go ahead, emergency plans may need to be implemented. All relevant bodies, especially local authorities and police, should be on alert. Security (24 hour) may be appropriate to protect especially vulnerable and sensitive pieces of land.

7.37 Should a mass gathering take place, enforcement action as detailed in Chapter 6 should be considered.

Box 28 : An Aide Memoire on Mass Incursions

Drawing on recent experiences of mass gatherings, the National Crime and Operations Faculty, Uniform Operational Support at Bramshill put together:

Mass Incursions : An Aide Memoire

Guidance on Managing Unauthorised Camping

8. Evaluation of the Guidance

8.1 The Office of the Deputy Prime Minister and the Home Office are committed to evaluating the impact of this Operational Guidance to check:

- the extent to which local authorities and the police have adopted the Guidance; and

- its effectiveness in bringing about improvements on the ground.

8.2 In the light of evaluation - and changing circumstances - further Guidance may be issued in future as appropriate. ODPM and the Home Office will be pleased to receive comments on the Operational Guidance and suggestions for ways in which it might be improved.

9. Useful References and Contacts

Various pieces of guidance have been referred to in this Operational Guidance. These are listed below, together with other useful references ordered in the relevant Chapters of the Guidance. Useful contacts are listed at the end. ALL INTERNET ADDRESSES ARE VALID AT DECEMBER 2003.

Chapter 1

Department of Environment, Transport and the Regions/Home Office (1998) Managing *Unauthorised Camping: A Good Practice Guide*, DETR; Revised Chapter 5 issued July 2000

Cowan, D, Donson, F, Higate, P, Lomax, D & Third, H (2001) *The Management of Unauthorised Camping: Monitoring the Good Practice Guide*, Research Paper 77, Edinburgh College of Art/Heriot-Watt University

Commission for Racial Equality (2003) *Gypsies and Travellers - A Strategy 2003-2006 Consultation Draft*, CRE (http://www.cre.gov.uk/downloads/docs/GandT_strat.doc)

Gypsy Sites Refurbishment Grant (GSRG) 2004/05: Bidding Guidance (http://www.odpm.gov.uk/stellent/groups/odpm_housing/documents/page/odpm_house_025116.hcsp)

Home Office (2002) *National Policing Plan 2003-2006 (http://www.policereform.gov.uk/natpoliceplan/)*

Home Office (2003) *Respect and Responsibility (http://www.official-documents.co.uk/document/cm57/5778/5778.pdf)*

Chapter 2

Counts of Gypsy caravans are published on the ODPM website at (http://www.odpm.gov.uk/stellent/groups/odpm_housing/documents/page/odpm_house_602529.xls)

Niner, P (2002) *The Provision and Condition of Local Authority Gypsy/Traveller Sites in England*, ODPM
(http://www.odpm.gov.uk/stellent/groups/odpm_housing/documents/page/odpm_house_602542.hcsp)

Niner, P (2003) *Local Authority Gypsy/Traveller Sites in England*, ODPM (http://www.odpm.gov.uk/stellent/groups/odpm_housing/documents/page/odpm_house_023012.pdf)

Chapter 3

Derbyshire Gypsy Liaison Group (1998) *Moving Base*, DGLG

Hopkinson, G, Ingram, M & Wishart, B (undated) *Where's the Real Choice? What are the accommodation needs of Travellers in Wychavon?* Evesham & Pershore Housing Association

Southwark Housing (2000) *Needs of the Traveller Community in Southwark*, LB Southwark

Morris, R & Clements, L (2002) *At what cost? The economics of Gypsy and Traveller encampments*, The Policy Press

Local e-Government Strategy (http://www.localegov.gov.uk/Nimoi/sites/ODMP/resources/20021127 Final NS with cover.pdf)

Commission for Racial Equality (2000) *Guidance for Journalists: Travellers, Gypsies and the Media*, CRE (http://www.cre.gov.uk/media/guidetj.html)

DETR (2001) *Local strategic partnerships - Government guidance* (http://www.neighbourhood.gov.uk/formatteddoc.asp?id=95)

Guidance on Managing Unauthorised Camping

LGA (2002) *Guidance on Community Cohesion (http://www.homeoffice.gov.uk/docs/cc_guidance.pdf)*

DETR (2001) *Supporting People: policy into practice,* see http://www.spkweb.org.uk

Children and Young People's Strategic Partnerships (within Local Strategic Partnerships)

Sure Start, see http://www.surestart.gov.uk

Connexions, see http://www.connexions.gov.uk

Home Office (1999) Guidance on Statutory Crime and Disorder Partnerships, see http://www.homeoffice.gov.uk/docs/partcont.html

Race Equality Schemes, see http://www.cre.gov.uk/duty/duty_schemes.html

Department of Transport, Local Government and the Regions (2002) *Homelessness Strategies: A Good Practice Handbook,* DTLR (http://www.odpm.gov.uk/stellent/groups/odpm_homelessness/documents/pdf/odpm_home_pdf_6015 17.pdf)

Chapter 4

DoE Circular 1/94: *Gypsy Sites and Planning,* January 1994 (see Annex B)

Planning Policy Guidance 3 *Housing,* ODPM (http://www.odpm.gov.uk/stellent/groups/odpm_planning/documents/pdf/odpm_plan_pdf_606933.pd f)

Planning Policy Guidance 12 Development *Plans,* ODPM (http://www.odpm.gov.uk/stellent/groups/odpm_planning/documents/pdf/odpm_plan_pdf_606929.pd f)

Chapter 5

Web-site of the Information Commissioner's - http://www.informationcommissioner.gov.uk

Chapter 6

Fuller v Chief Constable of Dorset, [2001] EWHC Admin 1057

Home Office Circular 45/1994

R v The Commissioner of the Metropolis ex parte Small (not reported)

Department of Environment, Transport and the Regions/Home Office (1998) *Managing Unauthorised Camping: A Good Practice Guide,* DETR; Revised Chapter 5 issued July 2000

DTLR, the Court Service and the Welsh Assembly: *Getting the best out of the court system: Claims for possession (http://www.courtservice.gov.uk/cms/media/best_court_system.pdf)*

Planning Policy Guidance 18 *Enforcing Planning Control* 1991 (http://www.odpm.gov.uk/stellent/groups/odpm_planning/documents/page/odpm_plan_606903.pdf)

DoE Circular 10/97 *Enforcing Planning Control: Legislative provisions and Procedural Requirements (http://www.odpm.gov.uk/stellent/groups/odpm_planning/documents/pdf/odpm_plan_pdf_606834.pdf)*

DoE *Enforcing Planning Control: Good Practice for Local Planning Authorities,* 1997

Chapter 7

Guidance on Managing Unauthorised Camping

Home Office (2003) *Respect and Responsibility (http://www.official-documents.co.uk/document/cm57/5778/5778.pdf)*

Home Office (2002) *A Guide to Anti-Social Behaviour Orders and Acceptable Behaviour Contracts (http://www.crimereduction.gov.uk/asbos9.pdf)*

Environment Protection Act 1990 s34, *Waste Management: The Duty of Care: A Code of Practice (http://www.defra.gov.uk/environment/waste/management/doc/pdf/waste_man_duty_code.pdf)*

Fly Tipping Stakeholders Forum, *Fly Tipping Guidance (http://www.environment-agency.gov.uk/commondata/105385/flytip.PDF)*

Home Office (2001) CCTV*: Implications for Public Space Surveillance in the Light of the Data Protection Act 1998* see http:// www.crimereduction.gov.uk/cctv7.htm

Home Office (2001) *CCTV and the Human Rights Act*, see http:// www.crimereduction.gov.uk/cctv13.htm

Mass Incursions: An Aide Memoire Contact: National Crime and Operations Faculty, Uniformed Operational Support, Bramshill (01256 602777)

Useful Contacts

Gypsy/Traveller bodies and support groups

Advisory Council for the Education of Romany and Other Travellers (ACERT)

Moot House, The Stow, Harlow, Essex CM20 3AG

01279 418666

Gypsy Council

(President: Hughie Smith) Spring Lanes Caravan Park, Bickerton, Nr Wetherby, North Yorks LS22 5ND

01937 842782

Gypsy Council for Education, Culture, Welfare and Civil Rights

(Chairman: Charles Smith)

8 Hall Road, Aveley, Romford, Essex RM15 4HD

01708 868986

Irish Traveller Movement in Britain

The Old Library Building, Willesden Green Library Centre, 95 High Road, Willesden, London NW10 2ST

020 8459 7638

London Gypsy and Traveller Unit

6 Westgate Street, London E8 3RN

020 8533 2002

Derbyshire Gypsy Liaison Group

Ernest Bailey Community Centre, New Street, Matlock, Derbyshire DE4 3FE

01629 583300

Guidance on Managing Unauthorised Camping

Friends, Families and Travellers

Community Base, 113 Queens Road, Brighton, East Sussex BN1 3XG

01273 234777

Community Law Partnership

Ruskin Chambers, 191 Corporation Street, Birmingham, West Midlands B4 6RP

0121 685 8595

Travellers' Times

The Rural Media Company, Sullivan House, 72080 Widemarsh Street, Hereford HR4 9HG

01432 344039

Central Government

ODPM

Gypsy and Traveller Branch , Eland House, Bressenden Place, London SW1E 5DU

020 7944 4400

Home Office

Crime Reduction and Community Safety Group, 50 Queen Annes Gate, London SW1H 9AT

0800 000 1585

Department for Education and Skills

Ethnic Minority Achievement Unit, Sanctuary Building, Great Smith Street, London SW1P 3BT

0870 000 2288

Department of Health

Primary Care Access, Quarry House, Quarry Hill, Leeds LS2 7UE

020 7210 4850

Other bodies

Commission for Racial Equality

St Dunstan's House, 201-211 Borough High Street, London SE1 1GZ

020 7939 0000

Local Government Association

Local Government House, Smith Square, London SW1P 3HZ

020 7644 3000

National Association of Gypsy and Traveller Officers

c/o George Summers, Estates Practice Department, Hampshire County Council, The Castle, Winchester, Hampshire SO23 9DS

01962 847315

National Association of Health Workers with Travellers

Guidance on Managing Unauthorised Camping

(Chair : Sarah Rhodes) Travellers Health Project, Central Health Clinic, Tower Hill, Bristol BS2 0JD

0117 922 7570

National Association of Teachers of Travellers

c/o Lucy Beckett, Advisory Service for the Education of Travellers, Room L25, Cricket Road Centre, Cricket Road, Oxford OX4 3DW

01865 428089

Annex A: DoE Circular 18/94

A: DoE Circular 18/94: Gypsy Sites Policy and Unauthorised Camping + Revision of Advice on 'Toleration' issued 26 July 2000

Annex B: DoE Circular 1/94

B: DoE Circular 1/94: Gypsy Sites and Planning

Annex C: Summary Points from Research Monitoring the Good Practice Guide on Managing Unauthorised Camping

In 2001 the results of research monitoring the impact of the DETR/Home Office Good Practice Guide were published[1]. The research was carried out by Edinburgh College of Art/Heriot-Watt University in conjunction with the Universities of Bristol and Cardiff. It involved a telephone survey of 263 local authorities which explored the pattern of unauthorised camping. Some of the main findings relating to unauthorised camping are:

Unauthorised camping is a widespread phenomenon - 92% of responding local authorities had experience of it in the twelve months before the survey.

The average number of reported incidents of unauthorised camping in the past year was 22, although this varied widely and almost half of authorities reported ten incidents or fewer. A separate incident could be the same Gypsy/Traveller group moving onto different sites in the area. The speed with which an encampment is moved on is one factor in the number of separate incidents experienced.

The average number of different locations in an authority area subject to unauthorised camping in the last year was 13, again with wide variation.

Unauthorised camps involving 20 caravans and more were far less common than camps involving a dozen caravans or fewer. Only 8% of responding local authorities had experienced an encampment of 50 or more caravans in the past year.

Local authority respondents said that most encampments were small scale and relatively unproblematic while a minority were extremely high profile and associated with crime, damage, dumping and other anti-social behaviour.

Irish Travellers were most often reported as having camped on unauthorised sites in the past year (70% of authorities), followed by Gypsy Travellers (58%) and New Travellers (23%).

The most common sites for unauthorised encampments were vacant or derelict land, industrial estates, car parks and roadsides or verges. Other types of sites, for example, parks and recreation areas, green lanes and bye-ways, farm land and wooded areas were used less often.

The three main factors influencing unauthorised camping were seasonal travelling, work opportunities and visiting other Gypsies and Travellers in the area.

Local authorities' experiences of changes over the past five years were mixed, with no clear trends emerging in terms of frequency of unauthorised camping, number of locations used, use of authorised sites or number of caravans in the groups.

---

[1] Cowan, D, Donson, F, Higate, P, Lomax, D & Third, H (2001) *The Management of Unauthorised Camping: Monitoring the Good Practice Guide*, Research Paper 77, Edinburgh College of Art/Heriot-Watt University

Annex D: A Summary of the Legislative Framework

This annex summarises the main legislative framework relevant to a strategy for managing unauthorised camping. Most of the provisions are described in greater detail in the text of the Guidance. Exceptionally, human rights and race relations responsibilities which are referred at various points in the text are set out in more detail below.

Site Provision

- The Caravan Sites and Control of Development Act 1960 s24 gives local authorities discretionary powers to provide caravan sites.

- While there is no duty on local authorities to provide Gypsy sites, DoE Circular 18/94 makes clear that authorities should maintain their existing Gypsy caravan sites, and should continue to consider whether it is appropriate to provide further permanent caravan sites for Gypsies in their areas.

- Government is currently reviewing policy on Gypsy site provision. Gypsy Sites Refurbishment Grant makes limited funding available for provision of transit and emergency stopping places.

- Private site provision is governed by planning legislation. DoE Circular 1/94 sets out the Government's policy on Gypsy site provision and urges local planning authorities to consider, and to look favourably, at applications for Gypsy sites in development planning and development control.

Dealing with Unauthorised Encampments

- There is no specific legislative duty placed on local authorities to deal with unauthorised encampments by Gypsies and Travellers.

- Local authorities can take action as landowners through civil actions against trespass using Civil Procedure Rules Part 55, heard in a County Court.

- Local authorities have powers given by the Criminal Justice and Public Order 1994 ss77 and 78 (see Chapter 6). These require cases to be brought in the Magistrates' Court.

- Common law rights to recover land from trespassers are also available to local authorities over land they occupy. Authorities are, however, advised not to use such powers unless there is exceptional justification for doing so and, for example, the police are unable to use their powers under s61 of the CJPOA (see 6.5 above).

- DoE Circular 18/94 provides guidance to local authorities on the exercise of s77 powers, and reminds them of their other duties towards Travellers in terms of education, children and homelessness legislation.

- Case law (starting with the judgement of Sedley J in *R v Wealden District Council ex parte Wales*) has developed and clarified the courts' expectations of the welfare enquiries and decision-making processes local authorities should adopt in making evictions under 1994 Act and other powers.

- Where Travellers camp on land which they own or on other private land with the consent of the landowner, district councils may take planning enforcement action, or prosecute for running a caravan site without a site licence.

- The Police have parallel powers granted by s61 of the CJPOA (see Chapter 6). Action under s61 is normally much quicker than under s77, and the welfare considerations less onerous although there are certain conditions in the legislation which have to be fulfilled before eviction can take place.

Guidance on Managing Unauthorised Camping

- The Anti-social Behaviour Act 2003 added new ss61A and 62A into the CJPOA which give police enhanced eviction powers in circumstances where there are suitable pitches on relevant Gypsy sites to accommodate the caravans affected. These sections come into force on 27 February 2004 and guidance as to their operation will be issued.

Other Enforcement Measures

- District authorities have powers to deal with statutory nuisance (which could include, for example, rubbish accumulation at unauthorised encampments) and noise (see Chapter 7 of this Guide).

- The Crime and Disorder Act 1998 places a duty on chief police officers and local authorities to work together to develop and implement a strategy for reducing crime and disorder. Section 17 imposes a duty on all local authorities (and others) to *'without prejudice to any other obligation imposed upon it . . . exercise its functions with due regard to . . . the need to do all it reasonably can to prevent crime and disorder in its area'.*

Service Provision for Gypsies and Travellers

- Gypsies and Travellers are entitled to access health, housing, education and welfare services as citizens in the same way as members of the settled community.

- There is specific recognition of the needs of Traveller children in accessing education, with a Traveller Grant payable under s488 of the Education Act 1996.

Human Rights

The Human Rights Act 1998 incorporates the European Convention on Human Rights into British law. Several Convention rights are relevant in dealing with unauthorised camping. The main relevant rights are:

Article 8: Right to respect for private and family life

1. Everyone has the right to respect for his private and family life, his home and his correspondence.

2. There shall be no interference by a public authority with the exercise of this right except such as is in accordance with the law and is necessary in a democratic society in the interests of national security, public safety or the economic well-being of the country, for the prevention of disorder or crime, for the protection of health or morals, or for the protection of the rights and freedoms of others.

Case law has established that, while neither eviction action against trespassers nor planning enforcement is incompatible with HRA, either could potentially breach Article 8 rights if not properly used. Authorities, and other public bodies covered by the HRA, must be able to demonstrate that all eviction and enforcement decisions are 'proportionate' in weighing individual harm (in the loss of 'home' for the Gypsy or Traveller) against the wider public interest. Potential challenge under the HRA means that all decision-making must be fully recorded and evidenced to withstand scrutiny.

First Protocol, Article 1: Protection of property

Every natural and legal person is entitled to the peaceful enjoyment of his possessions. No-one shall be deprived of his possessions except in the public interest and subject to the conditions provided for by law and by the general principles of international law.

The preceding provisions shall not, however, in any way impair the right of a State to enforce such laws as it deems necessary to control the use of property in accordance with the general interest or to secure the payment of taxes or other contributions or penalties.

Guidance on Managing Unauthorised Camping

This Article might be seen as protecting the settled community's right to quiet enjoyment of their possessions, which might be threatened by nuisance, noise or anti-social behaviour from a problematic unauthorised encampment. This should be one of the considerations to be borne in mind by local authorities and police when considering eviction action. To date there is no relevant case law.

First Protocol, Article 2: Right to education

No person shall be denied the right to education. In the exercise of any functions which it assumes in relation to education and to teaching, the State shall respect the right of parents to ensure such education and teaching in conformity with their own religious and philosophical convictions.

Education of Gypsy/Traveller children is frequently raised in cases dealing with eviction proceedings, and particularly with planning enforcement actions against unauthorised development. In such cases the question resolves itself to one of the balance between the individual harm to Gypsy/Traveller childrens' educational needs and the public interest harm in allowing unauthorised development to persist. To date there is no specific case law on arguments relying on this Article in this context.

Article 14: Prohibition of discrimination

The enjoyment of the rights and freedoms set forth in this Convention shall be secured without discrimination on any ground such as sex, race, colour, language, religion, political or other opinion, national or social origin, association with a national minority, property birth or other status.

While Article 14 rights are potentially engaged in any action concerning Gypsies and Travellers (as ethnic groups and national minorities), the Article can only be successfully argued if another Article is found to be breached. Where a claim under any Article is rejected, it follows that any claim under Article 14 also falls.

Race Relations and Equalities

The Race Relations Act 1976 as amended by the Race Relations (Amendment) Act 2000 gives public authorities - including ODPM, the Home Office, local authorities and the police - a general duty to eliminate unlawful discrimination, and to promote equality of opportunity and good race relations in carrying out their functions. It also gives listed public bodies specific duties including one to create and publish a Race Equality Scheme which details how they will meet the general duty. In developing new policies or strategies public authorities must assess their impact on different racial groups, and they must consult. If the impact is negative and disproportionate to the aim of the policy, it must be changed. Once implemented, policies must be monitored for their effect on different racial groups. Authorities must publish the results of monitoring and consultation.

Both Gypsies and Irish Travellers are recognised as ethnic minorities. Policies for managing unauthorised camping are likely to affect Gypsies and Travellers significantly. The RRA means that local authorities and police must assess the impact of proposed policies on Gypsies and Irish Travellers and must consult on them. If the policies are likely to have a disproportionately negative impact on Gypsies and Irish Travellers, authorities must ensure that this impact is not disproportionate to the aims and importance of the policies. If it is, it is important to take measures to reduce this adverse impact or consider other ways to achieve the aims, which would mitigate its negative effect.

Since eviction of unauthorised campers and enforcement against unauthorised development are likely to have a large effect on the public, and in particular on the Gypsy/Traveller population, they are functions highly relevant to the RRA general duty and should be prioritised in Race Equality Schemes. When evicting and enforcing, authorities need to ensure that they act in a way which meets the three elements of the general duty and so as to have the minimum negative impact on the Gypsies and Travellers involved.

Guidance on Managing Unauthorised Camping

Local authorities and police must always be able to show that they have properly considered the race and equalities implications of their policies and actions in relation to unauthorised encampments and unauthorised development by Gypsies and Irish Travellers. They must be able to demonstrate that their polices and actions are proportionate bearing in mind all the circumstances of the case.

Guidance on Managing Unauthorised Camping

Annex E: Interests to be involved in the Development of a Strategy for Unauthorised Camping

Organisation/party	Main topics of interest	Possible means of involvement
Local authorities **NB** In two-tier areas both county and district councils will be involved	Planning and information; race relations; site provision and land use planning; site protection; housing and homelessness; Traveller education; social services; refuse collection; unauthorised camping; communication and public relations	Lead development of Strategy development; key personnel involved in working groups or committees; others in ad hoc groupings and/or written consultation
Local politicians, councillors and MPs	All aspects including unauthorised encampment	Leadership and engendering support for the Strategy
Local Health Authority	Gypsy/Traveller health in all forms of accommodation and on unauthorised encampments; welfare assessments	Nominated officer to be consulted as Strategy develops; continuing involvement in implementation
Neighbouring local authorities	All aspects to inform own Strategies	Joint planning and shared working could be efficient and lead to a sub-regional approach
Police	Planning and information; race equality; dealing with crime, anti-social behaviour and threats to public order from unauthorised encampments; communication and public relations	Key player in developing the Strategy; continuing role in its implementation
Gypsies and Travellers	All aspects including needs assessment; service delivery; advice on site provision and unauthorised camping	Through national, regional or local representative bodies; consultation with local Gypsies and Travellers on their needs and aspirations. Written material, conferences and individual personal contact
Gypsy/Traveller support groups and advisors	Potentially all aspects including unauthorised encampment	Local contact, conferences, consultation through written media

Guidance on Managing Unauthorised Camping

Parish and town councils	Site provision and land use planning; site protection; unauthorised camping; and communications and public relations	Consultation on perceived issues, priorities and ideas; consultation on draft and final Strategy. Written material and conferences
Settled community	Especially site planning and land use planning; site protection; and unauthorised camping	Consultation on perceived issues, priorities and ideas; consultation on draft and final Strategy. Written material and feedback arrangements. Citizen jury?
Private landowners	Unauthorised camping	Consult on perceived problems and constraints and to agree respective roles in acting on unauthorised encampments
Crime & Disorder Reduction Partnership, Local Strategic Partnerships	Dependent on nature of partnership	Exchange information and consultation to ensure consistency and shared priorities
Highways Agency	Unauthorised camping	Consult to agree respective roles in acting on unauthorised encampments
Environment Agency	Fly tipping and pollution associated with unauthorised encampments	Consult to agree respective roles in acting on unauthorised encampments
Forestry Commission	Major land owner in some areas which may be affected by unauthorised camping	Consult to agree respective roles in acting on unauthorised encampments
English Nature	Unauthorised camping as it affects Sites of Special Scientific Interest	Consult to identify key areas and agree respective roles in acting on unauthorised encampments
National Trust	Major land owner in some areas which may be affected by unauthorised camping	Consult to agree respective roles in acting on unauthorised encampments
Ministry of Defence	Major land owner in some areas which may be affected by unauthorised camping	Consult to agree respective roles in acting on unauthorised encampments
Local press and other media	All aspects of the Strategy; especially site provision and unauthorised camping	Regular media briefings and invitations to all public events to ensure full appreciation of the issues and to encourage balanced coverage

Useful organisations

National organisations and government departments

Administrative Court Office
Royal Courts of Justice, Strand
London WC2A 2LL

Administrative Court (Wales)
Law Courts, Cathays Park
Cardiff CF10 3PG

Advisory Service for Squatters
2 St Pauls Road
London N1 2QH
Tel: 020 7359 8814

Advisory Council for the Education of Romany and other Travellers
C/o Felicity Bonel, Greenwich Traveller Education Service,
Boxgrove School, Boxgrove Road,
Abbeywood
London SE2 9JP
Tel: 020 8859 8755

Commission for Racial Equality
St Dunstan's House, 201–211 Borough High Street
London SE1 1GZ
Tel: 020 7939 0000
Fax: 020 7939 0001
E-mail: info@cre.gov.uk
Website: www.cre.gov.uk

Department of Education and Skills
Sanctuary Buildings
Great Smith Street
London
SW1P 3BT
Website: www.dfes.gov.uk

Department of Health
Richmond House
79 Whitehall
London SW1A 2NS
Website: www.dh.gov.uk

Educational Advice for Travellers
PO Box 36
Grantham
Lincolnshire NG31 6EW

Friends, Families and Travellers
Community Base, 113 Queens Road
Brighton BN1 3XG
Tel: 01273 234777
Fax: 01273 234778
E-mail: fft@communitybase.org
Website: www.gypsy/traveller.org

Groundswell
Elmsfield House
5 Stockwell Mews
London SW9 9GX
Tel: 020 7737 5500
Fax: 020 7733 1305
E-mail: info@groundswell.org.uk
Website: www.groundswell.org.uk

Gypsy Council
Greenacres Caravan Park, Hapsford, Helsby
Warrington WA6 OJS
Tel/Fax: 01928 723138

Gypsy Council for Education, Culture, Welfare and Civil Rights
C/o Aveley Clinic
Hall Road, Aveley
Romford RM15 4HD
Tel/Fax: 01708 868986
E-mail: Thegypsycouncil@btinternet.com
Website: www.thegypsycouncil.org

Irish Traveller Movement in Britain
Banderway House, 156–162 Kilburn High Road
London NW6 4JD
Tel/Fax: 020 7625 2255
E-mail: noelettekeaneitm@hotmail.com

Labour Campaign for Travellers' Rights
C/o 25 Clarence Road
London N22 8PG

National Assembly for Wales
Cardiff Bay
Cardiff CF99 1NA
Tel: 02920 825111
Website: www.wales.gov.uk

National Association of Gypsy and Traveller Officers
C/o George Summers,
County Estates Practice, Hampshire County Council,
The Castle,
Winchester SO23 8UJ
Tel: 01962 847315

National Association of Gypsy Women
C/o Rachel Ingham,
The CVS Building,
Church Row, Darlington,
Co Durham EL1 5QD
Tel: 01325 240033

National Association of Health Workers with Travellers
C/o Joanne Davis,
Balsall Heath Health Centre
43 Edward Road
Birmingham B12 9LB
Tel: 0121 446 2300
Fax: 0121 446 5936

National Association of Teachers of Travellers
C/o Advisory Service for the Education of Travellers
The Harlow Centre, Raymund Road
Oxford OX3 OPG
Tel: 01865 256620

National Romani Rights Association
C/o Basil Burton, 10 Dugdell Close, Ferndown
Dorset BH22 8BH
Tel: 01202 893228

National Romani Travellers Alliance
Lower Road, Hockley
Essex SS5 5NL
Tel: 01702 232020

National Traveller Action Group
Seddon, Woodside Caravan Park
Hatch, Sandy
Bedfordshire SG19 1PT
Tel: 01767 689736
Mobile: 07890 596718

Office of the Deputy Prime Minister
Gypsy Sites Branch, 1/J3 Eland House
Bressenden Place, London SW1E 5DU
Tel: 020 7944 3673

Ofsted
Alexandra House, 32 Kingsway
London WC2B 6SE
Tel: 020 7421 6800

Press Complaints Commission
1 Salisbury Square
London EC4Y 8AE
Tel: 020 7353 1248

Shelterline (24hour national housing help)
Tel: (Freephone) 0808 800 4444
Website: www.shelter.org.uk

The Land is Ours
Box E, 111 Magdalen Road
Oxford OX4 1RQ
Tel: 01865 722016
E-mail: office@tlio.demon.co.uk
Website: www.oneworld.org/tlio

Travellers Advice Team
Community Law Partnership
4th Floor, Ruskin Chambers
191 Corporation Street
Birmingham B4 6RP
LSC funded advice line: 0845 120 2980
Tel: 0121 685 8595
Fax: 0121 236 5121
E-mail: office@communitylawpartnership.co.uk

Travellers Aid Trust
PO Box 16
Llangyndeyrn
Kidwelly SA17 5YT
Tel/fax: 01269 870621
E-mail: info@travellersaidtrust.org
Website: www.travellersaidtrust.org

Traveller Law Reform Coalition
(now known as the Gypsy and Traveller Law Reform Coalition)
Banderway House
156–162 Kilburn High Road
London NW6 4JD
Tel/Fax: 020 7625 2255
Mobile: 07985 684921
E-mail: romanistan@yahoo.com

Travellers' School Charity
PO Box 2
Goodwick
Pembrokeshire SA64 0ZQ
Tel: 01437 532432
Website: www.travellersschool.plus.com

Travellers' Times
The Rural Media Company, Sullivan House
72–80 Widemarsh Street
Hereford HR4 9HG
Tel: 01432 344039
Fax: 01432 270539
E-mail: travellerstimes@ruralmedia.co.uk
Website: www.travellerstimes.org.uk

Treasury Solicitor
Queen Anne's Chambers
28 Broadway
London SW1H 9JS

Local organisations

There are a vast array of local organisations dealing with Gypsy and Traveller issues. Full details of local organisations can be obtained from one of the national organisations mentioned above. We list below some of the most active and prominent of these local organisations.

Avon Traveller Support Group
65 Hawthorn Grove
Combe Down
Bath BA2 5QF
Tel: 01225 835130

Brent Irish Advisory Service, Irish Travellers Project
Banderway House
156–162 Kilburn High Road
London NW6 4JD
Tel/Fax: 020 7625 2255

Bromley Gypsy Traveller Community Project
13–15 High Street
St Mary Cray
Orpington, Kent BR5 3NL
Tel: 01689 839052

Cambridgeshire Travellers Initiative
Tel: 01480 496010

Cardiff Gypsy and Traveller Project
114 Clifton Street, Roath
Cardiff CF24 1LW
Tel/Fax: 029 2021 4411

Children's Society
92b High Street
Midsomer Norton BA3 2DE
Tel: 01761 411771
Fax: 01761 417553
E-mail: dxh@childrenssociety.org.uk

Derbyshire Gypsy Liaison Group
Ernest Bailey Community Centre
Office 3, New Street
Matlock DE4 3FE
Tel/Fax: 01629 583300

East Anglian Gypsy Council
Plot 3, Oxney Road Caravan Site
Peterborough
Tel: 01733 347112

Herefordshire Travellers Support Group
Trefoil, Brinson Common
Hereford HR4 7AS
Tel: 01432 760350

Leeds Gypsy and Traveller Exchange
7 Shafton Street
Holbeck
Leeds LS11 9LY
Tel: 0113 234 6556
E-mail: info@leedsgate.co.uk

London Gypsy and Traveller Unit
6 Westgate Street
London E8 3RN
Tel: 020 8533 2002
Fax: 020 8533 7110
E-mail: lgtu@aol.com
Website: www.lgtu.org.uk

West Midlands Education Service for Travelling Children
The Graiseley Centre
Pool Street
Wolverhampton WV2 4NE
Tel: 01902 714646
Fax: 01902 714202

York Travellers Project
Community House
10 Priory Street
York YO1 1EZ
Tel: 01904 630526
Fax: 01904 630361

European organisations

Council of Europe
Website: www.coe.int

European Roma Rights Center
Website: www.errc.org

Bibliography

BOOKS ON GYPSY AND TRAVELLER ISSUES

Acton *Gypsy Politics and Social Change* (Routledge, Kegan Paul, 1974)

Fraser *The Gypsies* (Blackwell, 1995)

Hawes *Gypsies, Travellers and the Health Service* (Policy Press, 1997)

Hawes and Perez *The Gypsy and the State: the ethnic cleansing of British Society* (The Polity Press,1996)

Hyman *Sites for Travellers: a study in five London Boroughs* (London Race and Housing Research Unit, 1989)

Kenrick and Bakewell *On the Verge: The Gypsies of England* (University of Hertfordshire Press, 1990)

Kenrick and Clark *Moving On: the Gypsies and Travellers of Britain* (University of Hertfordshire Press, 1996)

Kenrick and Puxon *The Destiny of Europe's Gypsies* (Chatto-Heinemann, 1972)

Leigeois *Gypsies and Travellers: socio-cultural data, socio-political data* (Council of Europe, 1987)

MacLaughlin *Travellers and Ireland: Whose Country, Whose History?* (Cork University Press, 1995)

Morris and Clements *Gaining Ground: Law Reform for Gypsies and Travellers* (University of Hertfordshire Press, 1999)

Morris and Clements *At What Cost? The Economics of Gypsy and Traveller Encampments* (The Policy Press, 2002)

Okely *The Traveller-Gypsies* (Cambridge University Press, 1983).

Ò Riain *Solidarity with Travellers* (Roadside Books, Dublin, 2000)

Sandford *Rokkering to the Gorjios* (University of Hertfordshire Press, 1973)

Sheehan (ed) *Travellers: Citizens of Ireland* (Parish of the Travelling People, Dublin, 2000)

Stewart *The Puzzle of Roma Persistence* (University of Hertfordshire Press, 1997)

Vesey-Fitzgerald *Gypsies of Britain* (Readers Union, 1973)

LEGAL TEXT BOOKS

Arden and Hunter *Homelessness and Allocations* (Legal Action Group, Revised 6th edn, 2003)

Butterworths *Encyclopaedia of Planning Law and Practice*

Child Poverty Action Group *Welfare Benefits and Tax Credits Handbook* (2003/2004)

Clements *Community Care and the Law* (Legal Action Group, 3rd edn, 2004)

Jourdan *Adverse Possession* (Butterworths, 2003)

Jowell and Cooper (eds) *Understanding Human Rights Act Principles* (Hart Publishing, 2001)

Manning *Judicial Review: a practitioner's guide* (Legal Action Group, 2nd edn, 2004)

Palmer et al *Discrimination Law Handbook* (Legal Action Group, 2002)

Sweet & Maxwell *Encyclopedia of Housing Law and Practice*

OTHER BOOKS

Baumann *Modernity and the Holocaust* (Polity Press, 1989)

Lentin and McVeigh *Racism and Anti-Racism in Ireland* (Beyond the Pale, 2002)

Muller-Hill *Murderous Science* (Methuesen, New York 1988)

Walvin *There ain't no black in the Union Jack* (Routledge, 1973)

REPORTS

General reports

Commission for Racial Equality *Gypsies and Travellers: A Strategy for the CRE, 2004–2007* (2004)

Equality of Opportunity Committee, National Assembly for Wales *Review of Service Provision for Gypsies and Travellers* (2003)

Institute for Public Policy Research *Moving Forward: the provision of accommodation for Travellers and Gypsies* (Crawley, 2004)

Minority Rights Group *Roma/Gypsies: A European Minority* (1995)

Stonewall *Profiles of Prejudice* (2003)

Niner *The Provision and Condition of Local Authority Gypsy/Traveller Sites In England* (ODPM, 2002)

Niner *Local Authority Gypsy/Traveller Sites in England* (ODPM, 2003)

Niner *Counting Gypsies and Travellers: A Review of the Gypsy Caravan Count System* (ODPM, 2004)

Reports on education

Committee of Inquiry into the Education of Children from Ethnic Minority Groups *Education for all* (1985)

DfES *Aiming High: Raising the Achievement of Gypsy and Traveller Pupils* (2003)

Ofsted *The Education of Travelling Children: a Survey of Educational Provision for Travelling Children* (1996)

Ofsted *Raising the Attainment of Minority Ethnic Pupils* (1999)

Ofsted *Managing Support for the Attainment of Pupils from Minority Ethnic Groups* (2001)

Reports on health

Chartered Institute of Environmental Health *Travellers and Gypsies: An Alternative Strategy* (1995)

Council of Europe *Breaking the Barriers: Romani Women and Access to Public Health* (2003)

Derbyshire Gypsy Liaison Group *A Better Road* (2003)

Index

Eviction from unauthorised encampments *continued*
standing, 5.5–5.10
stop notices, 5.110
substantive defences, 5.3, 5.5–5.110, 5.150
sufficient interest in land, persons having, 5.5–5.11
tents, 5.31, 5.50, 5.69–5.70
threatening, abusive or insulting words or behaviour, 5.38
threats, 5.15–5.16, 5.38
time limits, 5.15–5.16, 5.34, 5.65, 5.71–5.72, 5.75
title, proof of, 5.11
towing vehicles, 5.39
transit pitches, 5.53, 5.150
trespassory assembly, 5.79–5.80
unknown persons, service on, 5.8
use of force or violence, 5.104–5.105
verges, 5.76, 5.79–5.80
video evidence, 5.42
Wales, 5148
warrants of possession and restitution, 5.18–5.24
Welsh Assembly Equality of Opportunity Committee, 5.148
Evidence
eviction, 5.42
home, family and private life, right to respect for the, 5.42
planning permission, applications for, 4.87
resume travelling, intention to, 4.87
status of Gypsy, of, 4.87
video, eviction and, 5.42
witness statements, 5.11
Exclusion from school, 7.33–7.45
appeals, 7.43
fair trials, 7.42
guidance, 7.37–7.40
hearings, 7.41
reinstatement, 7.43–7.44
standard of proof, 7.39
Expenses of carrying out works, recovery of, 4.107

Facilities
animals, keeping, 3.36
fire precautions, 3.38–3.41
guidance, 3.41
horses, keeping, 3.36
landscaping, 3.41
local authorities' powers, 3.36–3.37
official sites, 3.36–3.37
planning, 3.36, 3.41
sanitation, 3.41
security of tenure, 3.9
settled occupation, sites for, 3.41
transit sites, 3.41
water supply, 3.41
withdrawal of, 3.9
working space, 3.36
Factionalism, 3.26
Fair trials, 7.42
Fairs, 1.15, 1.16
Family life, right to respect for. *See* **Home, family and private life right to respect for**
Fees. *See* **Site fees**
Festivals, 1.44
Fines
bye-laws, 5.98
enforcement notices, 4.106
Fire precautions
conditions of sites, 3.38
duty of care, 3.40
fire authorities, consultation with, 3.38
guidance, 3.41
local authorities, 3.38–3.41
official sites, 3.38–3.41
standards, recommended, 3.39
Firle Bonfire, 1.4, 1.28, 8.42, 9.12
Fly-tipping, 5.37
Footpaths, 5.76
Forestry Commission
bye-laws, 5.99
eviction, 5.115
possession orders, 5.140–5.142
public law challenges to eviction, 5.115
Framework Convention for the Protection of National Minorities, 8.114–8.119
Function of travelling, 1.16

Official sites *continued*
Housing Bill, 9.10
Institute for Public Policy
Research, 9.11
judicial review, 3.25–3.32
lack of, 1.4–1.5, 5.147–5.148, 5.153
legal regime, 3.9–3.46
local authorities, 3.1–3.8, 9.3–9.12
caravans on, number of, 3.1
definition, 3.5
London boroughs, 3.3, 3.5
maintenance, 3.7
management of sites, 3.3, 3.26
material considerations, 4.23
Niner Report, 9.6
planning, 4.1
provision of, 3.3–3.8
race discrimination, 8.113
rent, 3.35
repairs, 3.33–3.35
repeal of duty to provide, 2.34,
3.47, 9.3
security of tenure, 2.56–2.60,
3.9–3.24, 3.47, 8.113
site fees, 3.35
Traveller Law Reform Coalition,
9.7–9.8
Travellers Law Reform Bill, 9.8–9.9
Wales, 3.3, 3.5
Welsh Assembly Equality of
Opportunity Committee, 9.9
Welsh county councils, 3.5
working spaces for Gypsies, 3.6
Old age, travelling and, 4.50–4.51
Open land
contaminated land, 4.34
designated sites, 4.34
DOE Circular 1/94, 4.34
investigations, 4.34
location of sites, 4.34
need, location of sites based on,
4.37
Operational development, 4.12–4.13
Opticians, 7.74
**'Order for the Avoiding of All Doubts
and Ambiguities 1554',** 1.12

Parks, 4.7, 4.30
Peace Convoy, 1.44

Peddlers, 1.14
Permission. *See* **also Planning
permission**
eviction, 5.40, 5.68
homelessness, 6.61–6.62,
6.64–6.65
Persecution, 1.14, 1.6–1.17, 1.21
Personal needs
designated areas, 4.60
DOE Circular 1/94, 4.59, App B
education, 4.64
eviction, 5.127
Green Belt, 4.60–4.64
presumption against
inappropriate development
on, 4.61–4.64
very special circumstances,
meaning of, 4.61–4.63
health, 4.64
injunctions, 4.117, 4.122
need, location of sites based on,
4.57–4.64
personal needs, 4.61, 4.64
planning permission, applications
for, 4.60–4.64, 4.87
Planning Policy Guidance, 4.61,
4.63
public law challenges to eviction,
5.127
Pharmacists, 7.74
Pikey, use of term, 1.1
Pitches. *See* **Caravan sites**
Planning, 4.1–4.127. *See* **also
Enforcement, planning and,
Planning permission**
accommodation, 1.35, 1.52
appeals, 4.89
caravan sites, 1.35, 2.15, 2.20,
2.23
county boroughs of Wales, 4.7
county councils, 4.7
definition of Gypsy, 4.41–4.49
designated areas, 4.30–4.33
development control, 4.11–4.33
development plans, 4.8–4.10, 4.29
district councils, 4.7
education, 2.64
ethnic Gypsies, Travellers and
Gypsy status, 4.41–4.49